MMBB

MERCER
UNIVERSITY PRESS

Endowed by
Tom Watson Brown
and
The Watson-Brown Foundation, Inc.

MMBB

A PIONEER IN EMPLOYEE BENEFITS

The First 100 Years

EVERETT C. GOODWIN

MERCER UNIVERSITY PRESS
MACON, GEORGIA

MUP/ H849

© 2012 Mercer University Press
1400 Coleman Avenue
Macon, Georgia 31207
All rights reserved
First Edition

ISBN 978-088146-383-5
ISBN 088146-383-3

Cataloging-in-Publication Data is available from the Library of Congress

This book is dedicated to the ministers and missionaries, past and present, who have provided the examples, inspiration, and crucial mentoring to make my own ministry possible, and on whose behalf it is the MMBB's purpose and privilege to serve.

CONTENTS

ACKNOWLEDGMENTS

This work has been made possible by many whom there is space to acknowledge and by a greater number that space does not permit to mention. To the Board of Managers of the MMBB, I express profound thanks for the opportunity to undertake this project. To Sumner Grant, Executive Director, I offer my personal gratitude for his support and encouragement along the way. I am also grateful to Harold Leibovitz, MMBB Director of Communications, who provided helpful assistance in shaping the scope of the project and in enabling its progress. Many other present and former MMBB staff members enabled and encouraged the project by their hospitality, encouragement, and insight, often when they did not realize it.

A number of former staff and board members were willing to offer candid conversation which enabled my ability to achieve some insights beyond the printed record; thus, thanks are due to all of them. Also, the time and energies of a number of readers who engaged the manuscript at a developing stage and offered suggestions for its improvement are especially appreciated.

Several persons invested time in reading the complete manuscript at an earlier stage and offered comments and suggestions that led to greater clarity—a work of great value. They included several who have had intimate knowledge of MMBB and its work, and scholars who provided helpful counsel in developing the narrative.

More personally, my wife, Jane Goodwin, provided innumerable insights and encouragements, and endured the sacrifices of time and opportunity that the project demanded. To her, especially, I express loving gratitude. Thanks is due also to my daughter, Leah Grace Goodwin (Baxter), whose expertise as a writer and editor served to provide cautions, advice, and practical counsel in developing the manuscript. To the Scarsdale Community Baptist Church in Scarsdale, New York, present and former spiritual home of several MMBB board and staff members, including one executive director, I offer my gratitude for tolerating the time required for this work. I hope that the realization of SCBC's role in MMBB's development serves as partial recompense.

One acknowledgment stands above all the others: Richard A. Huber, formerly Associate Executive Director of the MMBB, served as research assistant for this project and was of enormous importance in its development. Dick sifted through the minutes, supplemental minutes, annual reports, and other official records of the MMBB to create summaries, indexes, and lists of indescribable value. His painstaking preparations and his personal recollections of events and personalities made this work possible. Beyond this book, Dick's labors have also enabled the development of the MMBB Archives, a resource that will serve MMBB staff members and future historians in comprehending MMBB's history and progress.

At the end, I am also grateful for the editorial assistance of the Mercer University Press, notably Marc Jolley, for developing the manuscript into publishable form. After the best efforts of editors and readers, any remaining errors, omissions, or infelicities of expression are my own.

—ECG

AUTHOR'S PREFACE

The impetus for this book emerged from the MMBB's own awareness of the impending centennial of its creation. Among the many possibilities that emerged from considerations of ways to observe such a significant milestone was the idea of a history of MMBB encompassing its first hundred years. A book of memories, photographs, personal testimonies and cherished stories might well have served that purpose. Instead, a rather more comprehensive history was chosen as the goal. Ultimately, MMBB's Board and senior staff envisioned a history of MMBB that would be of interest to MMBB members and interested persons, and that might also offer those not familiar with MMBB, but who might be interested in its development, helpful information and perspective.

Thus, in the summer of 2008 I was approached to undertake the task. Both humbled and honored, I perhaps accepted more quickly than my abilities would merit. MMBB's creation and development is an inspiring story, especially for those who have had personal or professional contact with it or who have enjoyed its benefits. But it is also a story worthy of revealing to audiences beyond the boundaries of Baptist or even religious institutional development. Its successful narration has been my primary goal and I remain humbled by the challenge of shaping its narration.

In telling the story, I have elected to use a straightforward narrative style. What has emerged is largely an institutional history, embellished with the recognition of the personalities and events that shaped it. Having approached the material from the perspective of social and intellectual developments in the United States, I have sought to ground the narrative in the emerging conditions of philanthropy and charity at the beginning of the twentieth century. Chapters more or less follow the markings of decades throughout that century. Each chapter begins with a section which is intended to describe the themes of the particular decade's circumstances. Some readers who are only interested in the MMBB narrative may find that material extraneous. I hope they will reconsider: MMBB was both a creature of its time—and a shaper of things that were emerging. In both senses its development in context is exciting.

Pensions became an assumed right of professional persons and many other employees in the twentieth century. As this book proceeds to publication, the future of pensions, benefits, and deferred compensation in general is in doubt in the aftermath of a severe economic crisis and climate in the United States. The story, therefore, may in the end define an exceptional period of American history and, as well, an exceptional period of the history of American labor and professional services. For both reasons, I believe it is worth understanding.

A NOTE ON SOURCES

Founding documents and early publicity surrounding the MMBB's establishment are available at the MMBB offices at 475 Riverside Drive, Room 1700, New York, NY, 10115 (www.mmbb.org). Sources for the actions and deliberations of the MMBB's Board of Managers are available in the bound Minutes of the Board, which are also available at MMBB. MMBB Annual Reports, bound volumes of the Supplemental Minutes and complete sets of *The Ministry* and *Tomorrow* magazines are presently available in the office of the MMBB Director of Communications, and perhaps ultimately in the MMBB Archives. With few exceptions, printed or recorded versions of MMBB Luncheon Addresses are also available. A published history of the MMBB, *The First Twenty Years* by Everett Tomlinson and the unpublished histories of the MMBB written by Peter C. Wright and M. Forest Ashbrook are both available in the Archives. As the MMBB Archives are still in the collection and formation stage, footnotes referencing document availability are in some cases necessarily incomplete. A few pieces of Henry L. Morehouse's correspondence are available and will presumably be included the Archives, as are several letters from John D. Rockefeller and John D. Rockefeller, Jr., and M.C. Treat's original note to Morehouse proposing the challenge grant. Some additional historic correspondence is available in the Archive files. It is regrettable that much of the correspondence of the MMBB Executive Secretaries and Executive Directors is not available.

The American Baptist Historical Society, 3001 Mercer University Drive, Atlanta, GA 30341 (WWW.ABHSARCHIVES.ORG) is inarguably the best repository of historical materials regarding the development of Baptists in North America, American Baptists in particular. Its collections include the minutes and other documents of many Baptist organizations including the American Baptist Churches in the USA, and some materials related to the MMBB. Of possible particular interest is an extensive collection of brief biographical materials of ministers in the ABC collected at mid-twentieth century by the MMBB and now in the archives of the ABHS.

Much of the material for this book has been derived from the aforementioned sources. In addition, a number of secondary sources have provided context and insight and have been noted in the text. It is worth noting that very few histories of private or nonprofit pension organizations are available. In addition, a number of personal conversations with present and former MMBB staff members, MMBB Managing Board members, and others have contributed to understanding the flow of events during the last several decades. In some cases, such conversations were held anonymously, at the request of the individual.

Notes have been provided with a moderate touch in accordance with contemporary style. Informational notes offer the interpretation of the author based on sources available. Most other notes direct the reader to the sources in which events or decisions were recorded.

INTRODUCTION

The Ministers and Missionaries Benefit Board has been an important provider of retirement security and other benefits designed to ease life's challenges for ministers and missionaries since the MMBB was founded in 1911 and chartered in 1913. In pursuing its mission, the MMBB has been a pioneer in the development of pensions and benefits during the twentieth century, and has been a leader in its strategies in offering these pensions and benefits. MMBB's contribution to the development of private pensions in America, and employment benefits in general, is significant.

Although pensions ultimately became an expected feature of a great many professions and occupations in the twentieth century, they were, along with the other "benefits" that frequently accompanied them, essentially a twentieth-century invention. Prior to that, pensions were virtually nonexistent. Infrequently wealthy families or benevolent organizations provided funds or shelter for the support of a beloved employee, or to servants no longer able to work, but such benevolence was not routine. Private and commercial enterprises generally possessed little sense of responsibility for workers whose age or infirmity made them useless. Communally insured health care was not invented until the 1930s.

Religious organizations, notably the Roman Catholic Church, expected lifetime service from its clergy and religious workers. In return, they sometimes provided lifetime shelter. The Presbyterians provided meager monetary support to the widows or dependents of their clergy as early as the eighteenth century. Since the days of the Roman Empire, professional soldiers received pensions as rewards for their service, and an expectation of a pension was clearly perceived as a means to guarantee the loyalty of combatants; however, such payments were often considered a means of dividing the spoils of war. In a similar spirit, Revolutionary War soldiers, and combatants of America's later wars, often received modest pensions as tokens of gratitude and in recognition of their sacrificial patriotism.

With few exceptions, though, most people confronted their last years with only the resources they had inherited, saved, or otherwise acquired, or from family support. For that reason, "old" was often synonymous with "destitute." Statistically, of course, it was only a minor problem, as life was, to quote Thomas Hobbes's phrase, "solitary, poor, nasty, brutish and short." Life expectancy was limited. Illness and maturity in age most often meant impending death, and most people simply assumed that they would labor at their craft, profession, or calling until they died. The wealthy and well connected might anticipate a few years of dignified respect in their older years, but few people prior to the twentieth century had any expectation of a "retirement" in any modern sense. If they did, it was likely due to fortunate birth, good luck, or the beneficence of charity. Financial planning for retirement, including funds regularly contributed by an employer, an employee, or both, was virtually unknown. That, too, is an invention of a more recent time, and the MMBB was also one of the leaders in the field.

The history of the MMBB is rooted in the context of bleak beginnings. Only as the labor movement in America matured did the concept of benefits penetrate social consciousness as a matter of right. MMBB was among the first of a very limited numbers of organizations whose purpose was to support people in their older years out of a sense of communal responsibility and justice, and with a plan for long-term performance security. Speaking at mid-twentieth century, H. Pearson Hammond, MMBB's early, long-serving actuary and Board member, put it concisely: "Prior to 1900 pensions were generally considered as charity. During the early years of this century some formal plans were established but few were scientifically financed. It was in the late '20s that plans sound in principle began to be developed in any volume. A generation ago, churches in particular, and people in general, were not pension-conscious. The fund, therefore, was a pioneer in this field of endeavor." (H. Pearson Hammond, quoted in *MMBB Board Minutes*, vol. N [1971]: 123–24.)

What follows strives to narrate the story and to interpret the vision, origins, development, and maturation of the Ministers and Missionaries Benefit Board during its one hundred years. It does so from the vantage of describing the MMBB as first among many organizations that ultimately brought the concept of pensions into common expectation for laborers, professionals, educators, civil servants, and corporate managers alike during the twentieth century. To retire with sufficient resources, with a pension as a cornerstone, became the common expectation of the majority of Americans in that time.

The MMBB story has been told in parts before. The fund's early years were dramatically recounted in personal reflections by Everett M. Tomlinson, the first Executive Secretary of MMBB. Subsequently, at least two later executives, Peter C. Wright and M. Forest Ashbrook, contributed partially finished, unpublished manuscripts reflecting upon MMBB's history from their own perspectives as its leaders. And, on the occasion of MMBB's seventy-fifth anniversary, John S. Bone, an MMBB staff member, wrote an engaging volume that mixed a fictional narrative with factual material. A trail has, therefore, been previously marked. This attempt to recount the story through the lengthening sweep of a century is the first to be written by one not directly engaged in MMBB's daily operation. It is also the first attempt to present MMBB's progress in the larger perspective of its role as a social and economic pioneer in the context of the North American culture in which it functions, in addition to the obvious value to the ministers and missionaries it has served.

Prior to the development of pensions as a means to support older persons beyond their working careers, care for the elderly was primarily a family responsibility or the result of charity. Therefore, in approaching this subject, the unlikely power of Henry Morehouse's original vision to provide for the care of older ministers could not be adequately expressed without understanding something of its contrast with the past. Thus, the first chapter is devoted to summarizing some of the themes of the history of the motives and practices of charity and philanthropy that had emerged by the time of Morehouse's era. Remarkably little has been written about the history of charity in the United States. What little is available presents continuing and connected themes that have shaped both limiting and liberating characteristics in American society. Some of those themes are described at the beginning, primarily to enable an understanding of Morehouse's vision as the radical proposal it was. It will also underline how unlikely the success that MMBB achieved actually was. In addition, the initial chapter provides a background for the general questions, "What was going on?" and "What led to the rise of the pension?"

Subsequent chapters proceed in chronological order and in narrative form, with little exception. Each chapter describes the challenges, successes, failures, and dreams of the MMBB through a mix of materials highlighting the development of benefits for MMBB members. Each also suggests the economic forces that encouraged or prevented the offering of such benefits, the personalities and programs that delivered both the contractual and noncontractual benefits, and some of the surrounding social and political currents that shaped MMBB over both the short and long terms. Subsequent chapters also begin with a section titled "A Sense of the Times," designed to provide context for upcoming events. Those sections combine fiction with fact to achieve their purpose of invoking the ethos of each era; they are frequently presented in fragmentary style, intending to remind or infer, rather than to explain or prove a point. Portions of those materials may seem, on the surface, to have nothing directly to do with MMBB. But in reality they have everything to do with it: they explore the styles, themes, statistics, facts, and events that evoke the spirit of American society and culture at the time. In short, these sections describe the context in which MMBB was striving to provide for "the better maintenance of the ministry." Much of this material was inspired by, and in many cases was based on, a series titled "What It Felt Like" by Henry Allen that was published the *Washington Post* in late September 1999, on the eve of the new millennium. Allen's work is footnoted, but I wish to specifically acknowledge his unusual perception in that the sometimes-superficial trends of the twentieth century often added up to its substance.

It is a core purpose of this book to show that MMBB was created at a time when philanthropy was undergoing significant redirection. While MMBB was motivated by the desire of a religious organization to provide for its aging ministers, it became a pioneer in developing pensions that were an expression of support different from classic philanthropy and offered, instead, benevolent solutions that were built on the development of business and scientific principles. In so doing, MMBB became a pioneer in developing pensions that reflected a kind of delayed compensation as a deserved and just part of compensation for services performed.

A second, equally important purpose is to demonstrate that the key to MMBB's long-term success and durability may be understood by three things: First, in its earliest years it understood the necessity of developing significant financial resources and had the good fortune to achieve them. Second, it consistently balanced creative solutions with prudent and thoughtful actions. And third, it enjoyed the stability that resulted from effective leadership that was untainted by scandal or unnecessary controversy. To illustrate that point, the present Executive Director Sumner Grant once observed, in a casual comment, that perhaps the "one thing that defines MMBB is its endowment." Ironically, the Ministers and Missionaries Benefit Board began with no resources except Henry Morehouse's persistent vision. It proceeded with dedication by those who were its effective stewards and with the good fortune of financial generosity from individuals of both modest means and great wealth. MMBB matured by the grace of people with prudent judgment, shrewd perception, and above all, unbroken commitment to accomplish Morehouse's vision.

It is a remarkable story. A person of faith could argue that it was an achievement ordained by God, and even cynics would be hard-pressed to deny what sometimes seems the hand of a beneficent force guiding the MMBB along the way.

Henry L. Morehouse was the visionary "founding father" of MMBB whose dedicated persistence persuaded the Northern Baptist Convention to initiate action resulting in a pension program for ministers. He served as MMBB's Board President from 1911 until his death in 1917.

Col. Edward H. Haskell assumed Board leadership following Morehouse's death and served as President (1917–1923), leading the Board through the "Morehouse Million" financial campaign. He was also a significant early personal benefactor of MMBB.

Avery A. Shaw was a pastor and later the long-term President of Denison University. A long term Board member (1915–1941), he led MMBB through the Depression, and was MMBB's longest-serving Board President (1924–1941).

William R. Conklin served as Board President through World War II and the recovery period (1942–1950), and led the Board through its successful "Worry Free by '43" membership enlistment campaign.

Leonard J. Matteson was the son of early MMBB Field Secretary, William D. Matteson. His long-term Board service demonstrated the devotion of personal and familial commitment; he served as President (1951–1960).

Robert G. Middleton possessed negotiating skills honed as a successful pastor, and was Board President through the turbulence of the early years of a culture-changing decade (1961–1966).

John W. Reed, a legal scholar and professor, as well as an accomplished church musician, served as President on three separate occasions (1967–1974, 1982–1985, and 1988–1994). His leadership skill, wit, and wisdom enabled him to meet uniquely different challenges in each term.

E. Spencer Parsons served as an ABC pastor and Dean of the University of Chicago's Rockefeller Memorial Chapel and was President of MMBB (1975–1981). His insight and forthright integrity guided MMBB through the financial doldrums of the 1970s and effectively responded to ministers' concerns about MMBB investment experience.

Howard R. Moody served the Board frequently beginning in the 1960s, serving terms as Vice President and as President (1986–1987). As Pastor of the Judson Memorial Church in New York's Greenwich Village, he consistently brought sensitivity to concerns for social justice to the Board's attention.

Mary H. Purcell became MMBB's first female Board President. Her background in non-profit and charitable organization leadership enabled her to provide steady guidance as President (1995–2002) during transition in executive staff leadership and changing Board dynamics with the denomination.

George Tooze is a retired career pastor, author and astute observer of organizational dynamics. As President (2003–), he has brought both passion and insight to the Board as it has defined its vision and expanded its service beyond ABC/USA churches and institutions to new opportunity and growth.

Everett T. Tomlinson, pastor, educator and author of boy's books was recruited by Henry Morehouse to lead a campaign to raise $200,000 in response to Milo C. Treat's $50,000 challenge. After the campaign, Morehouse persuaded him to remain as Executive Secretary of MMBB until he retired in 1926. He remained as Advisory Secretary to the Board and wrote a history of the MMBB's first twenty years.

Peter C. Wright, pastor and a member of the original Board of MMBB, served as Executive Secretary (1926–1940), having previously served as Associate Executive Secretary from 1920 under Everett T. Tomlinson. His leadership guided the Board through the challenges of the Depression. Upon retirement, he was named Consultant Secretary.

M. Forest Ashbrook became Executive Director of MMBB in 1940 until his retirement in 1961. He had been recruited in 1935 by P. C. Wright and the Board to assume leadership upon Wright's eventual retirement. During his term, MMBB assets, services and organization expanded. After retirement, Ashbrook served as the Manager of the newly constructed Interchurch Center at 475 Riverside Drive.

Dean R. Wright, a minister and former Navy chaplain, followed M. Forest Ashbrook as Executive Director (1961–1990). Having been hired by Ashbrook with the thought he would stay about two years, his tenure as Executive Director became the longest. He led through three decades of notable change in churches, American culture, and at MMBB.

Gordon Smith was Executive Director (1990–1997), having served MMBB as Assistant Treasurer and Treasurer from 1975. His tenure was the briefest of the Executive Directors, but under his leadership the vision and core values of MMBB were clarified and strengthened, new technology was introduced, and the ground was prepared for MMBB's broader service.

Sumner M. Grant became Executive Director in 1998, after serving briefly as Acting Executive Director following Smith's retirement, and continues to serve until the present. Grant led MMBB through the period of expansion of contracted services to denominations, churches and organizations not affiliated with the ABC/USA, and through three major national economic crises.

John D. Rockefeller, a lifelong Baptist, became American's icon for both wealth and philanthropy. From his great wealth, he provided generous support to many causes including many Baptist schools, colleges, missions and programs. His contribution to the $200,000 needed to achieve Milo C. Treat's $50,000 challenge enabled MMBB to get started. Later, additional contributions provided about $7,000,000 to help underwrite MMBB's early benefit programs, and ultimately the endowment fund.

Milo C. Treat was an active Baptist layman from Washington, PA and later Pasadena, CA, who had profited through investments achieved in the oil and gas industry. In response to Morehouse's vision, he offered a $50,000 challenge gift if the Baptists would raise $200,000 among themselves. He insisted that the word "missionaries" be included in the MMBB name. He later provided several even larger gifts to MMBB. Insisting on anonymity, he always presented himself as "The Man from Pennsylvania."

Gardner C. Taylor, the distinguished pastor of Brooklyn's Concord Baptist Church, friend of Martin Luther King and a founding participant of the Progressive National Baptist Convention, was elected to the MMBB Board in 1970. Later honored by *Time Magazine* as "the Dean of American Preachers," his addition to the Board was one example of MMBB's desire to benefit from African American leadership.

Mary Beth Fulton, an accomplished writer and speaker, joined MMBB in 1936 as a "Special Representative" and as the first female member of the MMBB professional staff. She was originally tasked with developing communications with pastor's wives and women in general. Her communications skills soon brought her the responsibility for *Tomorrow* magazine which she developed into a popular magazine with varied articles of interest. She was a sought after speaker to women's' groups especially, and after her retirement served as an unofficial "ambassador" for MMBB.

William McKee brought a background in ministry with college students and youth to the staff of MMBB in 1961 as Field Counselor with Special Responsibility. He was the first African American field staff member appointed at MMBB. In 1963 he was delegated to work with state and city society executives in assisting pastors in personal or professional crisis as a result of their leadership efforts in civil rights. Later, McKee became the chief executive the Board of Educational Ministries of the ABC/USA.

C. Oscar Johnson was the Pastor of the Third Baptist Church of St. Louis, MO (1931–1958) and was a popular preacher, inspirational speaker and leader within the American Baptist Churches. As a current or former MMBB Board member he provided leadership on several occasions to raise funds or to enlist ministers, notably when Social Security was extended to ministers in the 1950s.

Arthur M. Harris became an original and long-term member of the Board as a result of contact with Everett Tomlinson during the first campaign inspired by Milo C. Treat's $50,000 challenge. Harris, a bond expert, was Vice President and Treasurer of the Banking firm of Harris, Forbes and Company. As a Board member, he provided unusual expertise and established high standards for MMBB's investment policies. He later served a term as President of the Northern Baptist Convention.

H. Pierson Hammond was an actuary with Travelers Life Insurance Company and later became head of Traveler's actuarial department. He provided consultation to MMBB at the time of the establishment of The Retiring Pension Fund in 1920 and soon was hired as the Board's actuary. His expertise and commitment to sound actuarial principles established an early habit of prudence in MMBB's fiscal management and his long term service, ending in 1951, assured its continuation.

Richard B. Fisher, then a young associate at the banking firm of Morgan Stanley and Company, became a member of the MMBB Board in 1961 and remained until 1998. During most of that period he served as Chair of the Finance Committee. His financial career became a Wall Street legend as he presided over the merger of Morgan Stanley with other banking and investment firms, an achievement that created great wealth even by Wall Street standards. His leadership in investments and financial management for MMBB was without parallel.

Margaret Ann Cowden was appointed in 1980 as the first Coordinator of The Women in Ministry project, a program MMBB funded for a three year period and later extended. She became a permanent member of the MMBB staff, and was later appointed Deputy Director. Following Dean Wright's retirement in 1990, she was a serious rival candidate to Gordon Smith to succeed Dean Wright as Executive Director. She later became the Executive Director of the American Baptist Extension Corporation.

Miriam R. Corbett joined the MMBB staff in 1965 as Special Representative with a focus on retirement counseling and services to those receiving pensions. She developed the annual visitation program to annuitants and later began a series of pre-retirement luncheons with seminars to assist those soon to retire. In 1970 she became Director of Retirement Services and later, Associate Director of MMBB. She briefly left MMBB to become the Associate Executive Minister of ABC/Metro NY and returned to MMBB in 1981 as Director of Special Ministries.

Leonard Ballesteros was appointed as a field representative on the MMBB staff in 1972 to increase MMBB's ability to communicate with and to serve its growing number of Spanish speaking members and constituents. As his service developed, he became widely popular as an astute but genial colleague. He worked persistently and gracefully to build bridges of understanding between groups of different ethnic, cultural and language backgrounds.

ACT OF INCORPORATION

AN ACT TO INCORPORATE THE BOARD OF TRUSTEES
and Missionaries' Board
OF THE MINISTERS' BENEFIT FUND OF THE NORTHERN

BAPTIST CONVENTION.
*Northern Baptist Convention, incorporated by Chapter 384 of the Laws of
the State of New York for the year Nineteen hundred and ten;*

Sec. 1.   All persons who are now or who hereafter may be members
of the ~~Board of Trustees of a fund for the relief and aid
of Ministers and Missionaries, their wives, widows and
dependent children,~~ *and Missionaries'* are hereby constituted a body corporate
with the name MINISTERS' BENEFIT *BOARD* OF THE NORTHERN BAPTIST
CONVENTION, and under that name shall have perpetual succession
and shall have the right to purchase or to acquire by gift,
devise, bequest or otherwise, and to sell, convey, or otherwise
dispose of any real or personal property.

Sec. 2.   The objects for which said corporation is established shall be

(a) To receive and maintain a fund or funds and apply the same
or the income thereof as follows: To provide temporary relief,
retiring pensions or annuities, without regard to race, sex or
color, for the ministers and missionaries, their wives, widows,
and dependent children, who by reason of long and meritorious
service, or by reason of old age, disability, dependency or other
sufficient reason, shall be deemed entitled to the aid and relief
of this fund, on such terms and conditions, however, as this Corporation may from time to time approve and adopt; provided, however, that the said temporary relief, retiring pensions or annuities shall be paid to such persons only as are or have been
members in good standing, or members of the families of such
persons as are or may have been members in good standing of
Baptist Churches. ~~affiliated with the Northern Baptist Convention.~~

(b) To receive and hold by gift, bequest, devise, grant or
purchase, any real or personal property and to use, invest or
dispose of the same for the purposes of the corporation.

(c) In general, to do and perform all things necessary to
encourage, uphold and dignify the vocation of the Minister and
Missionary of our Lord and Savior Jesus Christ, and to promote
fellowship and partnership in service, with full power, however,
to the Trustees hereinafter appointed and their successors, from
time to time, to modify the conditions and regulations under
which the work shall be carried on, so as to secure the application of the funds in the manner best adapted to the conditions
under which they were secured.

Sec. 3.   The direction and management of the affairs of the Corporation, and the control and disposition of its funds and property
shall be vested in a Board of Trustees, twelve in number, to be
composed of the following individuals; H.L. Morehouse,
of the State of New York, C. A. Eaton of the State of New York,
E. H. Haskell of the State of Massachusetts, W. H. Doane of the
State of Ohio, G. H. Thoms, of the State of New York, John
Humpstone of the State of New York, Henry A. Porter of the State
of Pennsylvania, Andrew MacLeish of the State of Illinois,
W. S. Shallenberger of the District of Columbia, G. H. Gallup of
the State of Rhode Island, E. S. Reinhold of the State of Pennsylvania, and F. C. Wright of the State of Connecticut, the four
first named to serve for the period of three years, and the four
next named for the period of two years, and the four last named
for the period of one year, or until their successors are elected,
who shall constitute the first Board of Trustees ~~and the members
of the Corporation,~~ and thereafter four Trustees shall be elected

MMBB Act of Incorporation: The Ministers and Missionaries Benefit Board was
incorporated in 1913 under Chapter 107 of the Laws of New York.

by the Corporation

temporarily

annually, on nomination of the Executive Committee of the
Northern Baptist Convention, to serve for three years.
Vacancies occurring by death, resignation or otherwise may
be filled by the remaining Trustees on nomination of the
said Executive Committee of the Northern Baptist Convention,
in such manner as the By-Laws shall prescribe.

Sec. 4.   The principal office of the Corporation shall be located
in the City of New York, State of New York, but offices may
be maintained and meetings of the Corporation or its Trustees
~~and Committees~~ may be held in other places, as   the By-Laws
may from time to time fix.

Sec. 5.   The said Trustees shall be entitled to take hold and
administer any securities, funds or property which may be
transferred to them for the purposes and objects hereinbefore
enumerated, and such other funds or property as may at any
time be given, devised or bequeathed to them for the purposes
of the Trust; with full power from time to time to adopt a
common seal, to appoint officers, and such employees not
members of the Board of Trustees, as may be deemed necessary
in carrying on the business of the Corporation, and at such
salaries or with such remuneration as they may think proper;
and full power to adopt such By-Laws and such rules and regulations as may be necessary to secure the safe and convenient
transaction of the business of the Corporation; and full power
and discretion to invest any principal and deal with and expend
the income of the Corporation in such manner as in their judge-
ment will best promote the objects hereinbefore set forth;
and in general, to have and use all the powers and authority
necessary to promote such objects and carry out the purposes
of the donors.

Sec. 6.   The services of the Trustees of the said Corporation,
acting as such Trustees, shall be gratuitous, but ~~such Corporation may provide for~~ the reasonable expenses incurred by the
Trustees in the performance of their duties *shall be paid.*

Sec. 7.   As soon as possible after the passage of this Act, a
meeting of the Trustees hereinbefore named shall be called by
any four of them, at the Borough of Manhattan in the City and
State of New York, by notice served in person or by mail,
addressed to each Trustee at his place of residence; and the
said Trustees named herein, or a majority thereof, being
assembled, shall organise and proceed to adopt By-Laws, to
elect officers and appoint necessary employees *or* fix their
compensation, ~~and generally to organise the said Corporation~~

The Corporation hereby incorporated may accept a transfer
of all real and personal property of any other corporation
created for similar objects, upon such terms as may be agreed
upon, and may receive, take over, and enter into possession,
custody and management of all such property, real and personal;
provided, however, that such property shall be applied to the
purposes of the Corporation hereby incorporated as hereinbefore
set forth.

Sec. 8.   The Corporation hereby incorporated upon accepting a
transfer of all the real and personal property of such other
Corporation, shall succeed to the obligations and liabilities
of such other Corporation and be held liable to pay and discharge
all the debts, liabilities, and contracts of such Corporation,
to the same effect as if such corporation hereby incorporated
had itself incurred the obligation or liability to pay such
debt or damages.

Sec. 9.   This Act shall take effect immediately, ~~on its passage.~~

MMBB's *Tomorrow* was the successor publication to MMBB's original publication, *The Ministry*, in 1941. Since then it has been published continuously. After a period of only occasional publication, and then cessation in the late 1970s, it was re-introduced as *Yesterday, Today and Tomorrow* in a larger format. The original "Tomorrow" title was restored after only a few issues.

"Worry Free by 43" was both the slogan and the title of an MMBB campaign in the early 1940s to enlarge its membership to the greatest possible number of eligible ministers, missionaries and others. The program was highly successful and greatly expanded MMBB's membership and ability to serve ministers' needs.

THE MINISTERS AND MISSIONARIES BENEFIT BOARD
OF THE AMERICAN BAPTIST CONVENTION
475 RIVERSIDE DRIVE, NEW YORK 27, N. Y.

RECEIVED

APPLICATION FOR MEMBERSHIP IN THE RETIRING PENSION FUND

I hereby apply to The Ministers and Missionaries Benefit Board of the American Baptist Convention for membership in The Retiring Pension Fund.

I understand that if payment of dues is made annually to the Fund in an amount equal to eleven per cent of my annual salary as determined by the Rules and Regulations of The Retiring Pension Fund, by the church or organization I serve, in part or in whole, and by myself for any part, or the whole thereof, not paid by such church or organization, I shall continue as an active member of the Fund, provided my services for which my annual salary is received are those which are ordinarily performed by an ordained minister or commissioned missionary, and provided such annual salary is received from a church or other organization fully cooperating with, or otherwise appropriately related to, the American Baptist Convention. I further understand that annual dues payments, assuming my continuing eligibility for active membership, are payable until my retirement at age sixty-five or later.

I will notify said Board annually on or prior to each anniversary date of my Certificate of Membership of the amount of my annual salary so that my annual dues then payable for the ensuing year may be determined.

I am a regularly ordained Baptist Minister or Commissioned Missionary of the American Baptist Convention and I am now engaged in active service and am receiving remuneration from a church or organization fully cooperating with, or otherwise appropriately related to, the American Baptist Convention for services which are ordinarily performed by an ordained minister or commissioned missionary.

1. Full Name **MARTIN**   **LUTHER**   **KING JR.**
   First Name   Middle Name   Last Name   Your Social Security Number

2. Residence Address **413 AUBURN AVE, NE**   **ATLANTA 12, GEORGIA**
   Number   Street   City or Town   State

3. Sex **MALE** Date of Birth **JAN. 15, 1929** Where born? **ATLANTA, GEORGIA** Citizenship **USA.**

4. Place and Date of Baptist Ordination or Commissioning as Missionary (state which) ....

5. Marital Status **MARRIED** ....(List Names and Birth Dates of Children below age 18 on Reverse Side)

6. Wife's Legal Name **Coretta Scott King** Wife's Date of Birth **4/27/27**
   Wife's Social Security Number

7. From what bodily or mental disease or infirmity have you suffered within the past five years? ....

8. Present Employing Organization **EBENEZER BAPTIST CHURCH** Position **ASSOC. PASTOR**
   Employer's Address **411 Auburn Ave NE. Atlanta 12, Georgia**

9. Does the Church you are serving cooperate with the American Baptist Convention, including reasonable financial support of work within its budget? **YES** ...., or

   Does the organization you serve have an appropriate cooperate, affiliate, associate or other relationship to the American Baptist Convention? If so, state relationship...........

ANNUAL DUES. Annual dues shall be equal to eleven per cent of the annual salary current on each anniversary date.

SALARY. The salary for payment of annual dues is the regular cash salary from sources properly related to the American Baptist Convention, plus an allowance for free parsonage (or other owned living quarters), which may be the full rental value, including the value of any utilities paid by the employer (but not less than fifteen per cent of the regular cash salary and any cash allowance for utilities). Add any cash rental, housing or utilities allowance in lieu of parsonage or utilities. Add free room and board at their estimated cash value.

10. Present Annual Cash Salary........$ **4000** ....(If shared by two or more organizations, list on reverse side)

   Cash Rental, Housing or Utilities Allowance $........ **6000 — 660 —**   **660. —**

   Rental Value of Free Parsonage and Utilities $ **2000** (Or value of room and board)

   Total Salary $ **6000** Annual Dues, 11% of Total Salary $ **660 —** Payable in **1** Installments
   (1, 2 or 4)

   NOTICE. Dues are payable annually in advance on the date and on each anniversary date of the Certificate of Membership and, after the initial payment, will be in arrears if not paid within sixty days thereafter, but by arrangement dues may be paid in semiannual or quarterly installments by the addition of an installment charge. The present installment charge for semiannual payments is 1% of the dues; for quarterly payments 2% of the dues.
   NO CHANGE WILL BE MADE in the amount of dues because of changes in salary except at the anniversary date of the Certificate.

   Signature of Applicant *Martin L. King*

Date **Sept. 18, 1963** ....19........
(All questions must be fully answered)   (Please fill out the other side)

Rev. Dr. Martin Luther King, Jr. enrolled in MMBB shortly before his assassination. MMBB supported Coretta Scott King (and their family) for the rest of her life and assisted Dr. King's children through college.

THE MINISTERS AND MISSIONARIES BENEFIT BOARD
of the
AMERICAN BAPTIST CONVENTION

475 Riverside Drive, New York 27, New York

ROBERT G. MIDDLETON
President
CHARLES C. TILLINGHAST, JR.
Vice President

September 25, 1963

DEAN R. WRIGHT
Executive Director
MALCOLM R. CARY
Treasurer

To All ABC Pastors:

This letter is sent as a special word of greeting and concern from The M & M Board to all our ministers who face a crisis in regard to civil rights in their communities or churches. It is not written to suggest what you should do, but to express a feeling of Christian solidarity with you.

The situation is changing with bewildering speed. The tactics for securing civil rights for Negroes lead us all onto unfamiliar and sometimes uncomfortable grounds. Yet we have never, perhaps, found ourselves confronted with an issue so lacking in ambiguity.

Many of us on national staffs are spared the hardest experiences because there is no controversy in our immediate fellowship about the basic issues of racial justice. But I know that the simplest reaffirmation of our Convention's repeated position on civil rights will, in some churches, cause serious tension and conflict. Some of our pastors may be forced out, even as is already taking place in the South.

Will you write me if there is anything you feel M & M can do to help you if you are under serious pressure. The social revolution that is taking place will constitute a major pastoral problem. Much healing will be needed and also much teaching--and a willingness to live with real disagreements will be required. The M & M Board stands ready to be of help to you in this situation in any way possible.

Dean R. Wright, Executive Director

DRW/seh

Many pastors, especially those in the south, suffered for their support of civil rights in the '60s. With justice and compassion, this letter from MMBB executive director Dean Wright assured these pastors of MMBB's continued support through job placement services and grants.

MMBB used a wide range of strategies to support the "Worry Free by '43" campaign to increase membership. It worked. By the end of 1943, MMBB announced that 72% of eligible clergy were enrolled.

"I'll ne'er forget, believe you me,
This Christmas, 1943,
And you who made me worry-free
With M and M Security!"

M & M
Crusade

1

THE MMBB IN CONTEXT

The MMBB grew out of a Northern Baptist Convention committee authorized to investigate ways to provide for retired or disabled ministers. In 1911 it was authorized to raise funds in response to a challenge grant. In 1913 it was chartered in the state of New York to develop and administer aid to ministers, with a mandate to "promote interest for the better maintenance of the ministry," a phrase that has been variously interpreted during its first century. The incorporators, however, clearly defined "maintenance" in monetary terms."[1] Over its century of service, the MMBB has remained focused on that goal, and its core service has been to provide pension, and later disability and health benefits for its ministers and missionaries. Until recently, those assisted were overwhelmingly affiliated with the Northern Baptist denomination.[2]

At times, "maintenance" has also included social and communal benefits, contractual and noncontractual benefits, and general support and encouragement for the profession of American Baptist ministry. More recently, the MMBB has also offered its products and services to a growing number of non–American Baptist churches and organizations that have met certain legal criteria and who have established an affiliation with the MMBB for the purpose of contractual benefits and services as well.

Throughout its history, the MMBB has generally sought to provide benefits that provided convenience and financial protection to churches and employers, as well as economic and social assurances to individual members and their dependent families. Priorities have occasionally changed due to circumstances, changing needs, and opportunities, but no other organization has defined its work as consistently using a word it helped to define: "benefits."

In order to fulfill that purpose, a number of conditions were necessary: the availability of financial resources, a developing sense of ministry as a profession, as well as a sectarian or God-inspired calling.

Changing social perceptions about compensation and its relationship to long-term security were among the conditions. Chief among these prior conditions and developing resources was a belief that worthy service deserved a just compensation that included a provision for retirement, the development of an organizational structure to administer it, and the resources and the will to provide it. Those preconditions provided the context out of which the MMBB could develop. But it was, in fact, a far more radical step than the founders of the MMBB likely perceived.

Old Virtues and New Possibilities

The idea of pensions—and even more, benefits—was new in the early twentieth century. It represented a profound shift from earlier concepts of "charity" and "benevolence." Charity often implied the uneasy and sometimes demeaning relationship that frequently accompanies money given by those who possess it to those in urgent need of it. In contrast, the concept of benefits emerged to imply a kind of normal and usual compensation that described a relationship that included responsibility on the part of the provider earned by the receiver.

Therefore, the MMBB's early development reflects the shift from an older notion of benevolent, individual charity to a more modern comprehension of communal and corporate responsibility expressed to recipients in the form of delayed or deferred compensation. MMBB itself was always a participant, frequently a pioneer, and ultimately a pilot of the leading edge of this development. An understanding of this development from older concepts of charity to the modern understanding of benefits is important in understanding MMBB's creation and its history of achievement.

The Seeds of Community Benevolence in Early American Perspective

North Americans have always perceived themselves to be inheritors of a revolutionary spirit, but their first political and social activities were more reactionary than revolutionary. The earliest English and European settlers in the colonies sought to escape the tumultuous, inequitable, economically unstable, and socially transient cultures from which they had come. The early purpose of these settlers, variously expressed in the colonies, was to create a more certain, simple, and predictable order of community life, one that approximated their image of the way things were and ought to be. Many were also inspired to conform human institutions to what they believed was the order of nature and of Nature's God. That order rested on a social contract under which everyone contributed and few would be dependent. Personal responsibility and a strong work ethic were central to creating and maintaining that order. Still, they understood the unpredictable misfortunes of life. Therefore, the early settlers also defined community responsibility to include practical concern for the poor or disabled, one undergirded by benevolence and charity.

Further, the foundations of early American institutions were established, in varying measure, on idealism, common good, moral purpose, economic necessity, social expediency, religious passion, and even zealotry. These strands ultimately merged in the political notion of fundamental equality and an inviolability of the "rights of man." The biblically rooted language of that simpler time expressed the belief that a "laborer was worthy of his hire." It also believed that laborers, once fairly paid, were obliged to provide for their own households. This applied to rich and poor, the highborn or those of low estate. A concept of benefits as a rightful, necessary, and expedient companion of wages, or compensation of value to whole communities as well as individuals, could not develop until a later and more complex time.

Whether motivated by religious vision or by personal and corporate greed, the goal of most early settlers was to accumulate wealth. Most were resistant to giving money away, and later, they were against taxation for anything beyond absolute and demonstrated necessity. Frequently their community goals were rooted in a parochial creed or a spiritual vision, and they often begrudged assistance to those who were not participants in their chosen covenant or system of beliefs. Few had the time or resources to tolerate others who could not, or would not, provide for themselves.

Early American Concepts of Community Responsibility

Nonetheless, a sense of charity was deeply rooted in the early American experience. For example, when Governor John Winthrop shepherded his immigrant flock onto the shores of the Massachusetts Bay Colony, he established charity in the community's founding principles. Deeply influenced by John Calvin's advocacy of an austere and socially rigid version of Christian piety, Winthrop believed that man must do good works to glorify God, and that personal habits of diligence and industry were as important as the discipline of prayer and faithfulness as signs of faith. In contrast, sloth, selfishness, and idleness were likely indicators of spiritual depravity, and thus signs of living beyond God's approval. Such beliefs encouraged self-discipline and rewarded the work ethic that led to stable communities and prosperity.

Therefore, Governor Winthrop's sermon "A Model of Christian Charity," delivered on board the ship *Arbela*, was a revealing description of the community the Puritan settlers in New England aspired to create: one of stability, social cooperation, high ideals, and service worthy of revealing the glory of God. Winthrop's seventeenth-century use of the word *charity*, however, was a synonym for love, not the more specific later sense of aid to the needy or to worthy causes. Winthrop's prescribed code of behavior for those who voluntarily entered into a covenant to create a new society in conformity with God's purposes was a simple one: work hard, live in harmony, keep the good of the community uppermost, and avoid wasteful and selfish indulgence. Charity in that sense, he believed, would encourage the brotherly affection and harmony which would, in turn, result in a community worthy of God's approval.

Nor did early American leaders like Winthrop condemn the inequality of wealth. Wealth was often perceived as a blessing, and poverty as punishment. But wealth was also understood as being granted for God's purposes and not to be used as an individual's prerogative. In Winthrop's vision, the poor must not rise up against their superiors, and the rich and powerful should not eat up the poor. It was a biblical vision used effectively to bind the settlers as "members of the same body." "We must," Winthrop said, "be knit together in this work as one man," and "we must delight in each other, make others' conditions our own, rejoice together, mourn together, labor and suffer together...." It followed that the common objective was "to improve our lives to do more service to the Lord." The "care of the public," including the poor, should take precedence over all private interests, but however much the suffering of the poor might evoke a Christian sympathy, charity of a financial kind was the obligation of the giver, not a right of the receiver.

During America's earliest years, the idea of "doing good"—the idea of worthy service—was the foundation of communal life. The great Puritan intellectual Cotton Mather, for example, sought to goad his Puritan sheep into living worthy, charitable, and meaningful lives. In his

Bonifacius, or *Essays to Do Good,* Mather advocated that everyone should be involved in a "perpetual state of doing good in the world." His core belief was that everyone, according to his means and opportunities, was God's agent, and the doing of good works was everyone's obligation to God. He is famously quoted as having said, "If any man asks, 'Why it is so necessary to do good?' I must say, it sounds not like the question of a good man."[3]

Charity Defines Individual Wealth and Virtue

Inevitably, Puritan discipline frequently led to a certain measure of prosperity. Wealth certainly provided opportunities for enjoying subtle refinements of life comforts, but ostentation was forbidden. Ironically, only displays of charity and good works were acceptable ways to display wealth. As American culture developed, it was permeated by an almost-universal connection between religious dedication and civic virtue, with charitable benevolence at its center. As the Quaker William Penn defined his holy experiment in Pennsylvania, he wrote, "True Godliness don't turn men out of the World, but enables them to live better in it, and excites their endeavors to Mend it."[4] His use of the word "mend" derived from the Hebrew word *tikvah,* translated as "repair of the world." And for Penn, repairing the world meant employing the wealth earned by diligence and frugality for benevolent and humanitarian purposes. Like Winthrop, he believed that God gave men wealth to use rather than to love or to hoard. Penn famously encouraged groups to organize and work for the common benefit of their members—values that continued in a direct line to Benjamin Franklin's later advocacy for volunteer fire departments, and for the building of schools, universities, and hospitals.

Thus the "founding fathers" of American culture and the generations that followed gradually defined an ideal of the public good that contained charity at its core. It was most often expressed as concern for community well-being and a dedication to common good that included both rich and poor. It did not particularly focus on special need. "Poor relief" in early America was nearly always a matter of almsgiving, often including the elderly as recipients. Here and there, "pensions" were occasionally present, but they were almost exclusively provided to the aging servants of wealthy patrons after a lifetime of service. Presbyterian and Moravian churches in the colonial period did pay pensions, but only as relief to the widows and orphans of deceased ministers. After the Revolutionary War, the new government granted annuities to Revolutionary War veterans in recognition of their service, but all of these examples, including those of the government, were uniformly expressed in terms of charity.

Virtues of thrift, sobriety, self-sufficiency, and responsibility saturated public ideals and encouraged success in America. But deprived of approval for ostentation, wealth brought, instead, an obligation to demonstrate charity. This ethical ideal was a stream that flowed through the merchants and industrialists of the early and mid-nineteenth century—straight to John D. Rockefeller, who, reminiscent of a good Puritan, believed his possession of wealth demonstrated God's approval, and also believed that in his use of it, God would hold him accountable.[5]

A Golden Age of Charity in the Early Republic

The inherent conflict about wealth in the early American public led, ironically, to a proliferation of benevolent activity. It was complicated: if ostentatious wealth seemed to demonstrate a kind of sickness of civic spirit, financial need and extreme poverty were also viewed as personal shortcomings and marks of God's displeasure. One proved one's godly worth by charity. But who was worthy to receive it? If a charitable spirit was to be encouraged, so were industry and self-sufficiency. The inherent conflict in those views sometimes birthed odd contradictions. For example, Amos Lawrence, the New England industrialist, was often extolled for his benevolent vision and charitable activity, but he was also admonished for expressing a kind of contempt for working-class men by paying low wages and creating working conditions in his mills that were worse than prisons.

Even generous spirits were criticized: Thoreau once commented that "he who bestows the largest amount of time and money on the needy may be doing the most by his mode of life to produce the misery he strives in vain to relieve."[6] Such remarks stung both rich and poor: the rich because then, as now, systemic poverty was often caused by the same people who then later sought to address its harsh effects, and the poor because it proposed that their poverty was a result of lack of diligence, intelligence, or hard work. Therefore, it was clear from an early moment that a growing tradition of monetary charity was a way for the rich to atone for their sins. Its purpose was to set the poor free from their sin and encourage them to become rich.

The Greater Virtue of Corporate Charity

Even extravagant charity ultimately came to be viewed as ostentatious. As a result, charity shifted from being a private activity of individuals to becoming an expressed public concern of communities and organizations responding to community health by addressing social ills. Somehow, in a group context, charity seemed more communitarian and more noble. As a result, in the first part of the nineteenth century a "golden age" of charity emerged, one that included the charitable creation of schools, colleges, hospitals, and other institutions deemed to benefit community life.[7] Regionally and nationally, voluntary associations were created to address countless spiritual, economic, personal, and community concerns. Even the Christian mission organizations that ultimately constituted the very structure of much of American denominational religion were a part of this movement. It was the era of the "Benevolent Empire" that shaped the benevolence in North America for the next century.

Charity that addressed the needs of those who suffered through no fault or cause of their own was especially popular in this period, and, therefore, orphanages were popular. Then, as now, disaster, famine, and hunger also evoked especially sympathetic responses. Response to the Irish famine of 1846–47, for example, remains as the broadest and deepest demonstration of compassion among Americans of all classes and abilities. Education, especially for the poor and lower classes, was a particular and enduring favorite because it was thought to provide a means for children to become responsible for their own lives and ultimately to provide for themselves. In time, such an ideal helped create the most remarkable system of higher education in the world.

America's emerging sense of order was highly moral. Therefore, much of nineteenth-century benevolence was focused on associations for moral reform that focused on an array of vices and deficiencies in human behavior. Still others sought to find solutions for social and political threats. One example of this motivation was seen in the American Colonization Society (founded in 1817), whose goal was the transportation and resettlement of free Negroes to Africa. The Society's activities ultimately resulted in the establishment of the nation of Liberia.

More broadly, strategies to address problems like poverty, drunkenness, financial mismanagement, and a long list of other ills emerged from organizations and institutions with goals to change behavior and to develop responsibility. Poor houses were founded to enable the impoverished to work for their own support and learn responsibility; prisons were established with the idea of mixing traditional notions of punishment with habits of spiritual growth and social reeducation, which would result in reformed community contributors; "wayward youth" inspired the establishment of programs of industry and education to shape youthful offenders to be socially productive; and stern moral perspectives united with social and economic realities to advocate both protection and moral reform for "unwed mothers."

Few of these corporate approaches completely fulfilled their goals, but that in no way diminished the generosity of their supporters. Charitable activity often demonstrated mere moralistic pity rather than true compassion. Yet its motives were positive, and its understanding of need was acute. Not surprisingly, many of these activities were sponsored, advocated, or supported by religious leaders and reformers.

Baptist Missions As an Expression of Charitable, Spiritual Good

Christian people and churches in the early nineteenth century provided a particularly passionate example of benevolence. In both small groups and large organizations they created associations and societies to accomplish specifically spiritual as well as charitable approaches to human betterment. Baptists, as well as others, perceived that spreading the Christian message with a benevolent hand ideally fulfilled the admonition to "go into all the world." These impulses combined to create a powerful mission movement, first in developing "overseas" missions, and soon, thereafter, missions within America itself. The American Baptist Foreign Mission Society was founded in 1814, originally to support Baptist missionaries Anne and Adoniram Judson in Burma. The American Baptist Home Mission Society (ABHMS) was founded in 1832 to "furnish occasional preaching, and to promote the knowledge of evangelic truth in the new settlements" and to "evangelize the Indians and western frontiersmen."[8]

The work of Baptist missionaries was, at first, almost exclusively focused on making converts, establishing churches, opening Sunday schools, and other religious and moral projects. That work soon enlarged to include the establishment of more corporate approaches as well: Bible and tract societies, temperance advocacy societies, reform groups in opposition to slavery, and especially later in the century, a variety of religious and humanitarian organizations that provided services to immigrant groups. From the mid-nineteenth century, the continuing influx of immigrants stimulated the publication of Bibles and other materials in several languages. In 1877 the Woman's American Baptist Home Mission Society was established "to proclaim the Christian faith and to minister to people of special need." Its programs often focused on aspects of public health, education, and practical and domestic skills that would ease the life circumstances of recent immigrants. Most immigrants were poor and isolated in the least desirable parts of urban centers; therefore, such societies also established or supported settlement houses and "Christian Centers" in many of the cities' most congested areas.[9]

The corporate model of Christian charity reflected in denominational mission efforts extended throughout the nineteenth century. For example, after the Civil War the ABHMS devoted considerable energy and inspired benevolent gifts to establish or support a great many educational institutions. Many of those institutions were focused on specific concerns, such as the education of the poor, black persons, immigrants, or the working class. Others were developed to provide future community leadership and pastors. Many of these colleges and universities achieved the top ranks of educational institutions.[10] The University of Chicago, for example, was forged from the union of a Baptist seminary and a floundering college and ultimately became one of the world's most respected institutions. Henry L. Morehouse, ABHMS Corresponding Secretary, was a catalyst in establishing that university under Baptist auspices.[11]

The need to publish evangelistic tracts, Sunday school materials, academic books, and inspirational materials resulted in the creation of the American Baptist Publication Society and its distribution network. These pamphlets, tracts, and books were directed at the moral improvement and inspiration of people both on the frontier and in the cities. In addition to their religious purpose, their publications assisted in encouraging a more literate public, especially in remote towns and villages of the frontiers, and often in poor uneducated urban areas.

Such Baptist societies, and many like them, were inspired by the continuing notion of community health and improvement in religious and spiritual forms. Their boards raised significant funds for the support of missionaries, schools, materials, and programs of assistance for those they sought to reach and assist. The mission societies also provided much of the impetus for creating denominational structures for interchurch cooperation, a sharing of administrative responsibility, and fundraising and support from churches and individuals for both foreign and home missions. They embodied the golden era of benevolence in a specific, sectarian way that was replicated by many other religious groups and denominations.

When the Northern Baptist Convention was created in 1907, it was in large part to unify these missionary, charitable, education, and publication societies under one umbrella, as well as to foster unity between the churches that supported them. It also created a platform from which common concerns, including salary and pension support for missionaries and ministers, could be addressed. Morehouse, the first and most passionate public advocate for a denominational pension program for Baptist ministers, recognized that there were mission societies with benevolent support for many purposes, but none to address the needs of ministers. He had lengthy service as Corresponding Secretary of the Board of the American Baptist Home Mission Society, and in that role he had formed broad perspectives and connections that later enabled him to enact his vision.

Toward Corporate Benevolence: The Social and Gospel
Necessity for Doing Good

Still, the development of the idea of providing pensions and benefits first required a culture with a preference for a systematic and routine approach to dealing with need. In American social development, the dual ideals of individualism and personal responsibility had come to dominate prevailing expressions of what it meant to be American—and even Christian. Charity and its cousin, benevolence, were clearly conceived and connected to the virtue of the person or groups providing them. But the effect of such benevolence, however generous or parsimonious, was still not projected as a matter of the recipient's right. Whether doing "good works" in the religious sense, or doing "good deeds" in the civic sense, both were assumed to be good for the giver to do. But it continued to be less clear that the recipients of such good works deserved the benefit.

The emergence of a more complex social order for the further maturation of American culture was needed in order to achieve what we might understand as modern philanthropy. With the rise of industrialization, greater complexity emerged, and the practical futility of random individual charity became apparent. By the mid-nineteenth century powerful forces were reshaping the American experience. Some of these changes magnified the need for charity. One was the remarkable geographic, economic, and population development within the United States. By 1850, for example, there were six times as many people in the United States than were present during the first census of 1790. By 1860 there were 31,500,000 people, an increase of more than 35 percent over the 1850 census. The period from 1840 to 1860 experienced a higher rate of growth than any subsequent period of American history. Large numbers of foreign-born newcomers entered the United States: "your tired, your poor, your huddled masses yearning to be free."

American population changed, and with that change there also emerged a loosening of older social ties and new structures of social and economic life. Not only was America's population changing, but America was changing. too. Energized by newly arrived immigrants and an expanding population in general, American mines and factories multiplied, cities grew, and in both urban areas and country villages, lines of social stratification became more pronounced. People became more isolated, and whole segments of the population were trapped by boundaries of poverty and disease. By the 1850s, symptoms of these changes included urban violence, anti-immigration sentiments, reactions to industrial working conditions, and social distress. It was also a decade of disease; cholera, for example, especially ravaged the immigrant and urban poor, but it equally attacked the prosperous and "respectable classes," creating anxiety and vulnerability for everyone. These developments fostered a growing new awareness that community good was linked to individual well-being.

America's sense of destiny changed, too. In 1850 most Americans had assumed that they were protected from the entrenched social problems that were then overwhelming European and English industrial cities. But one diarist observed, "Yet we have … our emigrant quarters, our swarms of seamstresses to whom their utmost toil in monotonous daily drudgery gives only a bare subsistence, a life barren of hope and enjoyment." Social and economic change was fostering conditions that would soon erase myths of complete self-reliance or economic independence by average people without assistance. In fact, the welfare of average people increasingly affected the well-being of their superiors. Likewise, the economically privileged seemed critical to the health of the less well off. As small-town American life disappeared, with it disappeared the assumption that people lived in simple independence where the elderly could count on a dignified security in small communities or on a family farm.

These changes initiated a long process that ultimately left behind the dominance of an agricultural economy and its social network. Until then, North Americans largely perceived themselves as members of small-town, independent, communitarian life, with its simple virtues. But increasingly America's cities created isolated lives, fragmented communities, and broken support systems. As the population increased and urbanization progressed, human suffering magnified, or at least appeared to, and such suffering seemed more frequently to challenge both American prosperity and character. Solutions to the challenges that accompanied the rapidly emerging changes soon needed large and corporate responses.

The Urgency for Charity: Urbanization and the Civil War

The acceleration of urbanization multiplied the categories of need. Children and youth were a popular and primary focus of benevolent concern: orphan asylums and foster homes attracted both public sympathy and private charity. For the elderly, help provided to poor or working-class families indirectly aided them, too. The founding of hospitals to isolate and combat disease, and, in some regions, institutional "homes" to care for the infirm elderly helped many others. Still, the plight of those too old to work and too healthy to die was not yet acknowledged. Instead, it was lumped together under the broad category of "pauperism."

By the 1850s, the national agenda was diverted, and then dominated, by constitutional, moral, theological, social, and economic controversies over slavery. The Civil War magnified the multiple realities of social chaos and was ultimately a major cause of widespread human deprivation and poverty. As regional tensions escalated, a rising tide of private generosity emerged for specific purposes as North and South armed and prepared for battle. Concern for the welfare of troops, especially volunteers, and their families, was primary, but broad financial resources had limited value if programs and structures to implement them were not in place. Therefore, by the time the war broke out in 1861, some of the most visionary had already made plans to create charitable structures. Religious leaders were among them. Henry W. Bellows, pastor of New York's prestigious All Souls Unitarian Church, for example, feared that "spontaneous beneficence" exercised without plan or direction would be wasteful and would likely overwhelm organizations and societies that received it. In 1861 Bellows led others to actively organize and coordinate the variety of soldiers' aid societies that had been developed in New York and elsewhere. The seeds of broad, corporate benevolence were taking root.

Bellows and his colleagues helped to inspire the creation of what was soon known as the "Sanitary Commission," a government-supported program specifically focused on the remediation of disease and infection inevitable from battle wounds and close living conditions among soldiers. Though government sponsored, it brought together a spectrum of private charitable organizations. Soon to follow was the United States Christian Commission, created in 1861 as an informal outgrowth of leaders of the YMCA. Its objectives were to promote the "Spiritual good of the soldiers in the army, and incidentally their intellectual improvement and social and physical comfort." The Christian Commission ultimately developed a broad organizational structure and succeeded in providing support, relief, and comfort to military men and, after the war, to others. Early in his ministry, Henry L. Morehouse served the Commission. Through crisis, charity began to clearly perceive corporate strategies to redress urgent needs.

The Civil War also resulted in a provision of pensions for the soldiers who had served, many of whom were maimed for life and thus faced poverty as a very acute reality. In 1862 the US Congress granted annuities to disabled Union soldiers, and later pensions were extended to widows and orphans of veterans and, ultimately, to all veterans. But the view of pensions as charitable gratuities continued into the 1860s, and they were meager in amount. Ultimately, laws regarding pension administration were liberalized, and by the mid-1890s Civil War pensions represented 43 percent of federal expenditures. By that time, federal Civil War pensions and large charitable organizations had emerged as examples of corporate, systematic approaches to problems that small-scale charity could not address.

Yet another benevolent response was to address the plight of the freed former slaves in the South. Among this population, suffering was staggering. In 1863 a gathering in New York of some of the same religious and other leaders who had inspired other war-related charitable causes petitioned President Lincoln to establish a Bureau of Emancipation, with the task of guiding the transition of the former slaves into new, "self-supporting industry." The resulting Freedmen's Bureau was a government-sponsored organization in partnerships with private organizations with related purposes.[12] It was a further example of a corporate, public approach to what had originally been perceived as a private, individual problem.

The Civil War also indirectly spawned a number of independent advocates and exemplars of charitable service. Clara Barton and Dorothea Dix were notable among these. Through their personal service and fervent advocacy, both gained wide respect. Others, such as Samuel Gridley Howe, contributed great theoretical vision to benevolence, even while expressing doubt about the effectiveness of charitable institutions. However, the efforts of these sometimes-maverick but charismatic personalities contributed directly or symbolically to the development of new organizations for relief, reform, or restoration following the Civil War. Many of those organizations continued into the next century.

A New Paradigm for More Effective Charity: Business and Science

The Civil War's legacy of suffering stimulated unprecedented charitable outpourings of money, volunteer participation, and social and economic programs. After the war, that spirit guided the transformation of many of the same benevolent and charitable organizations and created new ones. Renewed educational efforts, asylums for the mentally distressed and institutions for the blind, prisons, facilities for juvenile offenders, disaster relief, and a wide variety of other social needs resulted. In short, cataclysmic suffering stimulated a new understanding that only corporate benevolence in a systematic, cooperative spirit could create effective responses. Between 1861 and 1900 that spirit and its charitable activity merged into a more business-like endeavor, and more often sought to anticipate rather than to respond to needs.

New resources encouraged solutions on a larger scale. Meanwhile, the development and accumulation of previously unimagined wealth had a powerful impact. Between 1880 and 2010, several ultimately iconic figures assembled unparalleled fortunes. Through their wealth and their perspectives, they greatly influenced the course of the American approach to social challenges; two of them, Andrew Carnegie and John D. Rockefeller, revolutionized the charitable strategies of the wealthy. Each influenced both the philosophy and the practice of philanthropy. By focusing on their distributions of wealth, both demonstrated the vision of social architects, and both were ultimately instrumental in establishing pension funds whose underlying concepts rested on the idea of developing resources for retirement or disability as matters of compensation and a "right" based on professional service.

Carnegie, a cultural Presbyterian, sometimes tagged by the press as the "Star Spangled Scotsman," had immigrated to the United States in 1848. Within twenty years he was twenty times a millionaire. Though not a formally religious man, his economic practices were reminiscent of the Puritan philosophy: hard work, shrewd insight, remarkable instincts, and an eye for profit everywhere. Yet as early as 1868 he had remarked to a friend that he considered it "a disgrace to die rich." He believed that the wealthy should not bequest vast sums to heirs, but should instead administer their wealth as a public trust while they lived. In practical ways, Carnegie's views on charity mirrored those of John Winthrop and William Penn.

His beliefs, however, departed from the Puritan perspective. He believed the growing millionaire class possessed superior characteristics that shaped a unique fitness to survive and triumph in competitive struggle. Carnegie reflected an early social Darwinism that made him feel confident, superior, and obligated to do good things. In his view, the millionaire class was working toward the same objectives as Christ, but "laboring in a different manner," and by their united efforts would someday bring "peace on earth, among men of good will." In short, rather than achieving wealth that was God-ordained, Carnegie believed that rich philanthropists had the power to create lasting benefits for those who were weaker and poorer.[13]

Carnegie disliked almsgiving, mistrusted impulsive generosity, and was little motivated toward moral reform and personal rescue of the suffering. Instead, he believed that noble vision would inspire and empower people. He favored institutions and places that would enable that vision: libraries, parks, concert halls, museums, public baths, and educational institutions—places and circumstances that would improve the human spirit and direction. He was also a practical man and, therefore, was generous to Tuskegee and Hampton institutes because he believed they had elevated practical manual and domestic training into disciplines that built character and fostered economic capability. In 1889, when Leland Stanford revealed his plans for a grand university in the Far West (Stanford University) and gave what was believed to be the largest sum ever donated to assure its stability, Carnegie observed "Here is a noble use of wealth." The reason? Stanford's original design for the university was that it should emphasize the practical rather than the theoretical and teach skill training rather than liberal arts.

At virtually the same time, John D. Rockefeller had also emerged as the wealthiest among the millionaire class. His reputation became synonymous both with the "robber baron" mentality but also with the ideals of philanthropic generosity. Both identifications were correct. Like Carnegie, his wealth was achieved by persistent work; a shrewd business sense that, to later generations, appeared to be predatory; and by an organizational genius to discourage competition in order to maximize profits. Like Carnegie, Rockefeller was a giver, but from different motivation. His pious Baptist mother had an unwavering devotion to virtuous living. As a result he had practiced charity by giving away money, notably to churches and missions. Unlike Carnegie, he was not originally averse to "almsgiving," and he personally distributed numerous small contributions. His motivation was rooted in the view that God had given him the money and would hold him accountable for what he did with it.[14] By 1888 he was giving away $170,000 per year to various causes, and in both in 1890 and in 1892 he gave $1,000,000 to the fledgling, Baptist-led University of Chicago alone. In those years, his dividends from oil investments rose so rapidly that he complained that he could not keep up with the "surplus," as much as he tried.

Thus, where the Civil War had exposed the urgency of a great variety of human needs, the era that followed it was characterized by the rapid development of multiple, large-scale solutions to the problems. Private wealth, increasingly disbursed through the emergence of charitable agencies, provided significant resources. A strong tide of charitable, civic spirit focused them, and the contributions of the wealthy fueled them. By the 1880s, directories of charities required more than one hundred pages to list agencies that had been created to address the varieties of need they sought to ameliorate. Even "tainted money" found its way into American communities in significant amounts to fund hospitals, libraries, art museums, churches, relief societies, orphan asylums, homes for the aged, seminaries, colleges, universities, and specialized training academies. Similar funds were devoted to advance prospects for scientific achievement and to raise the standards of competence practiced by many professions devoted to human advancement.

Even more than the multiplication of needs and the agencies to address them, though, and more than the vast wealth that was focused on relieving them, the most significant development in philanthropy in the late nineteenth century was a transformed understanding of the purpose of philanthropy itself. Increasingly philanthropy was envisioned as a means of establishing a permanent approach to overcoming entrenched challenges. Two emerging assumptions shaped the nature of the work that philanthropy supported: The first was that solutions to social problems should be business-like. The second was that such solutions should be based on scientific principles. Both private philanthropy and corporate approaches to social challenges soon reflected those values.

The two leaders of the millionaire class, Rockefeller and Carnegie, profoundly influenced the change. Both were increasingly averse to random acts of individual charity. For one thing, their own significant funds could not be effectively disbursed by such means. Rockefeller, especially, was convinced that his notion of wholesale philanthropy was the only way to adequately distribute his "surplus." Carnegie's approach was to use large amounts of money to challenge communities and organizations both to raise more funds and to focus them on workable solutions. He believed such approaches seemed to offer the most likely means of addressing needs at their roots.

In short, wealth had again become a significant challenge for the wealthy. But now, the principles of the business that had created such wealth soon shaped a mechanism in which relief of current misery and the hope of solution in the future could be systematically addressed: the foundation. The idea of a continuing structure that could address problems in both the short and the long term was well suited to manage surplus wealth and to do good. With a philosophy, a vision, a purpose, and a staff of professional leaders to accomplish them, great things could happen by regular application of large resources. By 1901 Rockefeller, for example, recognized that even his "wholesale philanthropy" could not adequately distribute his "surplus." In that year, at the anniversary of the founding of the University of Chicago, he declared, "Let us erect a foundation, a trust, and engage directors who will make it a life work to manage, with our personal co-operation, this business of benevolence properly and effectively." His challenge was as revolutionary in American social and political life as any radical political party platform.[15]

Rockefeller's symbolic invitation was broadly accepted, and in the dozen years that followed Rockefeller, Carnegie, and many other millionaire donors established enduring foundations that outdated previous philanthropic efforts.[16] Foundations achieved a solution to the challenge of effective distribution and focused application of resources. Foundations also offered a systematic way of distributing private wealth over time with greater efficiency and vision than the donors could personally express. Later, funding for specific benefits such as pensions and insurance, including for the MMBB, followed a concept that combined private wealth with regular participant contributions to develop a continuing response to predictable, ongoing needs.

Since most of the millionaires of that period had achieved their wealth by astute, often shrewd, business practices, it was also only natural that theses social benefactors would affirm a business approach in evaluating needs, distributing funds, and monitoring their effectiveness. They advocated that philanthropic activity should be conducted with the same discipline and astuteness as a business. In that sense, the large foundations they created were effective instruments for this purpose because they could employ competent administrators and staff members to affect their purposes in a businesslike way.

These captains of the millionaire class also were convinced that science and scientific principles had a role to play in making philanthropy effective. The sentimentality and personal compassion that had often seemed to characterize much of earlier benevolence appeared, to these men and their colleagues, like it had earlier to Thoreau: to be both dangerous and counterproductive. Instead, their approach was to develop a means of evaluating the needs and the most effective strategies to meet the underlying causes, rather than to simply ameliorate individual examples of suffering. Thus, both Rockefeller and Carnegie, in very different ways, perceived that it was better to prepare for the old age and retirement of worthy social servants rather than to grant them charity. In pursuing these goals, they effected a profound change from benevolence and charity to social and political transformation.

By 1900 much of American philanthropy was still conducted in older, more sentimental, random, and individualistic ways. Ultimately, though, commitment to the principles of business and of science reconfigured the largest amount of philanthropic activity in the United States. Inevitably, the business approach would give rise to occasional charges that foundations and major charities were "big business in disguise." Also, the application of scientific principles to philanthropic purposes, administered in a business-like way, served as midwife for the rising social reform movements of the early twentieth century and afterward.

A New Vision: The Emergence of the Idea of Benefits

In the early twentieth century, philanthropy in the United States had come a long way from Winthrop's prosaic vision of community rooted in an Eden of communal charity. One reason was that life in the United States changed. Gone, or going, were many of the simple communities Winthrop had envisioned, and in their place had arisen cities of growing complexity; declining numbers of defined, natural communities and many perplexing social and economic challenges. Still, Winthrop's vision was curiously accurate about one thing: it was not possible to contain charity within individual motives and actions. More than ever, communitarian, or the newly developing idea of common, united purpose could achieve far more and be far more effective than isolated benevolence.

By the dawn of the twentieth century, the notion of "benefits" that addressed the needs of the working classes or those in modestly compensated, professional occupations was yet to be fully comprehended. But the long evolution of benevolence, charity, and philanthropy had laid the foundation for its development. This new and dynamic vision—which understood that extending philanthropy's developing vigor and principles to the ordinary, predictable circumstances of life would pay large individual and social dividends—

was revolutionary. What emerged were a variety of approaches that sought to combine private wealth, community contribution, and corporate supervision to offer resolution to troubling problems. Among the challenges was the emerging need to provide for the "retirement" of certain of the professions and in the working classes.

Those who grasped this possibility created the organizations and products that would apply business practices and scientific principles to assure life security. They developed products and services—life insurance, financial planning, and development resources for community, job, and career development—that would prevent or diminish obvious, and predictable, causes of human suffering. Pensions and programs to support not only veterans or widows and orphans but also aging workers and professionals beyond their time of active service were among the visible results. Such approaches had benefits for individuals, employers, and the communities in which they were situated. Those who established the MMBB were among the pioneers who first saw this need and opportunity, and were inspired by a vision to address it.

2

FROM CONTEXT TO CREATION: SEEKING REFUGE FOR THE OLD SOLDIERS OF THE CROSS

A Sense of the Times

In 1900 there were seventy-five million people living in the forty-five states of the United States—ten times as many as a century earlier. By 1910, a million new immigrants were arriving annually. The "Oughts" were an age of confidence: The *New York Times* proclaimed, "We step upon the threshold of 1900 ... facing a still brighter dawn of civilization."[17] A "can-do" spirit brought debates about solutions, not problems: a gold standard versus free silver, or unions versus free labor. The Wright brothers flew an aircraft for the first time, while railroads busily interconnected the nation. Vast new wealth had unleashed an age of prosperity, but Theodore Roosevelt busted the trusts, believing that too much wealth in too few hands threatened national well being. It was a time when unabashed Americans staked out commercial and military claims by starting to dig the Panama Canal, and Roosevelt sent the Great White Fleet around the world to flex American muscle and influence.

It was an age of contrasts: Gibson girls with confident, up-lifted hair and elegant clothes portrayed a new feminine independence and defined fashion. But hungry, grimy children were photographed trudging into textile mills to work; many of the children, while still young, emerged crippled, worn out, and uneducated. Farmers were driven off their lands, and whole communities were displaced by railroad expansion, while an emerging urban middle class found a fantasy of security in newly developed industry. In urban areas, slums spread their misery, while in fashionable Newport the Vanderbilts dined on bronze furniture surrounded by Algerian marble.

It was an age of confidence: It assumed a traditional faith and a certainty that God's will was being done. Nervous families dressed up for their minister's visit and feared God's judgment for the tiniest infractions. A variety of organizations, including the YMCA, sponsored missionaries to exotic lands, especially China. In addition to the creation of the Northern Baptist Convention, the Baptist World Alliance was founded at nearly the same time. Cooperative mission work led to founding the World Council of Churches and the National Council of Churches later. A popular Christian periodical renamed itself *The Christian Century* in the expectation that God's Kingdom, as imagined by the mainline Protestant establishment, would become increasingly apparent. Its contributors championed the Social Gospel, with an agenda of prophetic, practical application of Christian principles to assist the Kingdom's arrival. Meanwhile, immigration increased the numbers of Roman Catholics and Jews. Baptist John D. Rockefeller asserted with confidence: "God gave me my money."

Suffering often went unnoticed: Politicians spoke of the nobility of man, and of grand achievements to come, while, countless children died of diphtheria, whooping cough, typhoid, and malaria. Ice men sprinted up New York's five-story walk-ups carrying seventy-five-pound blocks of ice. In every city, ash men removed the debris of coal-fed fires while breathing unmeasured quantities of yet-unrecognized toxins. Blind people, those with cleft lips, the clubfooted, and hunchbacks were everywhere and were barely acknowledged.

It was a self-centered age. Senator Albert Beveridge of Indiana announced, "God has marked the American people as his chosen nation to finally lead in the regeneration of the world." But of such selfish self-centeredness, Henry James later wrote, "The will to grow was everywhere written large, and to grow at no matter what or whose expense." The displaced farmers, workingmen, immigrants, anarchists, and conquered peoples—from Filipinos to Puerto Ricans—believed they could testify to the accuracy of that opinion.

It was often an ugly age. Black people were lynched while Jim Crow laws justified it. But Negroes were not alone: Italian immigrants were also hanged for real and imagined infractions of social as well as legal codes. George Washington Carver advocated for the education of Negroes to serve in industrially useful occupations, while with entrepreneurial skill, found an industry on peanuts. In contrast, W.E.B. DuBois prophesied that America had "two-ness"—American and Negro—two strivings and two souls, unreconciled. He advocated for Negroes to prepare for competitive leadership and achievement. The differences between Carver and Du Bois stamped the education of black people in America with conflict for two generations.

It was also the era that first embraced the effects of science and technology. It imagined electricity to power the machines that would overcome every inconvenience and obstacle. Inventions underlined endless possibilities. Men gave up the mystique of the straightedge razor for King Gillette's new safety blades. Typewriters, Dictaphones, and the telephone were in the dreams of the moderately ambitious. Electric vacuum cleaners were a housewife's fantasy. And what of the land? "Drain the swamps! Clear the forests! The city skyline gets higher every day, and the wind tears the smoke and steam out of the stacks, banners of progress, an electric Camelot!" Albert Love could not know that the canal eventually named after him would stand, at century's end, as the symbol of flawed technology and desecration of the environment.

In a town east of Kearney, Nebraska, a minister sits down at his desk in the evening to begin his Sunday sermons. He hears the chuffing sound of a locomotive in the distance and the shrill of its whistle approaching a crossing. He has enjoyed a dinner prepared by his wife from the garden he tended in the morning and a chicken provided by a church member. He reads by the light of a lamp whose fuel was provided by another member. His mind is occupied neither by fashion, the marvels of electricity nor urban suffering, but upon the needs and occasions of his church, and upon the eternal destiny of his parishioners.

As he picks up his pen, a twinge in his shoulder from his morning's labor reminds him that, at age 47, he is not immortal. His useful career may end sooner than he wishes, and his life, too. He worries about his family in light of either circumstance. A newspaper had reported that the Presbyterians and Episcopalians were both trying to raise money for the support of clergymen in their old age. Sadly, his own Baptist denomination has no such program and he would have to look elsewhere for relief.

Sure I must fight if I would reign;
Increase my courage, Lord!
I'll bear the toil, endure the pain,
Supported by Thy Word.[18]
He hopes that the Word will be enough.

Components of MMBB's Creation

The role of the creator of the MMBB properly belongs to Henry L. Morehouse, but the success of Morehouse's vision would have been far less had it not been for the dedicated energies of a small number of supporters and an even smaller number of wealthy contributors. Milo C. Treat provided the monetary challenge that inspired the creation.[19] John D. Rockefeller, Sr., was ultimately the MMBB's biggest benefactor, guaranteeing the reserve funds that would promote its success. But even more, as both a Baptist and a philanthropist, Rockefeller was ultimately a critical shaping force among Northern Baptists and many institutions related to them. His financial generosity was the most obvious influence, but in many ways, his social vision and principles of benevolence were even more important.

Rockefeller soon developed a belief in addressing problems at their "root cause" by using business-like procedures and "wholesale methods." His insistence on the use of scientific principles in social development and philanthropic activity accelerated in the early twentieth century. His approach exerted great influence not only on Baptists but on much of American culture, too. The last quarter of the nineteenth century had sponsored the formation of numerous private, voluntary, and even government programs of relief that addressed specific, often overwhelming, symptoms of human suffering and need. The twentieth century was destined to place great faith in both business and science in addressing them. The unparalleled development of private wealth such as Rockefeller's also provided resources to fuel the engines of many of the organizations and agencies created to resolve them. MMBB was among them.

Although the nineteenth century had spawned many responses to pressing needs, one need remained unaddressed. The vast majority of the ordinary, working and professional population classes of people continued to face enormous uncertainty from three causes in particular: the frequent, early death of economic providers; the cyclical challenge of unemployment due to economic "boom and bust" cycles; and the economic uncertainty and deprivations resulting from old age. These harsh cycles wrought economic hardship and suffering on a large section of American society. Baptist ministers were among those who suffered. They frequently approached old age with no home, no financial resources, and no prospects for employment. However, the story of the effort to relieve their particular plight did not begin with Rockefeller, but with the Baptist minister, supervisor of Baptist home missions, and persistent advocate for ministers, Henry L. Morehouse.

MMBB's Founding Father

Beginning in the 1880s, Morehouse was at first a lone voice addressing the need for support for aging ministers, missionaries and their widows and dependents. Morehouse had been a pastor in both Saginaw, Michigan, and Rochester, New York, and in 1879 was elected Corresponding Secretary of the American Baptist Home Mission Society, the society's chief executive position.[20] As the Corresponding Secretary, he frequently addressed church and denominational gatherings, and beginning in the 1880s he frequently used such occasions to raise concern about the needs of Baptist ministers facing or in retirement. He often gained sympathy but little active response.

Morehouse's vision was at first rooted in the old precepts of charity and benevolence. Indeed, his original assumptions about ministerial retirement were defined by the possibility of a fund that would provide grants to older ministers who needed them, specifically those ministers and their families who lived on the edge of poverty and who experienced obvious hardship. Enlightened benevolence seemed the best way to address that need. At most, perhaps, he appeared to envision a program of pensions based on a noncontributory style—one reminiscent of government pensions in return for service rendered by former soldiers. How to accomplish that result was less clear, though, and there were major obstacles to overcome.

Obstacles Morehouse Confronted

One obstacle was the persistent and pervasive belief that able-bodied persons were responsible for their own welfare and that of their family, and that families were responsible for their own members who were unable to work or who had no means of support, especially the elderly. However, by 1890 the shift of population from countryside to cities, the greater social distance emerging between generations, and the consequences of downturns in industrial economic cycles that often deprived family units of their sole economic provider had reduced familial and community bonds and economic alternatives. In short, the accelerating phenomenon of urbanization and the growing reality of geographically separated families consistently eroded the informal but real "safety net" that had been provided by community life in more closely knit, family-based towns and villages.

Another obstacle was the growing stratification of social classes that geographic and economic expansion encouraged. In a rural town or village, the differences between farmers, tradesmen, craftsmen, teachers, lawyers, and educators were originally only a matter of degree. They associated freely, shared friendships, and did business with one another as equals. But as towns became cities, and as people migrated to cities to advance their opportunities, not only did the fabric of familiarity unravel, but social and economic class distinctions were magnified, too. One clear distinction was between "professionals" and "blue-collar workers," with "tradesmen" somewhere in between. Distinctions of prestige and privilege between these classes were assumed to be part of the natural order of things, and the distances on the scale of economic reward commensurately increased.[21] Class jealousy, suspicion, and even contempt increased.

Another challenge was the perception that old-age assistance of any kind was a degrading charity and threatened the idea of self-reliance. Pensions had been established by business only in a few cases. Veterans of the Civil War and the Spanish-American War, especially, had been granted pensions. At first such pensions had been perceived as a charitable reward for loyal service. Later they were assumed to be a matter of "right" earned by sacrifice. Few industries or services were inclined to offer pensions even to long-term employees, and where they did exist, they were offered with a spirit of benevolence accompanied by a sense of charity for those who could not care for themselves. Although a few industries established pension programs in the Oughts in response to union pressure, it was not until 1920 that the federal government established a retirement plan for its employees.[22]

Those who were among the prosperous entrepreneurial class or who rose to prominence in a profession, as well as those who had personal habits of discipline and conservation, generally could prepare for retirement or declining health. But those who worked for wages or for low-level salaries, or whose working careers were abbreviated by illness, disability, or age, often had no fortune or security. Without the mediating role of close and proximate family support to provide shelter, food, or even personal care, or without a closely related small community to intervene with compassion in circumstances of extreme deprivation, such persons often had little hope. One result was the development of a class of elderly impoverished that was previously unacknowledged. It was a common problem that crossed many lines of social definition. The elderly poor were becoming a numerous and growing population. A generation later this reality was partially addressed by the implementation of the federal Social Security program, but until that time persons among the lower economic classes faced old age or declining health with no income and thus often lived in grinding, life-threatening poverty.

Therefore, the financial challenges to aging workers, whether wage earners or the new professional classes, were often daunting. Those who enjoyed robust health could expect to work long into old age. But a comparatively low life expectancy limited working careers in sedentary professions and even more in physically demanding occupations. Health care was not universally available and in any case was limited in effectiveness, thus further limiting active work years for many. Most workers of all classes were "old" by the age of 50, and even if they were in good health, they often faced a discriminatory age that limited their employment possibilities even in good economic times. Those who were financially dependent upon aging workers were also faced with poverty as the breadwinner's employment ended or declined, whether as a result of health issues, economic circumstances, or overt discrimination.

Early Responses to the Need for Honorable Retirement

As urbanization, family separation, class stratification, and other shifts began to emerge in the second half of the nineteenth century, workers in several industries began to confront both economic insecurity and workplace accidents and their resulting injuries by demanding protection and, in some cases, organizing unions for these purposes. The railroad workers' unions were an early and effective force in advocating such protection. The networking of the United States by rail had become the most significant economic development of the last third of the nineteenth century. Railroads employed thousands of people, almost exclusively men, in work that ranged from manual labor to highly skilled jobs. In Chicago alone, for example, more than five thousand men worked in the railroad industries by 1910. At the industry's peak in 1930, Chicago's railroad and railroad-related workers numbered thirty thousand. Accidents were frequent, and they often resulted in death or work-ending injury. The critical importance of the railroads in the development of the United States, and the significant numbers they employed, ultimately encouraged protective federal legislation, voluntary programs of safety, and occasionally, limited compensation for those injured.

The magnitude of the railroad industry and the needs of its workers also ultimately encouraged the rise of multiple unions in other industries. Many of these unions demanded, and often received, benefits including insurance, pensions, and employment regulation. American Express, which was then a small railroad freight company, offered the first formal private company pension plan in the United States in 1875. One of the first pension plans offered by a major employer was that of the Baltimore and Ohio Railroad in 1884.[23] The demand for work protection, including pensions and insurance, spread to other industries, including mining, steel production, and manufacturing. Demands for such protections, in addition to demands for higher wages and improved working conditions, were at the center of the extensive, and often violent, strikes that characterized the late nineteenth and early twentieth centuries. So significant and controversial was the need for economic security and its proposed solutions that the history of industrial labor's progress was front-page news for more than half a century. Ultimately, some of the union organizers who led the pursuit of better wage and job security Eugene V. Debs, the most famous became significant figures in the general history of the United States.[24]

Among formally educated workers, teachers, professors, and other academics were employed in work that was much less physically dangerous, but equally insecure economically. Teachers labored in return for low compensation, and were often at the mercy of local town or city governing boards for long-term employment security. On college campuses, professors were often late to enter their profession because of lengthy academic preparations, and they usually commanded small salaries even at the height of their careers. Neither teachers nor professors had much opportunity to make effective preparations for economic security in old age, and they often worked well into their older years if they were permitted to do so. The term "genteel poverty" aptly described their circumstances.

The vision and ingenuity of Andrew Carnegie set an example for some of these professional workers to address at least the basics of long-term security. When Carnegie served on the board of Cornell University between 1890 and 1905, he encouraged the board to develop a largely grant-based pension program for the university's faculty. Later, in 1918, using that experience as a model, the Carnegie Foundation established the Teachers Insurance and Annuity Association (TIAA) and initially funded the program with $1 million. The program was, henceforth, fully funded by participating institutions and individuals. Beginning with thirty public and private institutions in the first year, TIAA ultimately became the primary provider of insurance, pension, and other benefits for a great many educational and nonprofit institutions in the United States.[25]

Pastors and missionaries faced a dilemma similar to that of the educational professions and labor unions in trying to develop resources for old-age support. Ministers' work was not as dangerous as railroad work, but it was frequently more insecure. Educational preparation for ministry varied greatly from region to region and from denomination to denomination. But, like academics, ministers' entry into their vocational work was often delayed. In much of the United States at the turn of the twentieth century, physicians, ministers, teachers, and professors were compensated at comparable levels. All shared the problem that it was usually difficult to make any provision for old age because of modest or very low salaries. For example, the most recent US Census prior to the formation of the MMBB listed the average annual salary among Northern Baptist ministers as $683, a figure that was the lowest among the most well known Christian denominations in the North. (The average among Unitarians was $1,221; among Lutherans, $944; Methodists, $741; and Episcopalians, $941.) In the South, the averages were even lower, and Baptists in the South claimed the lowest amount at $344. Many ministers were compensated at levels far below these averages. Some were "farmer preachers" or supported themselves in other bivocational ways, and received virtually no compensation for the ministry they performed.[26]

Challenges Specific to Baptists

Several circumstances combined specifically to challenge Baptist ministers' financial security—one being the dynamic growth of Baptists as a group. In the early eighteenth century, prior to the religious renewal and expansion known as the Great Awakening, there were only a handful of Baptists in the colonies—perhaps as few as five hundred. Two centuries later, their number was in the millions, approaching ten million by 1930. Baptists established and sponsored many colleges, seminaries, and hospitals during their expansion, but many of these institutions were largely the result of individual, local, or regional activity, not national intention. To some extent they competed with churches for funds. Simply stated, therefore, the rapid growth among Baptists outstripped their organizational structures and resources to provide for their creations. It also led to a wide diversity in preparation for ministry, procedural standards, and compensation expectations.

A second factor was that much Baptist growth was among rural people or in the growing cities among lower and middle social and economic classes. With a few notable exceptions, Baptists did not attract the wealthy classes, and where they did, such persons tended to focus their financial resources on establishing and maintaining schools, orphanages, hospitals, or increasingly, overseas missions. Ministers, who often were important in raising the funds for the support of those endeavors, were assumed to have simple needs and that those needs would be adequately provided by their churches.

Churches, however, were often inadequately funded. At about the time the MMBB was organized, Everett Tomlinson, the first MMBB executive, reported that, leaving out the churches of "ethnic" background, only 10 percent of churches in the upper Midwest, including Idaho, North Dakota, and South Dakota, raised more than $1,200 for their entire annual church budgets. In the more populated parts of the Midwest, 14 to 17 percent raised more than that amount; 30 percent of churches in metropolitan New York City exceeded that amount, and New England, with its "older money," varied greatly, with 20 percent of Maine churches exceeding the $1,200 benchmark, Rhode Island 45 percent and Massachusetts, including Boston, had 63 percent exceeding that amount.[27] Ministry salaries, even at their low average levels, frequently accounted for the majority of such meager church budgets.

Another factor that retarded or restricted ministers' financial resources came from the multiple demands placed on them despite their limited means. Having to perform varied roles in the community in addition to their church appointments, ministers were often obliged to subscribe or contribute to multiple church-related, denominational, or community causes, including their own church budgets. Then there were unmeasured costs as well: in many churches ministers (and their wives) were assumed to be responsible for providing hospitality to what often seemed an unending procession of visiting ministers, evangelists, missionaries, and the agents and officers of denominational activities in their respective regions. Of course, ministers had their own children to nurture and to educate, and their assumptions about education and its value often motivated them to want to provide a more-than-rudimentary education for their own offspring.

Prevailing social and theological attitudes also contributed to ministerial poverty. Ministers were assumed to be working in response to a spiritual calling and in confidence that "the Lord would provide." But in addition to the reality that a church often could not adequately provide, many congregations seemed nearly intentional in guaranteeing clerical poverty. A parody of a deacon's prayer of that era perhaps expressed best what often seemed to be a reality: "Lord, we pray for the work of our poor, humble pastor: We pray that you will keep him humble, and we will keep him poor." In response to descriptions of the low salaries among ministers, church leaders sometimes responded that ministers were "poor financial managers." That may have been true of some, but many church budgets would not have supported even the most basic of programs without the financial ingenuity of the ministers who administered them. Minister's wives seemed also to possess a remarkable ability to administer a household on insufficient income.

Ironically, yet another barrier to ministers' development of retirement resources was created by the rising standards for ministerial preparation. Ministers were increasingly expected to have at least a college education, preferably including graduate seminary training. This, combined with the practical career-ending age-barrier of 50, meant that many ministers had only about twenty-five years of possible compensated service. In addition, ministers who served traditional, local churches most often faced an additional challenge resulting from a lifetime of living in church-owned parsonages. They, therefore, often faced disability or retirement without a home and with no resources to acquire one. As a result, clergy in general were frequently motivated to extend their church employment beyond the endurance of their health, and often until death. In turn, some churches were served by ministers whose personal vitality and wisdom had long since passed. Some churches, out of compassion or loyalty, felt an obligation to care for such aging pastors while they remained in leadership positions. But in all too many cases, ministers were forced out of their positions by impatient congregations, or by circumstances of health or age, and often had no place to go and no resources upon which to draw.

At the extreme, it was not unusual to encounter old ministers living in abject poverty, serving as handymen or as servants, or forced to do manual labor beyond the ability of their strength or health. In a few cases, ministers were discovered disguised as beggars. For the most part, however, elderly or disabled ministers possessed such pride as to be unable or unwilling to seek assistance, and most often suffered and died in silent despair.

Early Responses to the Problem of Impoverished
and Retired Ministers

Among Baptists there was general recognition of the growing problem of ministerial poverty and the personal financial crisis of older ministers in particular. In some Baptist state and association organizations, funds were established to provide a modicum of retirement support through grants or assistance. Likewise, in a few cases, local or regional retirement homes were established to which aged ministers could retreat in retirement. But funds for assistance of any kind were woefully inadequate, and the homes for the refuge of aged ministers were generally substandard and inadequately supported.

Therefore, aged, disabled, or retired ministers commonly depended on aid from their children, or in many cases, lived with children or family members. In some areas annual "donation day parties" resulted in cast-off clothing and other necessities to be sent to missionaries and ministers. Such contributions were of limited value and were often demoralizing for recipients. In any case, retired ministers were often not included in the distribution. Everett Tomlinson, first executive of MMBB, frequently referred to these aging or disabled ministers as "Old Soldiers of the Faith," and Henry Morehouse, MMBB's visionary founder, frequently described them as "Old Soldiers of the Cross." Both phrases were apt, and both depicted tired, worn-out, battle-weary veterans who had nowhere to go and nothing to rely upon.

The plight of older ministers facing such impoverished conditions had an inevitable negative effect on churches as well. Without any recognizable means of supporting themselves and those who depended upon them, ministers were often driven to continue their work beyond their best abilities. In churches where compassion overcame self-interest, sensitivity for aging ministers often evoked sympathy even when their diminished energy became evident. Present life expectancy with accompanying health and vigor has advanced to such a degree that many professional persons can serve effectively to the age of seventy and beyond. But in 1900, the age of 50 was considered the threshold of "old age." It also became the barometer of declining ability and the starting point for age discrimination. At the same time, the Baptist ministry was an aging profession. At the turn of the twentieth century, 75 percent of ministers in Connecticut were over the age of 50, and in Massachusetts, more than 55 percent were above it. Even in the relatively younger region of Illinois, 30 percent of ministers were above age 50; and in Oregon it was 37 percent. In the settled Midwest, 16 percent were above the threshold. Only in the youthful "wild West" of Colorado was a mere 6 percent above 50. Even there, however, the proportion of aging ministers was higher than the population in general.[28]

Sadly, the churches that sympathetically recognized the economic needs of older ministers by continuing their service often exercised compassion at the price of diminished leadership and service. An aging pastor often could not provide the fresh vision and increased energy needed to build up or inspire his congregation in order to grow and to expand its work. The best interests of churches were thus often in conflict with the ministers' urgent personal financial needs. Henry L. Morehouse continued to be the Baptist visionary and gadfly who urged a comprehensive approach to ministerial support, retirement resource development, and care for aging ministers. But as he surveyed the needs of ministers, he also became acutely aware of the continuing leadership needs of the churches and the financial limits they encountered as a result of supporting an aging minister.

Parallel Responses

The growth of labor union influence created increasing pressure for the establishment of pension programs in large industries. The railroads had been the first to develop almost industry-wide pension programs, with some early pensions developed in the 1870s, and because of the sheer size of the railroad workforces, their programs became the most numerous. What had begun as an effective force in the railroads had, by the early twentieth century, spread to mining, steel production, and soon to follow, the young automobile industry. In all of these industries employers had gained by establishing pensions: industrial accidents decreased and productivity increased when skilled but aging workers had an opportunity to retire.[29] As a result, the notion of "benefits" gained ground as a business-like and practical way to plan for both individual and corporate stability as workers aged.

The dilemma faced by churches of caring for and replacing older ministers was shared by other professions, especially in education. Independent practitioners like physicians, lawyers, and accountants could, and did, continue their practices as long as their health permitted, and as long as their clients and patients had confidence in them.[30] Institutional contexts, however, created a different problem. Just as churches were sometimes handicapped by having to care for an aging minister, academic institutions were often weakened by aging or disabled teachers and professors in the classroom. The advent of the Teachers Insurance and Annuity Association (TIAA) program in 1918 ultimately led to more systematic, honorable, and dignified retirement for academics. This, in turn, led to a more dynamic educational profession without penalizing teachers and professors after a lifetime of service.

Morehouse: Persistent Prophet

Among Northern Baptists, Henry Morehouse had broad experience as a pastor and mission leader, twice serving as the Corresponding Secretary for the American Baptist Home Mission Society. His early personal life had been in the bucolic settings of New York's rich farm country, but as a young adult he had served with the Christian Commission and, briefly, in other roles of outreach and assistance. His pastoral experience had exposed him to a rude and developing city in the upper Midwest, and to another in the context of the growing industrial and educational environment of Rochester, New York. His work with the American Baptist Home and Foreign Missions had exposed him to New York City's urban challenges; his mission work, especially, brought him into contact with a great many pastors, churches and Baptist leaders.

As early as 1882 Morehouse had begun to raise publicly the need to provide financial support and security for retiring ministers—"agitate" was the world Tomlinson later used. His vision was broad and included concern for general financial support as well as a secure retirement for Baptist clergy. His original vision for supporting aging ministers originally focused on the establishment of retirement homes, and he declared that "the blessings of heaven would rest upon the generous donors who would provide them." He soon discovered, however, that ministers as a rule did not generally want to live in institutional "homes," but in their own homes.[31] At first Morehouse's concern for a way to aid older ministers in retirement was an isolated one. Gradually, he began to garner general support for his ideas, but for a long time there had seemed no possible way to implement them.

In the early 1900s Morehouse became aware of Andrew Carnegie's leadership in academic retirement programs. He, therefore, organized a meeting in New York, bringing together several denominational representatives with Carnegie's staff. His hope was that Carnegie might be interested in funding a pioneering program for ministers and missionaries that would improve their own circumstances while strengthening the communities in which they lived. It was a plan that, in theory, seemed to mesh well with the wealthy industrialist's interest in community, social, and economic development. Carnegie, however, was well on the way to developing a vision for his philanthropy on a larger scale. More to the point, he was also acutely disinterested in denominations and believed that the multiplication of churches in communities created wasteful duplication. He had no interest in any support that would perpetuate sectarian competition. Morehouse, therefore, abandoned that approach.[32]

Even more than discovering a lack of interest by major contributors, Morehouse also had to contend with the attitudes of pastors and other church leaders, which were often rooted in presumed issues of faith or biblical understanding. Tomlinson recalls opposition to Morehouse's vision by one pastor who said he believed the promise of the psalmist and had never seen "the righteous forsaken nor his seed begging bread."[33] Sometimes simple pride among the pastors themselves impeded progress. For example, one pastor archly claimed that a retirement program for the poor might be all right, but that a man of intelligence should provide for himself. It was thus apparent that

Morehouse's vision would be blurred by a variety of experiences and attitudes, even among those who might benefit from it. He concluded that it would be difficult to accomplish his vision and to raise the needed funds on an individual basis.

The New Northern Baptist Convention as Catalyst

Meanwhile, growing sentiment for greater Baptist unity and cooperation had encouraged the development of new Baptist agencies of collaboration. Southern Baptists had moved quickly to establish a denominational structure following their withdrawal in 1845 from the national Triennial Convention organizational structure. Most other Baptists in North America, however, had continued their united work through the American Baptist Foreign Mission and American Baptist Home Mission societies, the American Baptist Publication Society, and related organizations. These were loosely affiliated and operated independently. The creation of the Northern Baptist Convention in 1907 was in response to a need for greater effectiveness in missions and publications. At about the same time, a world Baptist fellowship, the Baptist World Alliance, was also created.

The establishment of the Northern Baptist Convention in 1907 provided Morehouse with a more effective platform from which to raise his vision and also served as a source for fund-raising to implement it. The first meeting of the new denomination following its 1907 organization was in Oklahoma City, in May 1908. At that meeting, twenty-five years after his first advocacy for the plight of aging or disabled ministers, Morehouse offered a resolution:

> Resolved, That a commission of Seven be appointed to make inquiry concerning the methods and the extent of aid to aged and disabled Baptist ministers and the dependent widows and children of deceased ministers; also to make a careful estimate of the number of such persons, by classes, within the bounds of this Convention for whom provision should be made annually, and the aggregate amount required for these purposes; also to consider whether there may be a better correlation of existing agencies for this purpose and whether some more comprehensive and systematic and measurably uniform plan may be devised for securing and dispensing the requisite means for these purposes;

said committee to make report at the meeting of the Northern Baptist Convention in 1909.[34]

Whether he was fully conscious of it or not, Morehouse's vision loosely conformed to the emerging spirit of philanthropy in offering a pioneering benefit: It was shaping a corporate response from the Baptist community; it sought to address a universal problem at its core; it was business-like in approach, proposing that whatever the program was shaped to be, it should be effectively managed on behalf of the denomination; and it was potentially scientific in application. The success of the resolution was made more likely because it was offered at a time when the emerging vision for the Northern Baptist Convention was new and exciting, with dreams of a mighty new structure upon which to support future Baptist work. The Convention response to Morehouse's resolution was not overwhelming, but it was affirming. The resolution passed, and the committee was established. It would be years before anyone would fully comprehend that Morehouse's vision and persistence had persuaded the newly formed denomination to embark on a pioneering enterprise that would become a model for the development of pension and insurance benefits for religious workers and for others.

3

LAYING THE FOUNDATIONS

A Sense of the Times

Virginia Woolf once wrote, "On or about December, 1910, human character changed."[35] Of course, a lot of people suspected that Virginia Woolf was a little crazy. Still, if you were to root around in the family photo albums you would see that before 1910—the Roosevelt years, the Age of Confidence—men with mustaches stared at the camera with the hard focus of self-command, and women looked at the camera as if it were an annoying intruder, or else they seemed to see nothing at all.

But after 1910—the Belle Époque and the Great War, the Age of Reform—the mustaches were gone and men tried to capture the look of college boys, "full of coy awareness and infinite possibility."[36] "Women's liberation" began as women slowly jettisoned their corsets, leaving chaperones behind, and hiking their skirts above their ankles. When they looked into a camera, it was with an "amused wise-guy wariness." Sometimes they posed with cigarettes. The face of innocence merged into the face of sophisticated sexuality.

For everyone, the idea was to be up to date and progressive—to put an end to greed, ignorance, inequality, disease, addiction, autocracy, and especially, the glooms of the late Victorian era. The decade's political icon was Woodrow Wilson, and he stood in stark contrast to Roosevelt. Wilson, the former president of Princeton, an idealist and a reformer, said, "I am a vague, conjectural personality, more made up of opinions and academic prepossessions than of human traits and red corpuscles." Youthfulness became a moral virtue, and John Dewey, the Progressive educator, disdained parents who "look with impatience upon immaturity, regarding it as something to be got over as rapidly as possible." He believed youth should learn by doing.

Energy. Adaptability. American writer Max Eastman promised what youth always promises—that his publication, *The Masses*, would be "frank, arrogant, impertinent, searching for the true causes; a magazine directed against rigidity wherever it is found. Meanwhile, the gross national product tripled in ten years, and the national debt went from $1 billion to $24 billion. Industrial excesses declined, partly thanks to child labor laws, pure food laws, and other reforms of the Progressive Era. Free verse radicalized poetry, and free love radicalized proper behavior. Paradoxically, Prohibition occupied the national agenda. Yale football coach Walter Camp's "The Daily Dozen" exercises promised fitness. "Everybody's Doin' It Now" sang the suffragettes as they marched up New York's Fifth Avenue: "Doin' it, Doin' it." American troops were sent to Mexico to put them in their place.

America was having one of its episodes of reform in the name of the American Dream—trying to be both prosperous and good at the same time. The new soldiers of youthful virtue, the Boy Scouts, tried to do a good deed every day, and positivism infused the air with its perfume. "A negative thought is a poison as deadly as arsenic. Every morning now when I wake up I think positive thoughts and say, 'Fogelman, get out and get to it!'" said one. Baptist preacher Russell H. Conwell bullied the laggards with an old American theme: "I say you ought to be rich; you have no right to be poor."

It seemed everyone was tired of the past and ready for something new and exciting. Despite his assembly line speed-ups and his anti-Semitism, Henry Ford was the new American hero. He paid his workers more because it meant they had more buying power for his products. When asked about the past, he said, "History is more or less bunk." Soon, enthusiasm for the Great War would seek to prove this by demolishing the old order. The tango became the rage in ballrooms, especially when the city fathers banned it, and ragtime was popular—perhaps especially because it originated with black musicians.

Sometime the pace of change was overwhelming. Once, the rich had been celebrities, celebrated at Newport's extravagant balls; now, the diamond-decked dowagers seemed dreary. Immigrants took commerce and city governments away from them, and the new rich were able to buy their way into Pullman cars and the best hotels. Upper class Senator Henry Cabot Lodge warned for years that a million immigrants a year would cause "a great and perilous change in the very fabric of our race." Robert Bacon, a Harvard athlete and partner of J.P. Morgan, headed to war, saying, "This world—our world—is not lucky enough to be snuffed out as was Pompeii. We have got to go through a long-sickening decadence."

In August 1914, after the war started in Europe, Wilson declared: "We're too busy with our reforms, we're too moral, we're 'too proud to fight,'" laying the foundation for his next election slogan. An Indiana paper supported America's presumed isolation from Europe's chaos, writing, "We never appreciated so keenly as now the foresight exercised by our father in emigrating to America," and a popular song of 1915 lauded, "I Didn't Raise My Boy to Be a Soldier." In 1916 Wilson ran on the platform "He Kept Us Out of War," but the war was bigger than his ideals. Later that year, the Germans sank the steamship *Lusitania*, killing 128 Americans, then to add insult, the Germans communicated to Mexico an offer to help it reclaim its lost territories in the United States. On 16 April 1917, America declared war.

Suddenly, everything changed. Americans soon experienced rationing, regimentation, censorship, and the draft. Wheatless, meatless, gasless, and heatless days marked the rhythm of the week. Women went to work in factories, and northern factory owners sent agents into the South to recruit black workers. It appeared that, for the time being, Americans liked regimentation, boot camps, and marching draftees. Wilson sold the war as the biggest reform movement of them all, "The War to End All Wars," the war "to make the world safe for democracy." Later, Charles W. Eliot, Harvard's forty-year president, would comment, "Like most reformers, Wilson had a fierce and unlovely side."

In truth, everyone had become sick of reform, idealism, promises, and "doin' it, doin' it." In their place, disillusion, xenophobia, paranoia, persecution, propaganda, bomb throwing, strikes, lockouts, and race riots become commonplace. More than half a million Americans died of the Spanish flu; black veterans coming home from France faced race riots; anarchists mailed dynamite bombs to public men; the government rounded up radicals in the "Red Scare." Then, in 1919, frustrated, angry, disillusioned, and deeply grieving his son's death in the war, Teddy Roosevelt died at 61. To cap it off, eight players for the Chicago White Sox were charged with conspiring to throw the World Series to the Cincinnati Reds. They were acquitted, but barred from baseball for life. Outside the courtroom a small boy confronted his baseball icon, Shoeless Joe Jackson: "Say it ain't so, Joe."

What was the result of all the energy and reform and idealism of the decade? Virginia Woolf wrote, "We must reflect that where so much strength is spent on finding a way of telling the truth the truth itself is bound to reach us in rather an exhausted and chaotic condition."[37] Maybe she wasn't so crazy after all.

Ministers' Urgent Need

Despite seeing a growing response to human need, Henry Morehouse had had an epiphany that there were no provisions for aging Baptist ministers. His persistent, prophetic voice identifying the need for support or assistance for aging ministers at formal and informal gatherings of Baptists over three decades gradually achieved sympathy and agreement. But fulfilling the dream for the enterprise that Morehouse envisioned required more than recognition of the dilemma or compassion for those in need. It required sponsorship, organization, and, most of all, money. The authorization of a committee to explore and develop a pension program by the newly established Northern Baptist Convention provided at least the theoretical sponsorship and the authority of organizational backing, if not at first the money. Behind the scenes, between 1908 and 1911 Morehouse labored to convince a handful of wealthy Baptists to provide the funds.

There were many ways in which the needs that Morehouse described could be met. Some state Baptist associations had already made tentative steps toward providing pension or grant funds for ministerial relief, and in a few cases there were regional attempts to provide retirement homes or financial assistance to retired or disabled clergy. But, with the exception of Massachusetts—whose funding for Baptist ministerial pensions was more significant, although not adequate—such attempts fell far short of even the most basic assistance. At an early stage, Morehouse considered the more widely accepted plan of providing retirement homes for ministers—a strategy considered and implemented by some other organizations. By the time of his proposal in 1908, however, some form of pension plan had become the dominant vision.

The Role of the Northern Baptist Convention

Although the fledgling Northern Baptist Convention drew together many churches and several Baptist mission societies, it was not yet a mature or fully functioning organization by 1908. The Convention did, however, provide a unifying banner: Its creation offered a way to develop resources for common goals, and a structure to enable their achievement. The Convention's affirmation of the resolution was, therefore, a hopeful indication that financial support could be achieved to meet such needs. As a result, Morehouse's efforts could focus on the specific steps required to bring his vision to reality.

Morehouse's resolution by itself did not bring about the creation of a pension program. Its only practical effect was the creation of an investigative committee of seven, with Morehouse as chairman. The committee was instructed to report back to the next Convention, scheduled to convene in Portland, Oregon, in 1909. At the Convention the committee did report, but the report contained only modest organizational accomplishments. The same was true for the next convention in Chicago in 1910. Part of the challenge was that the committee had no funds with which to do research or even to support its meetings, and it seemed that its work might ultimately prove futile. Appointing the committee had represented a positive step, but to actually develop a functional pension or retirement system required the creation of a functioning, permanent organization and, most of all, money.

As the 1911 Convention in Philadelphia approached, the committee was not confident that the slow pace of their efforts would achieve a significant advance by that meeting either. It was perhaps fortuitous, then, that the meeting in Philadelphia was in Grace Temple Baptist Church. The church's famous pastor, Dr. Russell H. Conwell, was a noted pulpit giant and popular speaker who had been distinguished by developing the church's ministries, by raising significant funds to support them, and by having a vision that had included the establishment of Temple College, later Temple University, which he served as its first president.[38] Conwell was personally a gifted motivational speaker and promoter, and his "Acres of Diamonds" sermon had raised multi-tens of thousands of dollars for the church's ministries and for the school, had inspired thousands, and was copied by many.[39] The Convention, still propelled by the dynamic of its creation, therefore gathered with enthusiasm and was undoubtedly inspired by the environment of the famous and financially successful Conwell and Grace Temple.

Tomlinson reports[40] that Morehouse had received a telegram. Correspondence indicates that the news it contained was likely the result of Morehouse having challenged a wealthy layman from southwestern

Pennsylvania to provide some seed money, and possibly followed one or more meetings between Morehouse and the layman in question. But when Morehouse presented his committee report to the Convention, he was prepared to make a significant and dramatic announcement. He stood before a capacity audience in the church's auditorium and read the following message:

> If the Northern Baptist Convention should appoint a permanent committee whose duty shall be the collecting and dispensing of funds for the relief of superannuated and disabled ministers and missionaries, it would appeal to me and I would pledge fifty thousand dollars for that fund, on condition that between now and next Christmas, at noon, they secure two hundred thousand dollars more.[41]

The donor wished to remain publicly anonymous, and his communication was, therefore, signed "A Man from Pennsylvania."[42] As the communication was read, the Convention broke into applause. The symbolism was unmistakable: it was a concrete and specific offer to challenge the newly formed denomination to deal with the established need for ministerial support in retirement. Even by the monetary values of 1911, $50,000 was insufficient to approach the challenge Morehouse had outlined. But its prospect brought to reality what Morehouse had long advocated, and what a growing number had perceived as important. There was, therefore, little dissent when the Convention voted to accept the offer and to authorize a campaign to meet the challenge to raise the $200,000 by the following 25 December 1911. It stated that if the quest for $200,000 in matching funds was successful, "thereafter the Convention will recognize the annual budget of the Ministers Benefit Board of the Convention as one of the objects of beneficence to be commended to the churches."[43] In spirit, the MMBB was born.

Creating MMBB Leadership and Corporate Structure

For MMBB to become reality, two things had to be accomplished: First, while Morehouse had personally expended significant energy on promoting the cause of financial assistance to aging ministers, he had given little advance thought to an organizational structure to accomplish it. Such a structure was urgently needed, both to raise the funds and to shape an organization. Second, and more immediately, there was the challenge to raise the $200,000 by the following Christmas. Both were significant tasks, and the latter seemed impossible.

In accomplishing the challenges of a financial campaign and organization, the MMBB's fortunes were again guided by Morehouse. He was a visionary and a creative administrator, but he knew his own limits and almost immediately identified Everett T. Tomlinson as the person to be the Executive Secretary to the newly appointed Board. Tomlinson had been pastor of the Central Baptist Church of Elizabeth, New Jersey, for twenty-three years. During that time he had become acquainted with Morehouse through their mutual service on the board of the American Baptist Home Mission Society. He had also been an educational administrator in Auburn, New York, and headmaster of the preparatory department of Rutgers College (now Rutgers University).[44] Just prior to the establishment of the MMBB, Tomlinson had resigned from his successful pastorate, with a desire to focus on his writing, preaching, and educational endeavors. He was available.

Using artful persuasion—and not a little pressure—Morehouse convinced Tomlinson that he was the only one qualified to undertake the task of leading the retirement program into reality, and that if he did not take up the responsibility, it would result in the failure and abandonment of the program. William Rainey Harper of the University of Chicago had failed to recruit Tomlinson for his new university enterprise. Morehouse somehow succeeded where Harper had failed. Tomlinson originally consented simply to lead the committee in the effort to achieve the $200,000. However, his gifts of insight, communication, sensitivity, and organizational clarity proved to be the combination that the Board needed in a successful leader and administrator for the new venture. He faced a formidable task that required courage and patience. His new challenge was to achieve a noble vision without structure, to serve a Board without institutional or legal charter, and to offer pension grants for which there were no funds.

Achieving the $200,000 under any circumstances would require quick action. Inexplicably, the Board did not meet until 15 August 1911, nearly two months after the Convention that authorized it and less than five months prior to the deadline imposed to raise the $200,000 by the "Man from Pennsylvania." The first meeting was held at the offices of the American Baptist Home Mission Society at 23 East 26th Street, in

New York City. The Board comprised the Rev. Henry L. Morehouse (New York), the Hon. William S. Shallenberger (Washington, DC), the Rev. Clarence M. Gallup (Providence, Rhode Island), Eli S. Reinhold (Chester, Pennsylvania), the Rev. Peter C. Wright (Norwich, Connecticut), Charles M. Thoms (Rochester, New York), Andrew MacLeish (Chicago), the Rev. Charles A. Eaton (New York), Col. Edward H. Haskell (Boston), W. Howard Doane (Cincinnati, Ohio), H.K. Porter (Pittsburgh, Pennsylvania), and the Rev. John Humpstone (Brooklyn, New York). When the Board organized, Henry Morehouse was elected President, Peter C. Wright was elected Recording Secretary, and Everett L. Tomlinson was declared Executive Secretary.

Raising the $200,000 Challenge

The Board's first order of business was to develop a strategy to accomplish raising the $200,000 needed to receive the $50,000 challenge gift. To do this, they sought to establish a Committee of Cooperation in every state and in many of the larger associations. They also devised a list of persons to whom financial appeals might be successful. To launch the campaign, a formal announcement was published and broadly disseminated that described the purpose of the program, the immediate financial challenge, the leadership, and an explanation that the campaign expenses, including the salary of the Executive Secretary, had been provided separately so that no amount for those purposes would be drawn from amounts pledged or received. The announcement also stated the Committee's plan:

—To devote all efforts September to December 1911 to raising the $200,000;

—To research the number, nature, extent, and effectiveness of similar organizations, and the conditions on which aid was granted by them;

—To evolve a plan to encourage the cooperation of similar agencies (among Northern Baptists) in pursuit of unity and efficiency;

—To discover the number and extent of those who needed to be provided for, and for that purpose to appoint Standing Committees of Cooperation in each state to identify that need.

It was a clear, concise, and well-prioritized approach. It was also a tall order, especially raising $200,000 in a four-month period. By then it was nearly September. Board members were not at all convinced it could be accomplished, but they approached it with conviction and commitment.

The announcement clearly stated the urgency of action in response. In fact, objectively considered, the project seemed doomed to fail. In most states and associations, the Board's announcement was positively received, but the limited time remaining before Christmas made timely responses difficult. In many cases, the schedule of meetings for state or association boards meant that it would be almost December before the plan could be officially received and a response determined. In one state, for example, the state board began its appeal with the statement "it is just three weeks till Christmas day."[45]

Under the time pressure, the urgency of the task was articulated forcefully and clearly. Both the MMBB and state communications frequently referred to the needs of ministers and missionaries who "are too broken for further service." The purpose of the envisioned Ministers and Missionaries Benefit Fund was described in specific, personal terms: "It will help solve the problem of the last days of the minister or his widow, their shelter, food, raiment, and medical care." Some points of the plans or their aspirations were vague or, ultimately, incorrect. For example, they variously stated the purpose was to build retirement homes for ministers or to provide for "those who need only a moderate allowance in order to continue in their own homes or in the homes of relatives." But the broad scope of the project was effectively communicated: "there are hundreds of ministers and missionaries who are subject to intense want."

In addition to the promise of $50,000, the Board's best asset was the critical need that shaped their cause. It would have required a hard heart indeed not to have been affected by observations depicting cases of "almost starvation or death where the medical care and funeral expenses are met by public charity … these conditions should 'make our faces burn with shame and spur us to hasten to wipe this blot from our Baptist escutcheon.'" Both Morehouse and Tomlinson frequently used the phrase, "Old Soldiers of Christ," "Old Soldiers of Faith," and increasingly, "Old Soldiers of the Cross" to describe those whose resources the MMBB would support. It was a particularly apt and powerful image in a time still familiar with past wars and with the sacrifices made by the aging veterans among them. A sense of denominational and competitive pride also urged action: "Baptists in the lead in many other matters trail the procession in this." Using a spirit of interstate, regional, and interchurch competition also helped: the Nebraska Baptists' communications, for example, included a challenge that "Illinois is aiming at $25,000. Nebraska should not be satisfied with less than $2,000 or $3,000. The David City Church has already raised $50."[46]

At the same time, columns, news stories, and advertisements were placed in denominational magazines and newsletters, and promotional talks were sponsored in many churches and at denominational and associational meetings. Local churches were urged to establish committees to advocate for the MMBB and its financial goals. Specifically selected individuals were solicited for large contributions. The fact that campaign expenses were being covered by external funds was a strong encouragement to many contributors. Still, aside from the original $50,000 challenge, there had been insufficient time to solicit large gifts in advance to encourage the campaign's success, and, therefore, progress was slow. Morehouse himself was discouraged and became pessimistic that the full $200,000 could be achieved in the time remaining. In fact, Tomlinson reports that Morehouse suggested that they ask the challenge donor whether he might consider prorating his challenge to match whatever amount was actually achieved.

Milo C. Treat, the officially anonymous "Man from Pennsylvania," was a Baptist from Washington, Pennsylvania, who had made a considerable fortune in oil and gas investments. After making his challenge, Treat had almost immediately continued a personal interest in MMBB's progress and had frequently communicated with Morehouse regarding MMBB's operation and strategic investments. In order to facilitate communication and work, the MMBB office had moved from Tomlinson's home in Elizabeth, New Jersey, to the American Baptist Home Mission Society offices on East 26th Street in New York. During one of Treat's visits to the office late in 1911, Tomlinson posed Morehouse's question regarding the possibility of prorating his challenge and extending the deadline. Treat immediately refused out of conviction that his plan was correct, and that to compromise the vision was equivalent to failure. Meanwhile, pledges and contributions came in ranging in amounts from $5 to $5,000. The larger amounts, however, were too few.

By the end of the first week of December 1911, the goal was still $100,000 short of the $200,000 needed. In an attempt to inspire greater response, Morehouse sent a letter to the Board members offering a personal pledge of up to $10,000 if others would join him in meeting the remaining amount needed. Morehouse's pledge represented the great majority of his personal financial resources, and it stimulated the Board to express both appreciation and further appeal. They communicated with Conventions and churches that had not already pledged or contributed, and they appealed a second time to those who had already contributed by asking them to consider an eleventh-hour extra effort. Their effort was largely effective, but still they were significantly short of their goal.

Treat joined in the strategy of solicitation by suggesting that a special appeal letter be sent to the "leading ministers" of the denomination using a comparatively new communication method, the telegram Night Letter, to deliver the request. He also provided the funds to cover the cost of the communication's transmission. This innovative appeal brought a renewed flow of pledges and contributions. Tomlinson led the Board to approach again those who had already made a significant contribution and to ask them if they could consider an additional amount. Among those who responded positively with a repeat pledge was Arthur M. Harris, of the investment and banking firm of Harris, Forbes & Company. Of even greater importance for the long term, Harris assented to Tomlinson's urgent requests to serve on the MMBB Board, a service that began in 1912 and continued until 1941.[47]

Morehouse's pledge, the Board's renewed energy, Treat's continued encouragement, the additional contributions from larger contributors, and news of additional pledges being sent from churches and individuals were all encouraging. As December 25 approached, pledges and contributions continued to come, but a significant gap remained that seemed unlikely to be filled to qualify for the $50,000 challenge pledge. Therefore, on Christmas Day 1911, Morehouse and Tomlinson were at the MMBB office nervously awaiting noon. By their own description, time passed slowly. It would later be clear that, as they waited, approximately $18,000 was still needed to achieve the $200,000 mark.

Meanwhile, John D. Rockefeller, Sr., had been among those solicited to make large pledges. By the first week in December, he had thus far declined to make a specific pledge or gift. However, as the deadline approached, a letter from Rockefeller was delivered to Henry Morehouse with instructions that it not be opened until Christmas Day at noon. When Treat's deadline hour arrived, Morehouse retrieved the letter from an office safe and opened it. It stated that Rockefeller would contribute up to $40,000 to fill whatever gap remained in achieving the $200,000. That amount covered the remaining $18,000 gap, and the $200,000 needed to meet Treat's challenge had thus been raised. With $250,000 pledged or received, MMBB had met its first goal and was solvent. Later, Treat would say, "I knew Mr. Rockefeller would help," although there is no record that Treat and Rockefeller had communicated on the matter.

For the longer term, Rockefeller's contribution was clearly a positive sign. It was reaffirmed when, only a few weeks later, his personal assistant, Frederick T. Gates, wrote to Morehouse on Rockefeller's behalf stating that he (Rockefeller) "will crave the privilege of having you as their guest in the matter of underwriting and assuming the part of the bill which would fall to you.... Whatever therefore falls to you and him under the guarantee, he begs the privilege to assume." Morehouse was thus excused from fulfilling his own pledge, which would have been at great personal sacrifice. It was not the last time that Rockefeller would provide significant support for the MMBB.

Organizing for the Long Term

In the space of a few months, the newly created MMBB Board had accomplished several major tasks that promised sturdy foundations for building the vision that Morehouse had so persistently described. Treat's challenge pledge had enabled Morehouse to gain the affirmation and ownership of the Northern Baptist Convention for a program to aid aging and disabled ministers and missionaries and their dependents. The appointment of a Board had provided institutional stability and strength to pursue effective implementation of the program. In recruiting Everett Tomlinson to be the Executive Secretary, they had achieved leadership that would prove to be persistent, shrewd, and confident. Raising more than $250,000 to fund the program gave it a beginning financial viability. Identifying and recruiting Arthur M. Harris brought into the corporate leadership of MMBB a man of the first rank in financial and investment skill, and set a standard for the quality of Board members that MMBB would pursue in the future. These actions established their direction. But they had barely begun.

The first challenge was to build stability and strength in MMBB's leadership. The original "Committee of Seven" had transitioned into becoming the MMBB Board, and had begun to enlarge in numbers. Morehouse continued to offer the inspirational leadership. Tomlinson reported that, in his own mind, he had always assumed he would only remain for the duration of the financial campaign, which had now ended. But, as he later ruefully reported, "I found myself very much in the position of a man who has grasped the handles of a galvanic battery. I could not let go." Thus, Tomlinson stayed on to lead in the next phases of the Board's work. The quality of the Board and the astute and persistent skill of its professional leadership established a strong basis for progress.

The second important task was to organize the Board and establish appropriate denominational connections. This included the complex political problem of identifying the source of authority and parameters of autonomy for the Board and its work, a task that had to be completed in order for the Board to incorporate. The chair of the Law Committee of the Northern Baptist Convention, Judge Edward S. Clinch, believed strongly that the Board itself should not incorporate, but that instead all power and authority should remain in the hands of the Convention. The Executive Committee of the Convention took early action favoring its own authority and active direction of MMBB's work. There were, however, legal and political questions that had to be dealt with in that case, and despite the initial hurried action of the Executive Committee, the debate on where authority and power should be vested took up most of 1912. At issue were matters such as the Board's right to elect its own officers and to define their duties, to establish its own bylaws, and to manage its own affairs. In the broad sense, these decisions would define whether the Board itself would be ultimately responsible for the operation of the MMBB and its hoped-for success of programs of assistance, or whether responsibility would be vested in the control of a superior authority, namely the Northern Baptist Convention.

The issues were ultimately resolved at a meeting of the Northern Baptist Convention's Executive Committee in Chicago in December 1912. Tomlinson attended the meeting and successfully argued the case for the more autonomous board approach to MMBB incorporation. Although the debate was vigorous, with Judge Clinch again advocating that the Convention's Executive Committee should have the full functioning authority, the vote, when taken, affirmed the incorporation of MMBB as a separate corporation, with only two votes in opposition. As a result, responsibility was placed directly on the Board, acting under the general direction of the Convention, and able to define its own bylaws and policies, although generally subject to the approval of the Convention. Judge Clinch, the advocate for Executive Committee control, now became an advocate for the Board and quickly moved to arrange for the introduction of a bill to incorporate to the New York legislature and pursued its progress to completion in 1913.[48]

Establishing Position and Resources

With incorporation complete, the Board then turned its attention to the other items on its plan list. The first was to further define its practicing relationship with the Convention in order both to achieve an orderly cooperation and, of course, to lay claim to Convention-wide support. As with any attempt at organization and development among Baptists, this proved to be a challenge requiring negotiation and diplomacy. Plans of cooperation were developed with a number of previously established funds that had been organized to provide assistance to ministers. Appeals to congregations for funding and donations had to be negotiated state by state. As a letter from 1915 shows, cooperation achieved with the Massachusetts Charitable Society, established that MMBB funds raised for assistance to ministers in that state must be used on a 60/40 basis in support of ministers who had served in Massachusetts.[49]

Several other states or associations had also established programs for relief of ministers' needs and possessed funds, but most often the amounts were small. MMBB encouraged these organizations to turn over funds under their control to be administered on their behalf by the MMBB. For example, Baptists in Pittsburgh, Pennsylvania, voted quickly to transfer their funds for such purposes. In Philadelphia, some funds could not initially be transferred for legal reasons, but in one case, that of the North Philadelphia Association, the funds were transferred to the Philadelphia Baptist Association and, through that agency, were made available for the MMBB's work. Elsewhere, from Maine to New York, and from the East to the Midwest, a number of funds were merged, transferred, or designated for the MMBB's work, often with the provision that the priority of use for the funds would go first to specifically stated beneficiaries or to people from the region in question.[50] In addition, the MMBB moved successfully to establish the privilege of appealing for funds from among the Baptists in several states and associations.

Consolidating Other Resources

The establishment of the MMBB had created a national, denomination-wide approach to the needs of retired or disabled ministers and missionaries. By the time of its organization, however, in addition to efforts within states and associations, several other organizations had emerged with the same or similar goals. One was the Ministers Aid Society with headquarters in Fenton, Michigan, which sponsored a retirement home in Fenton. That society's work covered the states of Michigan, Indiana, Ohio, Illinois, and Wisconsin. Negotiations between the MMBB and the society board concluded that the operation of the retirement home should continue, and that only one annual appeal for denominational support should be sponsored by the MMBB within those states. In return, the MMBB would provide for the needs of ministers in those states who were not part of or planning to locate in the Fenton retirement home. The greater burden of that agreement ultimately fell to the MMBB as, increasingly, ministers elected to live in their own homes rather than a retirement home.

A second challenge was to define the relationship between the MMBB and the Baptist Ministers Home Society, whose work primarily addressed needs in the states of New York, New Jersey, and Connecticut. One of that organization's leaders, Dr. George W. Nicholson, had been active in the work of the Home Society, but had also become a manager of the MMBB Board. At the time of the MMBB's creation, the Executive Secretary of the Home Society was the Rev. William B. Matteson, DD, who had been newly appointed shortly before the MMBB was authorized. Matteson was a dynamic and forceful personality. There was clearly potential for competition for the financial support of the churches in those three states. However, a merger was negotiated with the Home Society, and the primary amount of their funds was transferred to MMBB in 1917, with a small amount held back for the continuing work of the Home Society's board. As one result, Dr. Matteson became the Field Secretary for the MMBB and began his leadership with promising effect. However, after service of less than a year, he died unexpectedly while advancing MMBB work in Milwaukee, Wisconsin, in October 1917.

Developing an Administrative Model

In order to administer the funds to qualified persons, MMBB had successfully established Committees of Cooperation in each state. In some cases these committees were separate, independent groups with the single purpose to advocate and assist the MMBB's operation and to develop resources. In other cases, the work of the committee was accomplished by the state's denominational board. An important early role for these state committees was to investigate and approve applications from those seeking assistance before the applications were submitted to the MMBB Committee on Applications. This early organizational approach enabled local Baptists to personally experience the needs of aging or retiring ministers firsthand, and to develop a strong sense of identity with the MMBB as a nationally constituted organization.

In addition to serving an administrative role in qualifying applicants, the state committees also were encouraged to advance the MMBB mission. In reviewing the work of 1913, the MMBB Annual Report encouraged the committees and others to recommend that the work of the MMBB be included in church budgets, to seek opportunities to define and promote the work of the MMBB, and to encourage churches to take communion offerings for the support of retired ministers. They also enlisted young people's groups and Sunday school children in activities designed to develop a habit of concern for retired ministers. By these early efforts, the MMBB established the importance of a broad, positive, and continuing policy of promotion and interpretation among its constituency. It later continued through a variety of programs and publications that consistently served its purposes both practically and spiritually.

In 1913 the MMBB began making grants in assistance to approved candidates. In 1914 it issued its first annuity bonds, which had the short-term effect of providing predictable support for those who contracted for them, and the long-term effect of building up MMBB capital. The process of determining qualified applicants for grants became a critical, ongoing task. In making his original challenge, Milo C. Treat had insisted that "missionaries" be included in the official name of the Board and their support be included in the purposes of the MMBB. As the Board began to define its procedures, it also clarified that the "basis on which aid ought to be voted by the Board is not ordination, but services rendered." Therefore, service in wide variety and diversity of style was established early in principle. However, even with placing the entirety of MMBB assets at work to provide grants, the early grant amounts were pitiably small and were made to a relative few. It was clear that having laid an effective organizational foundation, the MMBB's highest priority was to enlarge its resources in order to meet the needs.

Enlarging the Resources

The achievement of the first $250,000 had been filled with drama and anticipation, but much more was needed to fulfill the vision Morehouse, and now Tomlinson, had put forward. One addition came quickly and relatively unexpectedly. In 1915, at the annual meeting of the Northern Baptist Convention in Los Angeles, Ambrose Swasey of Cleveland, Ohio, provided a boost when he pledged $200,000 as a memorial to his wife, Lavinia Marston Swasey.[51] His letter to Morehouse announcing the gift cited the creation of the Northern Baptist Convention as an "agency for the quickening and strengthening [of] our denominational life," and especially expressed interest in the MMBB in its capacity of "caring for those who have devoted their lives to the service of the Master."

At the same meetings, an anonymous letter was again received from "A Baptist Layman" commending MMBB for its good work and advocating that its resources should be enlarged to at least $1 million. To that end, the writer proposed that if during 1915 the Board should secure enough funds (including what they already had) to amount to a total of $600,000, the layman would give $50,000 in addition. If the strategy sounded familiar, it was: the layman was again "the Man from Pennsylvania," Milo C. Treat, donor of the $50,000 challenge pledge in 1911. Henry Morehouse again set the pace with a personal pledge of $1,000, and the Board again sponsored an appeal. Funds pledged, donated, transferred, and given enabled them to quickly meet that goal and to receive the pledged amount. As a result of the mergers and acquisitions from states and associations, the $600,000 goal was in fact nearly accomplished even before the campaign began. By the end of 1915, MMBB resources had more than doubled since its inception. By 1916, the Annual Report of the MMBB listed $777,455.45 in the Permanent Fund. Not long afterward, in 1917, Ambrose Swasey added $100,000 to the memorial gift he had given previously. At that point, Morehouse's dream and Milo C. Treat's visionary goal of $1 million was within reach.

Sadly, the event that enabled MMBB to reach and exceed that goal was the death of Henry L. Morehouse on 15 May 1917. Following his death, a variety of verbal memorials and written communications testified to his vision, persistence, service, and dedication. At the annual New York Ministers Conference in November 1917, Everett Tomlinson boldly proposed that "another million dollars should be added to the fund [of MMBB] and when raised it should be his [Morehouse's] monument. He was a big man and a big Christian."[52] The proposal quickly gained momentum as "The Morehouse Memorial Million," or, as it was quickly streamlined, "The Morehouse Million." The Board quickly organized a campaign through churches and denominational channels to raise the amount. It was wartime in America, and the Board's communication urged everyone to get behind the fund-raising effort in order to be "as loyal in caring for the soldiers of the cross as our country is in caring for our soldiers in arms."[53] The "old soldiers of the cross" continued to be a favorite phrase that Tomlinson used to good effect in honoring Morehouse.

The campaign for the Morehouse Million was well under way with its organization, advertisement, and approach to important possible donors and with about a quarter of its goal achieved when plans had to be deferred. A previous fund-raising program to raise $5 million for funding other projects in the Northern Baptist Convention had recently been approved, and that program took priority. It was assumed it would be unproductive to have two denominational financial campaigns in competition for the same funds. Therefore, the MMBB assented to a proposal that its own campaign should be postponed, and that its own goal should be merged into the general campaign for the denomination's goals. MMBB's efforts were, consequently, adjusted to supporting the general campaign from which it would presumably benefit. During that time, "A Baptist Layman" communicated again, this time offering $200,000 specifically to help reach the MMBB goal. When the campaign was completed, the Morehouse Million portion of the general campaign was successful. The MMBB now had resources of more than $2 million—an amount that, according to Tomlinson, Morehouse had once believed was the ultimate goal.[54]

But more was to come. John D. Rockefeller had provided important help in raising the first $200,000 to meet Treat's original challenge grant goal, but the now-iconic, wealthy Baptist had not been directly approached for the MMBB's purposes since that time. Tomlinson's personal view was that Rockefeller should not be approached for additional support until the denomination had demonstrated its own full commitment. Now, with $2 million in the Permanent Fund, he believed that he could do so in good faith. Under Tomlinson's leadership, therefore, the Board proposed to Rockefeller that he consider a gift of $1 million. With his characteristic diligence, Rockefeller researched the work, methods, procedures, and especially, the financial practices of the Board, in addition to the worthiness of its purpose. In response, he informed the Board that he was making a gift of $2 million. The gift was received in 1919.[55] By Tomlinson's later accounting in 1931, Rockefeller's cumulative gifts to the MMBB ultimately totaled $7,119,293.24.[56]

In 1920 the Board clarified that women, who were commissioned as missionaries by the Woman's American Baptist Mission Society and the Woman's American Baptist Home Mission Society, were eligible for grants and, later, eligible for membership in the Retiring Pension Fund.[57] In 1920 women in the mission fields were most often present as spouses of commissioned male missionaries, but in local churches, women exercised considerable influence and raised significant money for church and denominational purposes. By including the present reality and the future possibility of pension support for female missionaries, the Board gained the significant support of many churchwomen.

It had been central to Morehouse's vision for a pension program that funds would be organized in such a way as to provide a permanent source of funding for the future. This approach was not only prudent, but was necessary in order to provide the basis for long-term retirement support. It required great discipline, however, because the current needs were great, and despite their initial successes, the Board's resources remained inadequate to meet them. Therefore, commitment to developing resources for future, as well as for present, needs was an important foundation for future success and stability.

A decade after the Board's beginning, it was clear that broad commitment and generosity had greatly enlarged the vision and the resources of the MMBB. In addition to the funds donated by Milo C. Treat, John D. Rockefeller, and Ambrose Swasey, Board member Colonel Edward H. Haskell contributed more than $100,000, C.Q. Chandler more than $36,000, and many others had made gifts or bequests in lesser amounts. Many regional and state organizations established for ministers' relief had contributed or merged their funds into the resources of the Board. In 1920 the Layman's Committee of the Northern Baptist Convention had contributed $721,792.90.[58] The 1920 Annual Report of the Ministers and Missionaries Benefit Board could record that the Permanent Fund had accumulated $12 million. In less than a decade, the MMBB had been established on sturdy and lasting financial foundations.

4

TOWARD A FUNCTIONING PENSION PROGRAM

A Sense of the Times

The Great War is over; the proposed League of Nations has failed, mostly because the United States wants to be left alone; and sensible men—Coolidge, Harding, Hoover—occupy the White House. It is a time—although no one knows quite why—that some people are getting very rich, while others are descending deeper into poverty. America struts with pride. It is the "Roaring Twenties," and many see nothing but more good times and prosperity to come.

On a country club porch outside of Chicago, a young woman, enjoying the kind of party to which Baptist ministers are rarely invited, is in a pensive mood. She is one of the event's hostesses and is a little drowsy from the evening's revelries. She hears the strains of the orchestra's rendition of "I Want to Be Loved by You"—a song so popular as to be unavoidable. The woman sings along and reflects, "We are all boop-boop-a-doop girls now. Even girls back home." Everyone has learned their manners from the radio and magazines, and flapper slang like "scram" and "lounge lizard" punctuates their vocabulary.

The woman also reflects on the war: The army had been the place to be, "making the world safe for democracy," but now what? What good were all these social rules? Recently an open-mouthed movie kiss performed by Greta Garbo and John Gilbert had tested the boundaries of acceptable taste: "Shocking!" But it was modern, and modernity, in any case, implied the right to invent oneself: "Bob your hair, raise your hems, roll down your stockings, paint your lips, do the Charleston and you're changed in a moment!"[59]

Disillusionment was a mark of the time. And why not? There was chaos in Europe; strikes, bombs, and the Red Scare in the USA; and the Ku Klux Klan with its parades and rumored lynchings. The young woman, resting on the club porch with drink in hand, was herself aware of the hypocrisy of Prohibition that had made Al Capone, with his army of bootleggers, a bigger hero to most people than the president. And as for religion, people were having their souls saved by those you used to see only in the tabloids—people like the ex-baseball player Billy Sunday, or that attention-seeking actress Aimee Semple McPherson. Back home in Ohio the farmers were getting poorer while the preachers were railing on about Darwin and evolution more than about community progress or eternal salvation.

The book of the age was *The Man Nobody Knows*, Bruce Barton's book about Jesus. The men at the Rotary Club believed it demonstrated that Jesus was the founder of modern business because he understood the concept of "service." "If only Jesus could service their Buick so it started in the rain," the young socialite-on-the-porch bitterly reflected. She is married to George, a self-made man who is working on his second million by putting everything he has into the stock market. His life is an "endless self-improvement course," she muses. But she is a little uncertain about his love for her. He recites daily the mantra contributed by Emile Coue: "Every day in every way I am getting better and better." And he believes it, too, but he gargles Listerine at least daily so as to prevent halitosis, just in case.

It is an age of seeking cures—everyone seems to need to be cured of something: sexual repression, boredom, idealism, cynicism. George walks toward her on the porch, shooting out his jaw and looking manly—as though he were posing for an Arrow shirt ad, or was a returned fighter pilot from the war. George is upset because some of the party guests are debating modernist ideas, Freudian concepts, and admiring modern art. But what really upset him was that his bootlegger had called and wanted him to settle up for the evening's supply of beverages. "He seems to think the market is going to crash," he says. "But it isn't, though," responds his wife. "Everybody says it isn't." "Everybody but my bootlegger," George responds.

Bored, the woman looks over the party guests at tables, and sees a man who looks like Walter Lippmann. Whoever he is, he offers an opinion that what distinguishes the generation rising to maturity since the debacle of idealism at the end of the war is not their rebellion against the religion and the moral code of their parents, but their disillusionment with their own rebellion. He sounds like Lippmann, too, she thinks.

George reappears and offers an opposing view: "Everything wrong with this country can be summed up in two words: flagpole sitters." After derisive laughter in response, it appears to make more sense. He is serious. He asserts that Shipwreck Kelly achieved fame for just sitting on a flagpole. "Famous for just being there," he says. Or these athletes: "The last time I heard, baseball was a team sport, but now all you hear about is Babe Ruth. And Charles Lindbergh is a god now. For what? People have been flying across the Atlantic for years. But New York drops a ton of ticker tape and torn-up phone books on him because he did it alone, and he is so damned good-looking. All he did was to take his flagpole from New York to Paris."

Now chilled, the woman begs to leave. As they walk to their Buick she asks, "What would it mean if the stock market crashed and didn't come back?" Without pause, she answers herself. "We'd have to live in a little house with only one servant and you'd have to get a job where you had to do something real, invent fire hydrants or something." The undiluted bootleg Scotch had made her philosophical. "We complain now that we're bored, but we'd be terribly nostalgic for these times, wouldn't we? We'd teach our children to be nostalgic, too. And they'd teach their children. America will be nostalgic for these days forever. Except it will be like a lost chord—nobody will be able to figure out how we made meaninglessness seem so meaningful. And the thing is, if you can figure that out, what else do you need?"

"A good market," George says, answering her question, pleased that he had gotten off such a good line. "Besides, it's just until the end of next year. I'm getting out in 1930."

Not too far away—but mentally a world away—a minister sits on his front porch on the same warm evening. The evening breeze transports phrases of the club orchestra's music across the fields. Unlike George, he has not made his "first $1 million." He hasn't even accumulated his first $20 in savings. Club parties are far from his mind. His anxiety is focused on his family's basic security.

The Real World

In the 1920s, few ministers were guests at the country clubs of the affluent. Most were barely able to support families in respectable dignity. They were poor—not the poorest of the poor, but poor nonetheless. And as age or illness caught up with them, their situation was sometimes desperate.

The earliest support of ministers provided by the MMBB had been in the form of grants. Morehouse's vision had primarily been to address the needs of aging ministers and their needs in retirement, but the Board had also responded to critical needs regardless of age. Throughout its history, the MMBB responded to ministers facing financial crisis, especially in unexpected circumstances. But the Board's goal was always shaped by benevolent concern for the plight of aging ministers without income or resources on which to live.

The Board's first and strongest priority continued to be focused on creating a pension program which provided predictable and guaranteed long-term income to retired ministers. However, with only the modest funding available to them, a fully developed pension program was not practicable. The 1917 Annual Report of the MMBB had stated that until the Permanent Fund had increased to $2 million, plans to provide a pension plan were to be put on hold. Soon, however, two events allowed them to resume planning for the pension plan: the achievement of the Morehouse Million and Rockefeller's decision to give $2 million to the MMBB. Financially enabled by these new resources, the Board could consider a different approach.

Establishing the Retiring Pension Fund

The impetus for the Retiring Pension Fund came first from recognition that, even with its remarkable early success in raising funds, the MMBB was able only to distribute grants that were pitiably small, usually from $100 to $300 annually. Clearly a consistent process of funding was needed to enlarge the Board's resources to more adequately meet the retirement needs of more people. Second, the plan envisioned the Board's early goal of establishing a pension program on a continuing, sound financial basis. The only way this could be accomplished with any degree of security or guarantee for the future was by implementing a program that was supported through continuous contributions. The plan for the Fund thus emerged as one that would be contributed to by the ministers. The amount of contribution would be a percentage of the minister's salary, and its total determined by that percentage as it accumulated through the number of years the minister served.

By basing contributions on a percentage of salary, some argued that an inequity in retirement pensions would be inevitable. Therefore, the idea of a plan under which all retirees would receive the same amount— that is, a "flat pension plan"—was also proposed. But that approach would have required significantly more money on hand to guarantee sufficient funds be available for those who qualified. Virtually any other approach to pension funding other than regular contributions made on some basis by participants, or on their behalf, would depend on the future donations or contributions from churches, denominational sources, or nonparticipating individuals. Pension assumptions based on those sources seemed uncertain.[60] Therefore, the plan for the Retiring Pension Fund that emerged was ultimately based on:

—A 6 percent premium paid on the minister's salary; in 1921 the board declared that the value of the housing provided should be included in salary;[61]

—The member's church would pay the premium annually, or in installments as requested;

—$1 in annual pension would be achieved on each $70 in salary on which premiums were paid;

—Pensions would be paid to members quarterly;

—Pension payments would begin at 65 years;

—The MMBB would subsidize 65 percent of premium amounts in the second year and would later increase this subsidy to 70 percent.[62]

The proposed plan for the Retiring Pension Fund was, in part, the result of research and a review of the positive and negative features of plans adopted by corporations such as the Pennsylvania Railroad for its employees. It was also the result of a review of public and private education plans such as TIAA and a few others, including other denominational plans.[63] In addition, the final plan was sent to several life insurance companies whose actuaries reviewed its features and declared it both "sound and safe." The chief executive of one of the companies remarked, "I had a strong hope when we first received your proposed plan that our company might be able to make you, or through you to the ministers of the Northern Baptist Convention, a proposition that would be advantageous for all concerned. I must frankly tell you, however, that we have nothing to offer which can touch the plan you have formulated.[64] Another insurance executive reportedly said more bluntly, "Your ministers will be fools if they don't jump at the chance which is given."

When the Board was satisfied with the proposal, it voted to recommend the Retiring Pension Plan to the Northern Baptist Convention at its 1920 gathering held in Buffalo, New York.[65] When the MMBB Annual Report was presented to the Convention, it included encouraging news of the Board's growing financial resources and made specific mention of the recent gift of $2 million from Rockefeller. Then, amidst enthusiastic response to the encouraging news, the formal proposal to establish the Plan was distributed and outlined by the Executive Secretary, Everett Tomlinson. Several Northern Baptist Convention leaders, including F. Wayland Ayer, former Northern Baptist Convention President, and Colonel Edward H. Haskell, President of the MMBB, spoke strongly in favor.

The proposal was not received without some confusion and opposition. Some at the Convention simply did not understand the economic theories undergirding the Plan's features, and advocated delay. Others did not understand the structure of the benefits.[66] Still others objected to the requirement that ministers themselves would contribute a small portion of the cost. And, continuing support for a flat pension was expressed, despite the explanation of its negative financial requirements. The most substantive and intransigent opposition came from those who objected to the Plan on the grounds that it would encourage centralized control and autocratic leadership within the Northern Baptist Convention—a fear that was argued against many proposals that would later come before the Convention throughout its history. However, despite scattered opposition, ultimately the Retiring Pension Plan was strongly supported and approved.

By the time the Retiring Pension Fund plan was adopted, the MMBB was making grants to retired ministers in twenty-seven state conventions. The Board continued such grants for those who would not have the opportunity of time to be part of the new program and also supplemented pensions for those whose time in the new plan was brief. The new program, however, launched a new era. Its features were what would later be described as a defined benefit plan. Although the plan was later superseded, it represented the standard that served for more than a generation of pension benefit plans. It was pioneering leadership.

Soon after the new plan was adopted, a representative of another denominational plan visited the MMBB offices to inquire about the Plan's features. That denomination's plan was one that had previously been considered a model of a noncontributing plan. But it was in financial trouble with a nearly $1 million shortfall at that time. Soon thereafter, that organization adopted a contributing plan that re-established its financial viability. In subsequent years, several other corporate, educational, or denominational, noncontributory plans encountered similar financial troubles and followed the MMBB's example and establish pensions on a contributory basis. The Northern Presbyterians, Congregationalists, Lutherans, Disciples of Christ, the Reformed Church, and the Southern Baptists all, likewise, drew motivation, strength, or inspiration from the MMBB's new plan or affirmed it indirectly by adopting programs similar to it.

Commitment to Financial Prudence

One key to the MMBB's early and long-standing fulfillment of its mission was its dedication to sound financial principles. A very important part of that was its attention to actuarial discipline. H. Pierson Hammond, who served as a Board member from 1920 to 1943, was also employed as the Board's actuary. Hammond had significant experience as an actuary of the Travelers Life Insurance Company and later headed its actuarial division. He established the strong standard of using the statistics of predicted life expectancy to focus and conserve the Board's resources long into the future. His successors followed with the same conviction. MMBB, therefore, established very early on that compassion and assistance were its business, but that realistic comprehension of its resources and their limits were its critical tools.

Another key to the Board's success was the early establishment of a competent and effective investment procedure. Actuarial accuracy defined the needs, but investment returns defined the available resources. To shepherd that process, the Board established a Finance Committee. Milo C. Treat had frequently complained that the MMBB was not getting the returns he was able to achieve. For example, he pointed out that he got 6 or 6.5 percent returns on gas and oil bonds and, therefore, assumed that the MMBB could receive the same. However, the MMBB was incorporated under the laws of New York, which restricted the kinds of investments a pension board could hold.

A finance committee, therefore, had to be astute regarding both its investment limitations and acceptable investments that would support long-term returns. It was a challenge requiring both patience and shrewdness. The first Finance Committee included Arthur M. Harris, principal in the private banking firm of Harris, Forbes and Company; A.K. Van Deventer, who was, at that time, the Treasurer of the Southern Pacific Railway Company and George D. Dutcher, a lawyer expert in real estate mortgages. They were a winning combination of talents and dedication and established a standard of investment principles and procedures that later Finance Committees were challenged to meet, and consistently did so.

The Retiring Pension Fund was functional by the end of 1920 and was received enthusiastically with a steady flow of applications. The first certificate was issued to Dr. Robert E. Farrier.[67] One surprising development was the number of missionaries who applied for membership. Treat's early insistence that the word "Missionaries" be included in the corporate title of the Board thus proved to be prophetic. As the plan's operation got under way, complaints and concerns also arose, and some of them required resolution. One of the Board's procedural rules was that pension dues had to be paid in full the first year of the plan's operation.[68] This was a distinct hardship on many ministers whose salaries were, by any standard, quite small. The Board had voted to reduce the cost of pensions to members by 65 percent (later it was reduced by 70 percent). This arrangement did not entirely solve the dilemma. In sympathy, the Board then raised funds from private gifts, including a significant one from Rockefeller, that were to be used to reduce the dues during the first year of membership for those whose salaries were $1,500 or less.

A second financial challenge arose regarding those who, by reason of age, would have only a short-term opportunity to participate in the plan. The MMBB had begun as a grant-making pension board. After the Retiring Pension Fund became operational, they continued to give grants to two categories of members: retired ministers over the age of 65 and, in cases of dire need, to ministers under that age. However, a large number of ministers were nearing retirement, or had relatively few years remaining to develop their participation in the program. The Board, therefore, felt compelled to devise ways by which a minimum pension could be sustained to honor and support the work of those too old to practically benefit from the new contributory plan. Support of the widows and children of those who died with few years in the program also had to be addressed. The Board ultimately determined that the minimum annual pension for such persons should be $500, subject to certain restrictions.[69] In a similar spirit, in 1925, the Board established that the annual disability support would be $500.[70]

A third challenge was not strictly financial but, instead, procedural. There were two concerns: first that pensions should only be given to "worthy men," and second, that with regard to grants, only those in need of pension support would be provided them. The corollaries were that all those who were worthy should receive pensions, and that those who were truly needy should not be neglected. In these early years, the committees of cooperation in the local states, therefore, took on an increasingly important role in reviewing applicants. There was some fear that the Board's generosity might be abused, and an equal concern that, through ignorance, it might not be generous enough. The committees of cooperation generally performed their assessment with both scrutiny and compassion, and few circumstances of either unworthiness or unmet need were reported.

However, the question of "worthiness"—which the MMBB had to determine in the administration of pensions—brought up the role of ordination in considering the credentials of potential pensioners. In 1920 there was no universal standard for ordination among Northern Baptists, nor was there any point of reference or authority capable of imposing such standards. The purpose, role, and qualifications for ordination had become a denomination-wide issue and would remain so for decades. The MMBB could not independently require or impose standards without being perceived as attempting to impose "centralized power"— a perennial objection to the Board's potential power. On the other hand, without some standard or definition, it was difficult to define and evaluate what a Baptist minister was, and whether he was a worthy minister.

Ultimately, the Board determined that it was the nature of the service rendered rather than a specific credential or qualification that made its administration of a pension possible. In any case, pensions were, practically speaking, only available to those who had been ordained. Partly in recognition of that dilemma, the MMBB later inherited a continuing role in defining, organizing, and categorizing ministry represented in Northern Baptist churches: In 1929 the Convention asked the MMBB to create a registry of all the ministers and missionaries in the Northern Baptist Convention, including preparation, training, and experience.[71] This responsibility ultimately led to the MMBB's role in providing a quasi-placement service for ministers and a source of recommendation for churches seeking pastors.[72]

Defining Organizational Relationships

Still another challenge for the Board's development was a continuing need to define its role as part of the Northern Baptist Convention structure. At the time of incorporation there had been debate whether a separate board was needed for a pension program. MMBB and Convention leadership had concurred that a separate board would be preferable. However, the MMBB still was administratively related to the Northern Baptist Convention Executive Committee, and its major decisions and policies required the approval of Convention leadership. The continuing challenge was, therefore, to define a relationship that clearly identified the work and services of the MMBB with the Convention, but at the same time allowed for the Board's independence to the degree that would allow its mission to be fulfilled without unnecessary distraction. Two issues emerged that signaled both the importance and the delicacy of that balance.

The first of these related to appointments to major staff positions on the Board. Whether a vacancy resulted from resignation or death, it was a matter of some discussion whether the Board itself or the leaders of the Northern Baptist Convention had the authority to appoint new staff. The death of William Matteson in 1917 had brought attention to this issue through the subsequent appointment of his successor, Cornelius Savage. The intent of the MMBB had been that Savage would assume responsibility for fund development for the MMBB Endowment Fund and special programs. However, at just that time, the Convention's New World Movement financial campaign was getting under way, and the Convention seemed eager to include the MMBB's goals as part of it. That campaign was to be managed and led by the new Board of Missionary Cooperation. The MMBB acceded to the Convention's desires in a cooperative spirit, and Savage moved on to other service.

The second issue emerged as the New World Movement campaign developed and sought to achieve its challenging financial goals. The campaign officials advised MMBB's board that, "it is proposed to include the income received by the Ministers and Missionaries Benefit Board from investments, legacies and matured annuities in the anticipated receipts of the New World Movement Budget of $12,500,000 for the fiscal year 1920–21."[73] In effect, this would potentially significantly reduce the funding that the MMBB had expected and had been promised. Instead, the proposal would grant them only their percentage from the campaign, and not the gifts and legacies specifically designated for its work by the donors. The principal of the funding designated for the MMBB would, thus, be diverted to increase other Convention projects. In response, the Board resolved that income from such sources could not be diverted to any other purpose than that intended by the donors, and that both principal and income from such gifts should be used in the work of the Board and for no other purpose. This was a weighty and important confrontation as relationships between organizations of the Northern Baptist Convention were being defined. MMBB's actions not only preserved its own financial well being, but established a principle that ultimately served other Northern Baptist organizations and agencies well, too.

Administrative Development

As the MMBB grew in opportunities, assets, and responsibilities, administrative leadership had to grow as well. After Cornelius Savage had been appointed to succeed William Matteson, he served briefly until the formation of the Board of Missionary Cooperation created broad national oversight for the proposed New World Movement financial campaign, at which point the position of a separate MMBB Field Secretary was determined to be unnecessary. Administrative leadership needs, however, were expanding. Therefore, the Board elected the Rev. Peter C. Wright to the position of Associate Secretary of the MMBB in May 1920. Wright had been a pastor and a member of the Board since its organization in 1911.[74]

Also, following the establishment of the Retiring Pension Fund, the Board's operations and administrative responsibilities expanded, including more extensive record keeping, oversight, and communication with both program members and the denomination. Almost from its inception in 1911, the MMBB had been officially located at 23 East 26th Street in New York, in association with the offices of the American Baptist Home Mission Society. That building was then serving as the headquarters for much of the Northern Baptist Convention. With a need for more room and a more permanent administrative home, in 1921 the

MMBB moved to separate offices at 276 Fifth Avenue in New York. Then, in 1930, as responsibilities and operations expanded, the MMBB moved to 152 Madison Avenue in New York, along with several other Northern Baptist organizations.[75]

The organizational creation of the Northern Baptist Convention only preceded the founding of the MMBB by a few years, and it, too, was in a dynamic stage of growth and development. One of the Convention's challenges was to identify the ministers who served the churches associated with it. The specific challenge of defining ministerial qualifications and credentials, including standards of education and ordination, ultimately proved to be a century-long task. In addition, it was increasingly apparent that some kind of resource file would assist churches and organizations seeking pastoral or program leadership to identify and locate candidates for pulpits, organizational roles, and other purposes. The first step was simply to identify them.

Therefore, at the 1929 Northern Baptist Convention meeting in Denver, Colorado, the Convention delegates instructed the MMBB to secure records of all ordained ministers and commissioned missionaries currently serving the Northern Baptist churches or agencies and to build and maintain an active file of the information. The MMBB assented to this role, but with the clarification that its responsibility would be strictly limited to developing records and maintaining them. To accomplish that assignment, the MMBB developed a questionnaire that was sent to all churches, pastors, and organizations related to the Convention. The document asked for basic information regarding names and addresses, education, present place of service, and a limited amount of other information. It took several years for the files to be accomplished. The task was complicated by a continuing fear among some that the MMBB would become too controlling—a variation on the original concern that the MMBB would enable "centralized authority" within the Convention.

Nevertheless, the registry was successfully accomplished.[76] As a result, the MMBB began to be perceived as a key part of the "personnel system" of the Convention, and those seeking pastors, missionaries, or other religious leaders and workers began to rely on these records, as did ministers and others seeking opportunities. This role continued for more than forty years until a major denominational reorganization in the early 1970s established the office of American Baptist Personnel Services. The establishment and maintenance of these records further expanded the Board's role and also added to MMBB staff needs.

The MMBB administration persistently transcended record keeping. An increasingly important role was to develop and promote good relationships with members of the Retiring Pension program, and to serve their needs. One specific, pressing opportunity was to establish a closer connection with pastors and churches in the regions west of the Mississippi River, especially on the West Coast. Baptists in the Far West, only recently having developed beyond mission field status, generally felt less kinship with the Northern Baptist Convention than those in the Midwest and East.[77] The Board believed that a closer connection with the MMBB might help strengthen the Baptist association, and at the same time enable the MMBB to serve the pastors and churches more directly. They determined to establish an office in the region. As a result, in 1926, the Rev. George L. White was elected Western Secretary.

White's extensive connections with the churches and people of the western region had been established first by his residence in the West, and more practically his work for the American Baptist Publication Society. In that capacity, he served as a point of communication and interpretation between the Publication Society and the missionary pastors and colporteurs associated with the chapel cars that were instrumental in establishing many western churches and Sunday schools. One of White's primary tasks as Western Secretary was to strengthen connections with the churches and to develop donations and support for the work of the MMBB in the western region. White had an engaging personality and made friends easily, and his appointment almost immediately advanced the presence and the resources of MMBB in the western United States. After a year, however, the continuing leadership and administrative demands of the Board's work influenced the Board's decision to bring White to the headquarters in New York as Associate Secretary and extended White's work of encouraging gifts for the MMBB endowment and special programs.

The assets of the Board had grown primarily by gifts and donations, especially the large gifts by Rockefeller. Tomlinson reports that total assets of the MMBB in 1912, its first year of actual operation but prior to incorporation, were $140,031, which represented some of the funds raised to meet the challenge of M.C. Treat. By 1927 its assets had grown to $13,853,375, the most significant portion of which came from gifts from Treat and Rockefeller, assets from merged organizations, and a few other major donors. This was remarkable. Still, while this amount far exceeded the original hopes of Morehouse's vision and Tomlinson's expectation, it was insufficient for the Board's task. The total assets of the Board included the Endowment Fund, which were the funds given to the board to support the general work of the Board; the Retiring Pension Guarantee Fund which held the membership's contributions in the amounts determined for the purpose of guaranteeing the contracted pension promises to the participating ministers and the Annuity Fund, which held funds from annuities which were contracts with donors that required the MMBB to pay an established rate of annual interest for their lifetimes. Funds available for grants, however, remained limited.

Tomlinson reported in 1931 that the then total assets of the Board were $18,733,843. The Endowment Fund totaled $9,413,727.52; the Annuity Fund held $902,677.81; and the remainder of $8,417,537 was held in the Retiring Pension Guarantee Fund to provide security for the guaranteed pensions. Over time, all the funds would grow, but especially the Retiring Pension Guarantee Fund (and its successor funds), which received the systematic payments for pensions. In 1931 the Board reported that there were 2,475 enrolled in the Retiring Pension Fund and 1,358 beneficiaries (which included the retired pastors, their widows and children, and minor orphaned children).[78] The vision that Henry Morehouse had first brought to focus had become a reality.

The First Succession in Executive Leadership

In 1926 the MMBB's first Executive Secretary, Everett Tomlinson, was advised by his physicians to reduce his workload. True to his character and sense of responsibility, Tomlinson instead resigned from the position rather than serve in the role in a weakened capacity. The Board promptly elected him as Advisory Secretary and continued his salary. Peter C. Wright, who had served for seven years as Associate Secretary, was elected by the Board to assume Tomlinson's duties. This change of leadership, the first real leadership transition in the nearly sixteen-year history of the Board, might have tested Board effectiveness. However, it was clear that Wright possessed strong leadership qualities and good administrative experience honed in his work for seven years as Associate. In any event, Tomlinson remained available for consultation and guidance. Subsequently, George L. White, who had by that time served for nearly two years as the Western Secretary and had already moved to the MMBB offices in New York, was elected as Associate Secretary. It is clear that the Board established very early the importance of choosing and encouraging talented leadership and implementing positive succession planning. Those precedents would serve well in the years ahead.[79]

In 1930 George Clifford Cress was engaged to be a second Associate Secretary. Like George White, Cress had roots in the American West and was literally a "son of the covered wagons." He had served mission churches in several western states and later supervised mission work in Montana. He also had early service as a missionary in southern Africa, notably Rhodesia (now Zimbabwe), where he worked among the Zulu tribe. His abilities as a writer and his familiarity both with western American churches and with missionary activities abroad strengthened the Board's connections with several MMBB constituencies. His administrative experience assisted with the increasing staff responsibilities as the Retiring Pension Plan developed and grew.[80] Like George L. White, a significant part of Cress's responsibility was to develop good relationships with Northern Baptist churches and people and especially to encourage legacies and bequests as a method of developing MMBB assets.[81]

Communication and Interpretation

Almost at the same time as the establishment of the Retiring Pension Plan, in 1922 the Board began the publication *The Ministry*, a quarterly paper whose purpose was "to present to the denomination phases of the work that otherwise might be unknown or neglected."[82] It was published for the MMBB by the General Board of Promotion of the denomination, in part as a supportive tool of the New World Movement, the Convention-wide development program. The paper was distributed to Northern Baptist leaders and ministers, many churches, and to those who requested it. The first publication in October 1922 featured a front cover portrait of Henry L. Morehouse. The primary article was a brief history of the Board, tracing developments from Morehouse's presentation of a resolution in 1908, highlights of its organizational development, and major gifts that had secured its operation.

The first issue of the new publication established a pattern that would be followed for two decades. One article explained aspects of the

Board's financing and advocated for churches to provide for the pensions of their pastors by enlisting them in the Retiring Pension Fund. Another urged pastors to communicate with the Board to receive further information about their own participation. An article on average salaries of ministers participating in the Retiring Pension Plan hinted at the advocacy role that the MMBB would later perform in supporting more adequate ministerial compensation. There were articles advocating memorial gifts to the MMBB, and testimonials to the work the Board made possible. It was an effective beginning for a consistent and highly effective continuing communication effort with the denomination, its churches, and their pastors.

In the early years, issues of *The Ministry* focused on key personalities of the organization and leadership of the Board, including Col Edward H. Haskell, then President of the Board and major supporter of its work; Ambrose Swasey, whose $300,000 gift in 1915 established the Lavinia Marston Swasey Memorial Fund at a critical moment to both encourage the Board's prospects and to expand its service; and, in the fourth issue, John D. Rockefeller, whose several grants to the MMBB had greatly expanded its resources by 1922.

As publication continued over the next several years, successive issues highlighted Everett T. Tomlinson, the founding Executive Secretary; Avery Shaw, original Board member and later President; and Arthur M. Harris, early and long-serving Board member, Treasurer, and key investment advisor. These issues were followed by those featuring Peter C. Wright (then Associate Secretary and later Tomlinson's successor as Executive Secretary) and George L. White (Western Secretary and later Associate Secretary when Wright became the Executive). M.C. Treat—the "Man from Pennsylvania"—was featured in the April 1926 issue, a few months after his death on 19 December 1925. The back page of some issues displayed photos of board members, major contributors, and staff members in an effort to acquaint a broader public with them.

Board leadership personalities continued to be the subject of focus in later issues, especially as a means of announcing newly elected or appointed leaders, and, in many cases, as memorials. *The Ministry* consistently advanced understanding about the opportunities and procedures of the Board and included articles and essays on MMBB organization, programs, and achievements. In its earliest years, especially, the publication frequently offered articles clarifying how the Retiring Pension Fund worked, often comparing its investment approach to other denominational pension strategies. Non-MMBB experts were often quoted praising the contributing basis of the Retiring Pension Fund as a critical key to its long-term success. In a few cases, examples of other, noncontributing pension funds illustrated the superiority of the MMBB Plan.[83] In 1924 a brief piece titled "High Praise" noted that the president of a "foremost life insurance company" had said the Retiring Pension Plan "was the best plan in the United States." Articles also affirmed the actuarial basis of long-term projections to assure the Plan's success.

A brief early article noted the statistical longevity of ministers and their widows as a way of emphasizing prudent actuarial planning.[84] A focus on life expectancy was a consistent feature. Articles that reminded readers of the provision for a subsidy of annual dues by the Board and, likewise, a focus on minimum pension amounts for older members of the Plan were frequently included as examples to encourage membership. Board membership included many mature men who had successful business or financial backgrounds, and their presence was noted with reassuring effect. At an early stage, therefore, the MMBB became effective in selling itself as both a competent and compassionate organization.

Soon *The Ministry* began to feature retired pastors whose service was representative of Plan members. In October 1923, the cover featured Mrs. Nancy Judson Tolman, widow of the Rev. John Tolman, a pastor in New York and Illinois. Mrs. Tolman had lived nearly 100 years, and her ancestry included Adoniram Judson, the poet Robert Burns, and a Revolutionary War soldier. She had been a teacher and, in collaboration with her sister, had established a rudimentary school for girls, the Young Ladies' Institute, in Springfield, Illinois. At the time, Mrs. Tolman had been the oldest recipient of MMBB support, and had been among the first to receive a grant in its earliest days. The presentation of her dedication, character, and faithfulness was an effective means of demonstrating the high purpose of the Board and the worthiness of those who benefited from its support. This article initiated a continuing emphasis on older ministers whose dedication, faithfulness, creativity, or long service to their churches and the denomination made them exemplars of the theme "old soldiers of the cross" first established by

Morehouse. Acknowledging such service was likely effective in gaining both the appreciation and sympathy needed to motivate support and additional contributions for the Board's work.

Articles in *The Ministry* often revealed some of the challenges the Board encountered. One such challenge was to persuade ministers of the necessity of establishing financial priorities and habits to enable their annual contribution as a Plan participant. The idea of pension planning, and particularly personal participation in the planning, was still new, and ministers in most cases were financially stressed. In many cases they were doubtful about the sacrifice required for future security. Explanations and examples were offered to show both the means and the results of adopting the disciplines necessary to participate. Often, articles focused on investment alternatives, usually highlighting grim results for some who chose flawed approaches. The MMBB consistently had to compete for the participation and loyalty of its members who were frequently tempted to pursue other or more independent strategies of investment—or no strategies at all.

The Problem of Retiring Pension Fund Qualification

Another challenge revealed in *The Ministry* was the ongoing difficulty of assessing which persons qualified to participate in the Plan. Length of service was one, and the local committees' assessment of the applicant's service was another. But a desire to have a commonly accepted standard of accreditation was real and often led back to the question of ordination that, among Baptists, remained notoriously ill-defined. In June 1922, the Northern Baptist Convention had adopted a recommendation regarding ordination, and had passed it on to the states for consideration. Many had passed it, and were devising means of implementation of its standards and procedures. But many had not. In June 1923, an article on ordination concluded, pointedly, that "The Benefit Board will not be the least to profit when the denomination shall have an approved accredited list of ministers."[85]

Six years later MMBB was instructed to undertake the development of such a list. Inevitably this concern moved from the administrative convenience of accreditation to a concern about professional competence. An article in a June 1924 paper raised the question "Is There a Dearth of Men in the Ministry?" In a few words containing brief but pungent statistics, the article concluded that there was no dearth of men in the ministry, but there was needed a supply of "more well-trained, well-equipped, able and consecrated men." This concern became a consistent theme. For pragmatic reasons, therefore, the MMBB moved into a role of advocacy for competence and professional quality within the Baptist ministry, sometimes perceiving it to be one aspect of the "better maintenance of the ministry." [86]

A Continuing Spotlight on the Challenge of Ministerial Support

Difficulty in securing funds necessary to make the required personal contributions highlighted the relatively low compensation ministers generally received. This prompted a continuing series on adequate pay for ministers, sometimes illustrated in unique ways. For example, a continuing theme of the early years in *The Ministry* was a series focused on the number of ordained men who were not in the ministry any longer. It was a considerable number, and the poor economic reality of ministerial service was offered as a major reason for it. Sometimes the stories were heartrending. One article repeated a story first published in the *New York Times* regarding "Old Sam," an aged mill-hand in Massachusetts. He had turned to manual labor at the age of 63 when, in poor health, he was unable to support himself. He had never talked about his past, but upon his death, he was discovered to be a graduate of the University of Rochester and Rochester Theological Seminary and had served churches in the Northeast for more than thirty years prior to his work in the mill. "This is the tragedy of inadequate support and the conception of relief as a charity," concluded the article.[87] Another reprinted article from the *New York Sun* called attention to the pension plan as a means of "tardy and partial justice" for the "wrong done to the underpaid preacher [that] should have been righted long ago."[88]

Sometimes *The Ministry* used humor effectively to make its point. For example, a front-page story in 1924 was titled "The Oldest Horse in the World and the Old Minister." The story reported an old and retired Lutheran minister struggling as a result of recent illnesses in both himself and his wife. The minister's economic plight was exaggerated by the need to feed his old horse, Clover, which was reputed to be more than 53 years old. The story got into the public press, and it was determined that the horse might well be the oldest in the country. President Harding's wife sent $100 for his support, and the New York

Jockey Club offered a pension of $25 a month for the horse. After a much-publicized trip with Clover to Madison Square Garden in New York, the horse became a popular presence at bazaars, fairs, and community gatherings. His notoriety also rejuvenated the career of the old clergyman, who was occasionally invited to preach in churches near his home—if he brought his horse. The aged horse's fame provided the horse a more adequate income than the minister received for himself and his wife. The article thus drove home its point, with obvious reference to one of Jesus' teachings: "How much then is an old preacher of more value than a horse?"[89]

More often, the plight of ministers who lived a life of desperation in old age and poverty was presented in stark terms. Morehouse's term "old soldiers of the cross" lived on and provided a number of comparisons. A brief article in the April 1925 issue invoked the image of the Tomb of the Unknown Soldier, recently established at Arlington National Cemetery: "Many an equally heroic Soldier of the Cross struggles on—in old age—in a bitter conflict with poverty. Will some one tell us why he should not receive honor from those whom he served commensurate with the honor heaped upon the Unknown Soldier at Arlington?" The same issue announced the availability of a film, endorsed and sponsored by the MMBB, depicting the life of a pastor who goes through the community in ministry fulfilling needs of various kinds, and concluded by raising the specter of his own needs in old age.[90]

The Better Maintenance of the Ministry as a Profession

These early articles often combined the themes of ordination and qualification, adequate support, and planning for retirement. In a 1926 address titled "Making the Ministry Attractive," first given to the Ministerial Boards of the Congregational Churches, was reprinted in *The Ministry*. It stated clearly the need for high standards of learning, the need for pulpit freedom, the need for ministry to be perceived as a "career" and not simply random service, and the need for adequate support during ministers' years in active service. Failure to encourage these things, the author claimed, would "be to degrade the profession and fill its ranks with unworthy men." The MMBB's emerging agenda and continuing commitments were thus actively and clearly mirrored.

Careers in ministry were of advantage to both ministers and churches. But articles in *The Ministry* consistently exposed a major impediment to ministerial careers: the age limitations faced by many older ministers. A number of articles illustrated the reality that older pastors were frequently more effective in pastoral care, were less likely to be impulsive or "controversial," but that often churches were reluctant to engage them other than as "supply" preachers during interim periods.[91] The reason was clear: churches almost universally feared that they would be saddled with a minister in declining health or energy. Such concern made many churches cautious about engaging someone who was otherwise supremely qualified and, in fact, a preferred choice as a result of experience. Churches often had collective memory or experience with a pastor who had become old or ill, but who was not able to "retire." Articles addressed this issue forthrightly and in doing so, underlined the obvious advantage of both disability and pension coverage through the MMBB. By participating in the Retirement Plan, MMBB argued, churches were protected against the need of continuing the "old soldiers" who could no longer effectively serve the cause. From the opposite perspective, articles also featured stories of ministers who, at advanced age, were still serving with remarkable effectiveness.

Frequently, *The Ministry* also educated both laity and clergy about some of the nonfinancial problems within ministry. For example, in the 1920s, relatively short pastorates of two to three years were the norm, and resignations often were the result of conflict or dissatisfaction between pastors and churches. An article in June 1930 titled "Resigning" brought to focus many aspects of and many perspectives on the problem. The article revealed MMBB's growing awareness of the challenges of ministry and the contexts in which it was performed. Clearly, Baptist ministry was often a task requiring both boldness and delicacy, combined with faithfulness and hard work. The MMBB increasingly accepted the role of "better maintenance of the ministry" in more than financial terms, and increasingly led in addressing these challenges.

The Emerging Broad Role of MMBB

The MMBB's core mandate was to provide pensions and other forms of financial support in old age or in unusual circumstances of need. Therefore, *The Ministry* became an increasingly effective tool used to explain programs, advocate support, clarify benefits, and encourage financial planning for both ministers and churches. It also became a first line of response in the face of misinformation and rumor about MMBB programs and plans, and a useful instrument for announcing news and information about MMBB adjustments and new programs. *The Ministry* also educated many members about basic financial terms and concepts. As ministers were not generally knowledgeable about financial matters, this was an important purpose that served to broaden MMBB's value. The Northern Baptists, as a result, were becoming increasingly aware of the importance of the MMBB.

The June 1926 issue of *The Ministry* celebrated the fifteenth anniversary of the MMBB. Its expanded pages briefly reviewed the Board's history and focused on the present organization, especially the subcommittees that guided their work: Executive, Finance, Applications, Law, and Accounts committees represented a well-developed and maturing organizational structure. Fifteen months later, the October 1928 issue reported that the assets of MMBB at that time were $15,046,036, an increase of $1,192,660 over the previous year. The yearly increase was remarkable. However, it paled in comparison to the rise from virtually nothing at its beginning to more than $15 million in fewer than seventeen years. "What would Dr. Morehouse think today?" the fifteenth-anniversary issue asked. Morehouse once proposed that "the financial goal of the Ministers and Missionaries Benefit Board ... is a permanent fund of two million dollars."[92] Morehouse would no doubt have been astonished that the annual increase of MMBB's total assets was by more than half the ultimate amount he had originally only dreamed about.

In 1928 Arthur M. Harris, MMBB board member almost from the beginning, and its Treasurer and chief internal financial advisor, was elected as President of the Northern Baptist Convention. *The Ministry* announced his election and offered the opinion that "the M. & M. Board does not lose, while the Northern Baptist Convention shares, in a larger measure, the value of the experience, judgment and executive ability of Mr. Harris. We look forward to a year of increasing usefulness for both the President and the denomination."[93] The denomination was indeed well served by his election. But Harris's personal election to denominational leadership also signified the growing significance of the MMBB's broader role. In addition to providing pensions and other contractual financial benefits for ministers it was also rapidly emerging as an effective facilitator of communication and education for a still-young denomination coping with enormous diversity of geographic identity and theological opinion and experiencing many economic and social challenges. Though perhaps without clear intention to do so MMBB had mixed the ingredients to become, by a later generation's perspective, the "glue that held the denomination together."

No Longer a Charity

As MMBB's era of foundation that had been inspired by Morehouse and guided by Tomlinson and a remarkably able Board faced a transition to new leadership, it was reinforced by a growing change in perception about pensions and benefits as well. By 1928 the great educational and nonprofit pension board, TIAA, had grown significantly. TIAA's origin in 1918 was the result of necessity derived from many of the same social and economic dynamics that ministers experienced. In only ten years, it had begun to change perceptions about educators and careers in education. A career in education was now possible for the educated young to consider because it provided end-of-career security.

Likewise, large railroad pension funds had emerged from concern about the economic security of older and injured workers in a dangerous occupation. The growth of organized labor and the effective bargaining of their unions had propelled these funds to become large and prosperous. Regrettably, their resources had also become a temptation for graft and corruption. The temptation to use union funds as an instrument for wielding political power enticed some of the union and corporate leaders. Controls to assure appropriate funding of the pension funds were lacking, and the funds' resources were frequently raided for political, private, or personal purposes. So pervasive was corruption and incompetence in the railroad funds that they soon became bankrupt and had to be rescued by the federal government.

The MMBB was quickly able to establish the ministry as a profession and had shown significant progress in establishing long-term ministerial pension development as important to both churches and ministers. It had also established pensions as a just and important part of clergy compensation. Its sound principles of management and investment were building a strong base of support for its purpose, and its transparent and effective management completely avoided the incompetence that led to the bankruptcy that destroyed some early pension programs, and the corruption that had drained others. In the

1920s, therefore, the MMBB had transformed its original vision into a businesslike operation.

In same period, the MMBB had also largely shifted the basis of its purpose from charity to investment in leadership. An article in *The Ministry* in October 1928, titled "A Pension System, a Charity or an Investment, Its Value and Its Cost," revealed that evolution.[94] Morehouse's original vision had been inspired by concern for aging ministers, and he had appealed largely to both a sense of responsibility and a spirit of charity to meet their needs. The original, grant-based program of the Board had functioned on that basis of benevolent concern, and it continued in that spirit by providing limited pensions to ministers who were too old to have participated in the Retiring Pension Plan and grants to those in crisis. But now, with the lengthening experience of the Retiring Pension Plan, the article's author could state, "A pension system and a charity are not synonymous," and could clearly articulate the difference. He effectively argued that "a correctly established pension system is an excellent investment, an investment in living assurance.... I can assure you that the Retiring Pension Fund was established upon dependable foundations and has been since and will continue to be, administered along scientifically correct lines."[95]

What had begun as an expression of appreciative, sympathetic charity was rapidly emerging as a program rooted in effective social and economic planning. It was characterized by sound judgment, financial prudence, and scientific principles as a strategy to invest in present and in future leaders, by fostering an awareness of compensation and career benefits. In achieving that vision, the MMBB was again a leader and a pioneer.

5

RESPONDING TO THE CRISES
OF DEPRESSION AND WAR

A Sense of the Times

It was not that things looked radically different than before the Crash, but things were different: "Paint peels from houses. Cars get old, break down. Nothing you'd notice right away."[96] In Chicago, unemployment reached 50 percent, and it was not uncommon to see a photo of men fighting over a barrel of garbage. Out in the Dust Bowl, farmers threatened to lynch judges who foreclosed on their properties, and the second Roosevelt said, "I see one-third of a nation ill-housed, ill-clad, ill-nourished."

Between the Crash of 1929 and Roosevelt taking office in 1933, it seemed like everyone was trying to live the way they had before. It didn't work. *Fortune* magazine complained that the Flaming Youth of the '20s had gone and what was left was "a generation that will not stick its neck out." Many of the youth were now working in the Civilian Conservation Corps at $30 a month. If you were older and had once felt like a self-made man, you now felt like a self-ruined one. Whatever it was that you once did, you couldn't do it any longer—either no one needed your services or they couldn't pay for them. Everybody seemed to know a banker who was now working as a caddy in the club to which he once belonged.

Hemlines dropped and women once again had curves—the idea being to no longer look young, but to look mature. The studied look of boredom of a decade earlier had given way to an even more studied expression that conveyed, "I don't give a damn!" But they did.

Preachers and businessmen—in fact, nearly everyone—had something or someone to blame for the Depression: moral breakdown, a natural cycle, the Wall Street short-sellers, the installment plan, high tariffs, low tariffs, the British, the Russians, Stalin. How to fix it? "When you BUY an AUTOMOBILE You GIVE 3 MONTHS WORK to Someone

Which Allows Him to BUY OTHER PRODUCTS," said a poster advertising cars. It made sense. Except you first had to have a job to earn the money to buy the car.

Some people started to believe that only communism would save them, but people were scared of the "Reds." Someone testified before the House Un-American Activities Committee that Shirley Temple was "a stooge for the Reds" because, in an act of compassion, she had sent money to the Spanish Loyalists. She was only a little girl! Others believed that J. Edgar Hoover and the FBI would save them from the Nazi spies, gangsters, and the Wobblies.

Ironically, this was also the decade that established Hollywood: People went to the movies to escape. Hollywood knew that times were hard and that there was unrest in the streets, but they didn't show it in the newsreels. When Mickey Mouse came onto the scene, he was, at first, a mean little pest, but Walt Disney quickly turned him into a common-man hero—much like the men in the murals that the government artists were painting in post offices. Disney became a legend—and became rich.

Some thought Roosevelt would save everyone. They listened to his fireside chats, and when he talked, he said, "My friends." He didn't yell about the Reds or the Jews, like Father Coughlin, or itemize a long list of assumed enemies like Huey Long tended to do. Many people sensed that he knew them and that he knew how they felt. He famously said in 1932, "we have nothing to fear but fear itself." Several years later, things weren't much better, but most said he was still right about fear.

You hear what isn't there: On a Sunday afternoon it is quiet. No carpenters driving nails, no rivet hammers going in the city. There were fewer cars, and at many intersections stoplights were swaying in the wind. There were fewer whistles from trains or factories and no babies crying because people were afraid to have them. Men were home when they shouldn't be—laid off, let go by a sympathetic boss who knew he would soon be out of work himself. Sometimes you see men sitting by the window waiting for *Amos n' Andy* to come on the radio. You notice the movie theater audience is entirely men. They are hiding out there so others will think they are at work.

Not everyone was poor, though—some great fortunes were made during the Depression and great reputations, too. But there was a leveling effect on social habits and stations. Men no longer wore tops on their bathing suits, and girls of every class wore saddle shoes and apron dresses. If they had a nickel or two, they drank Cokes in a drugstore where they had crushes on the soda jerk—or he thought they did.

Eventually, no one notices the shabby furniture in hotels, the sagging phone lines along cracked highways, and the slow pace of life nearly everywhere. Churches become havens, places of nostalgia and refuge—and sometimes a free meal. At the movies, the newsreels display a funny, crazy little man whose German troops are marching first in a parade, and then into Poland. Huey Long is shot dead in Baton Rouge, the latest casualty in America's long love affair with guns. Soon, more and bigger guns are needed, and there are job openings to make them, and the ammunition to fire in them. It isn't long before there are jobs in plants where they build bombers and tanks to be sent to beleaguered allies.

The Second World War arrives in America on 7 December 1941, "a day that shall live in infamy," said Roosevelt.[97] Suddenly, everything is, once again, rows and bunks and barracks, marching in order and ordering more marches. Troops ship out to ports only dreamed of, where they receive "Dear John" letters from girls they only half remember. News from the war touches every family and every community.

But life goes on, sometimes strangely energized. Girls dance with servicemen at USO clubs, and with shortages of everything, some of them color their legs light brown to mimic silk stockings, drawing seam lines up their calves with a mascara pencil. "Use it up, wear it out, make it do, or do without." Scrap metal is collected in every neighborhood for "the war effort." It does no practical good—but it makes everyone feel like a participant in a war that is unspeakably distant. Roosevelt dies and is mourned; Truman takes office, and his decision to use atomic weapons in Japan ends the war and sparks a moral debate that continues into the next millennium.

Finally the war is over! A sailor famously kisses a pretty nurse in New York's Times Square—he never meets her again. Suddenly, there seems to be a different kind of explosion: traffic jams, factory whistles announcing work shifts, and everyone working at their jobs, with the exception of those on the GI bill. Colleges and universities boom and build Quonset Huts on campus to house the overflow. About five hundred Northern Baptist Convention military chaplains return to resume service to churches, and the Convention urges pastoral search committees to consider them. The MMBB urges that the churches enroll them in the Retiring Pension Fund.

One veteran, writing for *House Beautiful*, says "There will be a new and changed United States, and I want my house to be in keeping with this new spirit...."[98] He is right. Everything is changed. Soon, women stop building planes and start having babies while men translate war skills into careers—or at least some of them do. Black men go home to dusty towns and crowded urban neighborhoods, but neither the black men nor the women of every color will stay put very long.

Everything has changed.

MMBB Copes with the Turbulent Decades

In 1931 the annual report of the MMBB actuary H. Pierson Hammond described a record of significant progress. It noted that the membership of the Retiring Pension Fund was 2,421 and that the average salary of participants in 1930 was $2,846 (an increase of $500 over the average salary of $2,350 in 1920). During the previous ten years, 2,654 membership certificates had been issued, and, of those, only 113 had been terminated by cancellation, with another 70 terminated by death. During the same decade, 508 participants had become pension recipients, and 32 widows were also receiving pensions. Of the total number of still-active participants, 1,902 were less than 65 years of age. However, the average member age was 51.2 years—a figure that presaged early, looming pension obligations. During the first ten years of the Fund, $485,000 had been paid out in pensions. During the same ten years, $1,261,611 had been paid out as the MMBB's program of supporting or "discounting" pension dues for ministers. The Fund, which guaranteed the payment of pensions for the active membership, amounted to $8,200,000.[99]

Clearly during the 1920s MMBB had constructed a financial and institutional structure that brought its original vision into focus and promised its fulfillment. It had also effectively transitioned from an original vision that rested on a charitable response to human need to a new and developing goal of structuring benefits as part of professional compensation. But the next era of its development was to be tested. No part of American life, personal or public, escaped the economic ravages of the Great Depression of the 1930s, and likewise, every aspect of the nation's culture was re-shaped by the demands of World War II. MMBB and the people it served were no exception. Remarkably, by the end of the era of Depression and war, MMBB was not only still standing and progressing toward its goals, but it was arguably stronger and more effective in doing so.

The Immediate Effects of the Financial Crash and Depression

The decade of the 1930s began early in one sense: the stock market crash of 1929 and its aftermath of uncertainty and stagnation affected every financial institution and every financially related program in the American economy and culture. For the MMBB, the most immediate and obvious challenge was the preservation of its financial assets in the face of dismal market conditions. MMBB resources were protected, to some extent, by the conservative investment strategy required by state laws, but that concern was ultimately only one of many. The financial crisis proved to be a harbinger of profound disruption in a broad and devastating pattern. The failure of banking and financial institutions ruptured normal economic predictabilities, the peculiar convergence of weather patterns in many agricultural parts of the country contributed to crop failures, and depressed commodity market conditions throughout the world devastated the economics of agriculture, the most predictable and stable industry in the country.

Northern Baptist ministers were affected by both circumstances. Northern Baptist Convention churches were predominantly located in rural areas, towns, and small cities, especially in the central regions of the country. The largest and most rapidly growing churches were in the large industrial cities where the rising numbers of unemployed persons profoundly affected the income of even the largest and most prosperous churches. In the villages and small towns of the countryside where agriculture was the main economic base, the effect was even more marked. Normally supportive members were unable to continue their contributions, at least not at former levels. Some families were quickly transformed from independent and prosperous to dependent and impoverished. As a result, church budgets were stressed, and demands on church charity were greatly increased. In many churches, pastor's salaries were reduced or even terminated. Therefore, the MMBB experienced great demands on its resources while simultaneously experiencing a reduced stream of income.

By April 1931, an editorial in *The Ministry* reported that "correspondence indicates a considerable tendency at the present time in the direction of reduction of the salaries paid to pastors." It was a theme that would be repeated frequently over the next several years. When pastoral salaries were reduced—or abolished completely—there were multiple effects.[100] Salary reduction had obvious, immediate effects for the minister's financial survival, but salary reduction also had the long-term effect of reducing a pastor's potential pension payment. For MMBB, it had the aggregate effect of reducing current cash flow into the Retiring Pension Fund as well. In addition, over the next several years, salary reductions and terminations forced by economic circumstances caused a real decline in the number of active members in the Retiring Pension Fund. The dues-paying membership of the Fund had achieved a high of 1,902 in 1930, but by the end of 1934, it had only 1,668 participants. During the same period, there was a significant increase in the number of emergency grant applications from ministers in middle career who were not eligible to retire.

Despite the financial crises of the time, prudent policies and conservative investments initially had preserved Board assets. At the 1931 Northern Baptist Convention in Kansas City, Missouri, the MMBB reported total funds of $18,733,843.43, with $9,413,727.52 in the Permanent Trust Fund, income from which was available for pensions. The Treasurer's Report for the fiscal year ending 30 April 1931 reported that the market value of all the securities held by the Board was more than $600,000 in excess of book value. Although it was a remarkable achievement considering the brief history of the Board, the funds remained entirely inadequate to meet the needs even in normal times. The Depression challenged it further as the decade continued.

For one thing, as the resources had increased, so had the number of beneficiaries. In 1922, members in the Retiring Pension Fund numbered 562, but by 1931 that number was 2,475. Likewise, in 1922 the amount distributed to all beneficiaries was $160,918, and in 1931 it was $341,736. The Fund's reserves totaled $1,085,569 in 1922, and by 1931 totaled $8,325,584. On first review, the five-fold increase in Pension Fund members seemed to be more than matched by a nearly seven-fold increase in the Retiring Pension Fund assets, but the emerging problem was that a significant percentage of the Fund's membership were older members. And because of church budget reductions, many ministers were forced out of their positions, or had to seek retirement sooner than they had planned.

M. Forest Ashbrook, MMBB Executive Director from 1940 to 1961, later reported that in 1922, the first full year of operation for the Retiring Pension Fund, the expenditures on accounts of pensions paid was $401.98. In 1931 expenditures on accounts of pensions paid was $163,397.58.[101] With the high percentage of older age members expecting guaranteed pensions, the trend was not a good one. In addition, contributions to the Board's work from individuals and churches decreased by more than one-third between 1922 and 1931, and denominational support declined by a similar amount during the same period. The demands for grants outside the Retiring Pension Fund, especially, were escalating rapidly as receipts were declining at an even greater pace. Here the source of the problem was simple: older ministers and widows who had previously believed they could manage on what little they had, or with family support or assistance, were pushed into impoverished necessity, and a number of middle-life ministers also began seeking emergency help. Requests for grants therefore increased.

Limits to Retiring Pension Fund Membership

The core problem for the Retiring Pension Fund was that the prudent operation of the Fund was based on accurate actuarial expectations, which necessitated having a cash reserve in place for each member. In addition, the Board had historically covered the majority cost of the individual participants' dues, and as a result, the dues did not reflect the actual cost. Therefore, the Fund did not initially benefit financially but was instead additionally stressed by each new member enrolled. Conversely, the Fund had to grow financially in order to accept new members. Therefore, in 1931 the Board decided to accept new members into the Retiring Pension Fund "only as funds are in hand to make the necessary reserve."[102] The potential enormity of the problem was described in 1932: "At present but 2,519 are members of the Pension Fund. Provision should be made so that approximately 3,500 more, not less than 6,000 in all, may have the assurance of our pension system."[103]

The MMBB Budget for 1932–33 was, therefore, predicated on the funds needed from churches and individuals to allow for the inclusion of anticipated new members, an amount of $671,046. This was almost $275,000 more than the $395,000 that had been approved in the past several years. It was by no means certain of success even at the lower figure. As a result, a waiting list was established which, in 1931, held 130 names. The names were to be chosen in chronological order as reserve funds became available. The Board also proposed to the Convention that, when the Depression had ended, it would be necessary to raise "several million dollars with which to meet the very insistent demands of its pension and relief work."[104] Meanwhile, the "waiting list" of applicants for membership in the Retiring Pension Fund grew to nearly 500 in the years to come.

As a result, the Board was forced to curtail expenses and tighten limits. In 1931, for example, the Board voted that Retiring Pension Fund members "whose service will be outside the denomination will become ineligible for continuance of active membership in the Fund."[105] In 1931 the maximum pension approved had been $4,500, but in 1932 the Board established that the maximum pension that would be approved would be $2,500. Clearly the Board was confronted with a need to limit liabilities in a time of decreased income. And even with prudence and caution, the Board was prompted to aggressively seek additional income to meet the requirements of emergency aid to the older ministers and those in middle life without pastorates. Thus, by October 1931, the Board was seeking to establish a "Million Dollar Emergency Fund" through special gifts and bequests for the purpose of increasing their ability to provide emergency grants.[106]

A Persistence of Hope and the Practice of Prudence

There were, however, encouraging moments: Late in 1931, John D. Rockefeller gave an additional $800,000 to increase the MMBB endowment fund. In doing so, he asked that $100,000 of the amount be designated as a fund whose income would be used to assist ministers and widows in "emergency situations." The new emphasis on wills and bequests, especially through appeals in *The Ministry*, began to have success. Not surprisingly, appeals for gifts and bequests became a dominant theme of that publication in the early 1930s. A report identifying the states and regions from which persons were planning bequests and informing the MMBB of their intent became a regular feature of publications as a way of encouraging future gifts. Economic crises also seemed to diminish the fear of "centralized authority" frequently expressed earlier. One indication of that change in perspective was that the registry of ministry that the MMBB had been requested to develop in 1929 had, by 1933, received completed questionnaires from more than five thousand ministers.

Still, the Retiring Pension Fund's resources lagged in its ability to add new members, and the waiting list grew. Therefore, the Board in the early decade moved to increase available resources to meet needs. In 1932 the Board had already established $2,500 as the maximum pension to be received, thus limiting liability. In 1935 the Board transferred $500,000 from the Permanent Fund to the Retiring Pension Fund to eliminate, or at least reduce, the waiting list of prospective members to the program, which had reached 491 by September 1935.[107] The transferred funds established the reserve needed for actuarial integrity— a figure that at that time was roughly $1,500 per person.

Also in 1935 the Board voted that those joining the program after 1 January 1936, would have dues of 10 percent. The church would contribute 7.5 percent and the member 2.5 percent.[108] This change would significantly increase the actual income to the Board from the pension dues.[109] First, the salary percentage upon which dues were based was higher.[110] And the new standard required that sources beyond the MMBB would be contributing the entire amount of the dues without MMBB subsidy. This was the end of what Forest Ashbrook later referred to as the "Super Santa Claus" aspect of membership in the MMBB, which had included a significant MMBB subsidy for pension payments. Henceforth, with some exceptions, the Retiring Pension Plan and its successor plans were based strictly on business and actuarial principles, with occasional exceptions for unique cases of compassion or crisis.

Increasingly the most critical need for funds was to respond to emergency needs and the needs of ministers and their families who were too elderly to have benefited from the Retiring Pension Plan. At the 1935 Northern Baptist Convention in Colorado Springs, Executive Secretary Peter C. Wright proposed that convention churches be asked to receive a special offering for the MMBB on one Communion Sunday each year to "assist elderly ministers and their widows." With the convention's approval, the offering became the Communion Fellowship Offering, which served its intended purpose until the 1970s.[111]

The Depression's continuing grim economic circumstances further exacerbated the MMBB's overall investment position. For example, the Treasurer's report for the year 1935 revealed that securities of the value of $863,000 would be called for payment in about six months. While those funds were budgeted to receive a return of 4.86 percent, lower yield rates made its future return more likely 3.75 percent, or approximately 25 percent less in income. Such disappointing performance restricted available funds for all activities. And, at the local levels, discouraging news continued as many churches were forced to close their doors, federate with another Baptist church, or even unite with churches of other denominations. As a result, emergency grant applications increased, and the MMBB responded. Resources for emergency response remained few, however, and in 1934 and 1935 amounted to only $9,900 and $8,000, respectively.[112] Forest Ashbrook described them as only a "modest handout" that at best only offered temporary relief from extreme circumstances. Finally, almost as a symbol of the period's continuing negative news, late in 1934 John D. Rockefeller announced that he would no longer contribute to the Unified Budget of the Northern Baptist Convention. Practically speaking, his largesse to the MMBB also ended. Henceforth, he stated, his support would be directed to interdenominational organizations and enterprises.[113]

The year 1935 included several events that would ultimately prove to be formative for the MMBB; two were staff appointments. In 1934, the Board had recognized that they had been fortunate that Peter C. Wright had been available to provide effective transition when Everett Tomlinson was forced to retire due to health. They, therefore, passed a resolution to select and train a successor to Wright, "since the position of Executive Secretary is one which requires a person who has had long experience in the administration of the work of that office."[114] Treasurer Arthur M. Harris and Executive Secretary Wright began a search for someone to fill that role, and ultimately M. Forest Ashbrook was appointed as Assistant to the Executive Secretary. It was understood that he was "in training" to succeed Wright in about five years. Mary Beth Fulton was also appointed as a corresponding secretary, with a special focus on women. Fulton developed a more extensive and effective outreach and connection with pastors' wives, widows, and other women connected with the MMBB's work. Later she served a long and effective tenure as editor of *Tomorrow* magazine, which replaced *The Ministry* in 1942.[115]

The third event of that year was consideration of the new Social Security legislation proposed by President Roosevelt. That legislation provided both benefit and challenges for the MMBB. The original dilemma was that a central tenet of Baptists was the separation of church and state. To many Baptists, Social Security seemed a compromise of that principle. To those of that opinion, ministers should not be a part of the program because their faith should be in the provisions of God and God's people. But more particularly, if churches were to be considered employers, and thus taxed for the purpose of the Social Security program, it was considered to be a clear violation of the separation of church and state doctrine. It was most objectionable to those who feared the political or legal entanglements that taxation might bring. Some feared that if the government taxed churches, then it could also claim the right to examine church books and thereby influence church practices. Baptist organizations and the MMBB in particular, therefore, at first responded negatively to ministers' participation in the program.

Social Security did indirectly offer the MMBB an opportunity. It could point to the Social Security program as a demonstration of the standard that the "world" held up for average persons. The Board was enabled to challenge churches to do no less for their ministers. And, because, initially, ordained ministers and missionaries could not participate in Social Security, it focused an even greater necessity for churches to provide pensions as an alternative.

The MMBB's general commitment to prudent management of funds and conservative policies enabled the Retiring Pension Fund to continue in strong fiscal condition despite the Depression. By limiting pension maximums, by increasing the percentage of salaries on which the payments were based for the new members, and by the decision to transfer necessary assets from the Permanent Funds to the Retiring Pension Fund in order to provide the reserves required to enable the addition of the growing number on the waiting list, the Board had taken action that not only enabled new members to participate in future benefits, but had expanded the critical mass and the financial basis of the program as well. Then in 1936, in response to more liberal New York laws governing MMBB investment practices, the Finance Committee began to invest some of the resources in the Permanent Fund in common stocks for the first time. It was a move that would have profound, positive longer-term effect.

Building Church and Constituency Relationships

The MMBB consistently developed strategies of communication to build strong relationships with constituent churches and pastors and to encourage new membership. Between 1933 and 1938 the Board benefited from annuity gifts totaling more than $1 million. And in 1938, the Board received its first large legacy bequest without restrictions, an amount more than $100,000, from Mary Colgate.[116] Clearly, effective communication with supportive constituents was valuable, and the Board sought ways to expand its relationships. In 1937, for example, Peter C. Wright experimented in Connecticut with a series of dinner programs to which key leaders were invited to hear the advantages of membership in the Retiring Pension Fund. While Depression economics proved to be an obstacle to many new churches, the work of the Board and its advantages became more broadly known and laid the groundwork for success for similar approaches.

The years of the Depression created both the necessity and the opportunity for more communication. One necessity was to remind churches and individuals of the pressing need for funds for emergency grants. The MMBB was effective in conveying sympathy: "The hundreds of letters that have come to us … tell a bitter story of your trials, hardships, losses, sicknesses, sufferings and poverty. We have often been depressed in spirit on account of the need and suffering which some of you have had to endure."[117] Sometimes the tone of request betrayed an edge of desperation, complaining that churches provided only a fraction of the funds needed to respond to emergency needs. But it was not the usual style merely to complain. Virtually every issue of *The Ministry* printed excerpts from grateful beneficiaries, and many issues also carried stories about church budgets based on faith and personal generosity resulting from sacrifice that had helped to save lives and ministry careers.

Certainly the economic challenge of the '30s magnified the increased need for grants-in-aid to elderly pastors who had not had an opportunity to join the Retiring Pension Fund, or to others who had been caught in the Depression's circumstances. In 1936, delegates to the Northern Baptist Convention approved a program called Adopt a Beneficiary, which was implemented by the Board in 1937. It encouraged individuals of greater means to "adopt" a beneficiary by paying either the entirety or a substantial amount of a grant to those in need. This, combined with the new income from the Communion Fellowship Offering, strengthened the Board's ability to provide grants. Nevertheless, resources for grants remained inadequate.

The dynamics of need during the Depression years seemed to shake loose some structural and procedural challenges, some of which reflected the growing complexity of church life, and also of Baptist identity. Since its inception, the MMBB had been primarily focused on Northern Baptist Convention churches and their ministers. But not all religious workers were ministers in traditional settings, and not all Baptist ministers served churches. The denominational identity of many churches was not entirely clear, especially among recent immigrant churches, which often continued using a national identity and language from a previous cultural environment. In 1935, for example, the Board approved a policy that Swedish, Danish, and German ministers who were pastors of churches affiliated with their respective Conferences, whose churches were allocated outside the territory of the Northern Baptist Convention, and whose salaries were supported by their respective General Conferences could be considered as missionaries and would, thus, eligible for inclusion in the Retiring Pension Fund.

The inclusion of missionaries both in MMBB's name and in benefits brought challenges, too; payment of missionaries' pension dues were, by necessity, an obligation of the sponsoring boards. Thus, relatively fewer missionaries had been members, especially members of the Retiring Pension Plan. However, in 1937 and 1938 the American Baptist Home Mission and the American Baptist Foreign Mission Societies both approved the enrollment of missionaries sponsored by those organizations to be enrolled in the Retiring Pension Fund. In 1938 the General Board of the Northern Baptist Convention passed a resolution clarifying their eligibility.[118] In the same period, the Board voted to accept evangelists into the Retiring Pension Fund as long as 60 percent of the evangelist's income was based on service to churches affiliated with the Northern Baptist Convention.[119] The MMBB also encouraged state and associational organizations to enroll their staff members in the Fund, and some responded. In these ways, the MMBB expanded the circle of its service and, at the same time, extended its base.

The MMBB frequently appealed to readers to consider gifts and bequests or to become annuity bondholders. Many readers likely received a rudimentary education about methods of giving that had previously been unknown to them. Bequests, trusts, insurance policies, gift annuities, and more were all introduced through the pages of the magazine. In one especially heartwarming story, a retired minister who had entered in to an "old age home" where his care was assured returned his bond as he didn't "need it any more." In another case, a minister who had no children and whose wife predeceased him informed the MMBB that it had become the beneficiary of his life insurance. Soon, the framework of a fully developed program of long-term giving emerged—and it began to show results.

Balancing Compassion with Prudent Management

Many Fund members had difficulty paying their dues. The failure to pay dues was almost never an act of irresponsibility. Rather, it was a matter of deep embarrassment and broken pride. Often, when the MMBB attempted to investigate the circumstances of a minister who had fallen behind, they found a minister or a family already deep in debt. Yet the MMBB faced a threat to its own long-term program solvency if it exercised a policy of overly generous compassion. For the long term, the MMBB's strict adherence to maintaining effective long-term investment and accounting principles in light of actuarial prediction benefited the Board's financial integrity. But the ministers that they could not or would not assist were casualties as a result.

A frequent theme of articles in *The Ministry* during this decade revealed the nature of the problem. They addressed the urgent need for ministers to communicate with the Board, especially when they were unable to pay their dues. And sometimes the conflict between compassion and prudence was very clear. "Some are finding it difficult to pay their dues promptly," one such article began. "However, it should be recognized by the members of the Fund that ... the Fund must be kept sound. In order to do so, the payment of the dues is necessary. Their payment must be required." In another issue they were more direct: "ALWAYS MAKE SOME REPLY TO NOTICES OR LETTERS SENT FROM OUR OFFICE. Remember that you are replying to friends of yours."

The anguish of the situation was often clear, but the discovery of extreme need often created an opportunity to educate. In several issues of *The Ministry* during the 1930s, the condition of unemployment among ministers was highlighted.[120] "The church is responsible for these men. It helped in their education. It welcomed their call to preach the gospel. It ordained them. It cannot now lightly ignore their plight."[121] In 1931 *The Ministry* reported what appeared to be a "considerable tendency in the direction of reduction of the salaries paid to pastors."[122] The The article recognized the economic challenges of the day, but observed that such reductions were made against salaries that were disproportionately low in the first place. The same article quoted the harsh judgment of a State Secretary: "The churches seem to be putting on the thumbscrews and trying to secure the best for the least."[123] Clearly those at the MMBB who faced the chore of deciding upon grants became acutely aware of the need to broaden both sympathy and understanding of the problem as a result of their responsibility. "We are sorry that it has been impossible always to respond to your requests," wrote Peter C. Wright in 1933. "Denials made for good reasons often have their background in genuinely tender sympathy. It is our aim to serve the needs of all the best that we can."[124]

Those who continued to be pastors were remarkable for their continued loyalty in service. MMBB's communications, especially *The Ministry*, consistently described ministers and their families reduced to near poverty and mere survival, yet remained committed to their ministry and congregations. Sometimes the suffering was heartbreaking: One MMBB representative discovered a minister, aged 67, and his wife who had both been ill; one reason was clearly malnutrition. They had been living on $1.90 per week from a grant from the county welfare board. They proudly claimed that they had no debt, but when asked what they had to eat, the answer was, "Well, just plain food."[125] Laity and leaders of the churches were urged to share "as fully as possible the burdens borne by their pastors...." But because not all churches were able to sustain pastoral salaries, or unfairly balanced budgets by reducing their ministers' salaries, it became clear that some pastors might need to work longer. But this was a challenge because the prevailing attitude remained that pastors reached their "deadline" at early middle age.

The Issue of Age Discrimination Is Magnified

Therefore, it was likely necessity that motivated MMBB to push back against the continuing, predominant negative attitudes toward older ministers. The 1932 MMBB *Annual Report* asserted that the

Depression had "compelled the retirement from active service of some who in normal times would have continued in active service somewhat longer."[126] Often those who might otherwise have expected to retire found it necessary to continue for a while, and the MMBB advocated on their behalf. One issue of *The Ministry* featured a 78-year-old minister who, at age 75, had been encouraged to retire and take a place in a home for the aged. Instead, he took a supply preaching position for six weeks and that experience led to another, and then another. Each of his positions was in a church known to be nearly dead, or in difficult circumstances. The pastor confounded expectations and rescued them all.[127]

Another example in the same issue described a pastor in retirement in a resort community who turned a vacant house into a Sunday school and then secured pledges sufficient to build a chapel. This octogenarian minister, though a pensioner, obviously had life and leadership yet to offer. Still another wrote to say that he was considering retirement the next year when he would be 86 years old.[128] With remarkable sophistication and subtlety, the assumptions of age discrimination were persistently challenged, and at the same time, stories of high-achieving older pastors offered inspiration to all. The theme was a persistent one. In 1939 an issue of *The Ministry* observed that "a leading whiskey distiller" had recently advertised that the experience and skill of its older distillery workers totaled more than five hundred years, and that "every product of ours is the result of this long and rich experience." Doubtless the lesson caught the attention of Baptists who, in many cases, at least claimed to be "teetotalers."[129]

MMBB had a specific stake in the matter of age discrimination because premature retirement combined with unexpected requests for grants threatened the financial assumptions its programs were built upon and prevented it from accepting new members into the Retiring Pension Fund. And, of course, pushing a crusade against age discrimination was a just cause. At the Convention of 1933, the challenge of ageism in attitudes toward ministers was directly confronted by an address entitled "The Forgotten Man in the Ministry," no doubt in part inspired by the MMBB's persistent reporting and possibly with its direct support. The address implored churches to consider men "according to their merits and not their years." There were, proposed the address, "many unemployed ministers who would make wonderful pastors, yet they are left out in the cold merely because they are too old—they are past forty-five." And it prophesied disaster if churches persisted in placing "immature ministers direct from seminaries ... in the largest pulpits, at the same time, placing those who have achieved maturity of mind and heart in the service of Christ upon the shelf." It is not evident whether the MMBB officially or unofficially sponsored that address. But it was clearly approved: The MMBB offered that a copy would be mailed free to anyone who requested it.[130]

Naturally, an overwhelming and common theme of the era was financial security. It proved to be a strong recruiting theme for participation in the Retiring Pension Fund. In 1934 H. Pierson Hammond, the longtime actuary of the Board, delivered an address to the Northern Baptist Convention titled "The Security of the Retiring Pension Fund for Such a Time As This." It was a biblical, theological, practical, inspirational, statistical, and financial presentation that left little doubt as to the wisdom of being part of the plan. The address, which was printed in *The Ministry*, was later followed by articles, written by Treasurer Arthur M. Harris, on the effects of inflation, under the 1935 promotional theme of "Give Them Security That They May Face Old Age With Security." Throughout the 1930s, the themes of loyalty in the ministry, the challenges of poverty for ministers, the need to provide security, and the role of effective financial preparation through pension contribution for ministers and the special needs for grants for those whose ministry preceded the Retiring Pension Fund or who had become disabled early in ministry effectively raised consciousness for the MMBB's goals. By 1940 the Board could announce that more than 1,700 Northern Baptist Churches had dedicated at least one Communion Offering to the Special Fellowship Fund, which addressed the most acute of the needs.

A Second Leadership Succession

In 1940 Peter C. Wright's health became uncertain, and he announced his retirement, at the age of 70, to take effect on 30 November 1940. Following the precedent established with Everett Tomlinson, he was elected to the position of Consultant Secretary "that the Board might not be deprived of the benefit of his long and rich experience." The Board's earlier hopes that M. Forest Ashbrook might be qualified to succeed him were fulfilled, and he was elected to assume the duties of

Executive Director on the same date as Wright's retirement.[131] In writing about the accomplishments of the Board under Wright's leadership, Ashbrook wrote, "During these twenty years past, Dr. Wright has seen the establishment of the Retiring Pension Fund and has had a major part in its growth into one of the three outstanding Protestant Pension Funds in the country. At the same time he has carried a tender, sympathetic concern in ministering to the company of noble Christian ministers, their wives and widows...."[132] In turn, Wright wrote that Ashbrook "has given clear evidence of his fitness for the office to which he has been elected."

The MMBB was entering its third generation of executive leadership, and the Board itself was also increasingly relying on a new generation of elected members and leaders. Most recently, Charles E. Wilson, the iconic leader of General Electric, had been elected to fill an unexpired term. Arthur M. Harris had served in key Board roles almost since the beginning, but health issues caused his retirement in 1939. William R. Conklin was elected Vice Chairman to follow Harris as Vice Chair, and J. Herbert Case assumed Harris's long-standing roles as chair of the Finance Committee and Treasurer.[133] Avery A. Shaw had served as Board President since 1924, but resigned in 1941 after he retired from the presidency of Denison University and moved to live in California. Despite these changes, the Board continued to demonstrate a harmonious, seamless continuity.

However, the new Executive Director and the Board were faced with a clear challenge. Between 1935 and 1940 membership in the Retiring Pension Fund had declined from 1,901 members, 1935 to 1,501 members in 1939. In that year, a transfer of funds had allowed the waiting list to be admitted to participating status, and 145 new members were received. At the end of 1940 the Plan included 1,648 members, which represented only about 38 percent of those eligible to belong. The two primary causes for the Plan's membership stagnation had been the impact of the Depression on church budgets and ministerial salaries, and the shift from the older rate of membership contribution at 6 percent compensation to the new 10 percent requirement. The mathematics was simple: A number of ministers had been forced to drop out of the Plan, and new members entered at a slow pace.[134] Thus, the challenge of finding support to provide grants to short-term members, or to those in unexpected need, remained severe.

Help from the World Emergency Fund

The Northern Baptist Convention's support of the MMBB through the Unified Budget in 1941 amounted to $136,421.56. Much of that support, in addition to the Communion Offerings, funded grants and responses to unusual needs. In that year, the Convention also developed a World Emergency Fund to address some of the most critical needs in both churches and in the mission fields resulting from depressed economies and emerging war conditions.[135] The goal of the fund was to raise $600,000 each year for special needs for the years 1941–44. The MMBB was budgeted to receive $40,000 annually of those funds for a "ministry of compassion."[136] As the last issue of *The Ministry* went to press in 1942, it carried an urgent appeal to help achieve the goals of the World Emergency Fund. In 1942 MMBB received $33,497, and in 1943, $43,400 from the World Emergency Fund. But the gap between need and resources to meet it was growing, and promised to become more severe. The fundamental problem could only be met by expanding the number of participating members.

New Membership and Support for the Retiring Pension Fund

In spite of the Retiring Pension Fund's stability and general success, the low percentage of participation meant that the fundamental goal was not being fulfilled and that future financial growth would be limited. Therefore, Forest Ashbrook's early agenda focused on achieving the membership in the Retiring Pension Plan of as many qualified and eligible ministers and missionaries as possible. A companion goal was to convince churches to assume an appropriate portion of the dues. In preparing to accomplish these goals, the Board engaged two new Associate Secretaries: G. Merrill Lenox, formerly pastor of the Judson Memorial Church of Minneapolis, Minnesota, and William A. Shanks, who had served as the Executive Secretary for Northern Baptists in the state of Washington for ten years. The election of Shanks followed the logic of the earlier appointment of George L. White in choosing one who had strong connections and deep roots in the western region—an area that continued to require special attention and encouragement. Both were engaged to focus leadership especially on promotion and membership advancement. In addition, Herbert E. Hinton, a former missionary, was also appointed as a midwestern representative with an office in Indianapolis, Indiana. Ashbrook also secured the assistance of

George Moll, who operated an advertising agency in Philadelphia, to work with the Board in developing promotional strategies.

With a new staff, and after consultation in several directions, the only apparent way to invigorate Plan membership applications was through a comprehensive program of information, education and recruitment. By 1940 the denomination's constituent mission societies, national agencies, and some seminaries had all agreed to enroll their staff members in the Retiring Pension Plan. In 1941 the Board announced a campaign Every Church Paying Its Share of Its Pastor's Dues in the Retiring Pension Fund by 1943. The Northern Baptist Convention approved this campaign at the 1941 Convention. The pastor of the Third Baptist Church in St. Louis, C. Oscar Johnson, also a Board member, became chairman of the Pension Fund Crusade committee, which comprised key lay leaders and ministers throughout the denomination. Johnson was a noted inspirational and motivational speaker in the Convention, and was particularly gifted with a sense of popular rhetoric. Johnson delivered an address at the convention titled "Worry Free," and it was likely he who inspired or led the Board to translate the campaign's goal into the effective slogan "Worry Free by '43."

State conventions, associations, and city societies had been slow to enlist their staff members and, in some instances, slow to encourage their churches to participate. Having targeted these organizations for recruitment, responses began to improve. By the time of the Northern Baptist Convention in 1941, virtually all the city societies and conventions reported taking action, or having actions pending for likely approval. To stimulate further support, the Board enlisted the aid of key lay groups in the denomination, including the men's and women's organizations, and enlisted key pastors and denominational leaders to provide active public support. In early 1942, the Board added a practical incentive for churches and agencies to enroll their ministers or staff members in the Retiring Pension Fund by reducing total dues by 20 percent in the second or subsequent year of membership, with the amount reduced to be applicable to the 7.5 percent of compensation payable by the church organization.[137]

The campaign to extend membership was a success. By the end of 1943, 1,201 new members had been added, representing 38 percent of eligible pastors.[138] By early 1945, the MMBB could report that 72 percent of eligible pastors in the Northern Baptist Convention now belonged to the Retiring Pension Fund. One state (Utah) boasted 100 percent participation, and several others claimed 80–90 percent.[139] By 1946 the MMBB could report that it was one of the largest three church pension funds in operation.[140] Even more important, the long-term effect of the campaign was to establish participation in the MMBB as a standard expectation of benefits appropriate for every minister and missionary and a clear expectation for the churches, agencies, or organizations that supported them.

The Effects of World War II

The era that began with devastating economic events ultimately concluded with World War II. That war disrupted or permanently changed virtually every aspect of American life. Already-weakened churches were affected in many ways, and most visibly by the temporary or permanent loss of members as combatants or, in some cases, the loss of pastors who served as military chaplains. In other cases, the lack of church resources, members, or pastors caused severe cutbacks in programs, and some closed their doors. Mission fields close to war zones were disrupted, missionary personnel were recalled, or resources for programs were reduced because of economic scarcity or rationing or both. At home, the annual national conventions of the Northern Baptists were cancelled for the years 1943 through 1945 as a result of the war effort.

Yet it was an active time for the MMBB and Northern Baptists. The combination of Depression and war had resulted in the availability of the beautiful Wisconsin country estate, Lawsonia. The luxurious farm/estate was located on the shore of Green Lake, Wisconsin, and had variously served as a retreat for the Lawson family which had developed it, and later had been a country resort that had reputedly hosted some of Chicago's most notorious underworld personalities. The property included a number of substantial buildings, a small hotel, and outdoor facilities for camping and hiking. A group of Northern Baptist leaders proposed to purchase the property as a conference center for denominational purposes. In 1943 the MMBB provided $5,000 to the American Baptist Publication Society toward the purchase and, thereafter, was a strong supporter of its successful use. [141]

For the MMBB, the war years encompassed a period of planning. It was in anticipating the eventual conclusion of the war that the greatest challenges were evident. A 1942 letter from E.H. Rhoades, Jr., then the Budget Research Secretary of the Northern Baptist Convention, had raised the question of what post-war conditions would mean for the work of all of the Convention's related agencies. Though the overall economic consequences of WWII could not be accurately predicted in 1942, several trends were already clear. First, inflation was rising. *Tomorrow* magazine reported that during the first two years of the war, food costs had increased by 47 percent.[142] Second, it was conservatively assumed that a national debt in excess of $300 billion at the war's end was likely. As a result of the restrictions, regulations, and public expenditures that the war required, it was also likely that a large national debt obligation would impose higher taxation levels and that interest rates would be regulated at a low level that would depress investment return.

These assumptions pointed to specific challenges for the MMBB. Therefore, in addition to concerns about adequate resources to meet needs created by or as a consequence of the war through grants or special programs, MMBB leaders began to evaluate assumptions about the various demands that the Retiring Pension Fund would face for the longer term and, specifically, whether its reserves were adequate for the future. In addition to the already rising trends in life expectancy, a predicted postwar inflationary period might raise ministerial salaries, which were already trending upward and which, in any event, needed to be raised. Combined, these trends would likely raise future MMBB payout pension obligations. In 1944 H. Pierson Hammond, the Board's actuary, reported that his own review of the Fund indicated that its reserves should be increased by more than $2.2 million to keep in healthy balance.

The World Mission Crusade

Therefore, from 1946 to 1948 the Board decided to take a multistep approach to bringing the Retiring Pension Fund into conformity with expectations. It decided to suspend the Board-supplemented reduction of pension dues for both the 6 percent members and 10 percent members in order to adjust the reserve investment return basis from 3.5 percent down to 3 percent; second, it determined to base its future payout values on the new salary projections, and finally it would report to the denomination MMBB's needs for additional funds to secure the Retiring

Pension Fund's future. The suspension of the reduction of dues—which was a direct subsidy from the Board to ministers and churches—was calculated to save $200,000 annually. After consultation with denominational budget and program leaders, the Northern Baptist Convention then proposed that a onetime amount of $1,500,000 be included in the then-planned World Mission Crusade, with an additional $350,000 in a section of the Crusade's budget for recurring items. In addition, MMBB was apportioned $25,000 per year in additional money from the Unified Budget for the years 1945–47, and was assured that this amount would rise to $200,000 per year from the Unified Budget for the four years following the World Mission Crusade.[143] Finally, in 1948, the Board transferred $500,000 from the Rockefeller Fund, a part of the Permanent Fund, into the Retiring Pension Fund in order to bolster its reserves to conform to the new projection of reserves required by the Plan.

The Board's tradition of prudence had defined a problem and approached it with commitment and creativity. The World Mission Crusade was a denomination-defining success, and the era of economic development and church growth following the war made its provisions possible.[144] During a time of economic turbulence and international crisis, the MMBB's core goal of providing pension support for retired ministers had remained focused and its numbers had expanded, now encompassing more than 70 percent of those qualified to belong. Its projection of actuarial experience and investment return promised that the funds to fulfill its commitments would be available. A new generation of leadership was securely in place and had met its early tests. As a result, pensions were now firmly embraced as standard and necessary components of pastoral compensation, and churches and agencies increasingly relied upon the availability of pensions as a means of assuring support for their clergy, staff members, and leaders. Previous, older styles of relief for ministers, notably the Baptist Ministers' Home Society and the Baptist Ministers' Aid Society, had completely ceased operations.[145]

The only program segment where the spirit of charity predominated was in the need to provide for the needs of those elderly ministers and others who had insufficient time to participate in the Plan and accumulate resources, or to augment the pensions of those who, for other reasons, were simply inadequate. To that compassionate end, the Board reaffirmed the importance of the Communion Fellowship Offering and proposed that it normally be received on the first Sunday in December annually.[146] The first issue of *Tomorrow* reported that funds available for grant assistance in 1943 included income from the Northern Baptist Convention Unified Budget of $140,093, Communion Fellowship Offerings of $31,727 and $42,362 in funds designated by MMBB from the Permanent Fund for a total of $212,282. That amount made possible average grants of $212. An additional $40,400 was available for those in "destitute circumstances because of the war conditions."[147] In 1947 the Board voted special grants during the Christmas season especially to address the needs of those receiving pensions of less than $500 per year.[148]

The MMBB's survival and success during the years of Depression and war were, in large part, the result of continued prudence in both investment and management, and in developing highly effective and personal ways to connect with its members and its supportive constituencies. An important agent of the MMBB's ability to develop positive relationship with local churches for more than twenty years was Mary Beth Fulton, appointed as MMBB Special Representative in 1935.[149] She was, in effect, a one-woman army on the march. Well-educated in Omaha, New York, London, and Oxford, with music the continuing theme in all her education, Fulton had a rare instinct to instruct, inspire, and motivate audiences by both speaking and writing. After the creation of *Tomorrow* magazine, her written contributions and editorial influence shaped that publication into one offering something for everyone. Practical information, inspiration, good counsel to both ministers and ministers' spouses, in addition to well-informed articles of opinion on sensitive subjects, all built trust and familiarity between the MMBB and its broad constituencies. Fulton also established a strong presence of female leadership at the MMBB, an achievement that later continued in MMBB's female executive staff and in MMBB's support for women in ministry.

In 1947 J. Herbert Case resigned as Vice President and Treasurer and was succeeded as Treasurer and later as Chair of the Finance Committee by George W. Bovenizer.[150] In 1947 Peter C. Wright died in retirement, thus ending a period of service as Associate Secretary, Executive Secretary, or Consulting Secretary that spanned almost twenty-seven years.[151] In the same year, the Board voted to request the Baptist Youth Fellowship organization to annually nominate a young person as a guest representative at board meetings. In 1948 MMBB Vice President Leonard J. Matteson reported that MMBB assets had exceeded $33 million.[152] Also in 1948, the MMBB moved to new offices at 79 West 45th Street in New York City in pursuit of more adequate space for its administrative operations. With the world-changing war over, the Board anticipated and prepared for a new era.

6

THE CORPORATE FIFTIES—REFINING
BENEFITS AND EXPANDING PROGRAMS

A Sense of the Times

America leaves its dirty, sour cities in large cars that "smell of dusty sunlight" while they thump over Eisenhower's unfolding ribbons of interstate highways with joints oozing of tar that smells like industrial licorice.[153] They begin to explore the Arizona highways, going home to the pristine new suburban countryside that smells of fresh-cut grass and insecticide outside, and inside of the electrically baked air of new TV sets. Airwick sticks try to disguise the smell of stale cigarette smoke, and the knotty pine of paneled family rooms proclaims a relaxed, casual prosperity. "How sweet it is!" Jackie Gleason could exclaim with blunt irony from his urban, walk-up apartment. But much of America missed the irony.

Ike projects a "don't-worry" attitude as he positions himself for a tee shot. There is a cartoon-inspired fullness to things. Everything seems possible. You believe in the future, but it is hard to ignore the passing dread that settles into the paneled family rooms. Hydrogen bombs, tested first in the Nevada desert, then in the South Pacific, bring a shiver of apprehension. Senator Joseph McCarthy is unmasked as a fraud about the evil Communists, whom he claims are everywhere but never quite catches. Still, there is a suspicion that he might have been right that gives rise to movements of patriotically conservative anticommunism, and its odd, liberal offspring, anti-anticommunism. Then there is Sputnik, which inspires a national inferiority complex that America never quite leaves behind. It seems as though American scientists have been inventing 3-D movies while Soviet slave labor was implementing a plot to take over space.

Somehow the '50s came to represent the American Dream at its best. Later, the decade would be remembered with the same nostalgia as the '20s. People would remember a time when everyone went to church and tipped their hats to everyone else. There was civility, community spirit, and family values—Norman Rockwell idealism, some called it; whatever caused it, churches could not be built fast enough in the new suburbs and, once built, could not quite meet the Sunday morning needs. Were there too many families and too many children? Too much sincerity, maturity, and posturing of success?

Still, you can't ignore Marilyn Monroe's lament: "What good is it to be Marilyn Monroe. Why can't I just be an ordinary woman?" Then suddenly you remember what happened to Marilyn. You have to ignore the Korean War, too, which was unbroken ugliness except for the garish tiger-embroidered silk jackets the soldiers brought home. You can't ignore either the newspaper pictures of screaming, racist bigots threatening demonstrators even before Martin Luther King, Jr., assumed leadership of a peaceful army of boycotters, counter sitters, demonstrators and school children who actually believed that "we shall overcome." You would have to ignore a lot to keep the '50s the serene decade it came to represent.

Television helped in the delusion. Roof-mounted antennas sprang up in Levittown suburbs all over the country, and on city apartment buildings, too. From glowing screens came the images that secure the memories: *Father Knows Best, Life with Father,* and that wise and wonderful father of *Leave It to Beaver* who, each week, enabled the Beaver to become a better boy. Fathers were everywhere, and not one of them was too preoccupied, too abusive, or too wayward to give time to his true calling of being a good dad. It was quintessentially expressed in Mayberry, where Ron Howard, as Opie, forever lived as the healthy kid everyone wanted to raise, and Andy Griffith was the compassionate father/sheriff who never beat up anyone, and only spoke gruffly when he had to.

Organization Men in gray flannel suits were organizing things at work, teenagers were at home watching *American Bandstand,* and adolescent boys were innocently fantasizing about Mouseketeers Annette and Doreen as first dates—this was coverpage America. The Pledge of Allegiance was recited each morning in school, and summer band concerts were performed in the park on summer evenings. But there were also Jimmy Dean, and Marlon Brando, and J.D. Salinger raising objections to phonies and trying desperately to discover the darkness that gives balance to humanity. In *Rebel without a Cause,* Jimmy

Dean complains: "If I could have just one day when I wasn't all confused ... If I felt I belonged someplace." Elvis Presley, with swiveling hips, blue suede shoes and Hound Dog lyrics lit the fires of 'tween baby boomers on the rise and combined with Frankie Lyman's hit "Why Do Fools Fall in Love?" to begin a crossover of the barriers between black and white cultures. Pat Boone, the first commercial Christian entertainer, sought to bridge things with "Twixt Twelve and Twenty," but it all made parents nervous anyway. The newly invented "teenagerhood" outraged a great many of them.

It was a prosperous decade. Catching up with things after the war generated an unprecedented economy and a sense of security. For the impatient, there was always the allure of the big-money TV game and quiz shows where you might win as much as $64,000 if you answered the questions right. Charles Van Doren, a Columbia University professor, knew all the answers, or so it seemed. It turned out the producers were supplying him the answers in his soundproof booth to keep him on the show and build an audience. Van Doren was disgraced and the episode fed the voracious appetite of one of America's most virulent chapters of anti-intellectualism with its implication that intellectuals were not moral, not normal, and not "true blue American." Even more than that, seeds were sown for mistrust in America's most respected people and institutions.

A serene decade? In cherished memory, perhaps. What began with automatic transmissions in Fords driven by young men just back from fighting in Korea ended with civil rights era workers heading south to where they were known as "northern agitators." Some of them were killed just as dead as the soldiers on Korea's Pork Chop Hill. The decade ended with marijuana openly smoked in Harvard Square and on the Berkeley campus—and a lot of other places—where "pinko" artists Pete Seeger and the Weavers entertained them. LSD and much less gentle music soon followed in the next decade.

In fact, the '50s were a time of growing anxiety; there was belief in progress, but a doubt that it would happen very quickly. Church attendance had peaked and by decade's end began to decline; there were just too many other things to do, too many demands on time. Hugh Hefner proposed in his *Playboy* magazine that sex should be fun, and the old-fashioned virtues that limited its pleasure should be abandoned. But in its heart, America longed for enduring love. A new national hymn emerged, one composed by Leonard Bernstein: "There's a place for us," the cast of *West Side Story* reprised at the musical's conclusion, as if to reassure everyone that, despite Tony and Maria's tragic end, the hope of progress and future serenity prevailed, "Someday, somewhere, we'll find a new way of living." Maybe. Someday.

Even ministers began to dream of a leisurely retirement—someday—perhaps living in one of the new Sun Belt retirement communities, or in a cottage near their kids, with ample time to do some sightseeing or fishing. They tried to save, maybe even to invest a little. During the annual ritual of the "summer family vacation," they visited places where an idyllic retirement could be imagined—and dreamed.

The MMBB at Work

By 1950 much of America was at work restoring personal lives after the disruptions of war, rebuilding the economy after the combined impact of Depression and war, and refining its organizational and corporate structures to create a more efficient, progressive, and productive future. There is partial truth in the popular memory of the decade as one of increasing prosperity, rock-solid virtues, stability, and unceasing productivity. In many ways, and like the rest of the country, MMBB's advances during that period reflected a refinement, organizational definition, and a vision of social development. The MMBB benefitted from its own "organization men"—the good kind—who envisioned the financial security that commitment to goals and organization could bring. During the 1950s, an unparalleled number of additions and changes in benefits were established that resulted in more effective service to members.

Leadership Changes

The decade's early years brought some key changes to the management of the Board. First, the retirement of long-term Board member H. Pierson Hammond in 1951 necessitated changes in actuarial and planning insight if the MMBB was to follow its established, prudent course of scientific assessment and businesslike practice. Hammond had served as the actuary for the Board since 1920 and had brought the same acuity to MMBB's financial forecasting and projections that he had brought as chief actuary to the Travelers Insurance Company. MMBB understood the continuing need and elected Huggins and Company as its actuary.[154] Also in 1951, William R. Conklin retired as Board President, having served in that role since 1942, and having served on the Board since 1934. His successor was L. Jerome Matteson, Board member since 1924 and son of William B. Matteson, MMBB's first Field Secretary, who served briefly in 1917. Both Clifford Cress and George L. White, early MMBB Associate Secretaries, died in 1951.

In 1953, Wilmer A. Jenkins, Administrative Vice-President of TIAA, was elected to Board membership. Jenkins was a professional actuary and recognized leader in that field. His connection with TIAA brought the benefit of both experience and experimentation from a similar, but larger, pension organization.[155] Also at mid-decade, two further additions to MMBB leadership foreshadowed future changes. In 1954 Dean R. Wright, who later became M. Forest Ashbrook's successor as Executive Director, was appointed Eastern Representative. Wright's first assignment in that capacity was to direct the effort in the eastern region to encourage ABC ministers to enroll in Social Security.[156] And in 1955 the Board elected its first female member, Genevieve K. Johnston, a professional educator in the Minneapolis Public Schools and Trustee, Vice-President, and Chair of the Finance Committee of the Minneapolis Teachers' Retirement Fund Association.[157] Her presence on the Board was one of the first affirmations by the MMBB of women in leadership.

In 1951 the MMBB observed its fortieth anniversary and recounted the gifts and energies that had made it possible. A *Tomorrow* feature article observed that in the Board's forty years, $8 million had been paid in grants, and nearly $10 million in pensions for the benefit of more than five thousand people. Assets had achieved $40 million by 1951, and $45 million by 1953. Still, approximately 30 percent of eligible pastors were not enrolled in the pension program, and many of them, an article in *Tomorrow* observed, "Will be compelled to call upon us for assistance in old age." The article asked, "Is it fair that these men should be dependent upon grant funds which rightly belong in a program of supplementing smaller pensions?" Churches were challenged to give priority to the "social, moral and scriptural obligations to the pastor."[158]

Reaffirming MMBB Identity

More broadly, recovery from a decade and a half of depression and war brought the MMBB a challenge to reaffirm its identity, to aggressively pursue goals consistent with its purposes, and to establish boundaries that protected them. One boundary was to define those ministers qualified to receive its services. From its creation, the Northern Baptist Convention (NBC) had been constituted as a network of churches often divided by different cultural experiences and faith perspectives rather than a unified whole. Controversies about biblical and theological interpretation, the style of church life, and the nature and purpose of denominational missions often erupted.[159] In the late 1940s, diversity of opinion broke into institutional debate and in some cases, division. One result was the creation of separate, new denominational organizations shaped under the general Baptist banner. The challenge for the MMBB was to determine how far the stretch of its retirement plan inclusion extended.

For example, in 1945 the Conservative Baptist Foreign Mission Society had been founded partly as an expression of displeasure with aspects of the Northern Baptist Convention's theology and policies. Many of the churches or pastors affiliated with the new Society sought also to retain affiliation with the Northern Baptist Convention, or at least with the MMBB. However, the General Board of the Northern Baptist Convention voted to exclude that organization and its churches from the NBC. Following that decision, and affirming itself as a program founded to support NBC-related churches and agencies, the MMBB determined that those affiliated with the Conservative Baptist organization could no longer continue membership in the Retiring Pension Fund.[160]

As a further consequence of continuing theological controversy and competition, in 1949 the Board similarly determined that it would no longer approve membership applications for the Retiring Pension Fund from ministers who served churches or organizations affiliated with the Baptist Conference of America (formerly the Swedish Conference) and the North American Baptist General Conference (formerly the German Conference).[161] Departures from the Convention for theological or reasons of ecclesiastical identity remained an issue for the MMBB. On the other hand, in 1949 the Board launched a new effort to encourage qualified Northern Baptist Convention ministers to join the Plan. Several ministers were again engaged to make personal contact to encourage qualified potential Plan members.[162]

Careers were generally in transition in post-war America, and the ministry reflected that trend. In addition to those who left the MMBB because of loyalty to denominational structures other than the NBC, some left the Convention or the Retiring Pension Fund for reasons including career changes or alternative retirement programs. When a member was no longer qualified by reason of affiliation, or chose to withdraw from the Fund for other reasons, the status of his or her account had to be defined. Until 1949, departing ministers had received a refund of the entirety of their accounts. However, in the event of such a former member's death, the dependents of a member whose account had been refunded were left without pension benefits. The Board determined that this did not fulfill the goal of the Retiring Pension Fund. In 1949, therefore, the Board determined that when a member withdrew or lost membership eligibility and requested a refund, the refund would be based on dues he had paid into the Fund. However, payments made on his behalf by an employer would be held by the MMBB to benefit the member beginning at age 65, or in the case of death before achieving that age, were held to benefit his widow or widower, minor orphan children, or paid to his legal representative.[163]

Having endured a period of internal division and controversy, in 1950 the Northern Baptist Convention further clarified its own corporate identity. In consideration of a broader, more inclusive sense of legitimacy and, at the same time, to separate its identity from other Baptist theological positions, traditions and organizations, it voted to change its corporate name to the American Baptist Convention. As an affiliate of that organization, the MMBB's identity was likewise clarified as the Ministers and Missionaries Benefit Board of the American Baptist Convention.

It was not a decade of turning inward, however. While the MMBB found it expedient to clarify boundaries and definitions of service within the Baptist ranks, at the same time, the 1950s became an era of expanded interdenominational conversation and cooperation, and the MMBB frequently led in that process. The Board expanded its service to include some new groups of Baptists. Examples of an emerging, ecumenical spirit included cooperation with interdenominational consultations to reconsider the role of Social Security for ministers and strategies to achieve its extension to ministers. Similarly, interdenominational cooperation led to the development of an interchurch center in New York to provide administrative headquarters for the individual activities of several denominations and ecumenical agencies.[164]

A Decade of Benefit Expansion

The primary agenda of the MMBB during the '50s was to focus on the addition and expansion of benefits and to devise the management of resources to fulfill them. In 1951, New York state law, which governed MMBB investment procedures, expanded its law to allow 35 percent of trust funds to be invested in common stock. As one step toward building a greater investment return, the MMBB Finance Committee soon thereafter established that ratio in its investment policy and, as a consequence, was positioned to take advantage of the next two decades of Fund growth and development.[165]

In 1951 a new configuration of the pension plan was offered to holders of both the previous 6 percent and 10 percent plan certificates. The new plan was based on an increase of 1 percent of compensation in annual dues to a total of 11 percent of total compensation including housing and included a number of benefit additions. One significant addition was that of a death benefit prior to retirement in the amount of $1,000, or 25 percent of salary, whichever was larger. In addition, permanent disability benefits were increased from $500 to $900 per year, until the age of 65, when disability benefits would be replaced by the normal pension payment.

At the same time, the maximum pension was increased from $2,500 to $3,700, and minimum spousal survivor's benefits increased from $300 to $400 per year. The child's benefit increased from $150 to 200 per child per year until the age of 18, with a family limit of $800.[166] Normal retirement age to qualify for pensions remained at 65, but a revised feature of the plan allowed for increased pension amounts to be achieved as a result of working to a later age while continuing to pay dues. In 1954, benefits under the new plan were again expanded, with the death benefit rising to a minimum of $2,000, a spousal benefit to $500, and the children's allowance to $300 per year, with a family maximum of $1,800 rather than $800. The disability benefit rose to $1,200 per year with a children's allowance of $300 per child, not to exceed $1,200 per family per year.[167]

In presenting the new plan features it was recommended that 8 percent should be paid by the church and 3 percent by the member. Certificates for the new program were available as of 1 July 1951, by surrendering the old certificate and voluntarily agreeing to the new dues structure and paying a $20 initial payment fee that was applied to the increase in dues.[168] The benefits included in the new plan represented substantial increases for both retirement purposes and family protection. The new plan had increased in cost enough to suggest that some resistance might be expected. To help interpret the changes and advantages to MMBB members, churches, and the denomination, the Board turned to a group of sixty ministers under the leadership of C. Oscar Johnson, who had previously led in the Worry Free by '43 effort. In addition, several retired ministers were retained to assist in promoting the newly structured Retiring Pension Fund throughout the convention. The year 1951 was the fortieth anniversary for MMBB and a lead event in the new plan's promotional effort was a series of dinners for lay leaders of churches.

In 1952, the Board determined that the MMBB's own lay employees could retire at the age of 65 after twenty-five years of service and receive a pension equal to one half of their average salary of their highest five years, with a maximum of $3,750 annually. This formula included payments for the Retiring Pension Fund accounts, primary benefits under Social Security, and Penn Mutual Life Insurance policies. The retirement was prorated for those with less than twenty-five years of service.

The reality of the often pitiably low ministerial salaries had always been a priority concern for the MMBB. One outcome of ministers' typically low compensation was reflected in proportionately small pensions. The harsh effects were particularly evident among the oldest category of ministers whose years of service had included years of depression and war. Therefore, in 1953, following a period of study on the potential financial impact on MMBB, the Board began a program of supplementing smaller pensions of members and survivors who were age 76 and older prior to 1 May 1953. For those qualified, the minimum pensions were henceforth $500 for single pensions, $600 for joint pensions, and $400 for widows. [169] By 1956, the qualifying age for annuity supplementation was dropped to the age of 70, and the minimum pensions were set at $600 for single pensions, $840 for joint, and a widow's pension at $500. In 1957 the amounts were again increased to $760, $1,000 and $660, respectively. These supplements were made possible by income from the Permanent Fund.

A Family Health Plan

Perhaps the most significant new benefit introduced in the '50s was the M&M Family Health Plan for both active and retired members. Medical science had made radical advances in first half of the twentieth century, and health care was significantly improved as a result. However, such advances came at a steep price in the cost of diagnostic fees, medical care, and hospitalization. Blue Cross/Blue Shield and other health insurance programs were emerging to cope with such health care costs, but by the mid-1950s such programs were only available in large metropolitan areas. In any event, such programs were themselves costly, and only ministers on larger salaries could afford them.

Consequently, as health care costs trended upwards, many ministers were unable to provide for adequate health care for themselves or their families. In the early 1950s, the MMBB investigated solutions to this problem and determined that the expertise needed required partnership with a qualified insurance company.[170] They also determined that in most circumstances many ministers would be unable to afford health care protection and that any program would likely need to be subsidized for assistance. With those assumptions, a group plan was developed and presented to the American Baptist Convention in 1956.

The new plan became effective in 1957 and was underwritten by the Ministers Life and Casualty Union of Minneapolis. The annual cost for active ministers was $40 to $84, depending on coverage options and salary level. Actual cost for family coverage was $125.20, but the lesser subscription amounts reflected a significant subsidy by the MMBB. Enrollment required that a member be a participant in the Retiring Pension Fund. Married members with families, or widows with dependent children, with incomes less than $2,500, or unmarried members or widows without dependent children with incomes under $1,500 received the coverage without cost. A Senior Health Plan was initially free for annuitants who had been missionaries.[171] Non-missionary annuitants received the plan free if their income was less than $2,500 per year, or if single and annuitant income was less than $1,500. For those who exceeded those amounts, the plan was provided at $10 per quarter.[172]

Benefits of the plan included hospital and nursing care at $15 per day; childbirth at $100 with up to seven days confinement, plus a delivery fee of $50; a polio benefit maximum of $9,000 for up to 420 days and such surgical events as an appendectomy ($125), kidney removal ($250), or repair of a dislocated shoulder ($35) as further examples. The maximum hospital benefit for one person for a year was $3,000. X-ray examinations were covered at $10. Also linked to the Family Health Program, but for the member only, short-term disability income was available for up to 60 months at $120 monthly, accidental death at $3,000, and the loss of limbs or eyes at amounts ranging from $760 to $3,000.[173] The addition of health care for Retiring Pension Fund members greatly relieved a major financial challenge to ministers and their families. It also introduced a significant liability to MMBB that later demanded adjustments and changes.[174]

The Retiring Pension Fund Membership Expanded

The 1950s were a dynamic period both for church growth and expansion of the institutions that they supported. Denominationally related colleges and seminaries, for example, expanded. As one response, in 1955 membership in the Retiring Pension Fund was extended to professors of theological institutions that had a defined relationship with the American Baptist Convention. But in addition, schools, neighborhood and urban centers of ministry and mission outreach, denominational departments, and a variety of other programs had added staff members to carry out their work. They were often led or staffed by theologically trained but nonordained persons who were serving a church or denominational agency, or who were highly qualified by commitment, dedication, and training for the specific work they performed.

Therefore, in 1957, at the request of the General Council of the American Baptist Convention, the Board introduced a Lay Workers Pension Plan to cover the needs of the growing number of denominational lay workers. Because such a plan was outside the scope of the MMBB's original charter, it was developed on a contractual basis with the American Baptist Convention, with the Convention providing annual funding to pay for administrative costs and to assist in building up a reserve.[175] The MMBB served as the Pension Board and administered the program.

Also in 1957, MMBB received the assets from the Pension and Aid Fund of the Danish Baptist General Conference and agreed to assume the obligations of that fund. The Danish Baptists had historically been affiliated with the American Baptist Convention and were actively considering the dissolution of their own denominational organization. As a result, they sought to arrange for the continuation of the purpose of the Pension and Aid Fund. Assets turned over were nearly $50,000, and annual obligations totaled $3,405 payable to twenty-three individuals.[176]

Social Security Extends to Ministers

The dynamic economics of the '50s made it clear that all of these actions would still be insufficient to ensure a decent level of retirement support, especially for those who had been compensated at low levels. Therefore, the extension of the Social Security program to include ministers on a voluntary basis offered a supplemental source of income for retirement planning for those who participated.

When the Social Security program had been introduced in 1935, Baptists and many other religious bodies had opposed church participation.[177] Baptists had been opposed because by defining churches as employers for purposes of taxation, important barriers protecting church independence and freedom from state control might be jeopardized. Consequently, opposition to the original legislation establishing Social Security had resulted in excluding ministers or religious workers. Over time, however, many church or religious organizations had individually reconsidered their positions and had explored ways to preserve the principles of separation and independence while allowing ordained ministers or commissioned missionaries to participate in Social Security benefits.

In response to the later requests of some organizations that religious employees be included, in 1951 Social Security laws were amended, permitting the inclusion of lay employees of churches and religious organizations on an optional, permissive basis. Many state and national denominational offices, churches, and religious organizations quickly placed lay employees under the benefits of Social Security. This action further and decisively raised the question of whether the exclusion of ordained ministers and commissioned missionaries constituted an unwarranted and perhaps unconstitutional exclusion. Many denominational and religious leaders joined together to actively encourage reconsideration.

Following study of the issue by the MMBB staff and Board, and in consultation with leaders of other denominations, in 1952 the MMBB recommended to the American Baptist Convention that ordained members should also be allowed to participate in Social Security on a voluntary basis if it were possible.[178] In 1953 the Board voted to unite with the majority of other Protestant groups in testifying at Congressional hearings on proposed amendments to the Social Security legislation to promote an amendment that would allow ministers and missionaries to participate as self-employed persons, a category that required that they pay the combined amount of employer and employee taxes.[179] M. Forest Ashbrook, MMBB Executive Director, was a leading advocate for this position and actively pursued it with colleagues from other denominations. Their efforts succeeded, and by Congressional action, ministers were able to voluntarily enlist in Social Security effective 1 January 1955 through 15 April 1957, a deadline subsequently extended for two years until 1959.[180]

MMBB support for Social Security membership was such that, in 1954, the MMBB began to encourage churches to consider paying the entirety of the member dues for the Retiring Pension Fund for ministers who enrolled in Social Security. To that purpose, the Board hired temporary field staff under the direction of newly appointed Eastern Representative, Dean R. Wright, for the fall and winter months of 1954 in order to educate churches and ministers about the benefits and importance of participating in it.[181] In the September 1955 issue of *Tomorrow*, ministers and churches were encouraged to enroll in Social Security, and the MMBB quarterly asserted that "before long, it will likely be the almost universal practice for churches to care for the full 11% Pension Fund dues for their pastors."[182]

In 1954 and 1955, the Board also engaged several retired ministers for a period of months to encourage churches to pay the entire premium for the Retiring Pension Fund in an effort to encourage ministers to register for Social Security benefits. In January 1958, *Tomorrow* published a lengthy article explaining the details of inclusion in Social Security for ministers. In later issues *Tomorrow* published additional articles helping ministers understand the role of a provided parsonage or a housing allowance and other issues in determining the Social Security taxes for ministers, as well as continuing articles and brief paragraphs encouraging churches to cover pension dues. It also published a booklet on the procedural requirements for enrollment in Social Security and the details of its coverage. [183]

By encouraging the enrollment of ministers, and by successfully encouraging most churches to assume payment of the pension plan dues, the Retiring Pension Fund became truly a benefit, and not a contributory obligation, for most ministers. As of 31 December 1955, 78 percent of churches were paying the full membership dues for the Retiring Pension Fund.[184] For many ministers, the present and future transfer of responsibility for the total pension plan dues was, in effect, a small increase in compensation. It also removed the amount of salary used to pay pension dues from exposure to taxation. The savings accomplished thus allowed ministers to participate in Social Security with little or no additional cost. Their coverage was ultimately a major boost to retirement security.[185] In some respects the Social Security program presented MMBB with its first opportunity to consider the possibility of "partnerships" with government and private programs that could secure or increase retirement security for ministers and missionaries.

Noncontractual Benefits and Other Services

From its beginning MMBB had sought ways to support ministers, in addition to its original goal of providing retirement grants and, later, managing the Retiring Pension Fund.[186] Particularly during the Depression years, emergency relief assistance and many acts of non-financial personal support had been offered whenever possible. In 1955 approximately 20 percent of the Communion Fellowship Offering was used to provide emergency assistance and the rest was used for grants to retired ministers based on need. The MMBB also received support from 20 percent of receipts for the World Fellowship Offering. These funds were primarily used for services to missionaries, such as the cost of enrolling them into the Pension Fund, supplementing pension benefits, or grants for unexpected or unusual circumstances. The American Baptist Convention's Unified Budget funding provided similar services for ministers.[187]

Other examples of nonretirement or noncontractual services had included, since 1929, maintaining a registry of ministers for the Northern Baptist Convention, and countless roles of advocacy for ministers' salaries. The MMBB had also sought to enhance professional working conditions primarily through articles in *The Ministry* and, later, *Tomorrow*, in addition to supportive talks and addresses in churches and regional associations. By the late 1950s, the Board was also effectively advocating for professional allowances for cars, books, and professional expenses separate from compensation. Counseling and pastoral services were also informally offered to ministers and missionaries and their families. Through a variety of means, especially in *The Ministry* and *Tomorrow*, general counsel and helpful advice were provided on a variety of financial issues—from family budgeting to adequate life insurance or health coverage, in addition to the life, health, and pension programs the MMBB provided.

These services reflected an overall concern for the support and "better maintenance of the ministry," but were only infrequently defined or organized as ongoing programs. In any case, they were limited by lack of funds. During the 1950s, however, the MMBB developed a frequent and systematic program of what were later called "non-contractual benefits" and other services. Some were of financial assistance such as emergency grants. Others were adopted into the administration of pension and disability payments. As noted, in 1955 the MMBB began offering educational grants for the children of deceased or disabled members in the amount of $300 each and, in 1957, raised the maximum to $510.[188]

MMBB staff members had always frequently served to counsel its members. Although not a formal program, the very nature of the MMBB's mission and concerns sometimes brought access to the challenges and changes in members' lives. In addition, many ministers and others perceived personal conversations with state, city, and society administrators, especially Executive Secretaries, to be potentially threatening to their careers, and were thus reluctant to reveal personal challenges and frustrations or even professional concerns. Thus, the MMBB was in an unusual position to provide counsel on personal and professional matters, as well as advice regarding financial, medical, and insurance needs.. As one result, an undetermined number of ministers and others received personal support and assistance, or were referred to sources that could provide it. The *Annual Report* for 1957 noted that its Secretary of Grants "holds a certificate in Counseling from the William Alanson White Institute of Psychiatry."[189]

The MMBB also instituted a number of services that were once-a-year or relatively low-profile events. One small service that was greatly appreciated was a decision in 1952 to provide ministers with helpful tax preparation advice, including a four-page document of tax preparation information focused on ministerial deductions, and copies of J.K. Lasser's first edition of *Your Income Tax*. After 1955 the MMBB provided a booklet on Social Security taxation, and later, also provided a similar booklet on the tax implications of a supplied parsonage or a cash housing allowance.

Another valued service emerged from the MMBB's support and cooperation with the Ministers Council. The Council had sought to gather ministers for an annual dinner at American Baptist Conventions, with limited success. In 1952 the MMBB collaborated with the Council on this event and voted to provide the speaker, Paul L. Sturges, for that year's dinner.[190] It also helped to secure funding in order to make the event without charge to ministers.[191] Later, the annual dinner was assumed by the MMBB and ultimately became an annual and later biennial MMBB Luncheon. Often the speakers at these functions addressed timely and highly significant issues of particular personal or professional significance to ministers and missionaries.

New Emphasis on Programs in General Support of the Ministry

During the 1950s, several initiatives and programs reaffirmed the MMBB's concern and interest for the wellbeing of ministers both individually and professionally. These efforts focused on improving ministers' compensation, assistance with pastoral placement, professional development, and access to and participation in denominational decision-making.

Salary Support: Although the MMBB's core goals were to provide pensions for ministers, throughout its history, the board had consistently expressed concern for the low level of compensation active ministers received. Originally the MMBB's concern was the direct financial effect that low compensation had on long-term pension program results. Increasingly, and consistent with its mandate to support "better maintenance of the ministry," the MMBB had also advocated more adequate compensation to promote better quality of life, as well as long-term security. Both *The Ministry* and *Tomorrow* had frequently published articles, reminders, compensation planning advice, and other materials to encourage more adequate compensation. In 1951 the Board initiated a program with the Wisconsin Baptist Convention to determine whether churches might be encouraged to provide for professional expenses for ministers.[192] Later, the MMBB became a strong advocate of professional expense allowances for books and periodicals, auto expenses, continuing education, and hospitality.

In 1956 the Board approved a Minimum Salary Plan, initially on a trial basis, in cooperation with five states in the Central States Project. MMBB Associate Director John W. Thomas was delegated to develop the program and was authorized to hire a staff member for the time needed to complete the program's implementation.[193] This was consistent with the MMBB's long-standing general concern for ministerial compensation. During the 1950s a variety of alternative career choices became available to those who might otherwise respond to a call to ministry, and the MMBB's concern became motivated by a "clear recognition of the need for rapid development of Minimum Salary Programs ... if we are to maintain a competent ministry." Ultimately the project established a minimum salary, including the value of housing provided, and strategized to encourage churches to meet that level in compensating their ministry staff members. One persuasive feature of the program was the MMBB's provision of a supplement to support the salary at the minimum level during a prescribed time. Following that period, the church was expected to raise its resources to continue unassisted.

In 1959 the MMBB joined with several other denominations and the National Council of Churches in a Clergy Compensation Study that was supported by the Rockefeller Brothers Fund. The study was designed to investigate and analyze the varieties of clergy compensation and their effects on both the recruitment and support of ministers. The goal was to produce accurate data, clear comparisons between denominations, and helpful information that would be of value in encouraging churches to expand their understanding of clergy compensation. One practical result of the study was the production of a concise brochure titled "What Is Adequate Support for Ministers?" published in 1961. That brochure was effective in developing a model plan for determining pastoral compensation (cash salary and housing allowance), as well as allowances for health care protection, automobile and professional expenses, and the need for an annual evaluation of compensation in light of inflationary trends.

Pastoral Information and Placement: Always eager to have clear definitions of what constituted qualifications for ministry, the MMBB was concerned with strengthening and supporting the general competency and quality of the ministry. Ever since the Northern Baptist Convention had requested that the MMBB compile and maintain a list of ministers in 1929, it had gradually become a de facto resource for ministerial placement for ministers seeking positions and for churches seeking ministers.[194] Placement among American Baptist Churches had frequently been an ad hoc practice and was often influenced more by personal connections, necessity, and convenience than by systematic procedures to match needs, qualifications, and experience. In addition, a specific problem had arisen: Seminary students who attended non-American Baptist-related seminaries often faced a barrier for placement in American Baptist Churches. As a result, American Baptists annually lost some highly qualified candidates for denominational service.

Therefore, out of concern for the general level of ministerial service, specifically in the several participating states, the MMBB participated in the Central States Project during the early 1950s. Pastoral placement emerged as a critical issue. In response, MMBB provided funding for a Central Pastoral Information Bureau in Omaha, Nebraska, to serve Minnesota, North Dakota, South Dakota, Wyoming, Kansas, Nebraska, and Iowa for a two-year trial period, which opened in 1957.[195] The New England states were similarly interested and inquired about a possible placement bureau to be developed in Boston. Soon thereafter, also with MMBB support, offices were established in Boston and in Oakland, California, thus achieving pastoral information and informal placement assistance in the east, west, the center of the nation.[196] It was an incremental step toward a more comprehensive approach to a growing need.

The Ministers Council: In further support of the ministry, MMBB had offered active support to the Ministers Council since it was first organized in 1935, largely to foster greater professional and collegial fellowship among ministers. An MMBB grant of $1,500 supported its original organizational expenses. For its first twenty years, the Council had no salaried staff, but in 1954 Dr. Charles A Carman, a retiring staff member at MMBB, assumed responsibilities as the Council's executive on a half-time basis. He served in that capacity until the end of 1958. At that time, the Council then consulted with the MMBB regarding a closer relationship.

Subsequently, Dean R. Wright guided a process of discussion to include representatives of all national organizations related to the ministry. After agreeing that the MMBB and the Minister's Council had mutually supportive goals and that greater cooperation could be helpful to both, it was agreed that the Ministers Council would be administratively linked to the MMBB. The MMBB provided the Council with an office, a half-time executive, and a half-time secretary. MMBB's Director of Special Services, Fred Orion, assumed the executive responsibility and, in 1960, became the Council's executive on a full-time basis. Although administratively linked to the MMBB, the Council remained autonomous, and raised its own funds for program purposes.[197]

Commission on the Ministry: The MMBB had also been historically concerned about the qualifications and certification for professional ministry. Originally its interest was stimulated by the challenge of discerning which persons should be considered as qualified to receive grants and pensions. Originally, MMBB had concluded that it was expedient to consider the nature of the service provided, rather than specific qualifications. However, MMBB's contact with ministers and churches, and its role in providing a registry of American Baptist ministers, had encouraged it to develop more specific definitions of ministry and a broader concern for ministerial competence. In 1950 MMBB became a participant with several agencies in creating the Commission on the Ministry of the ABC. The Commission was a cooperative, inter-agency structure, not an official administrative body, and did not directly conduct programs. Instead, it delegated to constituent agencies the tasks and program possibilities that might result in strengthening the professional quality and service of ministers, and also to create opportunities for ministers' personal development.[198]

Throughout the 1950s, the MMBB consistently served as a catalyst for considerations and deliberations focused on strengthening and shaping the ministry. A continuing theme of concern was a sense of the lifetime developmental process of ministerial experience, a process that did not end at a particular age. In that context, in 1953 Lynn Leavenworth, Director of the Department of Theological Education, addressed the long-standing theme of ageism. His *Tomorrow* article "Too

Old at 55?" addressed prejudice against older ministers. He confronted the shortsightedness of churches seeking ministers who were "experienced but still young," as bartering a "Gospel birthright for a mess of pottage." Citing the experiences of a generation familiar with war, he wrote, "A line of 10,000,000 military men may be commanded by sexagenarians and septuagenarians, but a church of 1,000 members is certain that a man is 'too old at 57.'"[199] Leavenworth argued that older, more experienced pastors were often more dynamic and more competent than their younger colleagues and that, on the other side of the coin, young and old alike could be equally incompetent. To deal with both concerns, the MMBB continued its support of programs and resources for developing ministerial competence and quality.

To that end, *Tomorrow* frequently included articles provided by the most prominent contemporary Baptist preachers such as Robert J. McCracken and educators like Lynn Leavenworth that were focused on books ministers should read. Additional articles considered the beliefs ministers should address, by such diverse sources as L. Doward McBain and Howard Moody. It also provided brief, thoughtful essays on ministers' personal development, and the variety of ministerial roles a minister could adopt—from evangelist to personal counselor to interim minister. Mildred Palmer offered an article titled "Women Can Preach Too" a prescient subject in light of the already emerging desire of some women to be ministers. Mary Beth Fulton frequently addressed issues of the family life of ministers, and focused especially on the role of ministers' spouses—still almost uniformly women in the 1950s.

The MMBB also continued to advocate adequate financial support for ministers, even beyond its participation in the Minimum Salary Support program. By 1958 ministerial salaries had doubled from 1939, but Malcolm Cary, Assistant Treasurer, wrote a revealing article in *Tomorrow* suggesting that even paying a minister twice what he might have received in 1939 was inadequate. By then, he demonstrated, the average ministerial salary (including a 15 percent parsonage value) had reached $4,851. But to keep pace, argued Cary, it needed to be at least $5,200, and even that figure did not keep pace with the $7,600 salary that typified the average college graduate who headed a family in 1956.[200] The MMBB's relentless pursuit of more adequate salaries almost always fell behind its goals, but it had the effect of raising the averages, and stimulating increases for both the high and low ends of the compensation scale.

The growth economy of the '50s encouraged inflation and that, in turn, increasingly exposed the need for cost-of-living adjustments for pensions. However, "a most fortunate investment record over a period of years," as Executive Director Ashbrook put it, had resulted in surplus funds that were available to be used to adjust pensions to compensate. After a period of study during 1958, the MMBB voted in 1959 to provide funds for cost-of-living compensation to most of those who were receiving benefits from the Retiring Pension Fund in December of that year.[201] It was considered to be a first step toward a possible annual program providing a similar grant. Even more, it was, as Ashbrook later described it, "a major policy decision of far-reaching consequences."[202] The distribution was called the Gift, a supplemental income program for older, retired members. The basic gift was 10 percent of the member's pension, with additional percentages granted based on years of service. The Gift was again made possible in 1960 as a result of continuing positive investment performance.

In a related but separate action with profound implications for the longer term, the Board directed its Pensions Committee to study the range of benefits for its members, one aspect of which was to consider solutions to the pension erosion caused by inflation. One possibility that was identified to be reviewed was that of converting the pension plan to a variable annuity plan similar to what TIAA-CREF had implemented earlier in the decade.[203] That approach seemed to offer hope to link market performance to pension payments.

The Interchurch Center

The decade of the '50s included a renewed and general interest in ecumenism and interreligious cooperation among many denominations and religious organizations. By 1950 a new and vigorous National Council of Churches had recently been established. Similarly, a hope for eventual world peace had been modeled in the founding of the United Nations.[204] This spirit of collegial cooperation had its counterpart in a vision for increasing harmony and practical cooperation among denominations and religious groups. Among the possibilities imagined by those who actively pursued this dream was a vision for a common facility to house denominational administrations and ecumenical organizations, and to provide an environment for consultation and cooperation.

Although it was only indirectly related to its primary purpose, the MMBB played an important role in the development of what ultimately became known as the Interchurch Center. Earlier discussions of such a possibility had been tabled because the Depression and war had made such hopes unrealistic. In the mid-'40s, the Northern Baptists were searching for a new site to house their New York agencies, and several sites were considered, one of which would accommodate several denominations. The Presbyterians had expressed preliminary interest in using the same building, and, therefore, the MMBB proposed putting a hold on one site to allow time for consideration. However, no other denomination was willing or able to make funds available at that time. Correspondence with John D. Rockefeller, Jr., regarding his possible support received a tepid response, unless such a project would truly reflect a commitment by a number of denominations to join in the project.[205]

With the participation of the newly formed National Council of Churches in the late 1940s, the idea was reviewed again and a corporation called the Protestant Center was established. That group formed an inclusive vision for a national home for Protestant, Anglican, and Catholic communions in North America.[206] By 1954 the project was able to move forward, this time with the informal leadership of Francis S. Harmon, an active participant in Council of Churches' affairs and long-time Treasurer for New York's Riverside Church. By then, the National Council of Churches was actively seeking a corporate headquarters in New York City, and was considering a location in Morningside Heights. The proposed property, owned by Barnard College, included the entire block immediately south of Riverside Church, between 119th and 120th streets. Harmon sought the support of the MMBB and indicated that if at least five major denominations would contribute a total of $3 million for the project, he was confident that John D. Rockefeller, Jr., would invest as much as another $3 million. The MMBB took Board action in November 1954, and authorized $600,000 to be invested conditionally on the response of others. Other denominations did respond, and the project materialized. In 1955 a Board of Trustees was appointed for the project. The MMBB was represented by its President L. J. Matteson and by

Treasurer George W. Bovenizer, as well as by R.G. Fuller and Executive Director M. Forest Ashbrook.

Ultimately Rockefeller purchased the proposed site from Barnard College and made it available for a ninety-nine-year lease. In addition, Rockefeller contributed $2 million for construction of a building, with the additional promise of $650,000 if it was needed to guarantee an exterior construction of limestone to harmonize the building with Riverside Church and other structures in the area. The project had expanded from the original assumption of fourteen floors to a nineteen-floor edifice, and the denominational boards were ultimately required to invest $900,000 each. A variety of names for the project were considered, including "United Church Center" and "The Protestant Center." Ultimately it was built as the Interchurch Center.

Participant underwriters of the project included the National Council of Churches and the official boards of the Presbyterian Church, the United Lutheran Church, the Reformed Church, the American Baptist Home Mission Societies, and the MMBB, each contributing. In 1957 the MMBB voted to take a thirty-year lease for the 17th floor of the Center, predicated on the use of about half of that space by other Baptist agencies or organizations. On 17 November 1957, the construction began with a groundbreaking ceremony. The cornerstone was laid on 12 October 1958, with a cast of notables including David Rockefeller, prominent preachers Ralph W. Sockman and Harry Emerson Fosdick, and other well-known religious leaders. President Eisenhower laid the cornerstone before a crowd of spectators, estimated to be 30,000 to 50,000, lining the streets. The project had been completed within the budget at a total of $20 million.

The MMBB Remains the Lone American Baptist
Agency in New York

It was the hope of many that the new center would be the administrative home for the American Baptist Convention, as that Convention's agencies were scattered in several locations, mostly in New York and Philadelphia. For years it had been the denomination's goal to unite all of its operations in one location. The proposed Interchurch Center was one of two strong contenders to house their facilities. The other was in Chicago on property made available on the campus of the University of Chicago. The decision became competitive—at times acrimonious—

between regions and interests within the denomination. However, about the same time the Interchurch Center was being built, the Convention had unexpectedly compromised on a proposal for a headquarters to be built on land near the national historical monument grounds in Valley Forge, Pennsylvania. For a brief time, the American Baptist Foreign Mission Society leased the 16th floor of the Interchurch Center until construction was completed on the new American Baptist building, and then moved to the new facility.

The MMBB believed that the Board's best interests would be served by its continuing presence in New York City, both because it was the center of financial and investment activity, and because it was more accessible for key Board members, many of whom were New York-based. The MMBB held its last Board meeting at 75 West 45th Street in November 1959, and moved into the new Interchurch Center shortly before Christmas. The MMBB was the lone, long-term American Baptist occupant of the new Center, much to the dismay of those who had wished for the Center to be the ABC corporate headquarters, and equally much to the disappointment of those who desired the MMBB to move with other American Baptist agencies to Valley Forge.[207]

The MMBB continued as a primary force in the center's operation, and Forest Ashbrook, MMBB Executive Director, served for a time as the Director of the Interchurch Center after his retirement from the MMBB. Ashbrook reported that the attorney for the Interchurch Center once remarked, "The M&M Board is the best friend the Interchurch Center has." As time would indicate, the MMBB decision to remain in the Center, and especially in New York City, was a productive one for its core purposes and goals as well.[208] Its original investment of finances and energy supporting the Interchurch Center was a productive one over time.

Luncheon Speeches Point toward the Future

The 1950s generally justified its stereotype as an era of order and organization. Churches, as well as the culture at large, had sought to keep focused on the tried-and-true verities and values. Such stability encouraged an unprecedented decade of new church construction and program expansion. But by 1958 uneasiness seemed to settle in. Churches and their messages were encountering something new: If the '50s had been one of the best eras ever for the health and growth of churches, the impending '60s became one of the worst. In part because of the strength gathered in the '50s, the MMBB was ready to face the confusing road ahead. One resource was MMBB's development of effective communication with church leaders, especially ministers.

The MMBB's collaboration since 1951 with the Ministers' Council had often included dinner gatherings for ministers at conventions. In 1958, however, MMBB launched its long-standing tradition of Ministers' Luncheons at annual conventions. These gatherings soon became opportunities for reunion, fellowship, good humor, information about MMBB's benefits, and almost without fail, an inspirational, provocative, or prophetic address. The speaker at the first luncheon was Dr. Gene Bartlett, pastor of the First Baptist Church of Los Angeles, and later a seminary president and leader among American Baptists. His speech was entitled "The Gospel Confronts the Contemporary" and could not have been more timely. He suggested that the gospel was "confronting us where our goods have become our gods." He perceived that "self-confidence was becoming self-doubt," and finally, that the gospel "confronts us at the point where knowledge becomes intimidation." The '50s were not yet over, but in hindsight, on that occasion Bartlett described the agenda of era to come.[209]

The era of the Great Depression and World War II had defined much of American life since the 1920s. From 1960 to 1990, however, life would be completely transformed. In retrospect, the '50s, in religion as well as in the broad American culture, was a time of gathering resources and establishing habits and patterns for the time to come. Although many have tried to see the '50s as the norm—a kind of American cultural plumb line—it was more likely the exception.

7

A GENERATION OF TRANSFORMATION—
PART ONE

A Sense of the Times

How to describe the Sixties? Camelot? Twiggy? Or the Beatles—they were all young and alive then, George, Paul, John, and Ringo. There was the young Cassius Clay, soon-to-be Muhammad Ali, a young, black David who slew the corrupt old lions in the boxing ring: "Float like a butterfly, sting like a bee!" The stock market kept going up. There were Frisbees, hula hoops, and Chubby Checkers's "Twist." In cities, singles bars, came alive with "booted, pant suited, birth-controlled and pleasure-goaled young women" with big, teased hair who were on the cusp of the sexual revolution. On California summer weekends, the Mustang Sallys went to courtyard apartment pool parties in frilled bikinis.[210]

And what about the boys? They were cruising the boulevards in their Chevy 409s or bored-out Ford 289s mounted with slick tires and with the front hood blower scoops that sucked oxygen and blew out sexy, ear-shattering noise. They were cruising for chicks. No quarry? No problem—there was always the thrill of racing for pink slips, or drinking the beer stashed in the trunk! This was America—Opie all grown up with an edge. Of course, John F. Kennedy's and, later, Lyndon B. Johnson's war in Vietnam put a damper on all the fun. After 1964, many of the boys' cars spent years in garages.

Nikita Khrushchev pounded his shoe on the podium at the UN: "We will bury you!" The Cuban Missile Crisis created ominous dread. But when morning came and no one had been vaporized, Kennedy's courage and America's might temporarily glistened. Camelot ended in Dallas. "The President has been shot," a fellow student said vacantly, and I said, "Yeah, right." But he *was* right. Rockefeller Chapel was full to overflowing for the first time in decades. There were new terms like "catafalque," and the pomp and splendor of the military protocols. Jackie grieving, John Kennedy, Jr., saluting at the grave. We hated Dallas. Even then some wondered if they had missed out on something: a contemporary said, "Maybe I should've joined the Peace Corps."[211]

The Sixties. It was Freedom Riders going south, Governor George Wallace vowing "segregation forever," and Bull Connor with his ranks of fire hose-armed cops. It was little girls killed in a Birmingham church bombing, students helping with black voter registration killed on Mississippi roads, and in the end, Martin Luther King, Jr., shot dead, as he knew he would be. Ironically, he became the first enduring national icon since Roosevelt.

Camelot's idealism was replaced by a new cynicism. "We were going to change mankind," said one. "I thought we could make people peaceful," lamented another, "and then you see you are getting ripped off by manipulators—the SDS, Joan Baez marrying David Somebody because he was going to jail for draft evasion and that made them both cool." Timothy Leary and LSD at Harvard, and then everywhere else: "You bought into it, you thought you were going to have a revelation that would change everything, and then you didn't." Instead there were bad trips and bad dreams. For some it seemed a decade of bad trips.

If the '50s had fostered the belief that everything was possible, the '60s tried to prove it:

Consume, consume, consume ... sex, sports cars, ecstasy, Bermuda shorts, enlightenment, Playboy bunnies, freedom, justice, truth, art ... Everywhere the new smells of non-dairy creamer, tear gas, marijuana, Tang, Cool Whip ... Fake leather car interiors with big-button tufting, the cool rustle of beanbag chairs, the "think I can, think I can" of VW Microbuses straining to climb the Continental Divide.

Music lifted everyone: "California Dreaming" and "Little Deuce Coupe" by such innocently named groups as the Mamas and the Papas and The Beach Boys. Everywhere was Bob Dylan's nasal voice: "the answer, my friends, is blowin' in the wind."

Black Power! Some believed redemption, and maybe a little glamour, could be found in the company of "beautiful young gunmen known as the Black Panthers." Others saw the long-lost continent of Africa as the rediscovered Eden. Even white people tried to get in on the act and started calling everyone "brother." The students who had read

Frantz Fanon's *The Wretched of the Earth* wanted to join forces with them. But it was too much too soon. Many of the Freedom Riders returned home to suburban comfort or migrated to Wall Street careers. Vietnam's veterans began returning home and it seemed like no one noticed.

Reality and fantasy were hard to separate. Hippies, revolutionaries, and dropouts seemed present only on the news. Soldiers in 'Nam smoked pot. Reality? The preppies initially spurned Jimi Hendrix and thought Frank Sinatra and the Rat Pack were cool. There was also the antireality—those who tripped out, got high, and grooved on endless rock music. But all the divergent postadolescent roads seemed to come together with *The Graduate*, a film that united upper class arrogance, middle-class nihilism, flower-child innocence, and sorority girl superficial sophistication in a common, confusing destiny.

The medium was the message—so pick your medium. The news became drama. Walter Cronkite nearly became more important than anyone he covered. The nightly news body count of American and Vietnamese casualties measured America's growing cultural depression. The Beatles captured the seeming meaninglessness of events:

> I read the news today oh boy,
> About a lucky man who made the grade and though the news
> > was rather sad
> Well, I just had to laugh. I saw the photograph
> He blew his mind out in a car
> He didn't notice that the lights had changed
> A crowd of people stood and stared
> They'd seen his face before
> Nobody was really sure if he was from the House of Lords…

Nothing was quite real. What had begun as "everything is possible" became "nothing is real." Strangely, the same attitude encompassed the killings of King, Bobby Kennedy, and rioters in Newark, Washington, DC, Detroit, and Los Angeles. After King was killed, one New York TV station's total coverage for the evening was a single camera focused on a handwritten white card which said "SHAME." Most people switched to another channel.

Somehow the Sixties ended up with a sense of self-pity. Maybe it was because the flower children grew up, stopped acting like children, and instead started having them. SDS members and a few of those on the FBI Most Wanted List ended up in politics or making fortunes. In Vietnam, more than fifty thousand mostly young Americans and countless Vietnamese died. But somehow, it was those who stayed at home who felt victimized. A decade after the war, even the memorial designed to remember the fallen soldiers became, at first, a symbol of division, demoralization, and disgust. Jane Fonda, married to student radical Tom Hayden and vilified as a traitor by naively traveling to Vietnam to build a bridge of understanding, went home to rebuild her career.

And what about churches in the Sixties? The sexual revolution and Vietnam divided many congregations, and the new "generation gap" divided the rest. Later, the "culture wars" were perhaps an inevitable outcome. In cities, black preachers performed heroic service as leaders, ombudsmen, and intermediaries. Some of them later became politicians and statesmen. But integration, barely drawing its first breath after Johnson's amazing accomplishments in the civil rights agenda, was still nowhere to be seen in churches.

The Sixties? You had to be there. And even if you *were* there, you perhaps weren't. It was a decade that never ended for some, and couldn't end fast enough for others. America was young then, not the population, but America itself. America also felt a little dazed. Maybe it was the marijuana in the air. Or the tear gas in the streets.

MMBB in the 1960s

For the MMBB, the 1960s began an era of transformation that lasted a generation. The challenges were evident. For religious institutions, the 1950s had been preoccupied with reestablishing American values and making order out of war's chaos. Then, no sooner had things appeared "back to normal," a rising generation seemed to desire reinventing what normal was. Many of the young—traditional and revolutionary—had been raised in Baptist Sunday schools. Some of the era's development seemed to them to demand their prophetic response.

Ultimately, the '60s became an iconic decade in American history. The civil rights movement, evident in the streets, in the courts, in Congress, and in personal lives, precipitated profound social and cultural change, and change in the American Baptist Convention, too. Conflict in Vietnam, begun quietly in the late 1950s, continued nearly unnoticed into the 1960s, and then burst into a conflagration that inspired a youth rebellion-sponsored psychic trauma for many of America's families and, therefore, caused turmoil in a great many churches.

Also, by decade's end, the prosperity of the '50s had stalled, and war-induced inflation began a rise that threatened national and personal security. However one marks the beginning of the era, the mere mention of the Sixties invokes a time when change and challenge were everywhere. During that decade, the MMBB became actively involved in the national quest to achieve civil rights in very personal ways. To some extent, its policies incorporated changes in its own goals. It extended benefits, and then revolutionized its approach to providing pension security for its members. It reacted practically to the advent of the federal Medicare program, which, along with the Civil Rights Act, was perceived by many as among the most positive and lasting results of a fast-paced national political agenda. It reached out to personally support members and churches struggling to achieve or maintain reasonable compensation for clergy, and it sought to support ministers in both the North and the South, in cities and in small towns, who were in personal and professional crisis brought on by the social and cultural changes surrounding them. For the MMBB, as for the culture, it was an era of transformation. And it all occurred at a breakneck pace.

As the MMBB settled into its new quarters at 475 Riverside Drive in New York, the American Baptist Convention prepared to gather its several agencies into its new building being constructed in the historic, pastoral setting of Valley Forge, Pennsylvania. The American Baptists' new location was in symbolic contrast to the emerging themes of the time: At Valley Forge, its new address was not a street, but a Post Office box and, soon, a ZIP code. In truth, the ABC's move to Valley Forge was predicated on a corporate model of the church which required a headquarters for expanding administration. But, by that time, such a model of church life was already outmoded. Cities, challenged by their own transitional agonies, were nevertheless again becoming the locus of the future, and in church life "local," not "national," was the coming mantra. Although not obvious at the moment, the role and character of ministry, the function and character of the church, and the expectations of religious leadership were all being challenged. As Bob Dylan had put it, "The times, they are achanging!"

Investment Policy Changes

As the decade began, the MMBB was tending to the usual business of its core purpose: developing resources for the provision of pensions for Baptist ministers and missionaries. By 1960 New York state laws regarding investments for pension organizations had changed again. Therefore, at the Board's first meeting at 475 Riverside Drive the bylaws were revised to allow greater investment exposure to equities by stating that "not less than 50% of the Retiring Pension Fund should be invested in fixed-income producing securities."[212] This allowed for a more aggressive long-term investment in equities rather than the earlier 65 percent requirement for fixed-income securities. In 1965 all restrictions related to investment in common stocks were removed by a change of the MMBB bylaws. At the same time, the Common Investment Fund was created that allowed for all unrestricted funds of the Board, including those of the retirement plans, to be invested in common stock with increased diversification and a broader investment base.[213]

At that first Board meeting, there was also an extensive discussion regarding plans for the new American Baptist headquarters building in Valley Forge and possible MMBB financial involvement. There had been denominational tension over the MMBB's decision not to locate its own primary offices in Valley Forge. Nevertheless, the MMBB desired to support the ABC decision and approved a $500,000 loan to the American Baptist Convention for the construction of the new building. They also authorized a lease for space for an MMBB service office in the new facilities.[214] The MMBB's status as an anomaly within the American Baptist structure was becoming clearer: It was of, and for, the American Baptist Convention, but it was not limited by it.

Almost immediately, an acute introspection occasioned by the era's social and political movements caused many organizations to review their investment policies to encourage and support healthy and socially equitable businesses rather than unhealthy or oppressive ones. In 1964 the American Baptist Convention passed a resolution concerning the investment policies of the Convention and its affiliated agencies regarding investment in companies that did not include minorities.[215] Without reservation, the MMBB followed by reviewing its own policy.

Later in the decade, in 1967, a group of black churchmen presented demands to the Boston meeting of the American Baptist Convention, several of which impacted MMBB practices. Rather than accede to what some perceived as "demands," the MMBB chose to respond in the spirit of the "justness of cause" that the demands for reparations had presented. At issue for MMBB were two main concerns. The first was MMBB's reliance on two major banks that it used for transactions and subsequent discussions of whether those banking relationships should be abandoned because of their connections with South African businesses.[216] The second was a contingent concern that the MMBB should alternatively invest in black-owned or directed banking institutions. Both issues raised for the Board the urgency to define a balance between the Board's authority to invest funds at its discretion, its obligation to fulfill its fiduciary responsibility to keep funds secure to provide pensions, and a moral imperative to support the movement to achieve civil rights.

The MMBB's ultimate response was determined first by following its practice of maintaining a clear focus on its core purpose as steward for pension and other benefit funds. In receiving legal counsel, the Board was assured that it had broad ranging discretion in investments, but that it would be judged by its demonstrations of responsibility under the "prudent man" principle. The Board also investigated the banks in question and the alternatives to them, and concluded that the services MMBB needed to fulfill its responsibility were simply not available elsewhere and that the banks in question were positioned to do good, not evil. However, recognizing the moral issue involved, MMBB also decided to invest $300,000 in twenty banks in disadvantaged, mostly black, communities.[217] With a sense of diplomacy, the Board thus strived to steer a course that acknowledged its mandate while also affirming moral imperatives.

Leadership Changes

The '60s were a dramatically challenging time for leadership, including the MMBB. There, leadership changes symbolically and practically illustrated events already in motion or soon to be evident. First was the unexpected death of George W. Bovenizer in May 1961. Bovenizer was a long-serving personal link to the Board's first generation, having served the MMBB from 1925 onward and as Chairman of the Finance Committee since 1947. He was remembered as a man of "sharp business acumen," but also as a man of sensitivity and understanding. "He was," remarked Forest Ashbrook at his funeral service, "one of the most truly spiritual men I have had the privilege of knowing." His warmth, vision, unflappability and perspective had been valuable assets during the challenging times the Board had already faced.[218]

The second event was the retirement on 30 June 1961 of M. Forest Ashbrook as Executive Director of the MMBB. Ashbrook's service to the MMBB had extended over twenty-six years, with more than 20 of them as Executive Director. When he assumed leadership of the Board in 1940, MMBB assets totaled $23,817,141. Those assets had grown to $86,463,791 just prior his retirement in 1961. When Ashbrook assumed his responsibilities in 1940, the Retiring Pension Fund was the principal benefit offered by the MMBB, and about 38 percent of ministers who qualified belonged to the Fund. At his retirement, more than 90 percent belonged. Benefits had greatly expanded, and new benefits, non-contractual and contractual, as well as many services, had been added. As Ashbrook retired, significant changes and additions, including a shift to the variable annuity approach to pension funding, were under consideration or being implemented as a result of his leadership.

Ashbrook had been a strong and consistently demanding leader. Under his leadership, the MMBB had increased its membership, developed strong, reliable procedures, and enjoyed unparalleled stability. A somewhat shy and sometimes taciturn man who strived to listen impartially and to judge equitably, Ashbrook had become a highly regarded denominational leader. Edwin H. Tuller, ABC General Secretary, credited him and the MMBB with doing "more than anything else to hold our denomination together" during the frequently tumultuous and often threatening years of his leadership of MMBB. It was, as Mary Beth Fulton remarked in *Tomorrow*, truly a "passing of the torch."[219]

A third change was the Board's appointment of Dean R. Wright as the new Executive Director to succeed Ashbrook. On the face of it, the Board had once again carefully prepared the way for transition and succession. In the spring of 1961, Wright participated in the Advanced Management Program of the business school at Harvard University. He had previously served as the Eastern Representative, Assistant Director, and Associate Director at the MMBB, and prior to his service, he had served as a minister of the Judson Memorial Church in New York City, as a staff member of the Ohio Baptist Convention, and as a chaplain in the US Navy.[220] His credentials and experience were, therefore, broad, and his age was in harmony with the youthful spirit of the times.

Like all of his predecessors, Wright had a clear vision of the MMBB's core purpose, and he greatly valued the procedures and processes that would facilitate its fulfillment. Wright also had an instinct for the persons whose talents and experiences would assist the Board and, from an early moment, recruited unusually able men and women to serve. But Wright seemed not to be content for the MMBB simply to be a well-managed pension fund. Instead, he had a vision for the MMBB to nurture new directions and to influence desirable change. A somewhat shy and reserved man, there was nevertheless a sense about him that there was always more to come. Under his leadership, therefore, MMBB would ultimately travel in some new directions.

There were significant changes on the Board also. In 1961 Robert G. Middleton, then pastor of the First Baptist Church of Kansas City, Missouri, was elected President, replacing Leonard J. Matteson, who had served the board for thirty-eight years and had been President since 1951. Middleton's short but effective tenure on the Board had begun in 1958 and his service as Vice President since 1960 had demonstrated evidence of his potential for strong MMBB leadership. Middleton's first official act was to appoint Matteson, the outgoing President, as Chairman of the Finance Committee to fill the vacancy left by George Bovenizer's death. Matteson was later succeeded in that position by Alden C. Smith, retired partner of Price Waterhouse & Co., and long-term Board member.

The Board's business expertise was also reinforced by the election of Charles C. Tillinghast, Jr., as Vice President of the MMBB. Tillinghast had served on the Board since 1948 and had also previously served a term as the Board's Vice President. A lawyer by profession, Tillinghast had been a director and Vice President of the Bendix Corporation and, in March 1961, had been elected as Chief Executive Officer of Trans World Airlines, which, at that time, was one of the world's premier and largest airlines. During the years 1967 to 1978 Tillinghast was also Chancellor of Brown University, his alma mater.[221] He brought first-rank business experience and prestige to the MMBB Board along with a strong Baptist heritage: His father, Charles C. Tillinghast, Sr., principal of the highly regarded Horace Mann School in New York, had been a member of the Northern Baptist Board of Education for many years.

Five Board newcomers were also elected that year. Among them were three who began lengthy and especially fruitful service: Richard B. Fisher, an associate of the investment banking firm of Morgan Stanley & Co. in New York; the Rev. E. Spencer Parsons, then the minister of the Hyde Park (Union) Baptist Church in Chicago and soon to become the Dean of Rockefeller Chapel at the University of Chicago; and the Rev. Howard R. Moody, minister of the Judson Memorial Church in Greenwich Village in New York. The addition of William T. McKee, as Field Counselor, with Special Responsibility, brought the first African-American professional staff member to the MMBB's service. McKee had previously served in ministry among students in several positions in New Orleans, Rochester, New York, and New York City.[222]

As the decade matured, several African-American pastors brought leadership to the MMBB Board. Among them was James R. Holloway, pastor of the Zion Baptist Church of Minneapolis, Minnesota, who was appointed as the representative of the General Council of the ABC in 1966. Elected to the Board were Samuel D. Proctor, then a Dean of Special Projects at the University of Wisconsin (Madison) and later pastor of the Abyssinian Baptist Church in New York City, who joined the Board in 1968, and Gardner C. Taylor, pastor of the Concord Baptist Church in Brooklyn, New York, and former President of the Progressive National Baptist Convention, was elected in 1970. Because of their lengthy and broad national service, Taylor and Proctor, especially, brought unique perspectives to the MMBB, especially in providing service to African-American Baptist ministers and in expanding MMBB services to new constituencies.[223]

There were organizational changes, too. After more than forty years, the annual grant to the Massachusetts Baptist Charitable Society was discontinued, and the MMBB gained full use of the Communion Fellowship Offering received in that state, phased in over a four-year period. After more than fifty years, organizational changes affecting the relationship between the MMBB and the American Baptist Convention experienced a change also. As a result of denominational reorganization in 1961, several bylaw changes affecting leadership were required by the Board. One change reflected Convention concerns to retain control of the MMBB: The Board member elected by the denomination's General Council became a voting member of the MMBB, and the MMBB Executive Director became an Associate General Secretary of the

American Baptist Convention. The result was that future MMBB Executive Directors could only be employed after consultation with the denomination's General Council and nomination by the General Secretary of the American Baptist Convention.[224]

Early Decade Expansion of Benefits and Services

During the 1960s, the MMBB benefits developed at an unprecedented pace, and services multiplied in many new directions. It included an expansion of death and disability protection, a new and modified health care plan, and a plan for seniors that, after 1965, coordinated with the new Medicare provisions. At mid-decade, the MMBB introduced an entirely new pension program designed to reflect economic growth. This program was inspired by several concerns, two of which had been increasingly evident—a robust return on MMBB investments during recent years in contrast to the lack of an easy or obviously equitable means of adjusting for cost-of-living changes. The new retirement program promised to address both issues and, over time, promised as well to enable ministers' pensions to benefit from the nation's economic growth.

Even before the new program was introduced, however, benefits were consistently expanded. Early in the decade some benefits were adjusted based on the precedents of programs in place. For example, The Gift program, the cost-of-living supplement first granted in 1959, was continued through 1964 at increasing percentage rates based on ministers' lengths of service.[225] It was modified for 1965 when it was closed to new members in light of the new pension program. Likewise, educational grants were increased to $900 per year in 1961. Grants were also increased for minor children of the Retiring Pension Fund annuitants to $420 per year.[226]

Effective for 1963, the retirement program's death benefit for active members was placed on a benefit scale that was dependent upon age and compensation. As examples, death occurring before age 61 resulted in a payment of 150 percent of salary, and declined annually in increments, so that at age 65 or thereafter it was 75 percent of salary. Child allowances for deceased members were increased to $500 per year with a maximum of $3,000.[227] Death benefits were either paid to the survivors as a lump sum, or, if the amount was over $5,000, the widow or widower could elect installments or as a pension annuity. Later, in 1970, the Death

142

Benefit Plan was separated from the Retirement Plan and shifted to be part of a group term life insurance program to enable it to be tax-free to beneficiaries.

In 1963, after a period of investigation and a subsequent recommendation by the Finance Committee, the Board approved the Variable Annuity Supplement (VAS) as an elective addition to the Retiring Pension Fund. In developing this program, the MMBB had monitored the success of TIAA-CREF and a number of private corporations that offered such plans for employee retirement. VAS was, in essence, a means by which members of the Retiring Pension Fund could opt to contribute amounts in addition to the basic dues of the Retiring Pension Fund and thereby increase retirement resources. Premiums contributed to the VAS program were either contributed by the employer or deducted from the minister's salary and paid by his employer into the Fund on his behalf. The new option contained both tax advantages and additional pension coverage. VAS Funds were pooled and invested with other like funds for investment and invested in debt obligations and equities in the hope of long-term investment growth.[228]

Church leaders and ministers had varying degrees of experience or understanding regarding financial programs. Therefore, the MMBB was fine-tuning its expertise in presenting clear explanations regarding both noncontractual and contractual benefits and becoming increasingly effective in using its communications resources in doing so. In the case of VAS, it was important to stress that Social Security, the Retiring Pension Fund, and perhaps other insurance should be the first claims on a minister's available salary. VAS was not a replacement for the pension program nor was it insurance. It was, however, a powerful supplement in building long-term resources.[229] Several articles in *Tomorrow* communicated its importance to all members.

The Board also expanded for inclusion in the Retiring Pension Fund some ministry professionals who were not directly employed by American Baptist churches or institutions. Two examples included self-employed evangelists who could pay on annual income of not less than $6,000 if married, of $3,000 if single. Ministers endorsed by the American Baptist Committee on Chaplains who were employed full-time at governmental or private institutions were also eligible to participate in the Retiring Pension Fund at a salary of not less than $3,000 per year.[230]

In 1965 the minimum salary figure for pension contribution was raised to $3,600 per year in all categories.

Unemployed ordained ministers and commissioned missionaries were granted the right to continue in the restructured Retirement Plan for up to a year.[231] Later, in 1969, ordained American Baptist ministers serving as full-time faculty teaching religion at a public or private college or university were made eligible to participate in the Retirement Plan.[232] The Vietnam War and the draft reached deep into American lives. Thus, in the same year, premium-paying lay Retirement Plan members with at least three years of ABC-connected service who left employment because of the Selective Service Act were permitted to continue in the Plan based on their last-recorded compensation, or $3,600, whichever was smaller. In these ways, the Plan adjusted to continuing changes during turbulent years.[233]

Support of the Ministry and Ministers

In 1961, on the occasion of MMBB's fiftieth anniversary, a symposium titled "The State of the Ministry in the '60s" was printed in *Tomorrow*.[234] Symposium participants included seven leading pastors, scholars, and lay leaders within the ABC and the MMBB: Robert T. Handy, historian; C. Adrian Heaton; Lynn Leavenworth; Robert G. Middleton; MMBB President, E. Spencer Parsons; Robert G. Torbet, historian and expert on Baptist procedures and practices; and Anna Canada Swain, a former American Baptist Convention President. The symposium's insights clearly introduced several themes that soon defined much of the MMBB's expanding programs of support of the ministry. Among them, the effects of the emerging trends of urbanization, secularization, political polarization and turbulence, the erosion of tradition, and growing diversity of religious experience and the multiple, and frequently changing, congregational expectations of ministers all pointed to the need for new kinds of support for ministers.

Therefore, beyond the contractual provisions of pensions and related concerns for health, death, and disability insurance, the 1960s were characterized by a broader view of "the better maintenance of the ministry." MMBB traditional support of the personal and professional ministry continued and received new emphasis in the early '60s especially. For one, the MMBB's long-standing advocacy of higher salaries was again evident in frequent articles or emphases in

Tomorrow.[235] In the late '50s and early '60s, the MMBB's active leadership in developing the minimum salary plan and other programs in churches had affirmed its efforts in raising ministerial compensation, having positively raised average ministerial compensation. In 1968 a pilot Salary Support Program in the northeastern region demonstrated significantly increased minimum salary standards.[236] As a result, at the end of 1969 the program was being prepared for introduction on the national level in 1970–71. It was assumed to be the "most expensive program ever" for the MMBB, and was to be funded from the 1 percent portions of the Retirement Plan premiums, plus reserves amounting to over $2.1 million developed in prior years.[237]

Tomorrow articles by MMBB staff, ABC leaders and executives, and others persistently and vigorously continued. However, over its long experience in advocating for increased compensation for ministers, the MMBB had learned that churches were often slow to significantly increase cash salaries. In many regions, pastoral salaries were below national averages. During the 1960s, therefore, the MMBB also continued to strongly advocate for churches to establish the practice of reimbursing or paying directly for certain ministerial expenses. "Those Professional Expenses Add Up!" a *Tomorrow* article had proclaimed in January 1958, and into the 1960s continuing articles advocated establishing budget amounts to reimburse automobile expenses, expenses for attendance at denominational meetings, training or continuing education expenses, hospitality expenses at the church or the minister's home, office supplies, and memberships in community organizations in which the minister represented the church. Many churches had not routinely provided for these expenses, and when they included them, many ministers experienced real salary savings.[238]

In addition, the long-term financial problem and retirement challenge resulting from ministers not owning their own homes had increased. In fact, several small state or regional organizations dedicated to helping to provide housing for retired ministers had been merged into the MMBB early in its formation. However, it was becoming an increasingly acute challenge for ministers to face the difficult prospect of securing a home for retirement. Housing costs had been rising since the mid-1940s. Now, a reconsideration of the traditional role of church-owned housing—the traditional parsonages or "manses"—became an especially frequent focus.

The housing impact on ministers was complex. From one perspective, church-owned and supported housing expanded the real value of many ministers' compensation. And ministers benefited not only by having housing provided, but also by not having responsibility for maintenance, repairs and, in many cases, the cost of heating and lighting the homes that were provided. On the other hand, the value of a church-provided home was frequently overstated to the church's advantage in considering a salary's value. One result was that cash salaries remained artificially low. As one consequence, churches were the only beneficiaries of rising property values while ministers at retirement faced ever-escalating costs. At the same time, the value of provided housing that was included in determining the dues for the Retiring Pension Fund and later the Retirement Plan was most often heavily discounted in order to reduce premium costs. Ministers were, thus, negatively impacted on both counts.

The MMBB sought to open more focused consideration on ministers' housing from both a career and a retirement perspective. Two successive articles addressed the housing problem in *Tomorrow*: "Should We Get Rid of the Parsonage?" by L. Doward McBain, and "Let's Do Something about That Parsonage" by Jerome J. Hevey, in 1960 and 1961. Each effectively introduced the subject of individual home ownership for ministers.[239] The result of these articles and other, similar communications initiated a dialogue that resulted in many churches opting to enable ministers to own their own homes by providing housing allowances.[240]

The Board's long-standing support of ministerial preparation and qualifications also continued, most frequently in *Tomorrow* articles focused on pastoral reading habits, study disciplines, ethics, and increasingly, continuing education. "How Shall a Young Man Plan His Way?" asked a *Tomorrow* article by J. Martin England.[241] Charles Lyons Seasholes, a recognized master at training and mentor of recent seminary graduates, contributed "What to Do about Ministerial Assistants."[242] The preparation and nurture of ministers in a changing time was clearly a priority.

The MMBB continued to support uniform minimum qualification requirements for ministers. However, it also continued its original approach of asserting that, for purposes of pensions, there was no direct relationship between educational standards and eligibility for membership in the Retiring Pension Fund.[243] Administratively, MMBB's support of the Ministers' Council continued, as well as its sponsorship of the Pastoral Information Bureaus. During this time, the office of the Boston Pastoral Information Bureau was moved to Valley Forge when the American Baptist headquarters building was completed, and the office previously opened in Omaha, Nebraska, was relocated to Elmhurst, Illinois.[244] The MMBB's western bureau remained in Berkeley, California. In 1963 a Southern Regional Office was established in Greenville, South Carolina.[245]

In short, the profession of ministry had developed rapidly and had multiplied in its forms of expression over the previous two decades especially. That development exposed several needs. One was to discover a way of creating a more efficient and more equitable placement procedure. To that end, the Board considered a proposed Ministerial Placement Project in 1962 and later an additional study presented in 1966.[246] But much more broadly, cultural, social, institutional, and professional trends all indicated that the ministry itself was in crisis: the "dropout" rate was growing higher, seminary enrollments were declining, and crises in churches involving pastoral leadership were increasing. To help understand the dynamics of the crisis, and to focus means to conserve and advance the ministry, Oren H. Baker, a professor at Colgate-Rochester Divinity School and a Board member, was appointed to head a program called "The Conservation of the Ministry."[247] Part of his work resulted in a "Profile of the American Baptist Pastor" completed in 1962. The implications of that work's conclusions guided much of the MMBB's focus for noncontractual benefits and advocacy for ministers in the years to come.

Conservation of the Ministry

Oren Baker's study sought to construct a profile of American Baptist ministers, their contexts, and their circumstances with a methodology based on descriptions of a number of churches of different sizes, contexts, and cultures, in varying locations, and on interviews with more than two hundred ministers. The purpose was to develop a better understanding of ways that "the age of change and tension in which we live is making unprecedented demands upon the time and resources of our pastors."[248] Churches were described in categories such as Inner City, Urban, Suburban, and Town & Country. A powerful image of the diversity of church contexts resulted, and even more, the dynamics of communities undergoing change in America.

Interviews with ministers engaged them in reflection on categories of motivation, concepts of the church and the pastoral office, attitudes of congregations toward ministers, and ministers' outlook on the future. The non-professional lives of pastors were probed, as well as their professional concerns. Pastoral education (or lack of it), the ability to access resources, and their understanding of their particular church's dynamics were all assessed as variables. In addition, comparisons of the effect of pastors' particular seminary or other educational backgrounds, and the demands of particular challenges such as those of bilingual pastors or other unique situations were evaluated. Career changes were also considered, including the increasing phenomenon of those who had changed denominations or who had left the ministry. A particularly revealing component explored relationships between pastors and denominational executives and the pressures of fulfilling denominational expectations.

The result was a massive study. It provided the raw materials that prophesied the changes in ministry to come for a generation and more. At best, a summary could be provided to the MMBB for consideration. Emerging from all categories of consideration was an expressed sense of isolation and, sometimes, feelings of despair with "no one to turn to." The study identified issues of basic education, continuing education, the need for effective mentoring for new or young pastors, and the need for personal counseling for pastors facing sometimes overwhelming and complex roles as counselors, administrators, preachers, and leaders. Many of its conclusions guided MMBB policies and program development.

The Baker report affirmed the importance of ministerial assessment and support, both of which the MMBB had long advocated. Thus, as one result, in 1967, the Center for the Ministry, a project of the Commission on the Ministry, was opened in Wellesley Hills, Massachusetts, with MMBB financial support. The center's purpose and resources included personal assessment, career and continuing education counseling, and counseling for placement and salary support as well.[249] Like its intentional support of ministers facing the stresses of civil rights activity in the South and its support in the following year of the Interpreter's House in Lake Junaluska, North Carolina, the MMBB's support of the

Wellesley Center represented a broader view and more expansive interpretation of the "better maintenance of the ministry."

Field Staff Development

For the MMBB, considering its mandate and its resources, one striking, specific conclusion of the Baker study was its identification of pastoral isolation and professional loneliness. Providing spiritual and emotional support to ministers serving in various locations became a high priority. Therefore, to respond to that need, and to others accompanying it, the MMBB now focused on a stronger and more varied development of its own field staff resources.

Early field staff members had been primarily engaged to develop effective MMBB relationships with ministers and churches. The earliest example was George White, who, in 1926, had been engaged to raise funds and to promote membership in the retirement plan at first specifically in the West. Likewise, in 1934 the Board had determined to encourage better understanding of their work. One result was the appointment of Mary Beth Fulton, appointed in 1935 as a Special Representative. Her work was particularly focused through contact with women's groups and ministers' wives, both to encourage understanding of the MMBB, and also to encourage the women and to report to the Board their perspectives and concerns.

From time to time, the MMBB had also appointed field service personnel to expand contact with ministers. For example, in the 1940s William Shanks had served as western representative and Herbert Hinton the Midwest representative. And, on several occasions and for temporary periods, retired ministers were appointed to help accomplish particular goals such as the expansion of membership in the retirement program in the mid-1940s, and the program to enroll ministers in Social Security in the '50s, as two examples. The new Executive Director, Dean Wright, had originally been employed as the Eastern Representative at the time of the Social Security enrollment effort. The MMBB's experience with fieldwork had, therefore, been highly productive both in expanding its work and developing its supportive relationships. In the early '60s, new circumstances warranted an expanded vision of this resource.

Under Wright's early leadership, the field services staff was enlarged. One compelling need was the general ministerial isolation that sometimes led to discouragement and failure. The Baker study had specifically surfaced the recognition that many ministers were uncomfortable or even mistrustful of sharing personal concerns or professional challenges with staff members of state or city associations out of concern for professional consequences. Sometimes, it appeared, personal and professional isolation led to professional or personal desperation.

Another contributing need was an urgency resulting from the stresses experienced by civil rights activity. In the South, especially, both black and white ministers were under duress and sometimes under physical threat. Under direction of the Board in 1962, J. Martin England opened the Southern Regional Office in Greenville, South Carolina, in 1963.[250] All field representatives helped to interpret and explain the Retirement Fund to churches and members, and assisted in enlisting new members. But the Southern office, especially, was created to reach out to African-American churches and pastors experiencing stress and violence during this period, and to white pastors whose positions were displaced or threatened because of their leadership in or sympathy with the civil rights movement. Wherever possible, field representatives sought to provide personal support and encouragement, and, when appropriate, emergency assistance for ministers. Their presence of sympathy and support was also critical for demoralized or traumatized churches.

Due in part to MMBB outreach to African-American churches and pastors, African-American membership in the MMBB was growing. To provide support and to serve their needs, the field staff was increased and included several African-American representatives. Representatives were also appointed to work with churches in urban areas, and additional representatives were appointed for the South, West, Midwest, and New England regions. In 1967, the field program was expanded to more adequately cover all the geographic areas represented in the American Baptist Convention, with a total of ten field representatives.[251]

In addition, the MMBB's core concern for ministers' preparation for retirement, both financially and as a new stage of life, resulted in a new aspect of service, provided in part by field representatives. In 1965 Miriam R. Corbett was engaged as a Special Representative with a focus on retirement counseling and services to pensioners. Soon after her appointment, the MMBB developed a plan of visitation for all retirees. Later, under her leadership, the MMBB also developed a series of pre-retirement luncheons and seminars to facilitate the personal and professional preparations of those soon to retire. In 1970, Corbett became Director of Retirement Services.[252]

MMBB Luncheon Speakers Provide Inspiration and Preparation

The annual MMBB Luncheon, first established in the late 1950s, continued to be provided without cost to MMBB members by invitation, and was invariably scheduled on the day the Convention opened. Therefore, its speakers often set a tone for the Convention gathering. During the 1960s, those speeches tracked social, theological, ecclesiastical, and political events with remarkable clarity and enabled those who heard them, or later read them, to benefit from their insights.

Samuel H. Miller, an American Baptist Minister then serving as Dean of the Harvard Divinity School, inaugurated the decade with a look both backward and forward at the role of ministry in a talk titled "An Honest Man of God." In 1962, Culbert G. Rutenber addressed what was surely becoming the decade's most familiar faith theme, "Prayer and Politics." Colin Williams, from the National Council of Churches, brought distant biblical narrative and burning contemporary issues into one place with "Pentecost and Race" in 1964. And, in 1965, Harvey Cox addressed what was becoming a daunting challenge: "Mission in a World of Cities." Subsequently, the Old Testament scholar James A. Sanders (1968) rooted some of the developing themes of the decade in biblical precedents in "The New History: Joseph, Our Brother," and B. David Napier (1969) wrestled with the obvious changes affecting the nation in his "The New Land." These and others frequently enlarged ministers' understanding and perspectives, and frequently provided thoughtful inspiration for the work of ministry and that of the Convention.[253]

MMBB and Civil Rights

The 1960s exposed the deep roots of racial and cultural separation in America. In particular, white oppression of African Americans, rooted in slavery, was still robust in the '60s, especially in parts of the South where Jim Crow laws often sanctioned such behavior. But the South was not alone. In most of the nation, cultural and social racial separation was still the norm, nowhere more so than in churches. The traditional 11 A.M. Sunday worship hour was famously described as "the most segregated hour in the week." In the early 1960s, it was rigidly the case and, in some circumstances, legally the case as well.

Consequently, the demand of African Americans to be treated with dignity and equality was a deeply disturbing experience for many Americans, including many church people. It was a divisive time, creating friction not only between races but within communities as well—even racially homogeneous communities. African-American churches were bombed and burned; demonstrators and activists were jailed, abused, and in a few cases, killed. Many individuals, including both black and white pastors, were personally challenged and professionally damaged. During that period, the MMBB provided unique leadership through its service.

The MMBB's reactions to the aspirations of the civil rights movement were rooted in the spirit and ministry of its founder, Henry L. Morehouse. Through his exposure to the varieties of human need through the American Baptist Home Mission Society, Morehouse had been especially sensitive to racial inequality. His commitment to higher education for Baptists was influenced, at least in part, by his understanding of the educational needs of the poorest and neediest of Baptists, with black Baptists being chief among them. As early as 1864 he had advocated a program of higher education for freed slaves in every state of the Reconstructed South. His legacy in education ultimately included Shaw University, Morehouse College, Spelman College, and the predecessor institution that later became Virginia Union University, to mention a few of more than thirty institutions.[254] His connections with John D. Rockefeller later assisted the establishment of the University of Chicago as a world-class school, but his sensitivities had first been formed around the need for education for African-American people— many who had recently been slaves. In the 1960s, the MMBB built on that legacy.

The June 1963 MMBB Board meeting, particularly, reflected on recent civil rights developments, and especially on events of the ABC Convention. During its sessions, one chapel speaker, from Atlanta, Georgia, had been questioned because his church had refused to seat Negroes.[255] The same meeting also reflected on the heavy number of inquiries from Southern Baptist pastors looking for placement in the North—a need that likely could not be met. The home of Martin Luther King, Jr., had been bombed, and an offering of $4,000 was raised to help rebuild it. African-American pastors were also inquiring about help, placement, and support.[256]

At its September meeting, the Board expressed deep concern for American Baptist pastors, and a letter of support was shaped and sent to them. The letter shared the Board's concern for civil rights and for the challenges they would likely face in trying to implement recent American Baptist resolutions on civil rights. The Board also determined that MMBB Representative William (Bill) McKee might serve as a resource to work with the state and city secretaries to assist pastors in trouble as a result of their efforts.[257] Therefore, at the national denominational level, and particularly in the Southern region, the MMBB sought to provide service and support amidst the very public and personal crises of the time.

As tensions in the South increased, MMBB's new regional office in Greenville, South Carolina, under the leadership of J. Martin England, provided a new focus for service. England was originally a Southern Baptist, but while at Southern Baptist Theological Seminary in Louisville, Kentucky, he extended his network of contacts to include American Baptists. As a student, he aspired to serve as a foreign missionary, and sought connection with the American Baptist Foreign Mission Society. As one result, he finished his education at Crozer Theological Seminary in Philadelphia and then taught at Mars Hill College in North Carolina while awaiting appointment. Ultimately he was appointed as an American Baptist missionary to Burma, but his service there was interrupted by the onset of World War II. He subsequently returned to the USA. When the war ended, concerns for his wife's health prevented their return to Burma. In 1951 he was engaged as a representative by the MMBB, and after a decade of experience in that role, he was appointed to manage the Southern office of the MMBB.

There were a variety of specific reasons for the MMBB to open a Southern office. First, a number American Baptist ministers were Southern in origin, and tended to retire closer to their home communities in the South. Second, other American Baptists were finding the Southern climate hospitable for retirement. Very few American Baptist churches existed in the South, and most of them were dually aligned with the Southern Baptist Convention or the Progressive National Baptist Convention. But as civil rights activities intensified, a great many ministers beyond those affiliations also experienced stressful and threatening environments. An MMBB presence in that region, therefore, seemed to provide an opportunity to reach out to pastors with support and solidarity.

England was frequently a participant in the marches and demonstrations of the era, and often personally responded in support of pastors who had been dismissed or threatened by their congregations for being too "progressive," or had been traumatized by violence. One letter of gratitude described him as "always on the doorstep of those in trouble." Sometimes he responded to the news of a pastor's dismissal to bring support and, where possible, financial assistance. England frequently traveled to be present during demonstrations following church bombings or other acts of violence, and was often accompanied by Dean Wright and Howard Moody as well.[258]

J. Martin England's personal roots in the South enabled him to network with a great many pastors and leaders, both to support those taking difficult stands on civil rights and to convince others to exert pastoral and prophetic leadership. His personal contacts among notable Southern pulpit voices and writers such as Will Campbell, a spiritual "gadfly," author, and speaker, and Carlyle Marney, the eloquent pastor of the prestigious Myers Park Baptist Church in Charlotte, North Carolina, affirmed his credibility and access to those in need. His relationship with Marney, for example, led to MMBB support in 1968 of Interpreter's House in Lake Junaluska, North Carolina. Interpreter's House was a facility created by Marney to provide a communal context for support, reflection, and redirection for many pastors who had been personally wounded or were professionally in crisis, many as a result of the dynamics of social change.

According to MMBB records, it would be hard to overestimate England's work and its positive extension of MMBB's service. Letters of testimony and thanks came to the MMBB office and included such phrases as this from one community organizer: "About 6,000 names of Negro-white workmen come to us from his office. A dozen underground groups in Greenville, Jacksonville, Jackson, Mississippi, Birmingham, Baton Rouge, Memphis, Atlanta, [and more] look to him."[259] What many especially admired was that the "lonely Negro pastor, or buffeted white liberal isolated from support—all know [him] and turn his way." Through England's extensive connections and efforts, the MMBB was also able to be of support to the civil rights movement's symbolic and spiritual leader, Martin Luther King, Jr., and his family.

England had met King briefly on several occasions. They shared the personal bond of having both graduated from Crozer Theological Seminary in Philadelphia, although they attended a decade apart. England had become close to King's father, Martin Luther King, Sr., who was, understandably, concerned about his son's safety. England was in Birmingham in 1963 when King was arrested at a demonstration and was taken to jail. England pursued King through his booking process and was able to see him. They spoke briefly, and King was able to give him a piece of paper on which he had hastily written a statement of his vision and his position. England immediately sent the paper to Dean Wright at MMBB in New York, who, in turn, was able to have the essay published under the title "Letter from a Birmingham Jail."[260] It was only one of many times when England and the MMBB provided support for leaders of the civil rights cause.

In 1965 several MMBB board members attended a church-sponsored conference in Baton Rouge, Louisiana, on civil rights. They returned convinced that support for that cause was among the highest priorities of the time, and that the struggles it included would be difficult for educational, government, religious, and a wide variety of other leaders to encompass. Indeed, the Board was unified in its support, and therefore its outreach to ministers in need as a result of the turmoil was effective. In the same year, the Board sponsored a conference in Atlanta to acquaint denominational leaders, including the General Secretary of the American Baptist Convention and ABC agency executives, with the issues. A special focus was to expand understanding of the tensions American Baptist ministers serving churches in the South were facing.[261]

Martin Luther King, Jr., Joins the MMBB

MMBB's most symbolic point of service during the civil rights era was the result of King's decision to become a member of the MMBB. For several years England had sought to convince Martin Luther King, Jr., to join the MMBB out of concern for his safety and the financial security of his family. Martin Luther King, Sr., had strongly supported this idea and, indeed, was already an MMBB member. But the younger King always demurred, citing the reality that the Ebenezer Baptist Church in Atlanta where he was the associate minister with his father could not afford the premium. He repeatedly assured England that he knew the risks he was taking. Still England persisted and he always reminded King that the MMBB would pay the premium for as long as was needed.

One of the most tragic acts of the era was the 1963 bombing and fire at the Sixteenth Street Baptist Church in Birmingham, Alabama—an African-American church—that resulted in the deaths of three young girls. England immediately went to Birmingham in his usual attempt to provide support as he could. While surveying the rubble near the church, he encountered a man who he decided was deranged, and who threatened King's life. King was expected to arrive shortly to lead a protest march. England was deeply concerned and spoke to members of the FBI regarding his apprehensions. Then, upon King's arrival, England sought him out and, once again, pleaded with him to sign an MMBB application. On that occasion, Ralph Abernathy, King's associate in the Southern Christian Leadership Conference, and later his successor as Chairman, was present. King sought Abernathy's advice. "If Ralph says sign, I'll sign," declared King, and Abernathy, who was already an MMBB member, said in his deep voice, "Sign."[262] According to England's recollection, Abernathy then turned his broad shoulder to give King a surface to write on. Later, in April 1968, following King's assassination, the provisions of the MMBB death policy helped to support King's family.

One enduring result of the MMBB's persistent presence in the South was that it encouraged a number of African-American pastors to lead their churches to dually align with the American Baptist churches, partly in order to become members of the MMBB. Similarly, a few predominantly white Southern Baptist churches also dually aligned with the American Baptists. The work of the MMBB, combined with the presence of J.C. Herrin, also at work in the South on behalf of the Home Mission Society, resulted in a critical mass of churches that enabled the expansion of fellowship and ABC membership in the South. It also led directly to the eventual decision of several of the national African-American Baptist denominations to contract with the MMBB to manage their pension and other benefit programs.

American Baptist Black Churchmen Present Demands

The struggle for civil rights was a social, political, and moral revolution, and was accomplished by multiple means. Personal support, demonstrations, church networks, and many other strategies were successful instruments used to advance its purpose. The moral dimension at times focused on reparations, and the confrontational spirit of the era was present in churches: In 1967 a group of black American Baptist churchmen presented demands for "economic reparations" to the American Baptists meeting in convention in Boston. Among them was a demand that "no monies, including deposits and investments in financial institutions by the ABC or any of its affiliated agencies, be used to further any racial cause or perpetuate racial discrimination in any form."[263]

In response, the ABC urged all of its agencies to review their investment policies. The MMBB had been specifically criticized because of its investments and banking relationships with the Chase Manhattan Bank and the First National City Bank, both of which extended credit to or were invested in South African concerns. In response, the Board sought a careful review of the banks and legal counsel regarding the Board's authority and responsibility. At that time David Rockefeller, President of Chase Manhattan Bank shared with the Board his personal assessment of the bank's activities in South Africa and his opinion regarding the dilemma. Ultimately, the Board's Denominational Relations Committee concluded that the two banks had a negligible amount of business in South Africa. It additionally concluded that to urge the banks to withdraw would, in fact, further isolate South Africa from social pressure, and would cause financial damage to those most in need of support. And, as a practical reality, it further realized that to move its primary funds and investments to smaller, less experienced institutions might jeopardize the MMBB's core purpose because similar critical services were not available in alternative banking institutions. Therefore, it reaffirmed its relationship with the banks.[264]

However, another of the demands related to the investment or use of funds possessed by the convention or its agencies. In that case, choosing to respond not in the spirit of demands, but to the "justness of the cause," the MMBB was able to invest in the process of racial advancement and justice that the nation and many churches needed. Upon recommendation by the Finance Committee, the Board deposited $300,000 in twenty financial institutions in several areas of the country, chosen in consultation with black pastors and others who lived in the communities.[265] It was the intention of the Board that the funds invested might increase the amount available to loan to persons in the communities who had limited access to financial service institutions. It was both a symbolic and, over time, practical means of support.

In addition, and as an attempt to better meet the needs of black pastors and churches, three new field staff members were added to the expanding field representative program. They included black churchmen Joe Dancy in the southern region, J. Alfred Smith in the western region, and Ed Whitaker in the eastern region. All were distinguished pastors or denominational leaders.[266]

Primary Pension Benefit Shift to Variable Annuity

Despite these external activities, the MMBB retained its focus on its primary function: providing pensions for older ministers. The Retiring Pension Fund had been a remarkable success over the nearly forty-five years of its operation. It had maintained its purpose and its promise: it had provided secure and guaranteed pensions to its members. It had done so at times against great challenges, including the Great Depression and World War II. One of the chief virtues of the Fund was its guarantee of a pension calculated on a percentage of salary times the number of years served. In that way, it originally served the great variety and conditions of ministers. But the Fund's own success had pointed to a new dilemma—post–World War II economic expansion and market performance had driven up the Retiring Pension Fund's value faster than pension claims required. At the same time, inflation had eroded the value of the pensions it paid out. In addition, ministers' careers were longer, while greater length of service produced a declining, minimal additional benefit from their pension amounts.

To adjust for the joint phenomena of pension erosion caused by inflation and the Fund's increasing surplus, the Board had, in recent years, distributed The Gift, which often provided a significant percentage of the pension received. In that manner, annuitant's pensions were at least partially restored in purchasing power. But it was a makeshift procedure, and developing the formulas and equations that allowed for equitable and just distributions of the surplus was awkward and time-consuming. What was needed was a plan that allowed members' accumulated dues to benefit from market growth. TIAA had introduced such a plan some years earlier in the CREF portion of their program. Their experience had been positive. Indeed, the TIAA-CREF approach had been cited as a precedent in establishing the VAS program the previous year. VAS itself had inspired ongoing discussion at the MMBB regarding a possible new type of pension plan.

In June 1964 the Board passed a resolution recognizing, in principle, the need for a new plan and approved the idea as a possibility. The resolution recognized several key issues, the most important of which was that new memberships in the Retiring Pension Fund were increasingly career memberships and the RPF was not as favorable to career members as an accumulation plan might be. Therefore, it recommended a plan that would include investment in both fixed income producing securities and common stocks. It also reviewed a plan developed by the MMBB staff in consultation with the actuary and sought legal counsel regarding the Board's authority to make such changes. The plan was temporarily named the "Retirement Plan for the American Baptist Convention."[267]

At the November 1964 meeting the plan was approved, subject to the minor changes and modifications that might result from legal and actuarial consultation. The same resolution closed the Retiring Pension Fund to new members after 31 May 1965, and the new Retirement Plan became operative on 1 June 1965. On that date, $26,567,670 in assets from the Retiring Pension Fund was transferred to the new Retirement Plan. The same resolution provided direction on the actuarial formulas for converting the Retiring Pension Fund membership into the new Retirement Plan, and directed that realized gains in the Retiring Pension Fund be transferred to the new Retirement Plan.[268] The Retirement Plan was soon thereafter opened to lay employees who worked twenty or more hours per week. At its inauguration, the Retirement Plan was built on the assumption of a 13 percent of salary (including housing) contribution and was to be allocated as follows:

—Ten percent to an annuity accumulation plan invested by the Board in market instruments

—Two percent to provide death and disability benefits (both expanded from previous plan)

—One percent for a "Shared Protection" program to provide benefits to low-salaried ministers[269]

In subsequent Board meetings, a number of embellishments, definitions, and inclusions made the Retirement Plan more effective and positioned it for future expansions. In 1965 the Board established that membership in the new program required paying premiums on a minimum compensation of $3,600, a figure that also applied to institutional and governmental chaplains. This action tended to support a minimum level of compensation. It also was one strategy to prevent or correct a trend for some churches or denominationally affiliated organizations to report a lower salary for employees than was actually being paid in order to reduce pension dues.[270] Then, in order to establish a firm guideline for the value of annuity units upon retirement, in 1966 the value of annuity units achieved in the twelve months prior to September 30 each year was established as the basis for the subsequent year's payments.

Despite the increased cost of participation, the new M&M Retirement Plan was well received. In order to facilitate the new plan's interpretation and its acceptance, the MMBB drew upon previous precedent and engaged twenty-eight retired ministers to interpret and promote the new program. To reduce apprehensions, members of the Retiring Pension Fund were guaranteed that their annuities would not be less than those they would have received under the previous Fund.[271] By the end of 1965 about 95 percent of the Retiring Pension Fund members had converted to the new program. So confident was the Board in the ability of the new fund to adjust to changing economic patterns that The Gift program was closed to all new retirees.

The M&M Medical Plan

Experience in providing health insurance had led the Board to believe that health protection and retirement protection should be provided together as a comprehensive approach to supporting the ministry. During the June through November 1964 meetings in which the new Retirement Plan was approved, a new medical plan was also under consideration. The nearly ten-year-old M&M Family Health Plan, underwritten by the Ministers Life and Casualty Union, had increased in cost each year and was also perceived as not meeting the expanding needs. Medical costs had generally risen, but none were rising as fast as hospitalization for major surgery and long-term illness. The MMBB Pensions and Health Plans and Denominational Relations Committees had coordinated research and, through polling, discovered that a "major medical" style of insurance was what was urgently desired.

In 1963 two state conventions had proposed the establishment of a major medical plan that could be superimposed on the present health plan. However, this proved to be an unacceptable solution, and the MMBB thus authorized forward progress on the development of a new medical program offered by the MMBB, to be fully in accordance with MMBB specifications. Ultimately the Travelers Insurance Company was selected to administer a plan that the MMBB financed itself.[272] The Board communicated its gratitude to the Ministers Life and Casualty Union for its past assistance and partnership and terminated their relationship.

As a consequence of the MMBB's conclusion that health protection should be linked to pension protection, they decided that the dues for the Retirement Plan should provide for what they described as "Shared Protection." Their proposal was that part of the 1 percent of salary designated for "shared benefits" from the Retirement Plan dues be made available to help provide the new health plan to clergy in lower-paid positions. Initially, approximately $700,000 was budgeted to assist churches in providing both the new pension program and the new health plan for their ministers. The $700,000 was provided to churches as an offset for the increase in cost that the new plan required. It was distributed in amounts proportional to the increases over previous budgeted expenditures that the new plan represented for the churches. Soon the health plan was also offered to lay employees of churches and American Baptist institutions. By the end of 1969, acceptance of both the health and pension programs enabled the Board to terminate the Shared Protection program, and the MMBB thereafter provided supplemental financial assistance on an individual basis.[273]

The new M&M Medical Plan and its companion, the M&M Annuitant Medical Plan for retired, disabled, and widowed members, became effective on 1 January 1965.[274] The Board assumed the cost of $34 per quarter to widows and disabled members. The Medical Plan was also made available to lay employees. To assist in promoting the plan, the same retired ministers who were engaged to interpret the new pension plan, along with field staff, were also trained to represent the medical plan's features and advantages. In 1968 the Board determined that grantee widows younger than 65 who had not remarried, their minor children, and children in college, as well as wives under 65 of living grantee ministers over 65 would be eligible for coverage in the Medical Plan at no cost.[275]

Denominational Relationships

In its fifty years of experience, the MMBB had charted a course striving to provide maximum support for the "better maintenance of the ministry" for Northern Baptist and, later, the renamed American Baptist churches and ministers, while at the same time retaining a useful degree of independence for broader service. It had subsumed some regional or individual organizations for support of retired ministers into its own work, and had negotiated mutually supportive relationships with others. At the national level, by the 1960s the MMBB was clearly defined as an affiliated organization integrally related to the American Baptist Convention for a highly specific purpose. At the same time, events and opportunities were positioning it to serve a broader population.

For example, at the regional level, when the Communion Fellowship Offering had been initiated in the 1930s, Massachusetts had raised concerns because it administered an already existing state Baptist pension. As a result, the MMBB had negotiated a shared use of offering receipts in that state, to ensure that Massachusetts ministers would benefit. That arrangement had been modified in subsequent years. In 1966, however, the Board voted to terminate the shared arrangement, thus claiming full use of that state's Communion Fellowship Offering.[276] On the national level, however, the MMBB agreed that the Communion Fellowship Offering would become part of the Convention's Unified Budget, and in 1966 the ABC Division of World Mission Support assumed responsibility for promoting that offering.[277]

Recognizing that barriers and boundaries of many kinds were falling, in 1966 ABC President Carl Tiller proposed that ministers who left the American Baptist Convention to become ministers in other denominations might continue their membership in the Retirement Plan.[278] Therefore, in 1967, the Board voted that any member of the Retiring Pension Fund, the Retirement Plan or the Lay Workers Plan who had paid premiums for twenty or more years and who went to another denomination for ministry could continue membership in their MMBB plan. This represented a clear reversal of the policy and philosophy earlier established in the late 1940s and one that ultimately enabled MMBB to develop broader service to those who had dedicated significant years of service to the ABC.

Among other aspects of its denominational relationship, the MMBB had directly and indirectly provided financial resources for the new American Baptist headquarters in Valley Forge, Pennsylvania. In addition, the MMBB had assumed denominational responsibility for the Ministerial Information Bureaus, was engaged in exploring more adequate ministerial placement, and, in cooperation with the Commission on the Ministry, had enabled the establishment of the Center for the Ministry, first in Wellesley, Massachusetts, and later in other locations. It had also provided leadership and administrative support for the Ministers' Council.

By 1967 the American Baptist Convention was considering the possibility of a plan for a broad reorganization of the Convention. The primary motive was to more effectively centralize its operations and to function more efficiently and effectively. In an announcement that implied more change to come, Executive Director Dean Wright reported that the executives of the boards and agencies of the denomination were being asked to prepare statements of the purposes and functions of the respective agencies.

In 1969 the Board affirmed that the Retirement Plan would include a guarantee of 120 payments (ten years) to annuitants' beneficiaries—an addition that advanced the program into the realm of financial planning, as well as old-age security. In addition, Miriam Corbett was leading the Board to perceive retirement as a new stage of life rather than as merely a time of inactivity, and was developing programs to enhance that perspective and opportunity. The "old soldiers of the cross" that Morehouse and Tomlinson had imaged were increasingly perceived as among the new "senior citizens" of a rapidly changing new society in which they had a stronger and more powerful role. The MMBB was now instrumental in providing the security for the development of their participation in a new age. However, the specter of an ever-rising spiral of inflation was casting doubt on economic security in general.

In 1968 former Executive Director M. Forest Ashbrook died. His passing represented a symbolic breaking of the chain that had connected the challenging '30s and '40s to the relatively placid and profitable '50s into the turbulence of the '60s. In the time since Ashbrook's retirement, the MMBB had enlarged and changed significantly, especially in expanding beyond its mandate to provide pension support for older ministers and in its fulfillment of the "better maintenance of the ministry." Its financial house was in order, its programs were strong, its advocacy for ministers was successful, and its outreach had often been prophetic as well as consistent with its purpose. But a challenging decade lay ahead. In summarizing his Annual Report for 1969, Dean Wright recalled Ashbrook and quoted from his summary at the end of the 1950s. Then he offered his own assessment of the 1960s:

> The tensions, the uncertainties, the difficulties, which were a part of the '60s for all of us, will not vanish in the '70s. We have heard voices of the young, the black, the poor, that were not heard before. We did not hear them because we wanted to, but because they could not be ignored. We look to the '70s and beyond with hope that priorities will be reordered, a new life style will be found, and man may come of age. The Board looks to the future with confidence and is proud that in a time such as this it can have a part in serving those who serve others.[279]

Wright's summary was correct. The voices had not yet finished speaking, old priorities lingered despite attempts to reorder them, and the unexpected financial and political challenges of the '70s would prove to delay some hopes.

8

A GENERATION OF TRANSFORMATION—
PART TWO

A Sense of the Times

The 1960s had established new directions and new visions. The 1970s, in contrast, seemed destined to continue the '60s with more of the same, yet somehow with much less. The Civil Rights Act of 1964 and the Voting Rights Act of 1965 had defined the constitutional and legal terms by which African Americans and other minorities could participate equally in the American dream. The '70s continued the process of definition and adjustment. Women soon replaced people of color in the challenging role of demanding and receiving equality of opportunity and more equitable treatment. President Johnson's War on Poverty ultimately failed in its purpose to end poverty, but it did establish a new awareness of the least and the lost of the nation. The '70s tinkered with its legacy of success and failure, both socially and economically.

Silhouettes of helicopters against the sky had been a symbol of American combat in the 1960s, but by the '70s, they had became icons of the decade's failures: One tried to balance on the roof of the American embassy in Saigon while it rescued the remaining American personnel left behind after America's failed war in Vietnam. Another lifted a failed US President from the White House lawn. It circled briefly as if trying to get its bearings, and then carried its passenger into exile. The dynamic of social progress and economic prosperity in the mid-'60s devolved into the inflation and stagflation of the '70s. Whereas the previous decade had seemed an irresistible force, this one seemed to be an immovable object.

The shortage of gasoline for the age's bloated cars acquainted Americans with both panic and patience; combined with inflation, the shortage seemed to underline a new vulnerability. The media, which had portrayed Richard Nixon as a man of dangerous ego, bravado, and ambition, soon portrayed Jimmy Carter as a man who was dangerous because of his uncertainty, timidity, and disconnection. In between the two elected presidents the media portrayed Gerald Ford as only dangerous when he was playing golf. It was, wrote one journalist, "as if every locomotive in America was rusted to the rails."[280] News icon Walter Cronkite was America's most trusted personality as the hostage crisis in Iran unraveled the last threads of the decade. His sign-off phrase, "And that's the way it is!" seemed to hint at a nostalgia for a more confident time.

An erosion of both faith and structure appeared in churches, especially Baptist churches. Once solidly "center right" in the traditional mainstream religious hegemony, many American Baptists felt increasingly isolated by the development of more radical, liberal religion on the left, and the emergence of a dynamic new evangelical-dominated and conservative religion on the right. The era of church building and the expansion of the '50s and early '60s gave way to tightening budgets and eroding memberships for many American Baptist churches. Some, surrounded by decaying urban environments, debated whether to abandon the center city and move to the more inviting suburbs. Some did. Of those that did, many soon discovered that demographic and economic change occurred in the suburbs, too, and wondered if they had made a mistake.

The parachurch was replaced by the counterchurch and then by the television church. TV preachers created the illusion of transcendent community and "called on individuals in their living rooms and bedrooms to make a decision for Christ, be healed and expect a blessing." Of course, they requested a donation in return. Many became what Martin E. Marty described as "plural belongers" to both the church church and the electronic church.[281] It was not an even exchange; less than one-tenth of 1 percent of church members claimed to have been converted by electronic church outreach, but a far higher percentage of church members diverted their attention and financial support to television ministries. Pastors faced new pressures to preach and perform as the polished actor-preachers did, but without the benefit of a support staff or stage lighting. Uncertainty was as present in religious contexts as it was in politics. In religion, as elsewhere, this was the "Me Generation." Tending its own needs, the American Baptist Convention sought solace in its usual institutional manner: it determined to reorganize.

The MMBB at Work

Despite the organizational progress of the previous decades, no one was prepared for all that came next. The MMBB entered a time when its most important asset, other than its endowment, would be its ability to adapt, adjust, and change. As the MMBB continued its work, its agenda continued to be largely determined by continuing programs and concerns. Yet events imposed new items to be considered. As MMBB President John Reed reflected in 1974, "The theme from the '60s on—aside from traditional concerns of annuitants and retirement plans and medical plans—has been the intertwined fields of civil rights and social responsibility."[282] Sensitivity to the social justice implications of the Board's investment policies demanded consideration, and building and maintaining a field staff that reflected the denomination's increasing diversity became a priority. Still, the Board maintained its focus on broad personal and professional support for ministers. The ever-present need to encourage and raise ministerial salaries increased, as did the pressure to keep pensions current in value as inflationary trends became stronger and seemingly more intractable.

The MMBB also had to confront changes that came from beyond its own Board. Executive Director Dean Wright entered the second decade of his three decades of leadership, while in the national Convention, the Office of the General Secretary underwent transition from the leadership of Edwin H. Tuller, a centrist and a statesman, to that of Robert C. Campbell, an evangelical biblical scholar and teacher. In addition, uncertainties affecting church and denominational life had expanded concerns about the effective operation and cooperation of the Convention's agencies. That concern had resulted in the appointment of the Study Commission on Denominational Structure (SCODS). The Commission's report was received for study by the Convention in early 1971, and its proposed structural changes were authorized in 1972. The resulting changes in relationships ultimately brought long-term challenges for MMBB.

The Consolidated Investment Fund and Investment Strategy

Meanwhile, at the decade's beginning, the MMBB's long-term investment success had continued. One unintended consequence was the increasing challenge of effective management of its resources. In 1970, the total assets of the MMBB had reached a market value of $130,453,213, with $72,896,609 in the Retirement Plan, and $57,556,604 in the Permanent Fund and designated funds. Until 1970, the assets of the MMBB had been invested directly or under the direct supervision of the Finance Committee. As net asset worth climbed, however, that committee had reviewed their responsibility and had researched the procedures followed by organizations with similar purposes and greater resources. They reported that optimal results were best achieved by investment funds no larger than $40 million to $50 million and that investment funds that measured and monitored their investments tended to have the best long-term performance.

The Finance Committee, therefore, recommended several actions: First, MMBB funds should be accounted for separately, but for purposes of management and investment should be combined for reporting purposes in a proposed Consolidated Investment Fund. It further proposed that the new Fund should be divided into four parts, and that four investment advisory organizations would be engaged, each of which would manage a portion of the Fund on a discretionary basis. The Fund's managers were to be held to investment standards and policies established by the Finance Committee. It is likely that one consideration of the Finance Committee and the Board was a growing awareness of impending recommendations of the SCODS committee regarding the future constitution of the Board, which might have the effect of diminishing the Board's financial and investment expertise. The Finance Committee's recommendation for changes in the investment strategy was approved and implemented effective 1 August 1970.[283]

The changes were undoubtedly timely for long-term performance. However, overall investment experience in 1970 was, as Dean Wright reported, discouraging. But 1971 and 1972 were, once again, years of strong returns. In 1973, though, a national economic decline with commensurately poor investment results affected the funds, and initiated a period of essentially flat investment returns that seemed to last forever.

At the same time, gifts and legacies were a continuing source of MMBB asset development. Annual reports in the early years of the decade consistently reported the rising significance of these gifts: In 1970, $515,280 was received through such giving, $275,542 in 1971, $231,638 in 1972, and $432,023 in 1973. In 1974 B.R Pfaff, who had previously served on the staff of the MMBB, rejoined it as Director of Field Services. In addition to providing liaison between the New York staff and field representatives, Pfaff's primary responsibility was the cultivation of wills, legacies, gifts, and bequests.[284] The Board also continued its conscious self-education regarding social awareness and investment responsibility throughout the period. As one example, in 1972 William McKee reported on his observations during a visit to South Africa and the possible implications for MMBB investment policy. In several cases, MMBB exercised its stockholder votes to influence or change corporate policies.[285]

Board Leadership

Over its lengthening history, an important key to the MMBB's stability and effectiveness continued to be its ability to attract, groom, and, when needed, replace highly effective leaders on both the Board and on the Executive and Administrative staffs. Important developments in both Board and staff membership especially apparent during the 1970s: John W. Reed, who had begun his service as President of the Board in 1967, continued in the first of two significant periods of Board leadership until 1974.[286] Oliver J. Troster rejoined the board to continue service that had begun as early as 1934.[287]

Several new Board members reflected the growing diversity of the American Baptist Convention and the MMBB's commitment to serve it. In 1970, Gardner C. Taylor, pastor of the Concord Baptist Church in Brooklyn, New York, joined the Board, and in 1971 Floyd Massey, Jr., pastor of the Macedonia Baptist Church in Los Angeles, was appointed as the ABC's General Council representative to the Board. Santiago Soto-Fontanez, formerly the pastor of the Central Baptist Church in Brooklyn, New York, and also President of the American Baptist Hispanic Caucus, was also elected to the Board.[288] Additional new members included Clifford K. Beck, an administrator for the Atomic Energy Commission in Washington, DC, and Janet M. Clasper, a lecturer in theology and the arts at the American Baptist Seminary of the West.[289]

There were also changes and developments on the MMBB staff that reflected the expanding commitments of the MMBB. In 1970 William McKee was appointed as Associate Director. Robert H. Eads became an area representative assigned to represent Cleveland and Ohio, and J. Walter Sillen joined the staff to serve as the representative in the New England region.[290] Also in 1970, Miriam Corbett, who had served as a

Special Representative since 1965, especially in advancing understanding of gerontology, became Director of Retirement Services.

New assistants to the Executive Director were also appointed that year; they included Bennett Owens, former ABC pastor and staff member of the Executive Council of the Episcopal Church, and Charles J. Sargent, Jr., an MMBB area representative since 1968. In 1971 R. Dale Johnson, having served several churches in Colorado, Wyoming, and California, became a representative in the West, and in 1972, O.C. Jones, Jr., also became a representative for the western area.[291]As African Americans, Sargent and Jones continued and expanded Board commitment to serving the growing number of African-American churches in the ABC. Also in 1972, Leonard Ballesteros was engaged as a field representative to expand MMBB's ability to relate to Spanish-speaking members and constituents.[292]

As a marker of the receding past, Elmer C. Adams, a long time staff member of the MMBB since 1957, retired as Associate Director in May 1970.[293] At the MMBB he had served as Western Regional Director and had coordinated the Center for the Ministry in Wellesley Hills, Massachusetts. He had also developed the pilot program of Salary Support, and then, as his last Board responsibility, led in developing the nationwide Salary Support Program, which was inaugurated nationwide on 1 January 1970. Likewise, in 1976 Malcolm R. Cary also retired, having served for more than forty-three years on the MMBB staff, most recently as Treasurer. Cary was a Methodist layman, and according to his colleagues' testimony, his lengthy and dedicated service had significantly influenced and shaped the character of the Board.[294]

Later in the period, as indications of new responsibilities and directions, Barbara A. Freiert joined the staff as Assistant to the Director in 1976, and in 1977 Miriam Corbett was appointed Associate Director.[295] Hugh D. Pickett, a staff member since 1963, was appointed Director of Membership Services in early 1977. In May 1977, Gordon E. Smith, Assistant Treasurer since 1975, was appointed the Treasurer of the MMBB.[296]

Benefits and Services: Expansion and Restriction

Both the Retirement Plan and the Medical Plan had been recently reshaped and restructured in the mid-1960s. In 1970, the Lay Employees Retirement Plan was modified and refined so that lay employees would receive a retirement allowance based on years of service.[297] Otherwise, benefit changes were largely refinements or further definitions and extensions of existing plans' features. Many of them related to benefits for surviving spouses, rights of other survivors, beneficiaries, and guarantees to annuitants and their beneficiaries.[298] Twice during the decade the premium payment percentage was raised, first to 15 percent of compensation, and then to 16 percent. Otherwise, in the '70s, no radical changes to retirement plans were introduced. However, the economic challenges of the decade tested them and stimulated a number of adjustments.

One challenge resulted from the 1965 introduction of the new variable annuity basis of the Retirement Plan, which intended to allow members to benefit from market growth. In the face of discouraging investment returns in the '70s, the variable annuity concept was harshly tested. When the financial markets retracted significantly, or declined over significant periods of time as they did in the 1970s, the lowered value of member's accounts threatened to retard and even erode annuity payments. In 1970 the Board determined to supplement annuities for 1971 from the Permanent Fund in order that annuity payments would be equal to 1970 amounts. The same course was followed in 1971 for 1972 payments, and thereafter, supplementation continued for much of the decade.[299] By 1980, additional annual or biannual checks were also being sent to augment the lower than expected performance of the annuity funds as well as to correct for the significant and continuing rate of inflation.[300] Continued sluggish market performance combined with rising inflation would have potentially impoverished many annuitants were it not for the supplementation of payments from the Permanent Fund. By that means, the MMBB prevented crippling annual annuity payment declines.[301]

The combination of sluggish investment performance and inflation proved vexing for the MMBB and its members for a number of years. But despite mediocre investment performance, a number of benefits were enhanced. In 1972, for example, the maximum disability benefit was increased from $3,600 to $4,600, and the compensation basis of disabled members was adjusted: Thereafter, the basis upon which premiums were to be paid, and then waived, was increased to 5 percent each year. This allowed for future retirement benefits to be increased as if the person were normally employed during the disability period. In 1975, members without a spouse were given the option to designate as a joint annuitant a person dependent upon the member who was closely related by blood, marriage, or adoption.

In 1975 the Retirement Plan premiums were increased from 13 percent to 15 percent of members' compensation, including housing allowance or rental valued of housing provided. About 75 percent of the increase enabled higher contributions for retirement accounts, and the remainder enhanced short- and long-term disability benefits. In the same action, premiums and administration for disability coverage was shifted to the Medical Plan. Disability payments were coordinated with Social Security disability benefits to provide 66 percent of most recent compensation for long-term coverage.[302] In 1979 the Retirement Plan was again revised and became the Retirement/Benefit Program, and the premium was again increased from 15 percent to 16 percent of compensation. All of the 1 percent increase in this case was allocated to the member's Annuity Supplement Account (TAS). Additional changes raised the single life guarantee for members with twenty years of service or longer to "not less than 1/70th of the total salaries upon which premiums have been paid." The Board also established 70 instead of 65 as the age limit for short-term disability benefits, and broadened the program of assistance, previously restricted to active members, to include retired ministers as well.[303]

As the '70s ended, increased flexibility regarding disposition of, a member's assets included the ability to designate a beneficiary for the Death Benefit Plan who was not a spouse or a child under the age of 21, and new and more flexible guidelines for lump-sum settlements of the Retirement Plan were both introduced.[304] In addition, the Board established procedures to address the payment of benefits in the case of a missing person. The amount limits for possession of cash assets to qualify for special grants were increased from $5,000 to $7,500 for individuals, and from $8,000 to $12,000 for couples. The maximum grant was increased from $900 to $1,200 per year. Emergency assistance was also broadened to include financial assistance to provide an entrance fee to a retirement home in the amount of 25 percent of the total fee, with a maximum of $5,000.

In 1980 the Medical Plan was increased to include dental coverage, effective 1 January 1981. In the same year, the MMBB began providing Health Facts, a publication of the Center for Medical Consumers and

Health Care. This reflected a method of guiding members in effective preventative and personal health care, as well as encouraging members to be more cost effective in health care choices.

The investment returns of the '70s were a sobering experience. Some of those who retired during that period expressed regret that an investment option had not been available to provide refuge from the poorly performing equity markets. After deliberation, the Board considered exploration of an investment fund of less flexibility but also less vulnerability in declining markets. The fund would limit equity investments to 50 percent of the total and would only be open to those who were over 50. By application, they could transfer all of their previous accumulations and TAS contributions, plus future payments, into the new fund. Although the proposal was not immediately pursued, a similar concept was introduced at a later time.[305] However, that deliberation did present a willingness to consider wider options for Plan participants, the possibility of member participation in choosing investment options, and a consequent movement toward a financial services orientation for the MMBB.

Throughout the period several changes affected Joint Life Annuity options. The original practice was a 100/60 arrangement, with the member receiving 100 percent and the surviving spouse 60 percent. In 1973, however, two additional options of 100/100 and 80/80 were approved. In 1976 the Board also resolved that a premium-paying member without spouse or minor children was able to designate a beneficiary of his or her Retirement and Death Benefit Plans.

During the 1970s the MMBB also achieved several clarifying letters from the IRS, one of which broadened the definitions of those who were eligible to make contributions to TAS. Another declared that a portion of a retired minister's annuity could be declared as housing allowance. Ultimately, the IRS approved the designation of 100 percent of annuity and disability income as housing allowance, to the degree that such a percentage could be justified.[306]

Noncontractual benefits and services were expanded for annuitants and some others in unique circumstances. The Communion Fellowship Offering, first established in the 1930s as a means to provide emergency grants and respond to unexpected needs, was reshaped in 1976 to become the "Retired Ministers and Missionaries Offering." In its new form, the offering's purpose was not only to generate funds for emergency relief, but also to extend an annual "thank you" to all retired ministers and missionaries.[307] Approximately 40 percent of the offering was designated to meet financial needs, and the remainder for "Thank You" checks to all annuitants.[308] The "Thank You" offering was first received in 1977, the first distribution checks were sent in 1978, and the offering continues to the present. Although the checks were relatively modest, they often provided much-needed resources for such expenditures as medication for the annuitants living on extremely limited incomes. In conjunction with the promotion of the RMMO, "Thank You" offering, a new publication, *ABC People*, was created and featured the careers and retirement activities of retired ABC ministers and missionaries.

Looking to Future Retirement Security

In 1978 a staff Retirement Income Study encouraged a class of new retirees to assess the adequacy of retirement income for their needs. Income studied included the total of both the MMBB annuity and the member's Social Security payment as compared to the member's final compensation. Presented to the Board in 1979, the report indicated that while the MMBB was fundamentally achieving its mission, a great many annuitants experienced an income gap that was, in some cases, quite severe, especially after a decade of increasing inflation.[309] Several one-time or temporary actions resulted directly or indirectly: For 1979, an "extra" annuity payment was sent to all annuitants, funded by the Permanent Fund. The MMBB also joined in efforts to encourage federal legislation to allow an increase in contributions allowable to supplemental retirement accounts, and also to urge the IRS to increase the amount of annuity allocated as housing allowance for retired clergy. It also stimulated the MMBB to encourage members to develop additional sources of income for retirement, including investments and to encourage some form of professional activity in retirement.

Partly as a result of the Retirement Income Study, the Board in 1979 created and distributed to members the first "Annual Report of Account" detailing the status of their Retirement Plan activities. The report included 1978 premium payments, the number of accumulation units purchased during the year, the total number of units owned in the member's Retirement Plan, and the dollar value of the plan as of the end of the year. The report also provided a salary history, as well as a projected illustration of future annuity payments, based on age at retirement, a projection of future compensation increases, and projections of annual market return during the years still left prior to retirement. As a side benefit, the report made the correction of errors in salary history and payments more immediately possible. More importantly, it became an effective tool for members to use to project and to plan their resources for retirement. The report was continued annually thereafter as an aid to members.

Some benefits were revised or limited during the '70s. For one, the Board voted to eliminate their reimbursement for Part B of Medicare effective in 1976. And in 1977, members with fewer than five years of continuous membership in the Retirement Plan immediately prior to retirement were no longer eligible for the Board's provision of costs for medical coverage, which included Medicare Part B, but also a full subsidy of the MMBB Medicare Supplement insurance.

The most significant long-term development was one whose full consequences had not yet developed but whose trends were nevertheless emerging: The Travelers Insurance Company, which administered the MMBB's Medical Plan, informed the Board that premiums would have to increase by 35 to 40 percent effective in 1976. As a result, the MMBB decided to self-administer as well as to self-insure medical coverage. Space and staff in the MMBB offices were subsequently restructured to allow for personnel to handle claims processing, the issuing of checks, and correspondence and communication with members. For a time this avoided the escalating costs that otherwise would have occurred, largely because much of the administrative cost for the Medical Plan could be underwritten by the Permanent Fund, but it proved to be a short-term solution.

Broader Support of the Ministry

The Baker study from the early 1960s continued to inform and guide the MMBB's commitment to "the better maintenance of the ministry" in several ways. The enlargement of the field representative staff had sought to address ministerial isolation and loneliness, and efforts in developing counseling and assessment services in the Centers on the Ministry in Wellesley and Oakland additionally sought to encourage ministers encountering personal or professional challenges. The MMBB also acted to undergird and enlarge the placement process.

Most critically, however, the long-term goal of raising clergy compensation, especially in a time when local resources were often declining and inflation was rising, remained a high priority.

The Salary Support Program, which had been regionally piloted and tested, was introduced nationally on 1 January 1970. The program included a dual approach to raise salaries for ministers serving churches that were unable to pay adequate compensation and to establish a national minimum standard salary and raise the average level of compensation. The program's scope was large: 10 percent of all ABC churches qualified, though not all that qualified participated. The Salary Support Program was funded by the 1 percent portion of the then 13 percent of compensation salary premium payments of all MMBB members. Qualified churches willing to commit to raising a pastor's salary to at least the minimum level received financial support from the MMBB to fill the gap between previous compensation and a salary standard set by the Salary Support Program. At the outset that standard was $5,500, plus housing and professional expenses. Participating churches were subsequently expected to commit to a plan of stewardship emphasis and education, with the goal to enable it to achieve the salary amount from their own stewardship and resources over a three-year period.

In 1972 the salary objective was raised to $6,000. In 1974 the Salary Support Program was studied and evaluated under the leadership of Harold W. Richardson, formerly the Executive Director of the Board of Educational Ministries, and a report was issued for the Board's review.[310] The Board reaffirmed the program, which continued until 1992 when it was replaced by the Strategic Premium Assistance Program.[311]

Direct support of ministers, churches, salaries, and benefits was also demonstrated in other specific ways. For example, the MMBB had historically responded to disasters and unforeseen suffering by providing individual grants. In 1971, in a time of financial distress for the American Baptist Seminary of the West, the Board elected to pay the Retirement and Medical plans for the staff of the seminary.[312] In 1972 a massive flooding overwhelmed a number of cities and towns in northern Pennsylvania and western New York, resulting in whole communities struggling to rebuild. Many American Baptist churches had been affected, several of them in areas of low economic resources. The MMBB responded by paying or guaranteeing the salaries of six of the area's ministers for a period of time so that their churches could divert funds to rebuilding or rehabilitating their facilities.[313] In 1973 the MMBB cooperated with the American Baptist Churches of the Pacific Southwest to provide support for the Retirement/Death Benefit plans, as well as Social Security taxes, for pastors in Baja California, Mexico.

The MMBB also sought to encourage greater satisfaction and harmony in local churches. One finding of the Baker study had been a pervasive level of ministerial frustration. This had contributed to a continuing stream of ministers who left the ministry, or left the service of American Baptist churches. One identifiable cause was ineffective communication between church leaders and members, or insufficient feedback from congregations to pastors. To address this concern, during the '70s the Ministers Council developed and promoted the idea of Pastoral Relations committees within churches. The committees were envisioned to improve the understanding of the role of the pastor within congregations and to improve communication between pastors and their congregations. The proposed committees were to strengthen pastoral relationships by providing, on an annual basis, reviews of pastoral service and by advocating for adequate pastoral support, particularly compensation to encourage pastors to engage in continuing education. They were also to help identify and mediate troublesome conflicts between pastors and individuals or groups within the church. Through its administrative oversight of the Ministers Council, the MMBB strongly supported this effort in several ways, including the introduction and explanation of this initiative through its publications.[314]

To buttress the long-term security of the ministry, the MMBB during the '70s also initiated and supported two additional themes through seminars, workshops, and publications. One was the continuation of a traditional concern: increasing the compensation of clergy. Workshops and seminars brought key church leaders together in small contexts to consider this sensitive issue and to encourage solutions. The second was a relatively new initiative that sought to familiarize clergy personally with the need to save and invest beyond the resources represented by the Retirement Plan or TAS. The MMBB was not prepared to provide financial planning services, but it was an affirmation that most ministers needed to engage in such planning and discipline in order to secure their futures.

Women in Ministry

During the 1970s the role of women in work, professional, family, and community life came more broadly into focus. The role of women in American Baptist ministry also emerged more specifically as an issue requiring attention. American Baptists did not have a doctrinal position opposing the denominational or pastoral leadership of women. Indeed, examples of ordained women serving church, mission, or administrative purposes among American Baptists dated back to the nineteenth century. However, as a practical matter, only an isolated few women served as pastors, and relatively few served in the leadership of associations or the denomination. In 1972, in an MMBB Board meeting, Dean Wright, Executive Director, noted that a study had demonstrated that women in professional leadership within the ABC were discriminated against with regard to placement, advancement, and salary. He suggested that there was need for a conference in support of women in professional ministry to more clearly understand the challenges they faced. As a symbolic step, the MMBB revised its own bylaws and publications to rid them of exclusive language and took the lead among American Baptists in promoting gender-inclusive expressions.[315]

In 1974 the MMBB participated in sponsoring the first conference for American Baptist Women in Professional Church Leadership, held in Malvern, Pennsylvania. One aspect of the MMBB's support for the conference was to provide travel expenses for those traveling more than one hundred miles to attend. Sixty-five women representing local parishes, neighborhood centers, overseas missions, national and regional staffs, and counseling centers participated. Among the resulting formal recommendations was that a woman should be appointed within the ABC structure in a staff position to represent the career interests of American Baptist women in professional church leadership.

Another informal result was the creation of a network of caring and support for women, especially seminary students and recent graduates. The conference was ultimately the impetus for the development of a more specific effort to encourage women in ministry within the American Baptist Churches, USA, and its constituent churches. In 1980 a Women in Ministry Conference was again held at the American Baptist Assembly in Green Lake, Wisconsin. Following the conference, the MMBB elected to fund the project for the next three years. That decision signified a beginning for the MMBB's advocacy for women in ministry.[316] Margaret Ann Cowden was selected to give professional leadership and liaison to the Women in Ministry project, and ultimately also became a member of the MMBB staff.

The MMBB continued to have oversight of the Career Development Counseling Centers that had opened in Wellesley Hills, Massachusetts and Oakland, California.[317] The function of the centers was not directly therapeutic, but instead was "to help all who participate to use their capabilities more effectively." Its programs were designed to help ministers more clearly define their career goals and to assist them in developing resources and strategies to achieve them. At the same time, the MMBB was able to diminish its role in pastoral placement, a service it had performed in one way or another since 1929 as a "stopgap" measure. In recent years, several placement studies and experiments had demonstrated a strong need for more extensive placement services to pastors and churches. Therefore, in 1971, the General Council of the ABC created the American Baptist Personnel Services to assume overall responsibility for ministerial placement, in cooperation with regional "placement consultants" and under the supervision of the state, regional, and city Executive Secretaries or Ministers.[318] The denomination further refined and institutionalized a centralized approach to ministerial and other professional placement following the SCODS principles of reorganization.

The Church Alliance

The Federal Employee Retirement Income Security Act of 1974 (ERISA) sought to reform and regulate employee pension plans in order to protect such pension funds from abuse. However, in dealing with church plans, Congress had failed to understand the differences in polity and ecclesiastical structure among denominations. As one result, the legislation contained conditions and descriptions, which, unless resolved, might be interpreted to require the MMBB to conform to ERISA requirements in ways that would have excluded some MMBB members and might have prevented future potential members from participating. The MMBB exceeded the minimum vesting and funding requirements imposed by ERISA, and, thus, did not seek any variance in the operation of the Retirement Plan. Instead, the MMBB's concern was to seek clarification of who was *qualified* to participate in the Plan.[319]

At issue were hundreds of denominational employees or employees of church-related institutions and missions. The problem was largely an issue of language, with the IRS defining "Church" in narrow terms that did not encompass denominational connections or "non-steeple" professional affiliations. The implications were potentially significant, including the possible eventual exclusion of a thousand MMBB members from the Retirement Plan, including employees of seminaries, retirement centers, nursing homes, children's homes, hospitals, and potentially, missionaries and employees of mission boards. The provisions had taken effect on 1 January 1974, and as a result, the MMBB had not been able to accept as members any persons who served agencies or organizations that had not been previously recognized by the Board. Left uncorrected, in 1982, provisions of ERISA would make it impossible for the MMBB to have tax-exempt status if it provided coverage for members employed by agencies which the ERISA language did not define as churches.

Fortunately, the MMBB was not the only pension organization thus affected. In 1976 an alliance of more than twenty-five national church pension boards, including most Protestant denominations as well as Catholic and Jewish organizations, organized to seek clarification of the legislation and amendments to the bill if needed. From the MMBB's perspective, one aspect of the dilemma was also a failure to account for the constitutional issue of separation of church and state. Hearings were held in October 1977. Several denominations and church leaders formed an organization named the Church Alliance to vigorously pursue the common interests of religious organizations related to ERISA in hearings and in additional submissions of testimony and material. Subsequently, Congress amended and clarified the language sufficient to resolve the problems, and clarifications of ERISA were signed into law in September 1980.

The Church Alliance proved to be a unifying force between religious organizations, and an effective voice for articulating concerns unique to religious pension boards. It continued to address legislative and regulatory challenges and other legal matters that affected the member boards.[320]

Effects of the Report of the Study Commission on
Denominational Structure

The American Baptist Convention approved the SCODS report in 1972. The resulting implementation of the SCODS proposals effected the most important organizational changes for the MMBB since its founding. The official records of the MMBB testify to Board support and assent to the proposals. Executive Director Dean Wright confidently reported in 1972 that the "American Baptists made relatively few changes which specifically relate to their pension board." Nevertheless, implementing the changes brought about significant alterations in the Board's operation and autonomy and affected its long-term effectiveness and efficiency for more than twenty-five years.[321]

From its beginning, the American Baptist Convention had been a corporate expression of a relatively loose association of churches, regional associations, societies, and agencies derived from a mostly Northern (later American) Baptist heritage. Its primary societies, the American Baptist Home Mission Societies, the American Baptist Foreign Mission Societies, the American Baptist Publication Society, and a variety of auxiliaries and other organizations had cooperated and prioritized goals and actions whenever possible. The MMBB (then known by its full incorporated name as the Ministers and Missionaries Benefit Board) was a primary agency of the Convention, but because of its relative independence, its own traditional control over Board membership, and its highly specific focus, it was often perceived as something of an anomaly in its relationship to the other organizations in the ABC.

Nothing except a common heritage, shared vision, and covenants of good will, however, required the various societies and agencies to work cooperatively, and often they did not seem to do so. As a result, competition for support had been frequent, and controversies regarding priorities were often apparent. In addition, the relationships between churches and associations and the American Baptist Convention were also ambiguous. Churches, in reality, could come and go as American Baptist churches, and often did so. In the late '60s increasing concern had been focused on these issues, and ultimately a Study Commission on Denominational Structure (SCODS) was approved by the Convention in 1968 to concern itself with structure, organization, and relationships within the life of the denomination.[322]

SCODS had been empowered "recognizing that structure is needed to carry out program in terms of comprehensive goals and objectives of the A.B.C. and its constituent units." Therefore, its purpose was "to coordinate more effectively the various areas of denominational life."[323] Its mandate was to examine all national organizations affiliated organizations such as the regional, state, and city society units in relationship to the ABC; the representational structure of the denomination, with particular reference to proportionate representation for ordained clergy, lay persons, minorities, men, and women, and other categories; and the role of related and associated organizations such as schools, colleges, seminaries, homes, and hospitals. It was, to say the least, an ambitious and comprehensive approach to redefining denominational reality and relationships.

When the report was received, it contained specific proposals for altering the relationship of the MMBB to the new organizational creation. From a distant perspective, it appears that the Convention blurred some of the lines defining the MMBB's mission and took a greater-than-warranted responsibility for its achievements when it stated in the SCODS report that the "specialized support functions of the professional ministry ... have since 1909 been one of the significant aspects of the concern of the A.B.C. for its leadership." It defined those functions as "undergirding, support, and developing of adequate compensation, aid in time of emergency needs, protection through a well-developed health plan, guidance in career development, preparation for retirement, and use of time in those later years with retirement income."[324]

It is, in fact, hard to read the SCODS document and not perceive a desire on the part of the denomination to subsume the accomplishments and purpose of the MMBB, and likely other organizations, as a subordinate part of the greater denomination. The SCODS proposals were, at that time and later, generally perceived as an attempt to effect a centralization of the American Baptist Convention. Its structural changes were designed to transfer authority and autonomy from local and regional associations, as well as the national societies and agencies, to the national body, thus becoming subordinate to the General Board of the Convention. Eventually, the ABC/USA sought to more firmly link local churches to the national and regional associations as well. In time that intention became more apparent, and its negative effects became clearer.

Therefore, the majority of individual congregations resisted such increased connection.

Specific recommendations affecting the MMBB included a reduction of the Board of Managers' membership from a maximum of twenty-four to a maximum of eighteen. The Board was to be constituted by twelve managers nominated by the National Nominating Committee and elected by the General Board, one each nominated by the denominational program boards (e.g., Home Missions, Foreign Missions, Education), and three managers elected on the basis of particular skills deemed important by the MMBB. The Board's functions were to "be determined, assigned and evaluated by the General Board of the A.B.C."[325] In addition, the Board was given administrative responsibility for the Ministers' Council. The proposal from the SCODS committee was ultimately approved in 1972 for implementation between 1972 and 1978, with the public support of Executive Director Dean Wright and the Board.[326] The changes would become clear over time, both for the MMBB and for the denomination.[327]

Challenges to the Board

The new structural relationships within the newly renamed American Baptist Churches in the USA implied a greater-than-before sense of interdependence between the General Board, the regional boards, and the agencies. As one example, in 1977 Robert C. Campbell, General Secretary of the ABC/USA, brought before the MMBB a financial crisis related to the Michigan Baptist Homes. Following the denominational restructuring brought about by the SCODS proposals, the old Michigan Baptist Convention and the Detroit Baptist Union had become the American Baptist Churches of Michigan. But the older body (Michigan Baptist Convention) still existed, and it included two subordinate groups—a Michigan Baptist Foundation, which operated a retirement facility in Florida, and the Michigan Baptist Homes, which operated retirement facilities in Michigan. It was a complex corporate dilemma and was, in fact, an underfunded enterprise. By 1977 the Michigan Baptist Homes was in financial crisis.

The Michigan Baptist Homes had gone into receivership in 1977, and in May 1978 asked for help from the ABC/USA. In June 1978, the General Board had appointed an Advisory Committee to advise the General Secretary and the Executive Committee of the General Board.

The MMBB had no direct responsibility for retirement homes in Michigan or elsewhere, but some MMBB annuitants were living in the home in question, and others were apparently investors in The Michigan Baptist Homes without living there. Concern for the Michigan Baptists' reputation had to be considered as well. It was potentially a financial and legal dilemma, but it also introduced a crisis of institutional and personal relationships.[328] By 1978 the Michigan Baptist Homes was in Chapter 11 bankruptcy and the dilemma of its residents had been featured on the popular TV program 60 Minutes, casting the managers of the Michigan Homes and, to some degree, the ABC/USA, in an unfavorable light.[329] Robert Campbell, the ABC General Secretary, stated that it was "the most difficult thing the denomination has ever faced."[330]

The MMBB was, of course, one potential source of financial resources able to resolve the crisis among the American Baptist agencies and departments. However, to respond to such a request with MMBB funds seemed at least a departure from, and perhaps a violation of, the MMBB's original mandate and purpose. Dean Wright sought legal counsel to determine whether the use of MMBB funds was legal or permissible in these circumstances. He was advised that it was not. The MMBB Act of Incorporation narrowly and specifically spelled out the purposes of the MMBB, and legal counsel had further serious questions whether the use of Board funds to aid the Michigan Homes could withstand scrutiny from the criteria of prudent investment principles.

Wright was in a difficult position. Legally prevented from responding to a request for funds to accomplish a bailout, he and the Board nevertheless faced a challenge of perception. Rather than seem negative or uncooperative in responding to the denomination's request, Wright composed and later published in pamphlet form an allegorical story titled "The Rabbit Who Could Not Swim." The witty tale parodied some aspects of the MMBB and the ABC/USA, as well as some of the key players in both organizations. In the story, a rabbit was ultimately called upon to rescue a group of people drifting farther from shore on a raft. But the rabbit could not succeed in his rescue mission simply because he could not swim—a metaphor for the MMBB's prohibition from using funds for such a purpose. The ultimate effect was to extricate the Board from a likely illegal action that might have equally likely resulted in financial losses for the MMBB. But perhaps most importantly, it clearly established a precedent that the MMBB's resources were not available for general denominational use. And it did so with good humor rather than rancor.

A second challenge came from the action of the Conference of American Baptist Ministers in Massachusetts. At their meeting on 8 April 1978, the Conference had received a motion that proposed to sue the MMBB "predicated upon the return from investments that retirees are receiving, and that the Executive Committee be requested to study all facets of the problem and report to the Conference on 31 October 1978." It happened that MMBB Board Member James Ashbrook was present at the Massachusetts ministers' meeting, as were two MMBB staff members. They responded by correcting and clarifying several errors of fact in the presentation by the impassioned proponent of the lawsuit. As a result of their efforts, action on the motion was deferred, and instead a committee was appointed "to gain full understanding of M&M's retirement program and make comparisons with other denominational and secular plans and that the investment procedures be understood for the purposes of interpreting these procedures to our members."[331] A similar situation, short of a threatened lawsuit, had occurred previously in California. That circumstance had led to a positive outcome by MMBB staff members, who used the opportunity to explain and discuss benefits.

In the case of Massachusetts, the MMBB conversations with representatives of the Conference of Baptist Ministers of Massachusetts continued for more than two years and concluded in a meeting of the Conference board in November 1980. At that meeting, the recommendations from a "Task Force on M&M" were presented for consideration. They included six recommendations, some of which contained subcategories. In the course of receiving the recommendations, it became apparent that there were wide variations in understanding about the MMBB's policies, as well as a disparity of knowledge about investing. (A humorous moment occurred when, after a discussion of the recommendations regarding investments, one Conference member commented, "It's very hard for me to vote on that question of investments unless you can help me by explaining what equities are.")

It also became clear that there was some internal competition among Conference members over potential leadership roles, and one or more members had chosen to rally personal support by criticizing the MMBB. The criticism did not represent a broad level of dissatisfaction with MMBB, but it did surface some remediable concerns. The recommendations were received by the MMBB and little more transpired regarding the threatened lawsuit. Ultimately, several of the recommendations made to the MMBB by the Conference were adopted or adapted.[332]

What both challenges to the MMBB illustrated was the need for constant, effective public interpretation regarding the MMBB's chartered mandate, as well as of its policies and functions. In reality the shift from the old, defined-benefit structure of the Retiring Pension Fund to the new, variable annuity–based Retirement Plan was made smooth by the positive investment results of the mid-1960s. But in the '70s the new Retirement Plan had suffered an increasingly negative image because of the prolonged market stagnation, especially after 1973. The variable annuity had been introduced with the enthusiastic hope of persistently improving unit values resulting from rising markets, an expectation at odds with benefits that had not risen in the '70s. For still-active members, in most cases, account values had declined due to falling unit values. For the already retired, annuity payments were often less than had been projected, and they had only avoided additional, significant, crippling declines because MMBB's voluntary supplementation had stabilized annual payments. Worse, by the late '70s, rapidly escalating inflation was further eroding the value of active members' accounts, and diminishing the purchasing power of retired members' annuities. Thus, the perception that something was amiss was understandable.

It was especially clear that such perceptions were often built on flawed comprehension of investment procedures and strategies. Therefore, the MMBB was cyclically challenged to project a hopeful perspective for the variable annuity-styled Plan, especially in times of discouraging performance. Those who retired in the late 1970s, in particular, suffered a real loss in unit value and, thus, received lower-than-expected annuity payments as a result. In reality, however, active members, especially those entering the Retirement Plan in the '70s, potentially benefited from purchasing annuity units at low prices. It was a delicate task.

Later, the 1980s would offer an unparalleled period of investment growth, and the majority of MMBB members mostly recouped the losses of the '70s, and in many cases, enjoyed an exceptional increase. Still, as would be true in later periods—notably the mid-90s and twice in the 2000s—the MMBB often faced the challenge of finding a comforting message during a discouraging experience. MMBB investment expertise had never been a significant issue, either directly or through its financial managers, but interpretation of current changes, especially in sustained market downturns, became a continuing and formidable challenge.

Providing a Perspective: The Role of Luncheon Addresses in the '70s

Aside from the constant need to describe and define benefits, and to interpret financial activity and MMBB policy, effective communication was defining an important aspect of the MMBB's standard of excellence. The *Annual Report of Account*, as well as occasional other communications, focused specifically on benefits or member choices and kept members well informed regarding their special interests. The *Tomorrow* and *ABC People* publications regularly provided information to ministers and a broad understanding of the needs of ministers and missionaries to lay persons and church leaders. At the biennial conventions of the ABC/USA, MMBB luncheons continued their role as an opportunity for fellowship, reunion, and thoughtful stimulation. What had begun in the '50s as a good idea worthy of experiment had, by the '70s, become a valued tradition. Often the luncheon speakers introduced luncheon participants to new concepts, trends, emerging challenges, and theological developments that would likely affect their ministries.

As examples, 1971's speaker was Edwin T. Dahlberg. Dahlberg was a revered witness to the acceptance of God's presence in the lives of others, and a personal witness for peace. He reflected on his own life and experiences as a laboratory in which God's grace could be seen. In 1972 Edward H. Pruden, the retired pastor of the First Baptist Church of the City of Washington, DC, reflected on the role of Christian witness in the political arena. Pruden had been President Truman's pastor during the uneasy years of the emerging American ascendancy to world power. His personal reminiscences reminded the audience of the importance of asserting the value of principles during confusing times. In 1973 Jitsuo Morikawa, formerly the pastor of Chicago's First Baptist Church and, at that time, the sometimes-controversial Associate Executive Secretary of the Board of National Ministries (the American Baptist Home Mission Society), merged reflections of his own spiritual journey in the context of the often painful national experience of dealing with cultural differences. Morikawa had unique experience and had performed powerful

Christian witness as a person of Japanese extraction who was interned during World War II. Afterward he had sought to disarm cultural stereotypes and mistrust by effective use of the scriptures. Morikawa challenged an emerging generation to prepare for the challenges of a coming world in which differences of identity and cultural background would become the norm, not the exception.

Henri J. Nouwen, already emerging as a leading writer of spiritual concerns that transcended denomination and creed, addressed the 1975 Biennial on a simple, pastoral subject: "Care and the Elderly." His perspective pointed not only to the growing need to care for a rapidly aging population, but also to the spiritual rewards involved for those who did. And in 1979, Martin E. Marty's address "Dangerous Future or Quiet Turning: The Scope of Religions in the Eighties," identified many of the changes in religious structure, orientation, participation, desire, and organization that were soon to come. His projections of what seemed a strange and incomprehensible future soon were demonstrated to be accurate. In between those two presentations in 1977, Al Carmines, Associate Pastor of the Judson Memorial Church in Greenwich Village in New York, and also the "father" of New York's "Off-Off Broadway" theatrical movement, portrayed the first sixty-five years of MMBB history in a whimsical, musical, and insightful presentation in the style of an improvisational cabaret performance.

Old Themes—New Challenges

Few were sad to bid the '70s farewell. The end of the decade was punctuated by the noise of angry demonstrators holding the American embassy personnel in Tehran as hostages. The demonstrations and the hostage crisis created a specter of the nation in crisis. It seemed like national humiliation and powerlessness had run a full course. The demonstrators in Iran were perceived as having cast a decisive vote in the presidential election of 1980 by rejecting what seemed, at the time, to be an inept Carter presidency. Ronald Reagan was elected, but he was almost killed by a deranged assassin's bullet a few months later. It seemed that the era was ending with the same themes of violence and despair with which it began.

The MMBB had navigated rough waters. To be sure, the '70s were not the best era of its investment performance. By the end of 1979, the total assets of the MMBB were $235,140,563, which represented a relatively lackluster performance in comparison with the previous two decades. But the MMBB had met the enormous challenges of the financial market: Its assets continued to grow, albeit slowly; benefits and services had been expanded and adjusted for better outcomes; and its long-standing priority of securing reliable pension support for retired ministers continued. Its historic and vigorous advocacy for increased salaries for clergy also endured. In areas of outreach and nonfinancial support through the field staff and the centers for the ministry, informational programs, and support, it had kept its vision clear. It had even expanded some of its resources.

The growing costs of medical care, on the other hand, were developing a worrisome trend despite the decision to self-administer the program and underwrite much of the administrative cost. The need to support annuity payments during years of extreme inflation also stressed the MMBB's resources. Between 1971 and 1978, for example, the cumulative total cost of supplementing annuities had totaled $1,601,691, drawn from the Permanent Fund.[333] What might the next period include? The '80s would prove to be a decade of advances. But as one writer of the time phrased it, "No child can discern the face of its mother while it still lies in her womb."

9

A GENERATION OF TRANSFORMATION—
PART THREE

A Sense of the Times

"It's morning in America," declared the new president, not so much because it was, but because the doldrums of the 1970s and former President Jimmy Carter's "age of limits" had grown tiresome. Morning offered a chance to awaken from bad dreams. Everything was symbolic in the 1980s, or more accurately, nothing was actually as it appeared. At the beginning of the decade, it was unclear whether Ronald Reagan was a hero with character, or whether he was a character actor playing a hero.

And it was unclear whether President Jimmy Carter was sent home because he was judged to be inept, or at least inept in his handling of the Iran hostage crisis. Or maybe he just had the bad luck to preside over tedious times, or because a media frolic sneering at his cardigan sweater and depicting him fending off an "attack rabbit" while fishing in Georgia dissolved what little gravitas he had left. Later, the Baptist Jimmy Carter's true value would be described as "the best former President we have ever had," as Senator Sam Nunn phrased it.[334]

"Symbol is substance everywhere," observed one commentator.[335] In world affairs, Britain fought the "last war of the nineteenth century" in rebuffing Argentina's claims to the Falkland Islands. In Lebanon, American vulnerability was symbolized when a suicide bomber killed 241 Marines bunked down in an office building. Then American strength was symbolically vindicated when American forces liberated tiny Grenada from communism and Soviet/Cuban influence, making it, once again, safe again for democracy. The space shuttle *Challenger* exploded with a national television audience watching. Its mythical hero and enduring symbol was teacher Christa McAuliffe, who was neither a career astronaut nor a scientist.

Talk show kings Phil Donohue and Geraldo Rivera delighted in hearing the confessions of the famous and the notorious, but true repentance was rarely evident. Madonna achieved fame by transforming herself into, well, "Madonna." In politics, Jesse Jackson illustrated that it was not necessary to actually hold public office in order to become a successful politician. Robin Leach rode the material side of the "American Dream" to dizzying heights on *Lifestyles of the Rich and Famous*, and everywhere, from suburban cottages to strip malls to New York's towering skyscrapers, bright, brazen gold became ubiquitous in America's decorating schemes: It was gold that everyone wanted, although polished brass would do. As the King of Brass, actualized in his "Trump Tower," Donald Trump reigned as Midas.

Personal-sized bottled water was introduced and suddenly became a symbol of purity, good taste, and good health. Later it would become a symbol of waste and environmental harm. Young rock star wannabes perfected the art of playing the air guitar, and their elders hungered to decorate their suburban walls with art masterpieces. Or, if their budgets were restricted, they decorated with the works of unknowns who were, as they were often described, "major artists in the making."

Everything was a symbol. But a symbol of what? Good, evil, indifference? Tom Wolfe novelized bond traders in New York as agents of evil. But it was the Soviet Union that was proclaimed by the president to be the "Evil Empire." However, when the same president said, "Mr. Gorbachev, take down that wall!"—and the Russian leader did—was it a symbol of restored American confidence and strength? Or did it simply symbolize the Soviet Union's bankruptcy? Who knew?

The beginning of the Reagan Era was not the consistently robust period some later recalled it to be. Economic retrenchment occurred, again, soon after the decade began, and the recession of the early '80s was one of the longest in the twentieth century. Just past mid-decade, in 1987, Wall Street's dizzying descent on Black Friday badly frightened investors. Near the decade's end, a major crisis in the savings and loan institutions traumatized anyone with money in supposedly secure banks. This worst banking crisis since the Depression symbolized the growing complexity of financial markets and the super-charged greed of the era.

In religion, evangelical growth seemed to occur at the expense of traditional Protestant churches, which languished nearly everywhere.

The Roman Catholic Church was confronted with women who wanted to be priests while, ironically, male seminary enrollments dropped precipitously. The church began importing priests from abroad, while the women who desired to be priests went underground. Churches everywhere were confronted by the sudden visibility of gay persons in their communities as HIV/AIDS took its toll. HIV/AIDS was first wrongly perceived in the early 1980s as a "gay disease." Eastern religions and meditational disciplines held strong appeal for the former Christians who were giving up their churches, but not necessarily their desire for religion. Television preachers kept expanding both their empires and their influence, but the fragility of those empires was later exposed when first Jimmy Swaggart, and soon thereafter Jim and Tammy Baker, led a procession of religious personalities, caught in morally embarrassing or corrupt circumstances, into disgrace.

In many regions, located near the crossroads of suburbs and interstate highways where transportation was quick and parking plentiful, new megachurches were built on business models and marketing strategies more than defined by charisma or doctrine. Willow Creek Church in Chicago popularized the concept of "seeker religion," and in Southern California, the Saddleback Community Church demonstrated that even in secular California, religion packaged effectively and offered conveniently could be sold to a rootless and often friendless population. In Texas, one church opened a McDonald's franchise on a church campus. What did that symbolize?

The '80s, like the '60s, was a trend-setting and turbulent decade. But unlike the '60s, its trends were material and self-centered—not so much focused on changing society or achieving justice as on accumulating personal wealth. In many ways, normative values and traditional institutions suffered, but not because anyone was really challenging them. Instead, it was more likely that no one was paying attention to them. A few years after the decade began, with the stock market rising and American confidence resurging, it did indeed feel a bit like morning in America. But it was more like one of those spring mornings when the fog is slow to lift. Everything glimmered in the distance, but it was hard to tell what anything was. Things were more complicated than they seemed.

The Coming Apocalypse

The last biennial Convention of the ABC/USA of the 1970s had been held in Carbondale, Illinois. It was a location that somehow symbolized Middle American values and the midwestern roots of the Convention's solid constituency during much of the preceding century: rural, agricultural, small city, and a bit isolated. A highlight of that gathering was the MMBB Luncheon speaker's address presented by Martin E. Marty entitled "Dangerous Future or Quiet Turning: The Shape of Religion in the Eighties."[336] Marty, a preeminent religious historian and popular observer of religious trends, anticipated the direction that the turbulent religious developments of the '70s were about to take. He began his topic by speaking of resurgence in religion and in the things in which religion has a part, including cultural, national, and political self-awareness. He anticipated the drift to the right of much of American religious identity, and the radicalism of militant Islam, tribal self-consciousness in Africa, and cultural and nationalistic trends in Europe. At the same time, he projected a growing global awareness within the broad culture, especially within churches. America, he said, would seem a very different place from the "Me Generation" of the '70s.

At the same time, however, Marty also projected that many of the core beliefs and identities would become diffused, with doctrinal confessions and creeds giving way to privatized and customized shapes and links connecting goals, beliefs, and preferences. One result, he suggested, would be the diminishing of broad campaigns to win souls, to be replaced by a magnification of single-issue agendas that would link religious symbolism to carefully defined causes such as antiabortion, pornography, creationism in the classroom, or the advocacy of specific life values as just a few examples. Marty suggested that, as a result, the religious "map" would be redrawn, with less distinction between older concepts of "mainline" churches and less-approved groups, and with less clarity, and thus less unity, among evangelicals. For the longer term, he also perceived that various religious groups might experience a need to "tighten up," and even seek protection from harassment, a perspective that might conceivably lead some to seek the protection of a "moderate police state" in some circumstances.

Despite these disturbing images of profound change ahead, Marty claimed not to be picturing a situation of "apocalypse now" in America. Indeed, Marty believed that there were some positives ahead. One was that churches might be able to bridge the growing sense of loneliness and isolation and that opportunity might urge church people to more actively practice invitation to others to join them. He also predicted that the forces of diffusion might well force churches to better define the rationale for their congregations, and that one such rationale might be a stronger sense of fellowship and community. In contrast, the 1981 American Baptist Convention met in San Juan, Puerto Rico—a symbolic location that self-consciously underscored the denomination's growing diversity. The MMBB Biennial Luncheon speaker that year was T. Herbert O'Driscoll, an Episcopal priest noted for his lucid use of biblical perspective and sensitivity to social upheaval and change.[337] He more fully embraced the image of apocalypse in his address at the MMBB Luncheon. He spoke of the coming decade and beyond with unusual prescience and perception in a talk titled "People of the Apocalypse—Children of the Covenant." O'Driscoll described apocalypse as being a place and time where there is "nowhere to run" and, in 1981, described that circumstance as being the condition of humankind. He suggested that to be a generation of apocalypse is "to taste ambivalence, ambiguity and confusion."[338]

O'Driscoll implied that the signs of apocalypse in those days included growing pluralism, a succession of social earthquakes that would shake and crumble many of the present foundations, and that social fragmentation would characterize the age more than unity. He prophesied that the shaking would both destroy things of the past and at the same time reveal things yet to come. He predicted that the present generation would be caught between hanging on to the things it had known and striving to comprehend the things that would be revealed. He sought to describe the implications of the apocalypse for "ministry in its midst." He was prophetic for the events of the coming years for the ministry, and particularly for the MMBB. These two back-to-back addresses served well as a guide to the events and stresses of the coming years. For the MMBB, they served as an introduction to the agendas of the years ahead.

The MMBB at Work

For the MMBB, the '80s were years that were occupied with defending its financial and benefit gains, especially, at mid-century, against some of the changes implied by federal tax reform. It was also a time when changing lifestyles encouraged benefit adjustments and new approaches to addressing the ongoing effort to increase clergy compensation. But the defining characteristic of the MMBB's response to the issues of the era was the creation of programs to address ministry concerns beyond financial considerations. For example, it proved to be a significant challenge to advance the acceptance of women in church leadership roles. American Baptists were socially, if not always theologically, conservative, and while they acknowledged the importance of women in churches, most did not want a woman as a pastor.

It was even more challenging to try to equip clergy to deal with the pastoral and congregational issues inevitable with the onset of the HIV/AIDS epidemic, a disease then wrongly presumed to be unique to gay persons. In advocating preparedness for ministry in response to the plague-like disease, the MMBB's straightforward initiative ran head-long into the varied and complex biblical, theological, and social assumptions that had kept gay-lesbian-bisexual-transgender issues a carefully hidden secret. The MMBB had anticipated a range of resistance, but they could not anticipate that, in trying to prepare ministers for an effective ministry of compassion, they were touching an issue that would ultimately shake the foundations of the denomination.

It was a time when everything seemed straightforward, but nothing was as it seemed.

Communications and Publications

In defining its agenda and programs, as well as outlining the challenges that faced ministers, the MMBB had, from its beginning, used communications effectively. In its earliest attempts to build support for the vision of retirement, it had told its story through state and local denominational publications, meetings, consultations, and gatherings. Occasionally it used the newest technology: The then recently developed postal Night Letter used to encourage pledges sufficient to achieve M.C. Treat's $50,000 challenge grant in days of the MMBB's creation in 1911 was an early dramatic example. Later, the creation of *The Ministry* and its successor, *Tomorrow*, had effectively connected MMBB programs and purposes to the broad constituency of American Baptist leaders while it informed the active participants in the retirement plans of benefits and programs to assist them. Also, the development of the MMBB luncheons at annual and biennial conventions had fostered unity while at the same time offering new and helpful perspectives.

The MMBB also communicated in very specific, often highly personal ways. The MMBB's letter to ministers during the early days of the civil rights efforts had greatly assisted ministers and others to understand more clearly the issues before them. It had assured many that they were not alone in facing the difficult challenges of ministry during that time. Likewise, when urgent matters such as ministers' participation in Social Security needed to be addressed, or when a new or revised program such as the Retired Ministers and Missionaries Offering needed an effective introduction, the MMBB had used staff members and sometimes special, short-term representatives, to personal visits and phone calls. Most often they had combined several forms of communication, but the growing complexity and prevailing themes of the '80s demanded more, not less. It was a prelude to the Information Age.

A 1982 Field Staff report offered to the Board by Glenn Hill observed that vast geographic distances separated churches and ministers in many parts of the country. That, combined with the demise of formerly frequent association meetings and regional gatherings, diminished a sense of personal connection among American Baptists. Further, the growing diversity of the nation, and more specifically the denomination, served to isolate racial-ethnic and other sub-groups both from the traditional majority and from one another. In addition, since the denomination's reorganization in the early '70s, ministers had increasingly expressed a sense of isolation, impotence, and power-lessness in denominational affairs.[339] These realities seemed to underline the wisdom of both Marty's and O'Driscoll's luncheon talks. All of these dynamics were seen to be decreasing American Baptist connections and, potentially, threatened the MMBB's ability to serve its purpose effectively.

The recently resolved misunderstandings with ministers in Massachusetts regarding investment performance and benefits had caused the Board some concern about its public perception. The MMBB staff, therefore, prioritized further reflection on that episode. Richard Huber, Director of Field Services and field representative for New England, New York, and Metro New York, and Barbara Freiert, Director of Retirement Services, led in the reflection. Their resulting assessment concluded that at least some of the cause of the recent confrontation was the result of confusion about MMBB benefits and procedures. They concluded that an informed membership was likely to be an effective and supportive membership. That led, for example, to the publication of a *For Your Benefit* packet of explanatory materials regarding the range of MMBB benefits that was sent to all members. Brochures, seminars, and consultations were increasingly devoted to more effective communication about MMBB benefits, programs, and services.

In retrospect it seemed that the diminished role of the MMBB's most consistent and visible communication, *Tomorrow* magazine, led to some miscommunication. *Tomorrow* had been an MMBB publication since 1944 when it replaced *The Ministry*. It had effectively combined articles of interest to active ministers and their families, retired ministers, lay leaders, and denominational leaders. Its mixture of inspirational, devotional, promotional, and informational articles had effectively communicated the MMBB's mandate, vision, operations, and perhaps most of all, its concern. But inexplicably, by 1970 *Tomorrow* was being published only sporadically. It then ceased publication altogether, without public explanation. Neither Board Minutes nor Annual Reports reflect an overt decision to end what had been a very effective communication device.

The *ABC People* magazine, which was created in 1977 to support the RMMO offering, did not replace *Tomorrow*'s content. After an eight-year interval, however, in 1979 a successor magazine with a slightly revised format begation publication under a title, as Dean Wright noted, chosen became it seems to represent the way yesterday's heritage and today's decisions are woven into the fabric of tomorrow: *Yesterday/ Today/ Tomorrow*. By the third issue, in the spring of 1982, however, the new magazine had reverted to the familiar single word title: *Tomorrow*.

The first issue of the restored magazine featured Jitsuo Morikawa, then minister of the First Baptist Church of Ann Arbor, Michigan, and previously the Secretary of the Division of Evangelism and later Associate Secretary of the denomination's Board of National Ministries

(American Baptist Home Mission Society). Morikawa himself symbolized the diversity and expanding dimensions of the denomination.[340] In his article, Morikawa focused on the meaning and opportunity of retirement and the right time to consider retirement, especially in an era when people of presumed retirement age increasingly chose not to retire. The same issue also included articles on the costs of high inflation, how to determine a fair salary for ministers, and concerns about growing medical costs, all which were concerns that would occupy much of the 80s. The magazine also briefly introduced the new Retirement Plan with its increased 16 percent premium and the Death Benefit Plan.

The resurrected magazine was published on a variable schedule during the '80s, and focused largely on MMBB benefits, investments, retirement planning, and tax concerns, with special focuses on the Women in Ministry program.

Leadership

In 1981 E. Spencer Parsons concluded his lengthy service to the MMBB, first from 1963 to 1972, and then from 1974 to 1981. He served as MMBB President during most of this second period of service. As his successor, John W. Reed had returned to the Board and was elected President. Daniel E. Weiss was Vice President, and Richard Fisher continued to guide the Finance Committee. Dean Wright had entered his third decade of leadership as Executive Director, and Gordon Smith continued as Treasurer. In 1983 Daniel Weiss became the head of the Board of Educational Ministries of the ABC/USA and, therefore, left the Board. In his place, Howard R. Moody, minister of the Judson Memorial Church in Greenwich Village, was elected to serve as Vice President. C. Oscar Morong, Jr., joined the Board as a Manager at Large in 1981. Morong was the senior vice president and investment manager of the College Retirement Equities Fund (CREF).

In 1982, four new Board of Managers members representing other American Baptist societies and agencies were welcomed. Carl Appelquist, representing the Board of National Ministries, was Director of Industry Relations at the American Council of Life Insurance in Washington, DC. He was a former President of both the ABC of Minnesota and of the American Baptist Churches. Harley Hunt represented the Board of Educational Ministries, and at that time served a church in Clearfield, Utah. Richard Ice, President of American Baptist

Homes of the West, Inc., came as the representative of the General Board, and Walter Pulliam, senior minister of Judson Memorial Baptist Church in Minneapolis and President of the Ministers Council of the ABC/USA, also came as a representative of the General Board. In 1983 Harold Davis, Executive Director of the Housing Authority of Oakland, California, joined the MMBB, also representing the General Board.

On the staff, Miriam Corbett, who had left MMBB service two years earlier to serve as the Associate Executive Minister of the ABC of Metropolitan New York, was welcomed back as the Director of Special Ministries.[341] Cheryl H. Wade, formerly Associate Minister of the North Shore Baptist Church in Chicago, joined the MMBB as a field representative in 1983.

Financial Development and Investment Issues

The years 1979 and 1980 brought investment relief as the moribund equity markets of the '70s expressed renewed signs of life and provided strong returns. The Consolidated Fund had a cumulative return for those two years of 58.3 percent, or an annual average of 25.8 percent. For 1980 the equity return was 35.6 percent and total investment performance for annuities showed an increase of 18.9 percent. The annuity unit values were based on a fiscal year ending on September 30, and for that date in 1983, the annuity values had increased by 34.27 percent. Annuities were increased by that amount effective January 1. At the end of 1980, the total assets of the MMBB had reached a market value of more than $314,000,000. Persistent attention to gifts and legacies had also paid off: in 1981 the MMBB received $752,224 from those sources.[342] With the exception of a financially disappointing 1983 and the temporary trauma of 1987's dramatic market downturn, investment performance during the '80s made the decade an almost unparalleled period of investment gain.

Despite the favorable returns of the time, the potential cost of the experiences of the last decade lingered. For example, the 1980 MMBB *Annual Report* recorded that the annuity supplementation during the '70s had totaled $1,707,438. Therefore, in 1983 the Board terminated several of the policies of the 1970s, most notably the guarantee that annuity payments would not drop more than 5 percent in any given year. In addition, the Board determined that if in the future such a guarantee were considered, no funds from the Permanent Fund should be used to provide that support—the Annuity Fund would stand on its own. In short, the MMBB's assets had grown, but they were not insulated beyond danger.

Further, the economic climate of the '70s had served to underline the importance of the MMBB's long-term financial prudence. But it also delivered a sobering judgment on assumptions about providing adequate retirement resources. For example, rapidly escalating medical costs were projected to claim much higher amounts of future annuity income, thus diminishing the real value of retired persons' pensions. In response, the Board moved to put the Retirement Plan on an ever more solid footing with the early-in-the-decade decision to raise the Retirement Plan premium from 15 to 16 percent of compensation (salary plus housing value). The 1 percent increase was directed entirely to the members' supplemental retirement accounts in order to create stronger future value. In light of the consistently positive market returns of the '80s, the value of the increase was significant for most active MMBB members. But health care costs, including insurance, continued to challenge retirement planning with their relentless upward spiral.

The issue of social responsibility as exercised through MMBB investments had been focused by the experiences of the '60s and had never left the Board's agenda. At various times permanent or temporary committees appointed to explore issues of social responsibility or justice issues had been established by the Board to lead them. In 1981 Citibank's participation in a loan to South Africa precipitated closing MMBB accounts at that bank, and transferring its business to Chemical Bank. The Chase Manhattan Bank accounts were also closed in order to take advantage of Chemical's range of services. As circumstances and conditions in the Republic of South Africa further developed, the Board adopted a resolution in 1985 that formally stated its opposition to apartheid in that nation.[343] In shaping that resolution, and later its effective implementation, the Board's considerations were both broad-ranging and specific. A great many corporations did business in South Africa, and the MMBB held significant financial positions in several of them.

Several other investment considerations had potential implications either for the MMBB or for South Africa or its people. One consideration included the question of whether divestiture was a merely symbolic act, or whether it potentially brought economic force to bear either on the corporation or upon South Africa, and, as a corollary, whether it would bring harm to the black citizens of that nation. The Board thus had to consider whether divesting itself of corporations that passively or tacitly supported apartheid would have a negative effect on the MMBB portfolio, or whether alternative investments could reasonably be substituted. And, given the Board's chartered responsibility, it was imperative to consider potential legal implications in developing its investment policy. The Board unanimously supported a resolution:

> RESOLVED, That within the legal restrictions and fiduciary obligations to which the M&M Board is subject, the Executive Director be empowered, in consultation with the President of the Board and the Chairpersons of the Finance Committee and the Committee on Corporate Social Responsibility, to implement appropriate action which will vigorously demonstrate the opposition of the Board of Managers to apartheid in the Republic of South Africa.[344]

ABC Board consultant J. Andy Smith expressed the belief that "economic pressure is one of the few hopes for black South Africans" and also noted that such pressure had seemed to encourage several corporations to provide housing, education, and training programs.[345] All such progress, however, had to be seen in the perspective of apartheid laws, and those laws were, therefore, the primary focus of any effective pressure. Ultimately strategies for implementing the MMBB resolution included actively voting MMBB's proxies, cosponsoring shareholder resolutions, and the selective divestment of securities in corporations perceived to be favorable to the continuation of apartheid. In 1986 the Board sponsored thirty-nine stockholder resolutions calling for US corporations to withdraw from investment in South Africa because of its continuation of apartheid.[346]

Benefit Changes and Program Adjustments

Reflecting its concern for developing long-term member resources for retirement, in 1982 the MMBB expanded its ability to enable additional long-term member contributions by creating the Deductible Employee Contribution Account (DECA), an addition enabled by the Economic Recovery Tax Act of 1981. The tax-deferred accounts were based on IRS Section 219(e)(2) and became effective 1 March 1982. Under many circumstances, DECA allowed for member contributions of up to

$2,000 in addition to the IRS limits on the TAS accounts.[347] In 1983, Medical/Dental Plan premiums for disabled members and their dependents, and for widowed spouses of active members and their dependents, began to be paid out of the Special Benefits Fund.[348] Eligibility for free medical coverage was liberalized to include widows and disabled members' families, and disability benefits were updated and designed to coordinate with Social Security disability provisions.[349] Education grants to children of deceased or disabled members were first increased from $1,200 to $1,500, and in 1986, increased again to $2,400.

In 1987, disability benefits were designed to increase by the average annual percentage increase in compensation of ordained active members in the Retirement Plan. This action assured that disability income kept pace at least with average ministerial salaries, and also assured that eventual retirement income would keep pace as well. In 1988, several re-definitions of payouts to surviving spouses and to families of disabled members liberalized that support. As examples, the minimum annuity payable to a widowed spouse upon the death of a premium-paying member was doubled from fifty to one hundred units, and children's allowances were, likewise, doubled from $500 to $1,000, while the period of payment increased from ages 18 to 21. The same allowances were granted to children of disabled members. The death benefit for retired members who were active members on their annuity start date and had twenty or more years of membership was increased from $1,000 to $2,000.[350]

Also in 1988, the Board revised the manner by which joint-life annuities were paid. Henceforth joint-life annuities would be recalculated for the surviving spouse on a single-life basis, subtracting payments already made. Then, the single- and joint-life annuities were to be compared and the survivor paid the larger amount. The same single-life annuity guarantee regarding the minimum number of payments was extended to joint-life annuities as well. These provisions were designed to protect survivors from the precipitous drop in income that sometimes resulted when one partner died. As a matter of technological change and convenience, the Board also began advertising that annuitants could receive their annuity payments by electronic transfer and deposit into their bank accounts.

The Death Benefit was also revised. Ministers and missionaries, particularly those with children, were especially vulnerable financially in the case of an early death. Before 1986, death benefits were 200 percent of compensation for all members up to the age of 61, 150 percent plus 75 percent from 61 to 65, and from 66 until retirement, 100 percent plus 50 percent, with 100 percent additional in the case of accidental death. In 1986 group term life insurance from the Death Benefit Plan was revised to provide 500 percent of compensation for members under the age of 41. Thereafter it was 400 percent from 41 to 50, 300 percent from 51 to 60, 200 percent from 61 to 65 and 150 percent from age 66 to retirement. In all cases, an additional 100 percent of compensation was added in the case of accidental death. These revisions were designed to add security for younger families during child-rearing years when resources were limited but without significantly penalizing older members.[351]

Medical and dental benefits were also significantly adjusted during the '80s. In 1981 dental coverage was added to the ABC Medical Plan, and in 1986 a Patient Advocate Program was also developed and added.[352] In 1987 the Board elected to provide financial assistance to ordained ministers serving churches with low compensation. In 1988 the MMBB more clearly specified the qualification for assistance for those who had expended $750 of the $1,500 stop-loss provision of the Medical/Dental Plan and whose total cash income did not exceed $14,000. In 1989 that assistance was conditional on $1,000 of the $1,500 stop-loss provision and with cash income that did not exceed $16,000. During the same time, continuing Board consideration of the relentlessly rising health care costs led to the development of a Church Health Network with the purpose of identifying cooperative ways among denominations to provide a national managed-care system for health care among clergy and religious workers. With the growing intractability of medical care costs, that effort collapsed in 1992.

Broader Support of the Ministry

The MMBB's broad, noncontractual, nonfinancial support of the ministry expanded significantly during the 1980s. The Board continued its support of clergy compensation, assumed stewardship of the Women in Ministry program, again addressed critical social and political developments that were likely to affect the practice of ministry, and took further, positive steps to acquaint ministers with other programs and resources such as Social Security. By 1990, the Board had developed a comprehensive plan to encourage clergy compensation during the 1990s.

Continuing its role as an advocate for increased compensation for ministers, in 1981 Richard Arnesman and Terry Burch, MMBB Regional Directors, addressed the Board on "The State of the ABC Ministry." In their presentation they identified themes of concern ranging from personal and family considerations among ministers, professional and congregational relationships, skill development, family dynamics, social contexts, and the long-standing and recurring issue of low compensation. As a follow-up, in 1982 a Clergy Compensation Survey was sent to both members and employers to gather data regarding the ways and amounts clergy were compensated. The resulting data and conclusions were useful in the Clergy Compensation Workshops that were initiated in 1983 for ministers, Pastoral Relations Committee members and other church leaders, particularly trustees.

The Board's priority of maintaining a clear understanding of the challenges and concerns of American Baptist clergy continued. In 1987 L. Ronald Brushwyler and Linda C. Spoolstra presented the Board with "A Study of American Baptist Clergy" that monitored previously recognized issues and trends since the Baker study. In the same year, the Board sponsored a succession of "Know Your Benefits" seminars under the leadership and direction of Barbara Freiert. The purpose of the seminars was to provide and encourage a clear comprehension of the variety of benefits available to MMBB members and how to access them. These seminars built on the theme earlier established in the 1981 mailing of the "For Your Benefit" packet of materials—brochures, legal documents, and plan descriptions of the Retirement Plan, Death Benefit Plan, TAS, and the Medical Plan. The seminars added awareness of some of the noncontractual benefits offered by the MMBB.

The Board also continued to provide critical perspective and advocacy regarding ministers' taxation. Ministers covered by Social Security were historically required to participate as "self-employed" practitioners, which meant that their payments had to equal the combined amount of employer and employee contributions. In 1983 the combined employer/employee amount had increased from 9.35 percent to 11.3 percent of qualified income. In the case of ministers, the fair rental value of a parsonage, or the amount designated for a housing allowance, was required to be included in the income. The financial burden of participation of Social Security was, therefore, becoming heavy, especially because ministry salaries did not always increase enough to cover the increased payments, which were often influenced by the rising values of housing provided. The MMBB, therefore, renewed its efforts to encourage churches and ABC organizations to provide a Social Security Offset allowance, a nonsalary amount equal to at least 50 percent of the minister's anticipated Social Security tax obligation. Those churches that followed that suggestion provided a significant increase in salary value, and protected ministers from excessive erosion of the salary portion of their compensation in future years as rates continued to increase.[353]

In addition, the MMBB sought to keep its members informed about changes in governmental benefits that could affect their retirement. As a result of the Tax Reform Act of 1986, a limited window was again opened for ministers during the tax years 1986 and 1987. Ministers who had previously opted out of Social Security could register for it during that time. The MMBB sent out a communication alert to all members, a pamphlet titled "Did You Make a Mistake?" and also sent a questionnaire to assess who was participating and who was not. Those who had previously opted out of Social Security were contacted by phone, letter, and personal visit in an effort to get them to reconsider. The Board also offered financial assistance to help those who had opted out so that they might enter the program. An issue related to Social Security was the unique role that ministers occupied as employees. In order to assist in threading the course through the complex IRS implications of that role, the MMBB began to publish and offer "Questions and Answers for Church Treasurers" in 1984 as an aid to proper reporting of minister's income and housing allowances.

Having earlier identified the inequitable compensation and restricted opportunities for women in the ABC/USA, the MMBB had nurtured a structure of response for education and support of women over several years. The MMBB formally accepted responsibility for the American Baptist Women in Ministry Project in 1981. In 1983 the Board committed to financially support the Women in Ministry Project through 1985 when the project was scheduled to end. The Board's effort was assisted by a special gift to the MMBB for support of the project in the amount of $25,000.[354] Ultimately, the Board continued support for the project for several additional years.

In 1983 the Board also adopted the male annuity table and then, later, a gender-neutral table as the standard for determining annuity payments, and made the new payments retroactive to current annuitants. Previously, the MMBB practice had been the industry-accepted policy of using separate actuarial tables for men and women, which gave women lower annuity payments than men because of longer female life expectancy. The US Supreme Court had recently struck down that practice as discriminatory. The Board's action had the effect of benefiting female Retirement Plan members without penalizing male members.[355]

Later in the decade, Holly V. Bean, who succeeded Margaret Cowden as Coordinator of Women in Ministry for the MMBB, reported that in 1988 the MMBB helped to sponsor a Racial Ethnic Women in Ministry Consultation, with women invited to represent four major groups: Asian/Pacific, black, Native American, and Hispanic women. The conference included the Executive Director of the Commission on the Ministry and the Director of the American Baptist Personnel Services, with a goal of developing strategies for placement. In the same year, the fourth national American Baptist Women in Ministry Conference was held in November. For that event, the brochure was printed in Spanish and English, and some aspects of the consultation were offered in bilingual format.[356]

With the goal of having an "informed membership," in 1985 Glenn Hill and Richard Arnesman, both of whom had become Certified Financial Planners, began to offer personal financial planning seminars for Retirement Plan members. The MMBB also undertook several initiatives to increase membership knowledge of benefits and to prepare more adequately for retirement. These included an MMBB newsletter titled "Thinking about Retirement" in 1984 and Know Your Benefits seminars, which were initiated in 1987. Both efforts focused on enabling ministers to plan more effectively for retirement while they were in their active professional years.

Social and domestic changes during this decade also stimulated the board to adjust and respond to new concerns. As one example, in the past, social as well as theological pressures had made it difficult for ministers to survive a divorce and maintain their careers in ministry. However, by the '80s it had become possible for clergy to divorce and still continue in a ministry career. In response, the MMBB became more expert in responding to domestic court orders regarding division of assets, including pensions. And, in 1983, the Board determined to provide the divorced spouses of MMBB members with up to two years of medical coverage. The assistance was terminated if the divorced spouse obtained medical coverage through an employer or remarried.[357]

Tax Reform: A Significant Challenge to the Board

In 1984, in one of America's recurring attempts to balance its budget and reduce federal deficits, a federal deficit reduction tax bill was initiated by the US Treasury. The bill proposed a variety of methods to increase federal revenues and to reduce expenses. One of its provisions brought up for reconsideration was the long-standing, tax-free benefit for ordained ministers who lived in provided housing or received housing allowances. If passed, the proposal would have effectively ended the long-standing practice of excluding the value of church-provided housing or a housing allowance from federal income taxation. As a consequence, the proposed reform would also have significantly increased the average minister's federal income tax obligation. It was tracked to be included in a final tax bill that would invoke the reform. In first review, it appeared that the nontaxable provision for housing or housing allowances would be retained after congressional review. The MMBB urged its members to contact their legislators to approve the provisions that would retain it.

As the bill progressed, however, it was reported out of committee still including the proposal to end the tax-free status of provided housing intact, and further, did not include any provision for church, school, or hospital personnel to be considered eligible for the church pension plan. In addition, it placed pressure on the MMBB to provide a defined-benefit plan, rather than variable-annuity plan currently structured by the MMBB. Congress was under a great deal of pressure to deliver a plan radical enough to significantly reduce deficits. On the other hand, it was also heavily lobbied by a variety of special interests to retain favorable provisions and privileges. At a critical point, Congress determined to adopt a "lock-out" strategy, and was presumably sequestered against lobbyists or special interests.

The Church Alliance, reinvigorated for this common cause, had been hard at work attempting to interpret the devastating effect that the loss of tax-excluded status for clergy housing would have on both ministers and churches, as well as the effect of other provisions of the bill under consideration. The "lock down" decision also threatened to prevent them from bringing their concern to the Ways and Means

Committee at a critical time. The MMBB sought the assistance of an American Baptist minister serving in Washington who had a personal connection to Senator Robert Dole, who could assist in arranging a personal entrée to Dole's staff for discussion. He was successful in arranging a hearing, and Church Alliance representatives traveled to Washington, DC, to join him in meeting with Dole's staff members, who were the key to shaping the final form of the tax bill.[358]

In the meeting, staff members were not receptive to the argument that long-standing practice had included the housing tax exclusion. The staff responded that it seemed unfair and constitutionally questionable. Members of the Church Alliance team were effective, however, in conveying the practical reality of clergy and church hardship, and also in educating the staff on the realities of church institutional life as it related to employees of denominational, educational, or medical facilities. In the end, a persuasive point was noted that, by long-standing practice, military personnel also received similar tax exclusion for base housing or government-provided housing allowances. One Church Alliance attorney ultimately carried the day when he requested, "We only ask that you consider ministers in the same category as the military." When the bill was passed, it contained a restored provision of the exclusion of ministerial housing and allowances from taxation. MMBB founder Morehouse would have been pleased that his military analogy to the "old soldiers of the cross" had resulted in persuasive consideration.

The 1986 Tax Reform Bill did have consequences for MMBB plans and programs, however. As one result, all employer sponsored "IRA-type" plans, including the DECA tax-deferred accounts, were terminated at the end of 1986. Other anomalies and problems were addressed in 1988 by several proposals from the Church Alliance to correct them.

Supporting a Ministry of Compassion: HIV/AIDS

The apocalyptic sense of the era predicted by the luncheon speakers early in the decade found one specific expression in the development of HIV/AIDS. Ministers have historically been confronted with the challenge of responding to suffering among disapproved or marginalized populations. And American Baptist churches often reflected predominant middle American social moral values. Therefore, perhaps no social development of the '80s carried a stronger and more lasting impact than the emergence of HIV/AIDS as a health threat, and consequently, a challenge for American Baptist ministers. First identified as a medical challenge in the late 1970s, and emerging as a potential "plague" in the early '80s, HIV/AIDS provoked deep fear and pervasive anxiety, largely because its causes and means of transmission were at first unknown. Its early association with the homosexual or "gay" population quickly cast it as a "gay disease."

Even before that association, however, it represented and inspired a profound fear of an imminent threat. Its emergence had broad implications for ministry and the role of ministers: Some funeral homes refused to provide services to those who died of AIDS, many churches were reluctant to offer their services for funeral services or even a ministry of compassion to the families of AIDS victims, and expressions of compassion for families affected by it were sometimes limited because of its associations. The connection of HIV/AIDS with the gay population was accidental and erroneous. But, before that was known, it served to focus social attitudes toward the gay, lesbian, bisexual, and transgender population of both the nation and its churches. For many church people, especially Baptists, AIDS forced a confrontation between impulses for compassion and deeply entrenched judgmental attitudes.

In the '80s, homosexuality remained the "love that dare not speak its name." In general, the attitudes of the majority of Americans toward homosexuals were either ones of near-violent rejection, extreme denial, or alternatively, of unspoken, uncomfortable tolerance, as long as it was closeted. But HIV/AIDS propelled homosexuality to a national awareness variously condemned by politicians, self-appointed moral leaders, and many preachers. For a minority, it provided an impetus for compassion and greater understanding, and, in the way only a crisis can sometimes do, it empowered LGBT communities to become both more visible and more vocal. Either way, it tapped deep into the national dilemma of dealing with "difference" and created a debate that continued well into the next millennium. During that time, and especially as the origins of the illness and its patterns of transmission became better understood, some people in communities and churches came to realize that it was not only a problem of others, but one that connected with their own communities. As one preacher expressed at one of MMBB's HIV/AIDS seminars, "Compassion for those with AIDS will emerge when it affects their [church members'] grandchildren."[359]

The MMBB perceived the issue as also a matter of crisis for those who were most likely to be in a place of ministry to those who suffered from AIDS, or their families. It was clear that ministers would face personal and social responses that were negative and judgmental toward those who suffered. It was equally clear that ministers were positioned to provide ministries of compassion to AIDS victims, their families, partners and others. They were likely also to be pressured to be mediators in the midst of social and moral conflict. The MMBB, therefore, sought to devise a way to prepare ministers for the challenge ahead. In 1987 it approved a resolution directing MMBB staff to explore ways to assist clergy in their preparation for informed and sensitive pastoral care of persons affected by AIDS.

The staff of the MMBB gathered information and developed workshops about the realities of HIV/AIDS with MMBB staff. It identified pastors with AIDS or who were providing care for AIDS victims. Within the wider ABC/USA, it participated in an Inter-Board Task Force that included all the national Boards and the Ministers Council. In 1988 an AIDS consultation led by Craig Darling was held for MMBB staff members.[360] From that consultation, seminars for clergy were developed, and in 1989 ten such seminars were held throughout the country. In addition, MMBB staff members frequently provided personal counsel, assistance, and support to pastors who were providing pastoral care and support for persons with AIDS and to those close to them, often in the face of severe, negative social and moral judgment.

Providing "Better Maintenance of the Ministry" in Times of Stress

Just as the luncheon addresses by Marty and O'Driscoll had marked the beginning of the decade, so did they also call for the prophetic work in ministry that the time seemed to demand. These addresses defined sharpening edges of ministry in a nation undergoing profound and unnerving change.

In 1985, on what was deemed the twentieth anniversary of the civil rights events of the 1960s, the MMBB Luncheon address at the ABC Biennial in Portland, Oregon, was given by Gardner C. Taylor of Brooklyn's Concord Avenue Baptist Church. Prince of the pulpit, "Dean of American Preachers," compassionate radical, and friend and mentor of Martin Luther King, Jr., Taylor spoke on "Civil Rights Events of the 60s: A Retrospective and Forward Look." It reminded everyone of work still to be done, and Taylor galvanized the audience. He reflected on the progress that had been made in racial relations and equality, and at the same time, remarked on how much remained to be done. Reflecting on a recent preaching tour of South Africa, Taylor noted that the American South of his childhood (though he did not confine it to the South) "was then what South Africa is today." He reminded those present that in the '30s and '40s the US Senate was still debating whether there should be or even could be "anti-lynching legislation in the United States of America."[361]

"If Dr. [Martin Luther] King made a miscalculation," he said, "it was in his optimism about the nation's willingness, once it had placed on its agenda a question which had embarrassed it and from which it suffered untold psychic damage and which it had sought to sweep under the rug."[362] He challenged his audience by continuing, "Some attempt has been made, but you and I know that in no part of the country has Dr. King's vision at Washington been fulfilled, and it hardly bids fair to be fulfilled in our generation." He particularly decried the flaccid support for equal rights for all Americans demonstrated by the then political administration in Washington. "Our problem is still deep. Our journey is still a long one." He noted the rise of the political right and its happy relationship with "the rise of slick television packaging of religious pitchmen for greed and for self-indulgence."

Taylor called the denomination to reclaim its historic commitment to human rights and the fulfillment of the Christian Gospel "in its unmistakable mandate in the area of the liberation of humanity," rather than a "retreat into a pious, non-controversial Christianity, whatever that is." Still, his word was underscored by optimism: "This sad time will pass. Light a candle in the darkness and the darkness will not put it out...." But it was a challenge in no uncertain terms to ministers—and to the denomination—to fulfill the agenda of its destiny, one that he perceived lay in liberation and equality.

By 1987, the marriage of political and religious conservative agendas had become clear. Among Baptists, the association between Southern Baptist leadership and conservative political forces was particularly striking. The Rev. Honorable John H. Buchanan was the speaker at the MMBB luncheon in Pittsburgh, Pennsylvania. Buchanan was a Southern Baptist minister who had served for sixteen years in the US Congress until, in 1980, as he described it, "the Moral Majority beat my brains out in Christian Love."[363] Buchanan's theme was that it was the job of Christians to "lift the life of our society to higher ground."[364] He traced the themes of Baptist history from John Smythe in the 1600s to the 1980s and found that the predominating theme was liberation, justice, and equality before God. He took aim at religious exclusivism and intolerance and asked that people join him in accepting the burden of the problem of world hunger, support for the aspirations of the world's people for freedom and justice, and leadership for civil and human rights. They were items of faith, not politics, he asserted. Therefore, Buchanan called on Baptists to be true to their tradition of defending the voices and rights of others, and to lift their own voices to be heard over all.

In 1989 the luncheon speaker was the newly elected pastor of New York's historic Riverside Church, James A. Forbes. With his Pentecostal background, it was not surprising that Forbes introduced the call of the Holy Spirit toward the coming millennial crossing at the year 2000, still eleven years in the future. He outlined the sobering statistics of what the nation—and its churches—would be like in that year, and called the Baptist leaders to be at work to improve them and to transform them. "People of faith have been taught to believe that significant times will divide up between *chronos* (clock time) and *kairos* (event time)." Forbes was clearly focused on event time and invited those present to join him in working for God's events. "Be assured the event is going to happen!" he reminded them. Without being specific, he exhorted all present that the Holy Spirit was working toward that time, and that Baptist ministers should be working with it.

In 1991 Howard Moody, long-time Board member and former President of the MMBB and long-time pastor of the Judson Memorial Church in New York's Greenwich Village, was the luncheon speaker. As a pastor and friend of Dean Wright, Moody used his address, in part, to reflect on Wright's transformative leadership during his thirty years as Executive Director. It was a remarkable expression of MMBB history, reflecting especially on his own journey with Wright and the thirty years that encompassed the civil rights movement. Moody remembered the vision and work of early MMBB leaders, including Everett Tomlinson. He quoted Tomlinson to say, "Our supreme desire is to see that the deserving are treated justly and generously, and are not compelled to look upon themselves or to be looked upon as in any way receiving charity. The entire work of the Board is based on justice, and not on charity."[365] "That's it," he affirmed. "The basic task of M&M is justice, not charity."

A gentle man with a strong, prophetic voice, Moody marked the future with certainty:

> The Church copied the world at its worst, and we adopted as our own the values of the world of commerce and business with its priorities of competition, growth and profit. As a result, at the end of the twentieth century we are setting up as role models for the Christian community of faith, "mega-churches...."

Instead, Moody offered the models of Christian community that addressed human suffering and need, where the fight for justice and equality was going on, where it was possible to stand with the underdogs and the outcasts, the hated and the despised, and to share fellowship with the economically marginal and struggling. Unfinished agendas of racism and poverty and marginalization provided the examples of his talk. It was clear that Moody had been, if not an architect, then certainly a cheerleader, for the MMBB's advocacy of ministers to serve the lost and the least of the past generation.

At the close of his address, Moody approached the subject most dreaded by American Baptists—and indeed, most Americans at that time: homosexuality. "I need to say, as a pastor whose congregation is at least 25 percent gay and lesbian members, that regardless of where you stand on homosexuality, you must know that the people we are talking about are our gay and lesbian sons and daughters (mostly silent and invisible) struggling against fear and hostility and indifference, hoping to gain their rightful place among us." "They grew up among us," he reminded everyone, "children of God, precious in His sight." They were "brothers and sisters of Jesus, the Christ, and ... with all of us, by the grace and mercy of our Lord, were members of the household of God. That was and is the spiritual legacy we gave them."

And then he called upon the painful judgment of the word of God on those who bore the title of minister:

> And then, along with them—the parents of those "invisible people," suffering silently, looking for pastoral care that was almost never there, bearing their burdens alone, feeling the

isolation and judgment with the words of condemnation that came from every source, including the pulpits of their churches. Where was *their* pastoral care? Who would deal with *their* pain, produced by their ambivalent feelings of alienation and parental love for *their* sons and daughters? Wherever we may stand on this volatile issue, we must understand that we are not dealing with 'outsiders' or 'unofficial representatives.' We are dealing with our spiritual kin—disagree with them.

Despite the mixed reception in applause, Moody sat down in affirmation. He had spoken clearly of the deeply divisive issue within not only American Baptists, but within every religious communion in the nation. Ironically, at the same convention held in Charleston, West Virginia, the ABC/USA voted to reverse its long-standing resolution on homosexuals and their rights, and replace it with a mildly condemnatory statement that pronounced that homosexuality was contrary to the Bible's teaching. Transformation sometimes unfolds slowly.

Mile posts

In 1986 the MMBB observed its seventy-fifth anniversary with a Board review of accomplishments and achievements. In 1987 it published *The Better Maintenance of the Ministry* written by staff member John S. Bone. It was the first official publication of a history of the Board since Tomlinson's history in the early 1930s. Its format narrated a fictional story of a minister's life as he encountered the provisions and programs available through MMBB.[366]

In 1990 Dean R. Wright retired as Executive Director after a service of thirty-six years, twenty-nine of them as Executive Director—the longest service by a decade of any Executive Director in the MMBB's history. He remembered with amusement that when he joined the MMBB, he and Forest Ashbrook had agreed he should work for the Board for "about two years." In addition to his sensitivity to ministry in the midst of change, his era of leadership had overseen the effective shepherding of the Board's assets. On 31 May 1990, at the last Board meeting prior to the end of his leadership, the value of the Consolidated Investment Fund had reached $1,109,207,964.[367] Tracking the statistical comparisons, *Tomorrow* reported that from the beginning of his leadership in 1961 through fiscal year 1989, assets under Wright's management had grown from \$115,693,800 to \$1,120,446,288, nearly a ten-fold increase.[368]

Wright had also managed the transition from a defined-benefit pension plan to a variable-annuity retirement plan, the first denominational pension fund to do so. And even more dramatic than the increase in the aggregate total of funds managed, during his years of service MMBB retirement benefits had increased from \$1,319,360 to \$29,210,404, a nearly twenty-two-fold increase. Non-contractual benefits, including emergency assistance grants, the Medicare Supplement, and subsidies for the Medical Plan, among others, had risen from a little more than \$1 million to more than \$7 million. He had led in the process of re-shaping the original Communion Fellowship Offering to become the RMMO "Thank You Offering." By the end of Wright's term, concluding the nearly eighty years since its founding, the MMBB had achieved success and stability in its core purpose of providing for the financial support of American Baptist ministers in retirement and in need far beyond the imagination of the founders.

At the same time, Wright had expanded and transformed the Board's understanding of the "better maintenance of the ministry" to encompass new levels and circumstances. His leadership began in the era of civil rights, encompassed the economic and social challenges of the '70s, and aggressively enlarged the Board's awareness of marginalized social, racial, ethnic, and gender concerns of the '80s. Under his leadership, the MMBB Board had also moved to provide resources to support ministry in the midst of struggles for civil and human rights, resources to equip ministers to be more effective in their service, and specifically to maintain ministry more sensitively to those with specific needs, most recently and notably people with AIDS. With the possible exception of Morehouse and Tomlinson and their generation, whose efforts to create and establish the Board would be hard to equal, no other MMBB leader had left as strong a mark on the work of the Board.

Wright had continued the tradition of management excellence that had characterized the MMBB from the beginning. Richard Fisher, Chair of the Finance Committee, whom Wright had recruited for the Board, described him as "a visionary with the necessary skills to make the vision real." *Tomorrow* concluded an article recognizing his contribution by saying "His three decades of leadership have reflected skilled management in the use of the Board's resources to meet the needs of its members." Board member Floyd Massey's only complaint about Wright was that "he never stopped long enough for you to thank him."[369] Behind the scenes, he was a lion of a leader yet a truly humble (and shy) man. In public, he always seemed amazed that anyone would find his humor amusing or his insights important. Perhaps he would not have claimed the role, but he had presided over a generation of transformation in the ministry, and over the enhancement of the role and ability of the MMBB to provide support to those engaged in it.

Wright's legacy was ultimately described by board members as one that had developed a high degree of professionalism on the staff, led by his own high standards of personal and professional conduct. He had embraced the pastors of nonwhite, ethnic churches and agencies, and at the same time interacted with the Finance Committee in such a way as to improve benefits for retirees "to the point of amazement by their peers in other denominations." At the same time, he gave unquestioned support to women in ministry, and brought strength, stability, and corporate memory to an often-chaotic denominational structure. He had become, in fact, the unofficial pastor to the entire ABC/USA denominational community.

10

INTO THE NEW MILLENNIUM:
THE END OF THE TWENTIETH CENTURY

A Sense of the Times

"Sometimes," wrote Henry Allen in the *Washington Post*, in late 1999, "being alive in the '90s could verge on thrilling, like watching an acrobat stack impossible objects—a stool, a bicycle, a ball—then stand on top with triumphant hands in the air."[370] The '90s seemed to feature many acrobats; former gridiron magician O.J. Simpson's acquittal after the brutal dagger slaughter of his ex-wife seemed an act of levitation to many. Another was Bill Clinton's improbable choice as Democratic nominee for president and his even more unlikely win against incumbent George Herbert Walker Bush, owner of the most impressive political resume in Washington, not to mention Clinton's deft escape from impeachment. There were the "masters of the universe," the unseen puppeteers of Wall Street, whose gymnastic maneuvers quintupled the Dow Jones average for no reason that anyone could explain, except with words such as "momentum," which was only to say that "it was rising because it was rising." "Irrational exuberance," Federal Reserve Chairman Alan Greenspan called it. But the Dow kept rising in spite of his objections, until after the "tech bubble" burst: then it crashed.

The twentieth century's last decade didn't begin well. First there was the Persian Gulf War, which was over quickly and left unresolved. When it was over, President Bush commented, "People are worried, there has been talk of decline." Didn't he learn anything from Jimmy Carter and his alleged description of America's "malaise?" There was also the Savings and Loan crisis—the worst banking debacle since the Depression. Perhaps indifference and contempt were the only rational responses after all. That, at least, is what the younger generation concluded: "*Whatever*," became its motto.

But America had won the Cold War. Recently liberated East European nations reemerged in new or renewed forms. Congress—and the Media—publicly debated how to spend the resulting "peace dividend." But most people knew how to spend it and bought endless new technological toys like cell phones, Palm Pilots, laptops, and cars with air bags, and less technological pleasures derived from Spandex, latex, and Oakley sunglasses. Ordinary joys seemed humdrum. Who had time for reality? The age of epiphany had ended and the age of the endless download had begun. Daily life was under the spell of virtual-reality computer games, fax machines, MTV, Internet romances, theme parks (including Florida's own "Holy Land"), and new, more efficient jails in which to house the POWs from the War on Drugs.

Women, who had seemed liberated from domestic roles, were oppressed by new expectations: Fashion magazines reminded them they were not thin enough, Martha Stewart implied their homes were not perfect enough, and the TV talk shows—from Jerry Springer to Oprah Winfrey—reminded them that their relationships were not good enough. And men? "Manliness," as Teddy Roosevelt had glorified it a century earlier, was now a politically incorrect concept, and anyway, no one seemed to know how to do manhood anymore. So men set their jaws and steadied their gazes, and whether they were stars of the boardroom, the courtroom, the hospital, or a construction project, they discovered that bureaucracy kept them from commanding respect, regardless of the nature of their walk or their talk.

Despite American successes, Bush the Elder had been right: there *was* talk of decline, both personal and public. It seemed like everyone was searching for renewed vitality. Maybe it was because we were older. By the end of the '90s, the median American age was 36. It had been 30 in 1980 and only 23 in 1900. Or maybe it was just a lost sense of perspective. Anxiety was prevalent, but there really wasn't much to be anxious about. For a previous generation, "Commies" had at least described a real and historically identifiable threat—if only with paranoid ambiguity. Now anxieties were focused on imagined plots devised by mysterious committees that were responsible for super governments or the globalization that would erode American culture, or the "loss of family values." *They* were weakening American moral strength. But who were the *they* who were masterminding these plots?

There was no "Establishment," no bohemian fringe, no avant-garde phalanx to despise. But there were a few notable personalities. For some, Hillary Clinton loomed as a woman of unseemly and, therefore, dangerous ambition. Was she a Calvinist Eva Perón, or more of a Catholic Our Lady of Personal, Perpetual Sorrow, "with nobility that sprang from a refusal to do anything about them?"[371] Later, many realized that her refusal was not rooted in sorrow, but in having bigger fish to fry. Without the external threat of global communism, external threats became personalized: Slobodan Milosevic, Saddam Hussein, Moammar Gadhafi, Osama bin Laden—these were the people who might be responsible for a major Armageddon.

Neither were there any towering icons of cultural change: no Elvis Presley, no young John Lennon to replace the martyred one, no Jack Kerouac or even an Ernest Hemingway to galvanize a generation; there were no authors who outraged and confronted. Music and publishing were again under the presumed-to-be responsible control of the industries that represented them. Even rap artists stopped advocating the assassination of policemen, and the ones who blatantly demeaned women were quietly and persistently marginalized. No one advocated the overthrow of the government. Instead, the Million Man March, mostly black men, descended on Washington's Mall seeking personal hope and possibilities, and The Promise Keepers, a mixed-race group of men, rallied at Washington's RFK Stadium seeking to restore manly moral purpose and practice.

Sex, America's enduring taboo obsession, was still a popular pastime, and articles about improving, developing, and perfecting it displaced articles about sewing in women's magazines. Men were expected to "improve their performance," and Viagra rejuvenated the erotic lives of some. But an article in the *New York Observer* proposed, "They love sex, but not as much as they love their Prozac. Forced to choose between designer drugs and prowess in the boudoir, the most fashionably medicated people go for the drug every time." Maybe it was because there was no equivalent of Clark Gable for women to idealize, no Marilyn Monroe for men. Or maybe they were just worn out from multitasking.

In religion, newly empowered conservative evangelicals worshiped with praise bands and took up formerly prohibited pastimes like dancing, wine, and appreciation for personal sensual pleasures. Traditional Christian institutions continued to decline while small- and medium-sized churches struggled against the forces of demographic, cultural, and community changes. Diminished in strength, many of those churches lost their voices. Megachurches continued to grow, but their appeal was geographically and culturally bounded. Rick Warren's Saddleback Church rose, while New York's Riverside Church barely held steady with a Pentecostal preacher with liberal politics. In Houston, Joel Osteen took over his late father's religious enterprise and, as pastor of his stadium church-without-a-creed, projected an infectious positivism that seemed utterly devoid, perhaps charmingly so, of theological content. On-screen community and personal purpose—they were apparently the magic formula.

The MMBB: Understanding the New Reality

The previous MMBB era had been one of transformation. Dean Wright had retired to choruses of admiration, appreciation, and affection. But both the world and the MMBB had changed between 1961, when Dean Wright had assumed leadership of the MMBB, and his 1990 retirement. It was clear that the previous thirty years had been a time of unprecedented growth and development of the MMBB's ability to fulfill its core mission of providing retirement resources for ministers. But it was also characterized by an expansion of MMBB programs in response to issues of civil rights, human rights, opportunities for women, and ministry in the context of broad social, and lifestyle changes. The Board's support of these nonfinancial programs to enlarge a prophetic ministry and encourage the general competence of ministers had, in some cases, been in response to Wright's vision. Others had been in response to the mandates established by the General Board of the ABC/USA. Regardless of the origins of change, 1990 marked the end of an era that was defined by an ever-enlarging definition of the "better maintenance of ministry."

Wright's lengthy service had generally been harmonious, but it had not been without criticism. Conservative members among the denomination's constituency felt that some of the MMBB's programs were too liberal or too aggressive. For examples, the perception that it was the Executive Director who had advocated for the role of women in ministry, and the perception that Wright and much of the Board were sympathetic to homosexuality were especially uncomfortable for some. Others, in the retrospect that the passage of time enables, focused on two areas where his leadership had led to a need for correction. One was that Wright's more broadly focused program approach had diluted the core mission of the MMBB's role in providing benefits, and that the cost of those programs risked diluting MMBB assets. The other was that Wright had not been attentive enough to preserving the functional independence of the Board in its relationship to the ABC/USA. The two, in fact, were related.

Wright could not be held solely responsible for carrying out denominational programs that were assigned to the MMBB. Even most of those who originally resisted the demands of the civil rights movement ultimately agreed that he and the Board had been both courageous and correct in leading American Baptists to be on the side of moral right. Still, some recognized that many of the programs that were assigned to the MMBB were made necessary because the MMBB had lost some of its independence by becoming more fully integrated with denominational priorities. Wright had begun his leadership in the early '60s by resisting denominational attempts to directly supervise some aspects of Board activity, notably bylaw revision.[372] Wright had also resisted some requests for funding assistance that he believed exceeded the Board's legal and fiduciary responsibility. But to some it appeared that at the point of the SCODS reorganization of the ABC/USA in the early 1970s, he had simply "let it happen," and, thus, was responsible for the broadening of Board responsibility into areas not related to its core purpose and for the loss of control of Board member selection.

On that basis, some perceived then, and others later, that it was important to rebalance the MMBB's priorities. The need for transition was also demanded by the impact of a number of social, economic, and professional trends that converged to impact the MMBB's continued service. Some of those forces threatened the MMBB's membership growth curve. They included the continued weakening of American Baptist churches in general and ABC organizations in particular, a desire among many MMBB members to exercise greater choice and greater control over the investment of their accounts, competition from a growing number of financial service programs and organizations that pursued the potential profit in managing the pension accumulations of ministers, and the developing challenges of national and global economic trends. In a short time, the MMBB reviewed the obstacles it faced and as a result gave renewed, almost exclusive priority to its core purpose of providing retirement benefits.

Some of the contrasts between the eras are striking. For example, the tenure of the previous Executive Director, Dean Wright, was the

MMBB's longest; the tenure of his successor, Gordon Smith, was the shortest. Gordon Smith and his successor, Sumner Grant, were already mature and experienced leaders when they began their service, in contrast to the relative youthfulness of their most recent predecessors, Wright and Ashbrook. In addition, the succession planning that had characterized the MMBB's previous management transition was less clear, first in the choice of Smith and later Grant, as Executive Directors. In part this appears to have been due to the more complex relationship between the MMBB and the American Baptist Churches that had resulted from the SCODS denominational restructuring in the '70s. By drawing MMBB closer to the operations of the denomination and creating a stronger linkage between it and the office of the General Secretary, it allowed both the temptation and the opportunity for the General Secretary of ABC/USA to attempt more directly to influence the choice of candidates to head the MMBB.

In an ironic contrast, though, the MMBB had been drawn closer to the denomination after 1990, when the boards and agencies of the denomination were less able to provide support and resources to the MMBB. Instead, by then they more frequently requested aid or support from the MMBB, especially regarding subsidies for employees' retirement and medical premiums. This subtle shift had two results: it elevated an awareness of the MMBB's economic independence and, therefore, its comparative economic strength in contrast to other American Baptist organizations. Ultimately that disparity affected the exclusivity of MMBB's relationship with the American Baptists. The MMBB had begun as a Northern, and later American Baptist organization. More, it was chartered as a church-related plan related to the Northern/American Baptist organizations. That heritage was highly valued, and everyone assumed the MMBB would always be heavily invested in the American Baptist Churches, USA.

However, the passage of time had modified functioning relationships. Even within the ethos of the MMBB as an organization, contrasts with past operational priorities became apparent. From the beginning, the MMBB's service to clientele had been defined in highly personal terms. But as the twentieth century ended, it became clear that future success would be better achieved by efficiency and growth. Rapidly developing technologies of communications and information retrieval opened new opportunities for the Board's effectiveness.

Economic realities made growth of membership and the retention and growth of assets imperative. To accomplish both goals, the MMBB ultimately realized it had to move from being an organization that primarily served individuals to one that primarily served employers. And it realized that the varieties of employers needed to multiply.

Other significant contrasts became clear in the transition: The last decade of the twentieth century had been increasingly exciting, with the dawning of the new millennium and its possibilities. By comparison, the first decade of the twenty-first century was a deeply anxious time with rapidly emerging global social, political, and economic crises. As with every transitional age, it was clear that major changes were ahead. It was just not always so clear what the end result would be, and some of that ambiguity may have affected the Board's choice of executive leadership.

MMBB Executive Leadership

The Board's first and most pressing business following Wright's retirement was to elect a successor—something they had not had to do for thirty years. Under the terms of the relationship between the MMBB and the ABC/USA subsequent to the SCODS reforms, a committee of the MMBB was prescribed to "advise" the General Secretary in the choice of a successor to the Executive Director. Unlike most prior executive leadership transitions at the MMBB in which it was only necessary to gain the approval of the ABC/USA for the appointment of an Executive Director, the path of succession this time was not entirely clear. It was especially uncertain because the ABC/USA had itself undergone a change in the Office of General Secretary and was adjusting to major leadership style changes under Daniel Weiss's leadership.

The 1990 MMBB's leadership choice included several able candidates. Because of the MMBB's decade-old advocacy for women, there was general speculation that the next MMBB leader might be female. Margaret Cowden, who had led the Women in Ministry programs in the early '80s and later became MMBB Deputy Executive Director, was assumed to be the likely choice. Cowden possessed strong leadership and financial management credentials, had completed the Harvard management program that had become a preferred credential for MMBB senior management. She was broadly perceived to be Dean Wright's choice to succeed him. The search committee itself perceived that she was the "heir apparent," and she was, in the words of one contemporary staff member, "already wired in—a done deal." Nevertheless, it was Gordon Smith, MMBB's Treasurer, who was proposed by the MMBB's Advisory Search Committee and was ultimately the candidate proposed by the ABC/USA General Secretary.[373]

Smith's selection represented the first occasion of clear deviation from what appeared to be the succession choice of the Executive Director. Why that was the case is not entirely clear. One senior management officer recalled that during the search process for a new Executive Director, Wright had queried him whether he preferred Smith or Cowden.[374] Whether Wright ultimately changed his mind, or whether he had privately conferred with many members of the senior staff and Board members about the choice, is unknown.[375] It is also possible that the Board itself recognized the necessity of a different direction, and was concerned that Cowden might continue to move in directions established by Wright. What is significant, however, is that on this occasion the MMBB's leadership succession plan wavered in execution.[376]

Gordon Smith had joined the MMBB in 1975 as Assistant Treasurer and was elected Treasurer in 1977. He became Deputy Executive Director in 1986 in addition to his position as MMBB Treasurer. He was a graduate of Sioux Falls College and the American Baptist Seminary of the West. Like his predecessor, he had completed the Advanced Management Program at Harvard University. In addition to his management roles at the MMBB, Smith's resume included service as an administrator at two American Baptist seminaries: the American Baptist Seminary of the West (Berkeley, California), and Central Baptist Seminary (Kansas City, Missouri). He had also been Director of Education and Development for the Baptist Hospital Fund, Inc., of St. Paul, Minnesota, which sponsored and supported the Midway and Mounds Park hospitals.

At MMBB, Smith's specific responsibilities had included the preparation and management of the annual budget, analysis of income and conformity to requirements for the General and Permanent funds and the benefit plans. He was also responsible for the promotion and distribution of the RMMO (Retired Ministers and Missionaries Offering). Upon Smith's appointment as Executive Director, MMBB Chairman John Reed reflected upon the significance of the loss of Dean Wright, but said, "We look forward with confidence to Gordon Smith's leadership." He especially emphasized the value of Smith's long-term presence and experience with the MMBB and the ABC/USA. Almost immediately, in reviewing both the MMBB's operation and the emergent changes it faced, Smith asserted that it was imperative to establish clear organizational boundaries between the MMBB and the ABC/USA. His selection, therefore, initiated what was ultimately a decisive course correction for the MMBB's operating goals and processes.

By both length and achievements, former Executive Director Dean Wright's administration had achieved iconic status. But in the opinion of some, he had agreed too eagerly to MMBB's subservience to the ABC/USA. In reflection some years later, one Board leader commented that Wright had "almost given away the store" in reference to his passion for expanding MMBB's emphases beyond its more specific goals to provide for retirement, disability, or health concerns for ministers.[377] Smith admired and appreciated Wright and had worked closely with him, but upon assuming responsibility as Executive Director he sought to refine and refocus more specifically the core mission of the MMBB. Philosophically, Smith believed that while the MMBB was created to serve American Baptist ministers and churches, it served best and most securely with a strong wall between them. Over time, increasing attention to legal concepts such as "ascending liability" and concern for the ability to perform the Board's fiduciary responsibility supported his view.

In 1992 Smith led the Board to engage Brennan Associates, a Philadelphia-area consulting firm, to help identify strategies to increase the MMBB's effectiveness. One immediate and practical outgrowth was a decision to install a new computer system to replace the original, thirty-year-old system that was increasingly unable to perform its needed functions. It was a first, but important, step in an ongoing reliance upon technology to perform its functions.

In 1993 the Board adopted a revised mission statement:

> To manage entrusted resources for the benefit of ministers, missionaries and lay employees who have served American Baptists Churches/USA, and their dependents, to administer lifetime benefits and services with efficiency, compassion and justice, and to promote interest in the better maintenance of the ministry.[378]

In 1994 Smith emphasized administrative efficiency with a focus on customer service as a primary goal for the staff and articulated five steps to achieve that goal. The steps included: better service to members, increased personal contact, integration of functions, reduction of redundancy, and the establishment of performance standards for the staff and its individual members.

Significantly missing from the new goals was a rationale for programs of outreach and the support programs of advocacy, education, or preparation that had characterized aspects of the MMBB's mission for the preceding generation. As concrete examples of the implications of the new direction, in 1994 the Ministers' Council, the Women in Ministry, and the Career Development programs were transferred to the (ABC) Board of Educational Ministries and located for administration at the Mission Center at Valley Forge. MMBB funds were made available in some cases to ease the transfer and to provide ongoing support for the individual programs.[379] The proposed creation of a National Commission on the Ministry was the public impetus for the transfer of these programs. That commission comprised representatives from several ABC boards and agencies with a variety of concerns for professional qualification, development, personal support, and advocacy for ministers' personal and professional needs and fellowship.

As he charted this sea change in performance goals, Smith did not hesitate to recognize that it was a departure from some of the MMBB's more recent directions. He strongly affirmed Dean Wright's leadership and his development of a strong and competent staff. But he also suggested that until the 1990s, a broad interpretation of the MMBB charter had encouraged the Board to become involved in too many programs under the broad banner of "better maintenance of the ministry." And, he suggested, since the SCODS reforms of the early '70s, the ABC/USA had increasingly sought to view the MMBB as a program board. Many of the programs or initiatives the MMBB had been encouraged to undertake, he reflected, were related to ministry and to ministers, but, in Smith's view, they were not directly related to providing benefits for the security and protection of ministers and their dependents.

As a result, in 1994 Smith suggested that "our energies and financial resources often became diffused in issues and programs unrelated to employee benefits." He observed that M&M's financial resources had become "the deep pocket for the growing needs of The Ministers Council, Women in Ministry, Career Development Centers and, to a lesser extent, certain other programs."[380] Smith's summary consistently asserted his belief that "the human resources we diverted to programs may have caused us to lag behind in the development of a more efficient system of delivering benefits." He concluded that "although we will continue to be involved in issues critical to clergy, at the appropriate time those programs will be discontinued or transferred to a Program Board." It served notice that the MMBB's mission was both bigger and more legally defined than a denominationally directed role and, by implication, that the MMBB was not a program board. That perspective continued to guide his administration.

Smith exhibited a new dedication to the efficiencies available through the greater use of technology, especially including the new computer system, which became fully operational in 1996. Communication was also significantly enhanced by the use of the then-new telephone toll-free numbers for medical and dental questions, and the use of imaging technology to quickly review members files. These new tools led the way for changes in personnel administration and assignment. As one example, in 1993, upon the retirement of Terry L. Burch, Associate Executive Secretary responsible for services in the West, the Oakland, California, MMBB office was closed and an 800 number instituted for direct connection to the New York and Valley Forge offices. Burch continued to serve as Representative-at-Large, operated a limited office from his home, and continued to represent the MMBB on the Western Commission on the Ministry at conferences and in special assignments in order to ease the transition.[381]

Other changes included training for both executive and service staff to broaden their knowledge and skills and, thus, increase MMBB's capability to respond quickly and efficiently to members' questions and concerns. In order to reduce the bureaucratization that threatened to advance in the new administrative structure, the Board also approved the implementation of cross-functional teams in order to create a sense of interdependence and to expand the value of individual expertise. A key aspect of the new personnel administration was the establishment of performance standards for executives and the support staff they supervised. The result was to establish strong staff goal orientation with quantifiable measurements to gauge progress and achievement. In order to assure the ability to attract and retain competent staff members in several positions, Smith sought to establish an independent role for the MMBB in staff selection and compensation.

Smith's determination to refocus the MMBB on its core mission had several implications, not least of which was the goal to develop greater independence to achieve its goals. For example, a pragmatic result of the MMBB's status as an affiliated Board of the ABC/USA since the early 1970s was that it was required to conform to the denomination's personnel position descriptions and salary grid. This had proven to be detrimental to the Board's ability to attract and retain staff members with the financial expertise and professional skills required to advance the MMBB's program. MMBB argued that was especially the case in the New York City labor market, where expected staff salaries in general, and compensation for those with financial expertise in particular, consistently exceeded the salary guidelines of the ABC/USA.

Early in his tenure, therefore, Smith established the goal of achieving greater prerogative for the Board in matters of determining position descriptions and establishing staff compensation, and diminished any expectation of the Board as a provider of programs other than those that supported its core mission. At a 1993 meeting in San Diego, California, Smith, Dick Fisher, Mary Purcell, John Reed, and MMBB's legal counsel began to strategize ways to more clearly define the MMBB's independence and autonomy. In 1994 Smith opened conversations with leaders of the ABC/USA on the specific matter of staff description and compensation. He was strongly supported by long-term Board President John Reed and incoming Board President Mary Purcell, both of whom actively participated in the discussions and negotiations with ABC/USA officials.

It was the dawn of an especially litigious era, and Smith, Reed, Purcell, and their associates effectively established the legal importance of building a wall of protection to guard against the legal concept of "ascending liability," a doctrine by which it was possible that the MMBB's resources could become exposed to legal action against the ABC/USA. They also emphasized the reality of "fiduciary responsibility," the requirement that the MMBB Board's chief responsibility was to effectively manage and protect assets in its care. It was a contentious time, but the ultimate outcome was the freedom for the MMBB to establish its own descriptions of position responsibility and, even more important, its own salary guidelines. It was a first step in claiming a new and more independent direction.

Other Leadership Changes

Leadership transition also redefined Board leadership. In 1991, Richard B. Fisher announced his retirement as Chairman of the Board's Finance Committee, a position he had held for eighteen of his almost thirty years of service to the MMBB.[382] As a universally acclaimed leader in the investment world, his insights had clearly contributed to the considerable financial advances of the Board's assets during his tenure. Fisher remained on the Board until 1998. Meanwhile, C. Oscar Morong was appointed Chair of the Finance Committee.[383] In 1993 J.P. Person also retired as the Board's legal counsel, ending a thirty-eight-year service in that role, which began in 1955 while M. Forest Ashbrook was Executive Director.

In 1994 John Reed, who had served several terms on the Board from 1965 to 1994, and three terms as President of the Board (1967–74, 1982–85, and 1988–94) became ineligible for reelection. Reed's wisdom and wit, as well as his confident leadership style and skill, had greatly enhanced his leadership through both challenging and smooth times.[384] Reed was succeeded by Mary Purcell, the first woman President of the MMBB, whose leadership, honed by years at the helm of several national, nonprofit organizations, enabled an effective Board leadership transition.[385] Purcell strongly supported Smith's vision for greater independence for the MMBB and provided strong leadership in achieving them.

Howard Moody, who had served on the Board nearly congruent with Reed's service, retired from the Board in 1996. Moody had served three terms (1964–73, 1980–87, and 1989–96), with terms as President (1986–87) and as Vice President (1983–84 and 1994–96). Moody's sensitivity to social justice, especially the rights of the socially and economically marginalized, had greatly informed and sensitized the Board and its priorities. His insights and experience had specifically contributed to the Board's navigation through the turbulent years of civil rights, economic dislocation, developing opportunities for women, and, more recently, the controversy regarding homosexuals and sexual difference present in many churches.

Among the staff, Richard Huber, Associate Executive Director, brought his lengthening MMBB résumé to focus on issues of compliance with federal and state regulations—an increasingly critical concern. A few staff additions began to reflect the new emphasis of expertise rather than American Baptist affiliation. For one example, James Keegan, neither an ordained minister nor an American Baptist, but who possessed a significant résumé in management, some in financial service organizations, joined the staff in 1998. He initially shared the responsibilities of Coordinator of Member Assistance with Holly Bean.

Benefits

During the '80s and '90s MMBB assets had risen remarkably: the value of the accumulation units for active members had effectively quadrupled during the '80s from $22.73 per share in 1980 to $88.70 in 1989, and then doubled again by 1997.[386] The more conservatively invested Annuity Unit values for retired members doubled between 1988 ($31.06) and 1998 ($63.72). Since the inception of the variable-annuity strategy of the plan, accumulation unit values for active members in the Retirement Plan had increased seven-fold. It had exceeded the cost of living significantly during the previous twenty-five years, even including the high inflation and discouraging investment performance of the '70s. Therefore, as the Retirement Plan had continued to perform effectively in building retirement resources during the '80s, especially, it continued to function without fundamental change and produced strong returns during much of the '90s as well.

For the most part, recent changes to the Retirement Plan and Death Benefit Plan were, therefore, adjustments and expansions. In the early 1990s, the most significant changes were primarily focused on more liberal definitions of eligibility for individuals or the inclusion of categories ministers not previously qualified. And, in response to member interest, a variety of ways in which members could exercise flexibility in the use of their resources were also introduced. In part, these changes reflected growing pressure from members for personal control, and were also in response to growing competition from commercial alternatives that threatened to entice MMBB members to abandon MMBB to pursue alternative retirement strategies.

As examples, in 1991 a level-income option was adopted for those who desired or needed to retire early. That option allowed for those over the age of 55 to begin receiving a disproportionately large annuity before they were qualified to receive a Social Security benefit. Following that period the annuity level was adjusted to reflect the addition of Social Security benefits after the individual qualified for them.[387] In 1994 members were offered the option to annuitize 80 percent of their MMBB account at retirement and either to withdraw or defer decision on up to 20 percent of their account amount. By 1997, members could choose to annuitize only 50 percent of their accumulation units, leaving the balance to be invested for future withdrawals or eventual conversion to an annuity.

In 1993 Board decided to re-allocate the 1 percent of salary portion of the premium previously allocated to the TAS-D accounts to apply, instead, to the members' Retirement Plan accounts, an action that effectively consolidated the two accounts. In 1994 in deference to increasing life expectancy, the mortality assumptions for calculating annuity unit values adjusted, thus bringing the financial health of the funds supporting the annuities of retired members into prudent balance.

In 1995 eligibility for the Retirement Plan, Death Benefit Plan, and the Annuity Supplement was expanded to include those receiving compensation for nineteen or more hours per week of work related to any Baptist church or organization recognized by the ABC/USA General Board as cooperating with, associated with, or otherwise appropriately related to the denomination. This expansion allowed the plan inclusion of part-time church staff members, including lay workers, staff members of denominational or other organizational structures, and also potentially the staff members of denominationally related schools, colleges, or programs. However, this category of clients was not eligible for non-contractual benefits.[388] This was a first step that made later expansion of MMBB services, and, therefore, much of its future growth, possible.

Also in 1995 the Board determined that the annuity unit payout for the following year would be the highest of the average of the annuity unit values for the six months ending September 30, adjusted for mortality experience, or the actual unit value on the same date, or 95 percent of the annuity unit payout value then in effect. This decision was intended to protect annuitants from a drop in annuity income greater than 5 percent in any given year.[389]

Later, effective in 1998, the percentage of the Retirement/Death Benefit premium allocated to members' Retirement Plan accounts increased from 12.5 percent to 13 percent by reducing the amounts directed to the Special Benefits Fund and the Death Benefit Plan. In other actions, eligibility for the death benefit for retired members was based on fifteen-plus years of active membership in the Retirement Plan instead of twenty-plus years, and the amount of the death benefit for retired members was raised to $4,000 from $2,000. At the same time, the allowance for children of disabled members who were under the age of 21 was raised from $1,000 to $2,000, and the income for disability members was adjusted annually by an amount determined by the percentage of increase or decrease in the average annual compensation of American Baptist ministers.

In 1996, following a favorable IRS tax letter ruling, the Board determined that "non-steeple" (nonchurch or non-church-related) employers could participate in the Retirement Plan at a reduced rate of contribution (that is, at a participation rate lower than the 16 percent of compensation required for the ABC Retirement Plan) as negotiated individually in contracts.[390] Also in 1996, the Small Business Job Protection Act confirmed that self-employed ministers could be eligible to participate in MMBB benefit plans. The resulting extension of services to such individuals, who were categorized as "Wandering Ministers," an increasing ministry category, also opened a new opportunity for MMBB growth. That category included self-employed ministers engaged in specialized ministries such as pastoral counseling, program development, consultation, or other ministerial services, as well as institutional and military chaplains and those engaged in ministry functions sponsored by for-profit organizations. As a result, such persons could participate in the Retirement Plan/Death Benefit Plan and could also make tax-deductible contributions to 403(b) accounts such as TAS.

Additionally, the same Act affirmed that no Social Security taxes would be owed on pension benefits taken as housing allowance by retired clergy. This ruling brought a practical extension of pension value to retired persons, sometimes protecting as much as 100 percent of pension payments from federal taxation, and also provided a persuasive reason for active members to remain with the MMBB rather than to be enticed by another investment program. Pre-retired members were permitted to designate nonspousal beneficiaries, with the consent of a spouse.[391] Also in the spirit of flexibility, TAS contributions were shifted to allow quarterly opportunities for changes to contributions instead of the previous annual schedule.

Benefits: The Particular Challenge of the Medical/Dental Plan

The encouraging financial experience that undergirded the prosperous functioning of the Retirement Plan and Death Benefit Plan during the '80s and '90s, however, did not extend to the Medical/Dental Plan. Over several decades, the economics and delivery of health care had increasingly become a financial concern for the MMBB as, indeed, it was becoming for the American public. For several decades MMBB's efforts to maintain costs had been frustrated. Much earlier, in 1976, the MMBB had terminated its contract with Travelers Insurance Company in an effort to maintain effective coverage at lower cost. However, health care premium costs continued to rise exponentially in the '80s. In 1983 and 1984, especially, members were required to bear significantly higher premium costs and deductible expenses for health insurance, despite the effective subsidy of MMBB administration of the Health Plan.

In 1986 MMBB's Margaret Cowden had led a team of staff members to produce, in consultation with the Board, the "M&M White Paper on Medical Care and Cost," with sobering conclusions.[392] To better understand these growing trends in medical and dental care that increasingly impacted the MMBB, Dr. John M. Burns, Vice President of Health Management, Honeywell, Inc., was invited to address the Board on "The Crisis in United States' Health Care Delivery System" at the November 1990 Board meeting.[393] To underline this growing crisis in spite of MMBB vigilance and attention, in 1989 the Board had needed to transfer $1,313,653 from the Permanent Funds as a reserve for the Medical/Dental Plan. Even so, by 1990, the medical/dental premium increase was only able to be limited to an "affordable" 14.5 percent by means of an MMBB subsidy.

By the early '90s, future long-term health-cost projections were truly alarming. During much of its experience in providing health care, and extending over many years, the MMBB had established premium costs at levels significantly lower than anticipated actual costs. In addition the Board provided assistance for medical expenses for members receiving low compensation. Subsidies had been drawn from several sources, including the Permanent Fund. Without such assistance, premiums would have risen even more rapidly, likely exceeding the financial abilities of many members. The annual financial shortfall, however, was still growing, and these practices could not be sustained without threatening the long-term financial health of the MMBB. In 1990, for example, the Board authorized a transfer of $2 million from the Death Benefit Plan to the Medical/Dental Plan after being advised by its actuary that the Death Benefit Plan was overfunded. In 1993 the Board again approved a transfer of $3,228,133 from the Death Benefit Plan to subsidize Medical/Dental premiums. Such infusions could not be continued.

Therefore, in 1991, in order to contain rising costs, the Board determined that annuitants born after 1908 would be required to share in the premium of the MMBB Medicare Supplement. In 1993 the MMBB established the practice of monthly rather than quarterly billing in order to increase cash flow.[394] The Board also actively pursued administrative strategies to reduce premiums in certain categories. As one example, a regional rating structure was implemented for both traditional policies and the experimental managed care policies that were currently being explored. In that case, the membership was divided into three regions evaluated to be low-, high-, or average-cost medical expense areas and were charged greater or lesser amounts for the premiums, depending on the region of the member's residence.

In the early '90s, the MMBB had explored health care programs with other denominations and organizations who were members of the Church Alliance, hoping to find a way to create or adapt medical coverage for religious workers in several denominations or organizations in a unified program. Further, they had hoped that greater critical mass resulting from the participation of several religious organizations combined might result in lower premiums. However, a variety of legal barriers, differing expectations, and several organizational impracticalities caused that effort to collapse in 1992. Following that, the MMBB switched its medical consultants from Coopers and Lybrand to the firm of Towers Perrin in 1993 to pursue additional possibilities.

In 1994 the Board had initiated a pilot program of managed medical and dental care in selected areas, administered by CIGNA. The results were promising enough that CIGNA was authorized to offer a Managed Care program for the Medical/Dental Plan on a national basis in locations where there were at least ten members and a CIGNA managed care network. Results were promising enough that in 1995 CIGNA was given responsibility for the administration and processing of all ABC Medical and Dental Plan claims.

One underlying cause of the specific health care dilemma for the MMBB was that, for many years, the steady drain of the plan's younger and healthier members to other health insurance opportunities and options had caused the MMBB plan to serve an increasingly older and sicker clientele. One reason for this phenomenon was that the membership base was both aging and diminishing, partly as the result of cheaper options available to many members. For example, increasing numbers of clergy spouses had careers that provided them with health benefits that could extend to family members at relatively low cost. Both trends had an adverse effect on the MMBB claims experience. As one result, estimates projected a cumulative loss for the Medical/Dental Plan of $6.6 million by the end of 1998, and similar estimates also suggested that annual increases of between 13 percent for managed care policies and 15 percent for traditional coverage would be required in order to meet obligations between 1996 and 2000. By 1996 nearly a third of MMBB's endowment fund income was already being used to subsidize health care costs. And, if the trend continued, MMBB Medical/Dental reserves, already supplemented by transfers from the Death Benefit funds, would be exhausted by the first quarter of 1998.[395]

Therefore, in May 1996, after much deliberation, the Board determined to close the ABC Medical and Dental Plan.[396] Most immediately and critically, the decision was precipitated because the Medical Plan administrator, CIGNA, indicated its intention to terminate its services to the MMBB because the MMBB was not compliant with the Multiple Employer Welfare Arrangement (MEWA). Under the requirements of MEWA, the MMBB would have been required to gain approval from a number of individual state regulatory agencies in order to continue its Medical/Dental Plan. The legal and administrative costs of that process were deemed prohibitive. In making its decision, the Board initially believed that most members would have easy access to other programs and policies. In terminating the ABC Medical/Dental Plan, the Board also explored several options by which it might be able to subsidize members who participated in other plans.

However, it soon became clear that a medical plan was urgently needed by many of MMBB's members, especially those who had no alternative access to other medical care programs, or who had prior existing conditions that prevented them from finding affordable coverage. The Board determined that while it might not be feasible to manage its own health care program under current circumstances, it was still possible to sponsor a medical plan without actually operating it themselves. One key was the creation of a trust which could be funded by premium payments and which would act on the members' behalf with an administrator serving to manage the medical insurance programs. Having established such a trust as a pre-requisite, in November 1996 the MMBB sponsored a plan with the national Trustmark Insurance Company for active members and with the ITT Hartford Insurance Company for annuitants who qualified for Medicare. In addition, it selected Kirke–Van Orsdel, Inc., as a third-party administrator for the Insured Plan. The Board passed several resolutions that authorized and enabled the service of the two insurance providers effective in 1997 under the MMBB's sponsorship.[397] It was an imperfect solution—but a necessary one under the legal and financial circumstances.[398]

In a further refinement, in 1996 the Board determined that for widowed spouses and dependent children of members who died subsequent to 1 January 1997, the MMBB would pay the full cost of the premium for Trustmark health insurance, or a plan with similar benefits, provided that they had been previously covered under the member's Medical and Dental Plans. Disabled members not yet eligible for Medicare received coverage with Trustmark or any other plan with similar provisions. Likewise, Retirement Plan and Death Benefit Plan members who were age 55 or older as of 31 December 1996 would receive a premium subsidy in retirement; the MMBB also proposed to provide disabled persons not yet eligible for Medicare with full payment of the Trustmark Health Insurance, or a policy with similar provisions. Medicare-eligible persons and spouses would receive a premium subsidy of $52.50 per month (reduced to $50 in 1999). Retired persons and qualified spouses under the age of 65 and not Medicare eligible received a subsidy of $107.50 (reduced to $100 in 1999). By these means the Board sought to ease the medical expense burdens imposed by the escalating health insurance costs.

In consideration of lengthening life spans that sometimes resulted in the need for long-term care, the Board endorsed the long-term care insurance policies provided by GEGA for employees of ABC/USA and related organizations in 1999.[399] Meanwhile, federal legislation removed the obstacle for church-based pension boards to operate medical plans without individual state regulation. Therefore, in 2002, the MMBB returned to CIGNA for its range of medical/dental insurance coverage, but continued the supplemental insurance for Medicare eligible retired members through the Hartford Insurance Company.[400] Nothing, however, effectively mediated the rising costs of medical care for ministers and their families, and those costs became an increasing challenge for church budgets and ministerial compensation.

Non-Contractual Benefits and Other Programs

Because the ABC/USA largely comprised churches of modest size and budget, for nearly a generation the MMBB had resourced a program of salary support for pastors of qualifying churches. The Salary Support Program had proved partially effective, but a significant number of churches receiving support ultimately failed to achieve or sustain their financial goals. Thus, one unintended result was that the program artificially supported financially marginal churches for extended periods. To review this growing problem, in 1987, the MMBB had engaged in consultation with the Regional Executive Ministers Council, which in turn created a task force to review the program's effectiveness for churches participating in its more than twenty-year-old Salary Support program. After a lengthy consultation and review, the MMBB decided to phase out the Salary Support Program and replace it with a Strategic Premium Assistance effort, effective in 1993. This shift allowed the MMBB to provide assistance to a greater variety of churches, especially those with high-growth potential, or to pastors of churches in strategic locations or with strategic ministries. It was a program seemingly more consistent with maintenance of the ministry while still supporting the goal of encouraging and sustaining churches.

Communications

During the rapid and often dramatic changes of the 1990s, MMBB publications frequently provided information to pastors to help interpret and become better aware of benefits. In addition, benefits seminars were reaffirmed to assist ministers who were considering retirement. The MMBB also more regularly surveyed its members, both active and annuitant, to identify their needs and expectations. And the Board's long-standing advocacy of adequate pastoral compensation continued through regular *Tomorrow* articles and promotional literature, especially during annual periods of church budget formation and salary review.

However, *Tomorrow* published less frequently during the '90s, generally on an annual or biannual basis. The format remained the same, but the content focused more frequently on interpreting MMBB programs and announcing staff and leadership changes. It was less often focused on matters of human interest or inspiration, and the goal of providing a variety of professional help materials for ministers was largely abandoned. Articles that focused on personalities, especially retired ministers and missionaries, were increasingly featured as part of *ABC PEOPLE*, a magazine published on an annual schedule to support the Retired Ministers and Missionaries "Thank You" Offering.

Tomorrow introduced the concept of flexible benefits, first in the mid-'80s, then persisted with that theme, as well as the concept of accountable plans for qualified expenses. Accountable plans did not increase compensation, but they often helped squeeze maximum benefit from salaries that could, by different arrangement and practice, be protected in greater amount from taxation. The MMBB also joined with World Mission Support to develop tithing and stewardship seminars, the net effect of which was hoped to be greater income for churches, thus enabling the possibility of more adequate salaries to ministers.

Consistent with the MMBB's long-standing effort to nurture an educated clientele, and, specifically to better equip members with their own financial planning and stewardship, a new series of benefits seminars sought to help members to interpret the Retirement/Death Benefit Plans. Better communications technology both increased member inquiries and encouraged more frequent personal field representative contact with members. The goal to help ministers increase their own abilities as personal financial managers, and to assume greater responsibility for providing for additional financial resources for retirement, was advanced by personal investment topics in seminars and publications. That theme was later underscored by an MMBB Luncheon address by Nola M. Falcone in 2001.[401] Her address, Your Financial Future, was a thematic departure for MMBB's luncheons. It focused specifically and practically on the need for MMBB members to take greater responsibility to become educated about financial affairs, and to save, invest, and manage assets in addition to MMBB accounts for their financial futures.

Throughout the '90s, MMBB Luncheon addresses again reflected the broad sweep of events of the times and the intersection of those events with churches and ministers. In the midst of growing controversy surrounding the church's ability to accept homosexuals, Howard Moody's 1991 focus on the unfinished reformations represented by continuing conflict and confusion over issues of civil liberties and racism, gender role expectations, homosexuality, and sexual identity defined the issue in personal terms. In 1993 Yale University Chaplain Frederick J. Streets addressed the issue of violence, especially its impact on the black community, from both biblical and social perspectives. Both luncheon speeches raised the specter of emergent American division over controversial and sometimes disturbing issues. Ironically, Moody's address regarding sexual identity failed to prevent an action at that same biennial that reversed an ABC/USA policy on homosexuality and established a new, more negative one.

In 1995 Russell H. Dilday, then professor and Interim Dean at Baylor University's George W. Truett Seminary, reflected upon the past decade and a half of turbulence in Baptist life and the need to clarify who Baptists are and how they might be preserved in his talk, "Authenticus Baptistus: Endangered Species." In 1997 David L. Bartlett, Professor of Preaching at Yale Divinity School, advocated the importance of the gospel in preaching and pastoral communication in the context of a culture—including the church—which often seemed indifferent to its message. In 1999, six months shy of the new millennium, Harlem's Abyssinian Baptist Church pastor, Calvin O. Butts, III, addressed the expectation and anxiety of the coming new millennium with both humor and with prophetic insight, juxtaposing Genesis with Revelation, and focusing on a great variety of emerging cultural trends in between.

Changing Denominational Relationship Developments

Denominational relationships and connections were a continuing issue for the MMBB, even if they were often in the background. MMBB's creation in 1911 had established the Board's clear identity as an organization affiliated with the Northern, and later the American Baptist

Convention. In the early years, the denominational connection had helped the MMBB to achieve the necessary resources. However, as the MMBB became more a provider of support and assistance to the denomination and its agencies than a net receiver of resources from the denomination, the shift eventually affected denominational relationships.

As financial limitations increasingly affected ABC/USA boards and agencies, both requests to the MMBB and assistance from the MMBB increased. For example, in the 1980s the MMBB began an annual subsidy to the American Baptist Historical Society (ABHS) that, in turn, took over management of some of the MMBB's records and archives. In 1992 it also began funding the publication of the *American Baptist Quarterly*.[402] In 1990 the Board voted to provide an annual appropriation of $25,000 to the Baptist Joint Committee on Public Affairs on behalf of American Baptists.[403] In 2001 the MMBB provided a $125,000 grant to the Board of Educational Ministries (BEM) to assist with its staff Retirement/Death Benefit Plan premiums for the first months of 2002 and then continued that assistance to the financially stressed BEM the following year.[404] As financial limitations increasingly impacted the denomination, in 2005 the MMBB approved a 2006 premium subsidy of up to $275,000 for the Office of the General Secretary for the ABC/USA.

By 2007 the operation of the American Baptist Mission Center at Valley Forge, Pennsylvania, had become financially untenable largely because the denomination had, on previous occasions, refinanced the property to gain assets and because declining contributions from churches were insufficient to sustain the burden of its mortgage and debt obligations. In order to prevent, or at least forestall, the commercial sale of the Valley Forge property, the MMBB joined with the Board of International Ministries (American Baptist Foreign Mission Societies) and the Board of National Ministries (American Baptist Home Mission Societies) in creating an investment corporation called the Mission Partners, which then purchased the Valley Forge property. Ironically, with this action, the MMBB became a part owner of the property it had rejected for its own purposes forty-five years previously.

As the MMBB's role in helping to preserve the denomination's infrastructure increased, the effects of denominational intrusion in MMBB's own internal processes imposed by constitutional relationships to the denomination chafed more frequently. This was particularly the case regarding its need to recruit and to retain Board members who possessed significant expertise in the areas needed by the Board. It was also the continuing case with regard to staff salary administration: the salary guidelines and limits suitable for Valley Forge, and even more for regional staff compensation, were argued to be increasingly inadequate for the more costly New York environment and the specialized skills required for MMBB staff. These and other social and institutional trends made it apparent that for its own sake and survival, and certainly for its long-term performance success, the MMBB had to redefine its relationship to the constitutional processes of the denomination, and perhaps also redefine the parameters of its own mission.

In the MMBB's earliest years the functional independence of the Board limited the points of the denomination's supervisory contact primarily to the provision of an annual report from the MMBB to the denomination. In the case of the appointment of a new MMBB executive, the General Board of the Convention had the right to approve the choice. But following the SCODS reforms of the early '70s, the original procedures were revised and reversed. Instead of simply approving MMBB executive choices, the denomination's General Secretary could now recommend a candidate for the position of MMBB Executive Director. In addition, the MMBB Executive Director also served as a member of the General Secretary's staff team as a national Associate General Secretary. These changes had chafed many MMBB leaders. Smith, especially, was intent on preventing such limitations in the future.

The SCODS reforms of the '70s had also reduced the size of the MMBB governing board and reduced, as well, the number of members who served on an "at-large" basis in order to achieve their financial expertise or other needed skills. In the new, post-SCODS denominational structure, a number of Board positions were filled either by appointment from the General Board of the ABC/USA or as appointments by the three program boards: Educational Ministries, National Ministries, and International Ministries. Practically, many of the Board members served brief terms, and fewer came to the Board with usable expertise. This had a destabilizing influence on Board effectiveness.

Since the '70s, therefore, the MMBB had been increasingly governed by denominational policies, some of which were counter to what it believed were its best interests as a benefits organization. As noted earlier, the MMBB was required to conform its staff salary levels to denomination-wide standards, especially those for leadership at the denomination's Valley Forge Mission Center. Soon after his election, Gordon Smith's and MMBB Board members' persistence had achieved a measure of independence in dealing with staff recruitment and compensation. Sumner Grant later observed that Smith had given two great gifts to the MMBB: The first was that he had "confronted the increasing drain on MMBB resources by its service as a program board"[405] early in his term as Executive Director. The second was that he confronted the issue of MMBB's necessity to conform to the denominational salary grid. By "breaking the back" of that requirement, MMBB was more able to employ staff members who had the skills needed.

Challenges to the Board

By the mid-90s, the major challenge to the MMBB was that of asset retention and growth. In a 1995 report to the Board, the Executive Director, Gordon Smith, outlined the trend that members increasingly desired to gain control of their assets in retirement accounts. He noted that the trend was, in part, the result of broader social trends created by many businesses that had given up responsibility for providing benefits for employees in retirement by presenting them with their assets and advising them to invest them personally to provide for retirement income. He also believed that many members did not understand the MMBB benefit plans and were, therefore, susceptible to rumors that undermined confidence in the MMBB and its services. Most critically, he noted that competition for the management of invested retirement dollars had become a growth edge for the financial services industry. These challenges represented more than a simple competition with other providers of benefit services. As Smith observed, the MMBB had a "strong commitment to churches and other employers that have invested significant amounts in premiums, often at a sacrifice of church programs or mission giving, a responsibility to assure their employees, M&M members, that they will have adequate financial resources in retirement. We believe we have a fiduciary responsibility that we cannot relinquish to either members or to their financial advisors."[406]

It was, to pardon the expression, a declaration of war. For the immediate term, such challenges stimulated a variety of immediate responses, including a video titled "Spirit of Service" to interpret MMBB programs and plans, the development of new seminars for interpretive purposes, and several print interpretations, including *Tomorrow*, to confront the communication haze. Meanwhile, Smith's report had laid down the broad guidelines from which would be built the longer-term agenda for the Board.

In 1996 longtime Board member Howard Moody issued both praise and caution to the Board. He noted that in the last few years the MMBB had been equipping itself with the most up-to-date and efficient communication tools available. While this "was a good thing," he said, he also warned, "Technology takes its toll. Without diligent care, miraculous electronic machines can control our lives and decisions in ways that are imperceptible, gradually diminishing person-to-person conversation and making human contact unnecessary."[407] The prescience of his comment was increasingly apparent. Only with technology could the MMBB offer its services and fulfill its mission, yet the danger of increasingly less personal connection with members was clear. Managing that tension would soon become a high priority.

Gordon Smith retired at the end of 1997, having served the shortest tenure of MMBB's Executive Directors to date. However, Smith's commitment to restore greater independence for the Board set a direction for the MMBB that shaped its future agenda long beyond his tenure as Executive Director. Just before his retirement, on 30 September 1997, funds under management by the MMBB totaled $2.1 billion. Sumner Grant, MMBB Treasurer, was named Acting Executive Director and served in that capacity until he was named permanently to the position effective July 1998. Richard Fisher, longtime Board member and Chair of the Finance Committee over several terms, retired completely from the Board in 1998. His contributions to the Board, especially in the realm of investment management, were recognized as being without parallel.

11

BEYOND THE NEW MILLENNIUM

A Sense of the Times

The first day of January 2000 brought anticipation—and relief—that Y2K had not ushered in a technological apocalypse. But the relief was temporary. The theme for the decade soon crashed in on a "heartbreakingly beautiful September day"—11 September 2001. It seemed like the end of time was at hand. Airline flights were suddenly cancelled, first to New York, and then to all other destinations. An attack on Manhattan's "twin towers" resulted in their total destruction, with the loss of thousands of lives. Soon, a plane struck the Pentagon in Washington, DC, resulting in hundreds of deaths, and a failed attack on the White House ended with a passenger-facilitated plane crash in a field in Pennsylvania. The sixty-four passengers who died in that crash were perceived as heroes for preventing the completion of the plane's mission to strike the White House. That day ultimately marked the decade. America again had "isms" to hate: terrorism, fundamentalism, and "Islamism."

As a result of the attacks, the stock markets crashed, shedding thousands of points, before gradually recovering. American confidence and security crashed too, but did not rebound as quickly. The nation went to war in Iraq to oust Saddam Hussein, and in Afghanistan to find Osama bin Laden, and push back the Taliban, under the assumption that Hussein, bin Laden and the two nations were directly or indirectly responsible for the attacks. But few really believed that either effort would make the nation safe or the world free. America became obsessed with issues of security and defense against an enemy that could not be accurately described or even generally located.

By mid-decade, a new normal that included an underlying anxiety began to emerge. With the recovering financial markets, the MMBB funds under management regained ground, and by mid-decade totaled $2.22 billion. Still, the national debt grew with ominous effect on the financial markets. America's first black president was elected in 2008—

having defeated Hillary Clinton in the primaries and a Vietnam War hero, Senator John McCain, in the national election. As one result, overt racism went underground.

Just prior to the 2008 election, but with causes rooted much earlier in the decade, the economy crashed: Banks were blamed for irresponsible mortgage lending, consumers were blamed for too much personal debt, automakers and other manufacturers were blamed for lack of competitiveness in the world marketplace. Nearly everyone was bailed out—except the consumers. Red and blue states continued to harden their identities. A new, populist "Tea Party" movement emerged on the political right to turn up the temperature of political debate. Then, in early 2011, an evidently deranged young gunman attempted to assassinate popular Arizona Congresswoman Gabrielle Giffords, who survived, but barely; a small crowd of others attending the same event did not. Temporarily, debates used a calmer rhetoric. By late summer a new group occupied New York's Wall Street, and the movement soon spread to Washington, DC, Boston, Oakland, and other major cities demanding resolution to close the extreme gap between rich and poor, among other issues.

American traumas in the 2000s did not stimulate the historical returns to religion and religious expression characteristic of previous times of crisis. Instead, domestic responses to church bureaucracies expressed a growing sense of the irrelevance of churches. The personal mantra of "spiritual, but not religious" continued. Some Christians reached out to their beleaguered Muslim neighbors. Others, likely the majority, chose simply to fear them or hate them—or both.

The decade became one of eerie anticipation—of the next crisis, of the next attack, of the next scandal. Roman Catholics struggled with the shame and the legal ramifications of priests who abused children. A Colorado evangelical preacher, who was vociferous in his condemnation of homosexuals, was exposed as having sex with a gay prostitute. Traditional denominational affiliation declined, and even the megachurch movement stagnated. Swollen by war expenses, the national debt skyrocketed, suffering from low-wage competition, and the balance of trade went out of balance. Several states, impatient with the perceived inability of the federal government to protect the borders, established laws to eject undocumented aliens. Most of them afterwards found it difficult to harvest their crops or to employ critical staff.

The 2000s were a decade of change and uncertainty. Unlike the '60s, they had neither folk songs nor flower children to break the monotony. Few would admit to being "liberals" and instead favored being known as "moderates." The few liberals who remained hated conservatives with the same vehemence with which they themselves were hated. George "W." Bush, with low approval polls, gave way to Barack Obama, who soon inherited his low approval. It was grim-jawed crisis time. Optimism seemed a fanciful exercise.

MMBB Executive Leadership in a Time of Crisis

It was perhaps inevitable that a decade that lurched from one extraordinary crisis to the next would leave some things unsettled. In that climate, the MMBB approached the end of its first one hundred years in transition. The decade began with the continued Board leadership of Mary Purcell. In 2003 the Rev. George Tooze, Senior Minister of the First Baptist Church of Indianapolis, Indiana, was elected President of the MMBB Board of Managers. Tooze had served on the Board since 1997 and had also served previously on the Board of National Ministries on its Investment Committee and on the General Board of the ABC/USA.

Following Gordon Smith's retirement, the selection process for a new Executive Director again demonstrated the potential conflict of decision making between the MMBB Board of Managers and the ABC/USA. A delay of some months resulted because it took time to reconcile the differing preferences expressed by the General Secretary and the MMBB. Both candidates were eminently qualified: Sumner Grant had credentials that included both pastoral ministry and regional ABC administrative responsibility. He joined the MMBB in 1992 as Assistant Treasurer and then became Treasurer in 1993 upon the departure of former Treasurer Cheryl Wade, who left to become Treasurer of the American Baptist Churches USA. Grant was later also designated Deputy Director at the MMBB. The candidate preferred by the General Secretary also had strong credentials, having achieved strong academic certification and also having served in a senior management capacity with the MMBB as Treasurer. But more than a matter of qualifications, the selection choice reflected the dilemma of an unresolved nomination prerogative that later became one focus of the MMBB bylaw revision approved by the 2005 Biennial.

Sumner Grant was perceived as Gordon Smith's heir apparent and was the Board's choice as Executive Director. Grant's leadership résumé was strong: Prior to his service with the MMBB, Grant had been pastor of two churches in New Hampshire and Maine, an Area Minister in New York State, and Executive Minister of the American Baptist Churches of New York State from 1984 to 1992. He had been educated at Gordon-Conwell Theological Seminary and Gordon College and, while working with the MMBB, had completed the Advanced Management Program of Harvard University's Graduate School of Business Administration. He had a nearly lifetime affiliation with the MMBB that had begun in adolescence. His father, an American Baptist pastor of small churches in rural Maine, had died in 1957, only two years after enrolling in the MMBB Retiring Pension Fund. Grant's family had subsequently been the beneficiary of the MMBB's benefits, including children's allowances and educational allowances for undergraduate college degrees. "M&M opened doors of opportunity to me and my family and I hope to give back a portion of that which was given to us," he stated in an interview printed in *Tomorrow*.[408]

In presenting his first report to the Board in May 1998, Grant related the story of his own early relationship with the MMBB as a means of reminding the Board of its mission. He added that the mission had most often been fulfilled with a sense of intimacy with MMBB members. He then described a balanced vision to fulfill the mission for the future. In doing so he advocated a need to anticipate trends that would shape members' expectations and to evaluate members changing needs. Based on known survey data of the time, he proposed several organizational, administrative, and staffing goals, and particularly prioritized the goal of building a knowledge-based organization that communicated more effectively with technology to support effective service to members.[409] Over the next several months he refined his goals into a vision statement that defined the ministry of the MMBB in the future: "A ministry which places a high value on personalized service, achieved through partnering with world-class companies."

Staff Additions and Changes

Soon after Grant's appointment as Executive Director, early staff assignments and appointments reflected a preparation for the new era. James Keegan, who had previously joined the MMBB and shared the role of Coordinator of Member Service with Holly Bean, was appointed sole Coordinator in October 1998. In that role, he was given leadership responsibility for both internal and external services. Meanwhile, Bean moved to become Coordinator of Member Education, a newly created position to address the need to develop a more educated and informed membership regarding benefits and financial awareness.

Also in October 1998, Louis P. Barbarin joined the MMBB as Assistant Treasurer, and following the Board's affirmation in November, was appointed Treasurer, effective 1 January 1999. Barbarin was the first Treasurer of the MMBB with CPA accounting credentials, certified in both New York and Pennsylvania. Barbarin brought a refined expertise to financial procedures and internal accounting. Previously he had served in positions with the accounting firm of KPMG and as Vice president for finance at Cheyney University of Pennsylvania. He had also served as the Deputy Director and Treasurer of the American Baptist Board of Education and Publication Society. Later, in 2010, he became Deputy Executive Director of the MMBB.

Continuing staff member Walter Parrish, III, was promoted to Associate Executive Director in October, as well. His new responsibility was to lead the MMBB in developing denominational relations.

The Unfinished Business of MMBB Autonomy

Grant's affirmation as Executive Director did not erase uncertainty and tension regarding the nature of the Board's functioning relationships to the American Baptist denomination. In fact it had been exaggerated in the process of Grant's selection. The long-established tradition that the MMBB would select its candidate, subject to the approval of the governing body of the denomination, was a procedure that had been routinely and harmoniously followed through the selection of Dean Wright in 1960. Following the restructuring of the denomination in the '70s, however, the prerogative of proposing candidates for MMBB's Executive Director had been reversed, and was then placed in the Office of the General Secretary of the ABC/USA, subject to the approval of the MMBB. Gordon Smith had been selected by the Board in consultation with the General Secretary with relative harmony. But in the selection of Smith's successor, Grant, the General Secretary's strong support of a candidate who was not ultimately the choice of the Board's selection committee heightened a growing tension."[410]

Indeed, according to participants, the selection process was surrounded by controversy and some drama. Following interviews and committee deliberation, the MMBB Selection Committee, of which the General Secretary was a member, reported that there was unanimous committee support for Grant. The General Secretary reportedly responded that the committee had "made a mistake," and temporarily disengaged from the committee's work. Mary Purcell, Board Chair, engaged the General Secretary in private dialogue. She reportedly reminded him of the serious political ramifications for both the Board and the denomination if he persisted in his choice, with the result that a decision was deadlocked. After further consideration, the General Secretary acceded to the majority committee and Board decision. However, before publicly announcing the choice for validation by the General Board of the ABC/USA, he reportedly sought, but did not receive, concessions from the Executive Director–Elect that would advance his and the denomination's interests in Board affairs.[411] About two years later, according to Grant, the General Secretary commended Grant as "doing a great job" and affirmed "you were the right choice."

Some Board members undoubtedly assumed that the dust would settle. However, at least one Selection Committee and Board member recalls continuing strong concerns regarding ABC/USA administrative controls in the MMBB processes. He gained the support of several Board members, notably Mary Purcell, Chair, to seek clarification of the Board's autonomy, especially its priority in selecting an Executive Director. In addition to interpersonal and procedural concerns, the tension was heightened by the conviction of some Board members that in the past, MMBB's Board had served too often in a passive role. In contrast, there was a strongly expressed conviction that what was needed was a strong, more efficient, active, "hands-on" Board. They further believed that the impending new era required new direction and strategic responses to rapidly changing circumstances.

In addition to the specific issue of leadership selection, the Board had been frustrated that, over time, the appointment of Board members had largely devolved to denominational control. In the opinions of many Board members, this had resulted in a majority of Board members serving relatively short terms while frequently lacking the expertise needed for appropriately exercising its fiduciary responsibility and oversight of financial management. Board members Mary Purcell,

George Tooze, and Executive Director Sumner Grant began to strategize constitutional revisions that would further clarify responsibilities and relationships and, most of all, enable the MMBB to build Board expertise that was capable of fulfilling its function.

As a result, in 2005 a resolution largely shaped by the MMBB and its legal counsel and led by George Tooze, Board President, and Sumner Grant, with the intent to amend MMBB bylaws and those of the ABC/USA, was prepared and proposed for action by the ABC/USA. Its primary thrust was to modify the Board to include a larger number of Board-identified and Nominated members who possessed needed skills. A secondary purpose was clearly to clarify Board operating autonomy. To do so, the resolution increased the number of MMBB Board memberships derived from the ABC/USA and its affiliated boards to a total of seven—five from the General Board, and one each from the Board of National Ministries and the Board of International Ministries.[412] The minimum number of members on the Board was also raised from thirteen to seventeen while the maximum was reduced by one to twenty-five. This proposal effectively created the potential for a greater number of MMBB-generated appointments to the Board from sources other than ABC/USA institutional connections.

The same resolution expanded the number of at-large managers chosen by the MMBB to "not less than nine" and "not more than twelve," at least three quarters of whom had to be members of the ABC/USA at-large. But it also provided that "not less than two" and "not more than seven" members, also chosen by the Board membership, were to be known as Public Managers. It was not required that the Public Managers be American Baptist affiliated and were instead to be chosen because of their particular skills deemed to be helpful in performing MMBB functions. Public Managers most often served on the Finance Committee, which was later revised as the Investment Committee.

The resolution was passed at the ABC/USA Biennial in Denver, Colorado, in 2005. Also, as an outgrowth of conflict between the General Secretary of the ABC/USA and the Board in the nomination of Sumner Grant as Executive Director, the same resolution revised the nomination procedure for that position. As a result, the General Secretary's preferred appointment for the position could be rejected by the MMBB. A consultative process was defined to mediate disagreement. These revisions effectively reestablished functional autonomy for the Board and provided a mechanism to nominate the Board members needed. Henceforward, denominational appointees were less able to unduly influence Board decisions.[413]

Benefits

MMBB benefits in the late 90s and early 2000s were influenced by Grant's management vision. In order to satisfy the desire for participation in fund management by members, the Board continued on a track of greater flexibility and options. In order to help in the management of funds, daily unit valuations became available and members were able to select investment options on 50 percent of their Retirement Plan accounts and 100 percent of TAS, TDA, and qualified rollovers from individuals' non-MMBB sources. Other adjustments included further definition of Death Benefit and Retirement Plan account payouts for various categories of circumstances and relationships.

The MMBB's newly focused vision for growth also specifically stimulated certain benefit changes. For example, in 2001 it approved a tax-deferred annuity (TDA) primarily to serve the contracted retirement programs of churches or institutions unable or unwilling to participate in the full range and cost of the Retirement and Death Benefit plans. Likewise, it approved IRC 457 plans, a form of nonqualified deferred compensation plan for non-steeple religious organizations.[414] At the same time, the Board also affirmed the ability of employers to make contributions to the TDA. It further expanded the ability of members to make personal investment choices on 100 percent, rather than 50 percent, of their Retirement Plan accounts. These changes reflected a benefit program that functioned well and was the MMBB's most attractive product. One motive for changes to benefits that would expand products consistent with the tax and regulatory codes was to offer services with a maximum flexibility that would be attractive to current members as well as potential affiliates.

Establishing a New, Revised MMBB Vision

The 2000s, therefore, were dedicated to exploring, implementing and providing structure to the vision for growth that Grant had described. He proposed six operating principles: (1) commitment to the vision, (2) clear, measurable goals, (3) benefits and services customized to members' needs, (4) outsourcing operational functions not part of the

MMBB's core competency, (5) increasing and sharing knowledge, and (6) spreading cost through attracting new business. Grant had quickly demonstrated that his leadership would be characterized by attention to management plans and evaluative tools, both to measure success and to sharpen the focus of staff energies to achieve it.

In the short term, Grant sought to streamline administrative processes and reduce staff "handoffs," to standardize and document work flow to decrease errors in judgment, to decrease turnaround time, to educate employers to better understand billing processes and procedures, to develop incentives to reduce errors through focus on a corporate goal, and to reduce member complaints to less than 1 percent of total call volume. An additional goal was to increase the skill level of the operational staff through strategic hiring. In order to increase staff awareness of members' goals and needs, Grant directed a new round of focus groups to anticipate members' and employers' concerns. Additionally, he proposed to equip and train Service Representatives with additional technological tools to enable their work, and to redesign and introduce new financial planning modules, more flexible benefits, and retirement planning seminars. In short, it was a decisive focus on member service, efficiency, and effectiveness in pursuit of greater satisfaction and success in both MMBB service and growth.

For the longer term, Grant also affirmed that the MMBB should offer individually selected investment options to members. This option had been a frequently expressed desire as surveys revealed that a third of the membership wanted to be able to determine the investment mixes of their accounts. Personal investment choices (PICs), therefore, offered another important marketing resource as the Board actively explored the potential of offering retirement services to other, nonAmerican Baptist groups through an Affiliated Retirement Programs concept. Such groups would likely insist on choices. Grant proposed that this was a place where partnering would best achieve their goals by working with one or more major mutual funds. A goal to have Personal Investment Choices in place by 1 January 2000 was accomplished. PICs were to be administered by Dreyfus Retirement Services, a subsidiary of the Mellon Corporation.

Outsourcing some operations to financial service providers had multiple effects: It enabled savings in administrative personnel costs; it pleased the many members of the MMBB who wished to exert greater personal direction over their investments and, therefore, strengthened the Board's bond and the member's commitment. It also enabled the MMBB to conserve, both through savings of direct costs and through member retention and potential growth.[415]

As a result of the new goals and operational emphases, positive changes resulted quickly. Within about six months the Retirement Plan assets grew by nearly 2 percent, the TAS Plan grew by 6.6 percent, and the Field Member Service Representatives contacted a majority of both active and retired members. Results included a reduction in administrative expenses of 9.7 percent. Billing research time dropped from over two months to 4.6 days. In addition, the time required for annuity projections and calculations was reduced to 7.5 days instead of one month, and daily pricing of unit values, also a client request, was instituted.[416] In addition, a new financial planning module, developed by a team led by Jim Keegan, was introduced, and a new workshop for American Baptist employers was offered as a tool both for promoting benefits and services and in assisting employers in their relationship with MMBB's billing units.

One additional outcome of the change in operational style and direction was a 40 percent turnover in staff in the two years from Grant's beginning in 1998 until May 2000. Grant saw this as a benefit "allowing us to initiate a program of strategic hiring," by which he meant the ability to "employ staff whose competencies are aligned with our strategy." As one result, four new field representatives were added to build personal relationships with members, new phone representatives were engaged to respond to member questions, and new staff members with expertise in technology and finance were also employed to support administrative goals. The fundamental approach of providing retirement benefits had not changed, nor had the variable annuity-style investment approach to achieve it. But the adoption of Grant's principles enabled the MMBB to undergo changes as significant as those of the '60s when it had coped with the issues of civil rights struggles and the introduction of the variable annuity plan at the same time.

A Strategy for Growth

It was the achievement of the sixth of Grant's principles, that of attracting new business, that brought about the most significant shift in the MMBB's long-term goals and development. The case for the goal was persuasive: Demographics, social trends, and denominational stagnation had resulted in an aging MMBB membership and declining enrollment. In 1999, Grant pointed out that in the previous year the MMBB had expended $73 million more in benefits and services than it had received in premiums.[417] Greater efficiency and expense reduction could only accomplish a little in closing that gap. If the trend continued, he suggested, in the future the MMBB would be serving an aging population with a diminishing asset base. The inevitable cuts and reductions resulting from that development would reduce the MMBB to being merely an annuity board requiring only a minimal staff to enroll and service a declining number of members' accounts. In order to sustain a larger vision, it simply had to expand and grow.

MMBB's original vision had been proposed with a highly personal focus on the suffering or need of individual ministers facing their older years. Morehouse had used that vision with great effectiveness in advocating for his "old soldiers of the cross." He perceived that those individuals were the essential clients of the MMBB, and only secondarily emphasized MMBB's value to churches. But in recent years, it had become clear that the primary clients of the MMBB were employers— churches, organizations, institutions, and corporate structures. The MMBB's services indeed met the need of individuals for retirement incomes, and protection in the case of disability or death. However, in meeting those needs, the MMBB was providing a critical service to employer organizations. This had implications for growth.

The clearest path to growth was, therefore, to expand the MMBB's potential membership base to include employer organizations beyond those affiliated with the American Baptist Churches/USA—that is, to explore relationships with churches and organizations that might bring new members to the MMBB. To be qualified to serve members beyond the ABC/USA or its affiliated organizations required three things: the approval of the state of New York to a revision of the MMBB charter, assent from the IRS by means of a Private Letter Ruling that such service would be within the taxation guidelines, and the approval of the MMBB charter revision by the ABC/USA. By May 2000, New York had approved the charter revision, preliminary indications from the IRS were positive, and the American Baptist approval was pending. All three were finally accomplished within a few months.

In many ways it was a propitious time to accomplish this goal. The religious landscape, especially among Baptists, had been changing for more than two decades. Many Southern Baptist churches had chosen to distance themselves from the Southern Baptist Convention following its decade-long turmoil over theological and organizational directions. Some of those churches and organizations needed benefit services for their ministers and staff members. Early examples of new MMBB clients included the Baptist General Conference, which was approved for affiliation in 2000. The Alliance of Baptists, representing about ninety churches, had already endorsed the MMBB's plans, and marketing the MMBB benefit plans had begun in Alliance churches. The Board was also in dialogue with the numerically larger Cooperative Baptist Fellowship by 1999, and the MMBB became the administrator for that group's Retirement and Death Benefit plans in 2000.[418] In addition, two African-American denominations, the National Baptist Convention and the Progressive National Baptist Convention, also included many churches and agencies that were interested in MMBB services. Enrollment for the Progressive Baptists began in January 2001, and the ecumenically styled International Council of Community Churches also formalized a relationship with the MMBB that began in 2001.

By the end of 2000, the MMBB's adjusted vision was ready for full implementation, transforming what had begun as an exclusively ABC/USA pension and annuity board into a more complete benefits agency that served a broader constituency. Most of the new operational procedures and measurements had shown productive results, and the development of additional new clients was imminent. There were, however, hurdles that had to be overcome.

Challenges to the Vision—The Early Decade

One hurdle was a crisis of confidence in the MMBB's recent investment performance. After a recession in the early '90s, the US economy had gathered momentum, and between 1996 and early 1999 investments markets had generally produced robust returns, led predominantly by the domestic and technological sectors. MMBB's portfolios, which had been weighted in international markets, did not share the overall market success and resulted in comparatively anemic returns. This resulted in a loss of member confidence in MMBB's investments. It was a reminder that the primary expectation of members, both active and retired, was to develop financial security and growing account values.

As a consequence, the MMBB developed a new investment strategy more aligned with domestic markets, including new technological companies—just in time for the "tech bust" to further shake member confidence as market volatility dampened expected results. Market volatility also cast a pall over the early experiences of individual members with the new PICs. To demonstrate that MMBB products were among the best available, the Board had work to do in reshaping investment performance. It also had to produce new informational and public relations materials to explain benefits and to interpret the revised investment goals and performance. This was especially critical as the Board sought both to retain current members and to seek new clientele.[419]

A second hurdle was one that Sumner Grant identified as "financial accountability," that is, to be more effective stewards of the resources with which the MMBB had been entrusted. MMBB members were accustomed to attentive service, but it was not always as quickly delivered as members expected. This, too, eroded confidence. Effective, efficient service delivered quickly was expensive. Up to this point, members had received MMBB services without cost as the administrative expenses were paid for out of the Permanent Funds. It had been a standing Board principle not to exceed a 7 percent annual draw on the Permanent Funds, but in the years between 1998 and 2000, the Board had been forced to pass budgets that exceeded that limit. Cutting costs and enhancing revenue resources had, therefore, become an urgent challenge.[420]

To respond to this challenge, Grant again expressed his faith in the use of goals and strategies combined with evaluative tools to measure progress. By the May 2001 Board meeting the Executive Director and staff had developed what Grant called a "Balanced Scorecard." Using the MMBB vision statement, the scorecard was a tool that measured core survival questions concerning member expectations, management of human assets, financial progress, operational effectiveness, and the Board's effectiveness at dealing with the environmental, regulatory, or community forces that had an impact on the MMBB's goals. The Balanced Scorecard had almost immediate results in bringing new focus to the achievement of goals and, consequently, success in meeting them.

It also brought a material motivation to bear for the first time: For the subsequent year of 2002, departments that did not meet the cost savings structured into their budgets would put at risk 10 percent of newly introduced incentive pays if they failed to meet them.

Revenue flow was enhanced by progress in achieving additional clients. By the May meeting of 2000, it was announced that the National Baptist Convention of America, Inc., and the Eastern Baptist Association, a cluster of 225 churches in eastern New York, would begin enrolling members in 2001. By 2002, the Association of Congregational Christian Churches had also been added to the list of client organization. Baylor University was offering TAS as one of the offerings of its retirement plan, and informal conversations had begun with the Baptist General Convention of Texas. By 2005, the National Missionary Baptist Convention of America, Inc., and the General Baptist State Convention of North Carolina, Inc., had also been added to the list of MMBB's clients.

Meanwhile, at the November 2001 Board meeting, the MMBB modified its previous practice and authorized an administration charge to members of a fee up to 50 basis points on all funds managed by the MMBB. Members, therefore, for the first time would be paying for at least a portion of the services they received. The decision was based on the reality that continuing to over-draw on the endowments would ultimately lead to financial disaster. In 2000, for example, the MMBB had experienced a net loss of $9 million in Permanent Funds. A modest, below-market, standard fee on member's assets would close the gap and allow for positive growth in the future. That action "may not be celebrated today," observed Grant, "but a decade from now it will be cited as a prudent and measured response to stem a looming crisis."[421] The action resolved a current budgetary shortfall, but it also invited greater scrutiny and expectations of accountability by plan members in the future.

No challenge was as great, at least temporarily, as the psychological and economic effects of the terrorist attacks on the country on 11 September 2001, especially in New York. That event and the market turmoil it created were compounded just a few months later by corporate scandals that successively included AOL/Time Warner, Sunbeam, Enron, Arthur Andersen, Global Crossing, and ultimately, Xerox. Combined, the result was a "crisis in corporate governance," as *Business Week* described it.[422] The shock waves created, first by the malfeasance and then by the failure of some of America's most celebrated corporate and professional structures, quickly engulfed every institution and organization involved in public financial affairs.

Following the terrorist attacks, Grant had reported to the Board:

> I regret the challenges that we are facing as a Board have become a matter of focus within the context of the greater challenges we face as a people. But then, we have been aware for some time that the glow of our golden years is not radiating as brightly as it once was. Member loyalties, which were built on our 90-year history, have been tested by competition. Those who once would endure uneven service have hardened their ears to excuse. Retirement accounts which once doubled in value every five to seven years have been beset by market volatility, for which some blame us.[423]

His description was ultimately magnified by the corporate debacles that followed, which added to already abundant public feelings of mistrust, suspicion, and fear in regards to virtually all financial institutions. The later financial meltdowns of 2008 and beyond added to what by then could arguably be described as the decade of greatest challenge the MMBB had faced since Great Depression of the 1930s.

MMBB Responses to Challenges

In response to the multiple crises of confidence and operational disruption created by the 2001 events, the MMBB responded in several ways. The first was to rely on more frequent and pervasive communication. In 1998 the MMBB had developed its first Web site, which brought basic MMBB information into daily contact with the growing numbers who used computers for news, information, and socialization. It also made more extensive use of teleconferencing for sharing information. In addition, in 2000 the staff developed a variety of expanded print materials explaining benefits, procedures, and observations about retirement planning.

In 2002, a new seminar to enhance member knowledge about financial planning and investing was created. In addition, noting his belief that in times of economic crisis "it is important to be visible," Grant traveled to meet extensively with both annuitants and active members in several regions of the country to communicate the MMBB's focus, stability, and commitment to service.[424] During the same period, Grant and Associate Executive Director Dick Huber spent significant time lobbying to preserve the housing allowance tax exclusion for clergy, which had been challenged in court. Ultimately, successful legislation mooted the court case and preserved an important tax benefit for the time being.

Also, in response to continuing member concerns, now recently magnified as a result of national crisis consciousness, the MMBB created, by 2003, a "hot site" at Valley Forge, Pennsylvania, which made it possible for it to be fully operational within two hours following a disaster at the New York office. In the same year, it decided that members could make investment choices on 100 percent of their retirement plan accounts, rather than the previous limit of 50 percent. Both actions gave members a stronger sense of access to their accounts and control over their ultimate goals. In addition, the renewed vigor of communication with members was successful in underlining the MMBB themes of transparency and accountability. In 2002 trend lines for asset retention and growth were moving up, and by mid-year, the $1.8 million negative outflow in member accounts of the previous year had been reversed and had become $1 million positive.

More, a member survey indicated that member satisfaction had held steady and even increased by 2.5 percent. Dissatisfaction seemed directly linked to the impact of the financial markets on their accounts or to specific complaints about medical plan issues. In contrast, the broad array of member visits, seminars, general publications, quarterly reports, and interaction with the Web site had been positively received. Between 2004 and 2006 the increase of those who rated the MMBB as "excellent" in a client survey jumped from 35.7 percent to 52.8 percent, an almost unheard-of increase according to survey consultants. One especially bright result was that members rated the MMBB significantly higher than other providers. As marketplace competition for clients was one challenge MMBB had taken especially seriously, it was encouraging news.[425]

The persistent use of goals and measurements—the Balanced Scorecard—continued to reveal areas of strength, weakness, and need, encouraging reductions of cost and better deployment of resources. By 2003 the staff had been reduced from 84 to 75 persons. Even more significant was the shift in categories of personnel: "back office" staff members had been reduced from 40 percent of the staff to 28 percent, and those working in marketing, service, and communications increased from 29 percent to 37 percent. Some reductions of personnel and cost had been achieved by greater use of technology, while others were the result of outsourcing some administrative functions to investment services providers. Also by 2003 the increasing reliance on endowment funds for administration had been reversed by cost-reduction measures and by the decision to claim a small administrative fee. The administrative fee, originally established as 40 basis points, had reduced the draw on the endowment to a manageable 4.7 percent rather than the more than 11 percent of 1999 and 2000 experience. An influx of new clients had also elevated the amount of incoming funds while better communication and education had cut the outgoing fund rollovers by about 40 percent.[426]

Indeed, by the middle of the new century's first decade, most indicators were up and positive for the MMBB. The year 2004 was especially notable: 1,544 new accounts were added, which brought $2.8 million in new premiums, and $9.7 million of new money was rolled in. That resulted in a net increase in cash flow of $7.8 million over the previous year. Meanwhile, costs were contained in a year in which the endowment funds were up over 11 percent and the draw from those funds continued at a less-than-5 percent rate. In addition, survey information defined a growing membership satisfaction, with 43.6 percent describing the MMBB with overall ratings of excellent. In short, its major challenges were being met or effectively addressed: costs had been contained, new membership had greatly lifted cash flow, monthly billings diminished errors, and staff members felt both accountable and valued. As a result, member confidence was rising. A decade that had begun in tragedy and discouragement now seemed destined to achieve a happier and more prosperous ending. Personal service and efficiency were clearly strong drivers of recent success.[427]

The Eye of the Storm

The relative calm of 2004 and 2005 enabled the MMBB staff to tighten internal controls and costs and to enhance and underline training and staff development. "Good thinking means good products," was the motto that Sumner Grant borrowed from Toyota, and he sought to inculcate the habits of good thinking into the heart and soul of the

MMBB. As they moved into 2005, it remained a time to celebrate. But the Board was challenged to lift the vision to new, and as yet unachieved, horizons and to lay foundations for future success through effective marketing. In order to grow the endowment, and its ability to support the MMBB's core purposes, Dr. John Sundquist, a popular and seasoned American Baptist denominational leader, had enlisted his ABC colleagues Dr. Roger Fredrickson and Dr. James Scott to invite contributions to the MMBB endowment on an annual basis. This Heritage of Sharing campaign focused opportunities to enhance the MMBB's future resources through gifts and bequests. Charity, in cirumstances of emergency or times of crisis, remained an important part of the MMBB's ministry.

In 2005 several organizations with which the MMBB had been developing relationships and contracts came officially into service. The addition of the National Missionary Baptist Convention meant that the four largest African-American Baptist Conventions had now identified the MMBB as their benefits provider. As in 2004, the bottom line was strong: 1,463 new accounts represented an increase of 17.4 percent. MMBB funds under management, still in recovery after the shock of the twin towers attack, regained significant ground and totaled $2.2 billion by 31 March 2005.

But mid-decade brought signs of new or seemingly intractable continuing challenges, too. One was a continuing problem of asset retention. The retirement assets owned by ministers in the MMBB were increasingly perceived as rich prizes by brokers and financial managers, who often sought to convince ministers that their assets could be better managed by their services. Between 1 November 2004 and 30 April 2005, for example, members had rolled out $2.5 million from their accounts to other managers. Often, member departures from the MMBB resulted in disaster for their own financial security; their departures also meant a decrease in fees for the MMBB that put pressure on the budget. It also often tested MMBB compassion: some of those who rolled money out to other management lost a significant portion of their funds. Many ultimately decided to return to the MMBB, and, upon returning, often did so with diminished resources and greater needs. Stopping the flow of rolled out funds was, thus, a critical challenge for asset retention, and one, the MMBB believed, that was necessary to continue to serve its members. It was also one that required constant attention to communication and education.

Yet, despite the MMBB's vigorous program of communication and education, especially with members who owned larger accounts, the challenge continued. In November 2005, Grant reported that in the previous twelve months more than $6 million had been rolled out of MMBB members' accounts—one of the worst years ever. By 2006, a strategy team studied the impact of rollout trends and learned that 406 members held more than 24 percent of the accumulation fund assets or about $277,090,715. As a result, a strategy of services and support was developed to assist "key members" in two groups, those whose assets were in excess of $500,000, and those whose assets were in excess of $750,000. With several staff members newly trained as Certified Financial Planners, and with new software that enabled sophisticated financial planning, those with larger accounts were given personal assistance and investment education. This strategy was designed to provide them with information that would discourage disastrous decisions and that would demonstrate the benefit of leaving their assets in the MMBB plans.[428]

Two additional major challenges were presented by developments within the American Baptist Churches. First, for more than two decades American Baptist churches had been increasingly divided over matters of theological beliefs and denominational priorities, especially over the inclusion of homosexuals as pastors, leaders, or church members. By the mid-2000s the controversy had reached a crisis point, and following the 2005 ABC Biennial in Denver, Colorado, a number of American Baptist churches and one administrative region determined to withdraw from the ABC/USA. At question for the MMBB was whether employees of the churches that withdrew would have access to funds contributed while under ABC auspices, and whether the same employees might continue participation in the MMBB benefit programs.

Faced with a similar circumstance of churches leaving the ABC to form a new denominational organization in the 1940s, the MMBB had then followed the principle that they served only ABC-affiliated churches. Therefore, those who left could no longer participate in the MMBB. But circumstances in the new century were different. The MMBB itself had sought non-ABC-affiliated churches as clients, of course, and, as Sumner Grant observed, "this is a justice issue, and access to benefits is a basic right." The Board determined that employees of withdrawing churches, therefore, had a right to funds contributed on their behalf while they were American Baptists and, under most circumstances, were permitted to continue as members even if they changed their affiliation. However, certain noncontractual benefits, such as the annual RMMO "Thank You" Offering checks, and such things as premium assistance, educational allowances, and grants that were paid from the endowment funds would no longer be available to employees of churches or organizations withdrawing from ABC/USA affiliation.

Second, among churches affiliated with the American Baptist Churches, there had been a decline in the number of employers enrolling ministers and other staff members in the ABC Benefits for Life program, the most comprehensive and the most expensive MMBB product.[429] Instead, some opted only for the tax deferred annuity, which could be contracted for lesser percentage amounts of 12 percent, 10 percent, or even 7 percent of compensation, and did not include death or disability benefits. Among the newly affiliated groups, the trend lines were similar. Obviously, such lower levels of benefit coverage led to decreased retirement security, as well as potentially catastrophic results in the case of accidental or early death or disability. Practically for the MMBB, it also resulted in lowered asset development and fees. It was a convergence of an old theme: the importance of providing retirement security, and the need to encourage churches to be responsible in compensation— including long-term retirement planning.

The Emerging Storms

The MMBB further confronted a continuing dilemma from its earliest days: the circumstances of those who were qualified to be members, but who were not members of its plans. In its first generation, the MMBB had sought to enroll as many qualified ministers as it could and had achieved great progress by the mid-1940s. But following that effort, it had been difficult to encourage churches to enroll and enlist lay workers, part-time staff, and, indeed, in the majority of churches, any other staff member except the minister. It remained a clear priority of the MMBB's vision to expand services to any and all who needed retirement security and insurance protection and who would qualify under the guidelines of the MMBB charter and federal tax codes. This was, in addition to the MMBB's own need to grow, an important motivation to extend services to groups beyond ABC affiliation. It was also a spur to enlist church participation for a larger group of employees, including lay employees.

Executive Director Sumner Grant observed that this challenge was compounded by two primary realities. The first was cultural: the MMBB continued to be perceived as a culturally "white" organization, and building trust among potential ethnic minority clients took time. Also, within some cultural and racial sub-groups, the whole concept of pastoral retirement was foreign: in some church contexts a person was called to be a pastor until he or she died. In that circumstance, the MMBB sought to emphasize the protections offered to both the pastoral family and to churches through the death and disability protections. It was assumed that the appeal of honorable retirement might become more evident to churches and pastors alike. A second obstacle was largely economic: as the century's first decade matured, many churches suffered membership losses and increasingly restricted financial assets as a result of successive financial downturns. As a result, resistance to the broad provisions of the full Benefits for Life program grew, especially resistance to enrolling additional staff members in Benefits for Life coverage.[430]

As a result of a focus on Balanced Score card measurements and on attention to stated goals, by 2007 the MMBB was generally moving in positive directions in all areas. Strategies for handling complaints had intensified, outsourced administrators and providers had become more fully acquainted with the MMBB's "culture" and approach to servicing its clients, new accounts continued to increase, administrative expenses were under budget by nearly 5 percent, and the draw on the endowment had dropped to only 3.7 percent while its yield had achieved 13.6 percent. The MMBB was again in a position to practice "strategic spending" for future development. One result was the employment of additional regional representatives to assist in meeting member's needs. Another was to take a leading role in support of the broad Baptist movement leading to the "New Baptist Covenant" with its inaugural meeting in Atlanta, Georgia, in early 2008. The MMBB was once again performing a leadership function by not only providing for the financial security of ministers and others who depended on it, but by returning to a more comprehensive understanding of the "better maintenance of the ministry."

But 2008 brought new trouble. First, in January, the Cooperative Baptist Fellowship disaffiliated with the MMBB. The CBF, the umbrella organization of affiliation for many former Southern Baptist Churches and one of the first and most significant of the new, non-ABC/USA organizations that the MMBB had begun to serve, desired to develop its own retirement and benefits program. At issue was its desire to control the delivery of services and to assert a CBF branding on the benefits and services CBF negotiated. In the immediate term, however, many of the individual churches affiliated with the Cooperative Baptist Fellowship remained with the MMBB despite the CBF's official departure.

By far the biggest challenge, however, was the arrival of the largest financial meltdown since the Great Depression. The Dow Jones Average, having flirted with 14,000 in 2007, fell to 6,547 in 2009, its dizzying descent caused by multiple crises in the mortgage markets, numerous bank failures, and the failure of at least two major investment firms and countless smaller ones. There was, again, a general public perception of mistrust of financial service organizations and rapidly declining consumer confidence. The entire American economy went into a prolonged recession of debilitating scope. Psychologically, to many it was not *like* a depression, it *was* a depression. The MMBB's entire structure of services was linked to the health of the financial markets. Thus, the national economic crisis brought immediate crisis to the MMBB's services and operations, and also brought threatening stress to its long-term plans.

The least of the problems were immediate ones: the continued payout of annuities at amounts established in more favorable economic circumstances, and the MMBB annual operating budget which was suddenly based on inaccurate projections of returns. To deal with the budget, the Board approved an immediate salary freeze for all MMBB staff, furloughed all staff for ten days during the summer of 2009, and offered early retirements to selected members of the staff, which six accepted. One executive staff member was laid off. In addition, the annual visitation program was suspended, and several publications were re-conceived or terminated, including a health care newsletter. The number of staff representatives the MMBB sent to the 2009 ABC Biennial in Pasadena, California, was reduced to conserve travel costs and planned marketing was curtailed. The effect was to create a budgetary savings of more than $2 million, a 12 percent budget reduction that enabled an endowment draw of only 5.5 percent. But, as the Executive Director observed, "At the same time, opportunities have been lost."

To deal with the health of the Retirement Plan, a second, more stressful effect, was the need to inform retired members—those currently drawing annuities—that their income would be reduced. For the initial reduction, a 5 percent figure was imposed for the following year. But annuity recipients were also advised that a further reduction would likely be repeated for 2010 and possibly beyond in order to restore the health of the fund for the long term.

Still, potentially the biggest casualty of the economic crisis was the long-term growth plan for the MMBB. In response to the pervasive pessimism of economic crises, the temptation to abandon programs in order to cut expenses was great. At the November 2009 Executive Board meeting, Executive Director Grant explained that the Board faced a choice. The choice was shaped by the reality that long-term growth was not going to come from ABC/USA churches. He proposed that the stakes were dramatic, and, for him, the choice was clear: MMBB needed to continue in its direction of expanding assets by aggressive action toward growth by actively seeking to serve non-ABC institutions and accounts. The alternative was that it needed to prioritize the preservation of assets consistent with a vision that the future of the MMBB was to be only a pension and annuity board servicing a declining number of members with declining assets and staff.

To clarify the choice, Grant reiterated the impending retirement of baby boom members in the next few years. The effect for the MMBB would be increasing payouts for annuities, and declining revenues from premium payments. He also pointed out that in recent years 43 percent of new members had come from non-ABC affiliates. Even accounting for the decision of the Cooperative Baptist Fellowship to create its own pension organization, 41 percent of growth had come from affiliate membership since 2001. As of November 2009, 25 percent of MMBB members were non-ABC/USA affiliated. Continued growth could be expected to offset and even exceed American Baptist reductions in membership.

To demonstrate the alternative, Grant also described a scenario based on several assumptions: that the Board would opt to become simply an annuity board with a conservative investment strategy to ensure market viability. It would maintain fixed, low administrative charges and provide basic services to assure orderly financial transactions. It would be likely that the MMBB would have to rely more heavily on outside financial institutions for asset management and benefit administration. And it would be forced to eliminate programs providing such things as visitation, annuitant gatherings and in-depth financial planning. The growth initiative would be greatly curtailed, and any future enlistments beyond ABC/USA would come from informal connections. In that scenario, the endowment would be focused on core costs, and the annual draw from it would necessarily be reduced to preserve maximum principal in order to sustain the MMBB through the difficult years of decline. Financial institutions would be used to outsource asset management and to administer benefits.

Grant believed that the only rational path to long-term health and stable financial viability was to continue on the path leading toward membership growth, and it was that direction he asked the Board to affirm. In considering the choice before them, the Board of Managers was challenged to choose between the two strategies, one to achieve more members, the other to preserve current assets. There was a risk: if an aggressive policy of growth were the choice, it would require significant long-term investment in staffing and staff training. Such funding would necessarily put pressure on the endowment funds, and, in light of the current financial crisis and the challenges for the MMBB it was tempting to think this tactic was questionable.

In facing the choice, Grant shared that he was convinced of the wisdom of a *Harvard Business Review* article that argued that "The danger in the current economic situation is that persons in positions of authority will hunker down. They will try to solve problems with short term fixes, tightened controls, across-the-board cuts, restructuring plans."[431] The article's author had suggested that the present was an extraordinary time, "a time not to cling to the past but a time to hew to the future."[432] The Board concurred and chose to keep its vision focused on the future, not the present.

By 30 September 2009, MMBB funds, heavily battered by the economic crisis, had regained much ground and totaled $2,167,709,000. By early 2010, it appeared that the financial crisis was at least in a stable mode and possibly even abating. The equity markets were trending gradually upwards. At the May Board Meeting, the Finance Committee reported that the several measures to reduce spending that had been instituted in early 2009 had been effective: actual administrative expenses compared to budgeted expenses had been reduced in both the General Fund and the Endowment Fund.[433] By the end of 2009, the spending rate of the Endowment Fund had dropped to 4.1 percent, and as of March 2010, had fallen to 3.2 percent. In the Benefits Committee, however, there was extensive discussion regarding the valuation of the retirement funds based on previous years' losses, their 30 September 2009 values, and what the effect on the 2010 annuity payments should be. Annuitants had been protected to suffer only a 5 percent drop in income in 2009, which was significantly less than the real drop in the value of their units. The Board had long-term optimism, but acted with short-term prudence. They determined that, depending on market values, reductions would have to be imposed for one or more years in the future to bring the annuity payouts in line with true valuation in order to maintain fund health.[434]

Out of the Chaos—Regaining the Direction

The effects of the 2008–09 financial crisis continued to influence MMBB strategies and decisions as the MMBB entered its second century. Grant confessed that he wanted to repress it, "Block it from memory— bury it in the deep recesses of my subconscious ... I am haunted by the terror of the worst financial meltdown since the Great Depression, its near devastating blow to our organization, its potentially crippling impact on those we are called to serve."[435] But of course he couldn't— and didn't. Instead, Grant observed that the MMBB had learned that it was nimble, that it did well at managing risk, and that its commitment to prudent management paid off—especially in crisis. The experience of the financial crisis also seemed to affirm the MMBB's emerging new direction. It had become clear that mere survival was not a sufficient goal, and that growth was clearly the best alternative. Therefore, the direction the MMBB had already begun to take was reaffirmed, increased, and strengthened even as all eyes nervously watched the indicators for market recovery and restoration of financial stability.

Meanwhile, the staff was reorganized to further separate member service functions from member recruitment. Emerging technology and the growing inefficiency of attempting to have field representatives maintain personal contact in the field in order to answer questions and to resolve concerns had demonstrated that the greater use of phone, e-mail, and other communications was both more effective and, in many ways, more personal. Therefore, Field Representative Sara Day was called in to lead in centralizing all former member service functions in the New York office. Staff training and development positioned member service representatives to serve this function effectively.

Second, greater commitment to outreach, especially in the task of identifying and enlisting new members, was confirmed by the addition of Tom Huber as the new director for that work. Huber had extensive experience in sales, which, in more direct terms, was what field representatives were now focused to accomplish. James Keegan, who had directed field services, enabled the transfer of personnel to Huber's leadership and to help clarify new responsibilities. Retirement opportunities were granted to several staff members who did not feel comfortable or capable of making the shift in emphasis toward marketing. Through MMBB's first half year in 2010, new accounts numbered 582, a number representing more than half the annual goal of 1,060 for that year. By year's end, the goal had been exceeded with 1,062 new accounts.

At the November 2010 Board meeting, a number of revisions to the Benefits for Life plan were accomplished that clarified a number of emerging questions raised by the growing variability of approaches to retirement, withdrawal of funds, and the annuitization of member accounts. Additionally, the recent crisis had demonstrated the dangers of over-paying from the accounts of already annuitized members. The 95 percent guarantee, by which annuity payouts would not be decreased by more than 5 percent of the amount received in the preceding year had exposed the funds to potential disaster had the crisis not stabilized and had the market not rapidly regained strength. Therefore, a new, 90 percent guarantee was introduced which allowed for steeper 10 percent subsequent reductions in annuity payouts following an initial 5 percent. This steeper reduction would be implemented under circumstances when the annuity unit values dropped precipitously, or continued over a long period of time. This removed a certain degree of serenity from the previous 95 percent guarantee, but it offered greater overall protection in unpredictable and dire circumstances.[436]

In his report to the Board in November 2010, Grant borrowed again from the article Leadership in a Permanent Crisis from the *Harvard Business Review*. "Are you waiting for things to return to normal in your organization? Sorry. Leadership will require new skills tailored to an environment of urgency, high stakes and uncertainty—even after the crisis is over. You'll have to: Foster adaptation, helping people develop the "next practices' that will enable the organization to thrive in a new world, even as they continue with the best practices necessary for current success." In further clarification, Grant added, "Best practices are technical in nature; next practices are adaptive."[437]

Several technical advances were introduced at that meeting: a Stable Value Fund, a new conservative investment option, was introduced for members; changes to the outsourced Medical Plan to bring the plan into conformity with the Patient Protection and Affordable Care Act of 2010 were also announced. But the primary communication of the meeting was description of the adaptive changes that were under way. Tom Huber (Outreach), Sara Day, assisted by Matthew Hoffman and Frank O'Brien (Member Services), Harold Leibovitz (Communications), and Bill Hunnix (Human Resources) joined in reviewing the directions and changes that were under way. Illustrative materials included a new logo; Web site design; descriptions of strategy, markets, and approaches; and a variety of other arrows to point the way ahead.

Interim Outcomes

As MMBB's ninety-ninth year drew to a close, the MMBB had endured a financial crisis that was, perhaps, even more threatening to the present Board than had been the Great Depression of the '30s, largely because of the MMBB's comparatively greater complexity and larger size. The Board was confident that it had reacted conservatively to preserve its core financial mission. But it was also satisfied that, in a time of danger, it had refashioned itself in a more aggressive and confident form, and charted its future course through the sometimes-turbulent waters of growth rather than remain in the quieter pools of controlled stagnation. By 31 December 2010, MMBB assets under management had reached $2,378,999,000.

Clearly, long-established MMBB resources, traditions, and practices had enabled it to weather a decade of severe storms. First, the endowment, which was temporarily threatened with severe erosion, nevertheless provided stability and security in the worst of times. Second, the long-standing habit of prudent management had continued: the Board had avoided panicked or precipitous decisions that might have crippled programs or caused long-term fiscal dilemmas. Third, a clear focus on the core vision of the MMBB encouraged a steady continuation of both current practices and accomplishment of established goals. And, not least, the MMBB continued to benefit from the integrity and commitment of its Executive Director and senior management staff just as it had in previous times of crisis.

As the MMBB's one hundredth year began, the "new normal" of uncertainty was evident throughout the world, in American culture, and in the corridors of the MMBB's offices at New York's Interchurch Center. International affairs were challenged by domestic demonstrations in several Middle East capitals; the United States had become, at least temporarily, a debtor nation with old enemies and new competitors holding some of its debt. Congressional paralysis in the determination of just how high that debt would be allowed to go created yet another market crisis. The world of religion and religious institutions, with measurable losses of members and support, was clearly in a time of change and transition. Social Security, the federal insurance and retirement "safety net" established more than seventy-five years earlier, was among the top priorities for revision, reform, and restructure by some of the budget reduction forces in the US Congress. In short, old and new uncertainties continued to plague economic stability and threaten the well-being of those planning for security in retirement and those already in personal economic crisis.

In 2011, reflecting on events of the recent past, and perhaps hinting at those ahead, Sumner Grant commented, "The greatest challenges have been dealing with a very uncertain investment environment; meeting or exceeding member expectations with static resources; and growing our asset base with our outreach initiative to ensure the continuation of our ministry for generations yet to come."[438] Of course, the MMBB could not control or even accurately predict the future. But it could be certain that the need for the benefits and protections it offered would continue. It prepared for the time to come by paying attention to its goals and insisting on excellence in service. Its vision, now expanded, included service to not only American Baptists in particular, and other Baptists as contractual opportunities arose, but in addition, to like-minded organizations and structures ranging from individual churches, some religiously affiliated hospitals, child-care organizations, schools, colleges, and other organizations as yet unidentified and perhaps unimagined.

In late June 2011, one hundred years after the original establishment of a committee to investigate the possibility of a program to care for the "old soldiers of the cross," American Baptists gathered for their biennial convention in San Juan, Puerto Rico. During the business sessions the bylaws of the ABC/USA were revised to provide for a more flexible administration of the denomination, and as a result of those revisions, the MMBB's autonomy was further assured.[439] At that occasion the MMBB inaugurated a two-year cycle of centennial celebration with a grand display of its history. Sumner Grant, as Executive Director, addressed a plenary session of the assembly to call attention to some of the achievements of the Board. As the Morehouse College Choir provided some of the inspirational music at the event, both Henry Morehouse, whose name the college honored, and John D. Rockefeller, Sr., whose funds had stabilized and supported the college, as well as MMBB, both seemed present. And one could imagine that M.C. Treat, whose challenge grant had empowered the MMBB's creation even as he jealously guarded his own anonymity, was lurking in the challenges of the era to come.

CONCLUSION

Since 1911 a great many corporations have been chartered, under-taken, and planned to provide retirement security for older or disabled employees. Of those, a great many—the great majority—have failed. Why did the MMBB succeed? The short answer is that the MMBB's success was the result of Henry Morehouse's vision, John D. Rockefeller's money, and a succession of wise and effective leaders who sustained its vision and were effective stewards of its resources.

Vision is a compelling force, and necessity is a powerful motivator. Henry Morehouse combined vision and necessity effectively and added yet a third component: persistence. For more than a generation, from the early 1880s until 1911, Morehouse held up the plight of impoverished, aging ministers and advocated a proposal to provide some means of relief for their circumstances with a persistence that kept that concern in the light, if not always in the limelight.

Morehouse's vision led to the MMBB's role as a pioneer in the development of retirement benefits in North America and helped to establish pensions as a matter of compensation planning rather than as charity. As H. Pierson Hammond, the Board's first actuary-phrased it at mid-twentieth century, "The fund, therefore, was a pioneer in this field of endeavor."[440] Two generations later, Howard Moody reflected, "We must never think of ourselves as a charitable and benevolent dispenser of fiscal goodies ... we must always remind ourselves and those we serve, in the words of Everett Tomlinson in his 1912 Annual Report, 'Our supreme desire is to see to it that the deserving are treated justly and generously and not compelled to look upon themselves as in any way receiving charity.'"[441]

Milo C. Treat caught the vision and understood the necessity. Treat's challenge gift of $50,000 if Baptists were successful in raising $200,000, in addition to his other gifts, made it possible for Morehouse's vision to become a reality. His challenge gift, in effect, primed the pump, which resulted in Rockefeller's donated millions and the many other gifts, donations, and bequests that followed in due course. Treat was confident that if he made the challenge, others would respond. Perhaps he even knew that Rockefeller would respond generously if he opened the bidding. Treat himself was an able businessman and investor, as well as a committed Baptist layman. He goaded early MMBB leadership to achieve maximum returns on every investment to the MMBB that he made.

The result was that the MMBB was created to serve the "old soldiers of the cross" as they reached the end of their careers. At that point the MMBB was a pioneer, not only because pensions were very rare at that time, but also because many similar, well-meaning attempts were inadequately conceived. Many more attempts at providing pension support in a variety of occupations and vocations, though adequately conceived, soon failed because of bad management, poor strategy, corruption, or a failure to stay focused on the vision that had empowered them.

But many things that are successfully created also have short lives due to unforeseen challenges and circumstances. The MMBB was created on the verge of a world war that soon preoccupied the entire nation, and within its first twenty-five years it was also faced with an economic depression of legendary magnitude. Soon thereafter, another world war drained the nation's resources. Many institutions and organizations of long standing and with more significant resources did not survive those years. Yet the MMBB not only endured but emerged stronger, and has, since then, grown to broader and greater service. There are several reasons:

First, the MMBB's early organization and charter enshrined its vision in practical purpose. That charter seems to have been engraved in the minds of all who served its purpose. The purpose of serving elderly and retired ministers and missionaries was embedded at its core and was easily remembered by that most concise and inspiring phrase of its purpose, "for the better maintenance of the ministry."

Second, the MMBB's charter itself and early negotiations with the Northern Baptist Convention and its subsequent iterations established the MMBB with an important sense of autonomy. With a need only to make annual reports to the Convention and to achieve Convention approval of its most senior employees, the Board was able to operate efficiently and with consistent focus on its core purpose. It was also able to recruit Board members with unusual, sometimes legendary financial acumen and investment expertise. It was mostly able to avoid the inter-organizational politics that can so often and so easily drain institutional resources and confuse purpose. When the SCODS reforms of the early 1970s pulled the MMBB into a closer relationship with the denomination, the contrasting effect was almost immediately evident. It was corrected a generation later.

It would be hard to overstate the importance of the long-standing, functional independence of the MMBB. In the 1960s, reflecting on the MMBB's image, Miriam Corbett mused:

> When I shifted to the M&M Board after nearly 20 years of work for other church agencies, mostly Baptist, I had two new problems to contend with—money and freedom. These are two significant elements of our image. Always before, the entire budget of the agency for which I worked could be clearly stated on one sheet. I would be involved with discussions such as "Shall we give 20 ministers scholarships of $15 each, or shall we really make it worthwhile for fewer people and give 15 ministers $20 each to attend whatever we were planning."[442]

The Board's significant assets enabled it both to fulfill its purpose with generosity and to remain focused on its goals.

In addition, its early accumulation of financial resources from Treat, Rockefeller, the Morehouse Million campaign, and other individual and organizational sources provided it with a substantial reserve that was a significant buffer against both internal and external financial disasters. The American Baptist Churches/USA, like other denominations, presumes to serve a kingdom not of this world, but in this world financial resources are the source of many blessings. Money begets more money; lack of money ensures little more than stress. The MMBB was blessed.

Third, the MMBB's early dedication to prudent and business-like principles encouraged a discipline that preserved and nurtured assets for their stated purpose. The MMBB was able to resist the temptation to let passing opportunities for compassion erode its long-term health and strength. Equally, its early recognition that donations, no matter how generous, would never be enough to meet its goals, led to its early decision to move from grant-based pensions to a contributory retirement fund approach. The MMBB has always maintained a charitable dimension for emergencies and special needs, but its early establishment of a contributory fund for its pension put its programs on a sound long-term basis. It also enabled the MMBB, thereafter, to use its accumulated donated assets as a Permanent Fund that could be drawn upon to protect, advance, or creatively support its long-term goals, while pension funding itself came from member participants or their employers. More, its early and consistent dedication to what that early period referred to as scientific principles shaped it to rely on actuarial projections and rational, systematic procedures. That practice helped the MMBB to preserve and enhance its assets through accurate calculations of future retirement obligations against accumulated capital and income.

Fourth, throughout its first one hundred years, much of the MMBB's success in achieving its purposes was advanced through consistently effective leadership. From the early leadership of Everett Tomlinson to the present, each chief executive has stamped the MMBB with a tradition of faithfulness, excellence, and dedication. It is notable that there has been never been a suggestion of executive malfeasance, irresponsibility, or personal ambition that might have been counter to the purposes of MMBB's chartered goals. In addition:

MMBB's early and consistent choice of Board members, who were highly skilled, experienced, and effective financial and business leaders and managers, resulted in a high degree of financial competence and investment success.

MMBB's long tradition of order, harmony, and commitment to the purposes of the Board enabled efficient, effective, and sometimes highly creative solutions to challenges the MMBB regularly faced.

MMBB's consistent awareness of its need for effective executive leadership led to clear attention to staff development, preparing staff leadership skills, and succession planning, which, with few exceptions, enabled seamless transitions of executive leadership.

A further clear example of MMBB leadership has been the ability to keep its founding vision in focus. In addition to the efficiency of Board autonomy and freedom from denominational quarrels and entanglements, freedom from pressure to use funds for other denominational purposes than the stated goals of the organization has been immeasurably important. More than one benefits organization has failed because its funds were diverted to serve other purposes instead of remaining as resources for retirement security. MMBB leaders have clearly, and sometimes courageously, articulated and reclaimed the vision to preserve its core purpose. On the few occasions when alternative temptations arose, the Board has clarified its purpose and exerted its conviction by not responding to needs beyond its charter definitions, no matter how worthy or important such requests might have seemed.

In addition, autonomy often gave the MMBB the ability to tackle issues that were not safe or palatable for denominational agencies or divisions to embrace. Religious organizations, like any other human assembly, are frequently pressured to defer to the varieties of opinions present on governing boards and within the organization's constituency. In that respect, perhaps unintentionally, the MMBB became an anomaly within the American Baptist Churches. The resources the Board commanded enabled a practical independence with regard to establishing policies consistent with its charter, and also allowed the Board to escape the worst aspects of current fads or disputes within the denominational body. Such legal and institutional separation from both the denominational structure and its constituencies gave it the freedom to pursue its mission without feeling obliged to take political or operational detours that might otherwise have compromised both its mission and its effectiveness.

Finally, independence also provided the MMBB with a potential only recently fully realized: that of providing leadership to disparate but sympathetic groups that might find strength and unity in working in partnership with others to offer pension, insurance, and other retirement or disability benefits. This is clearly the established future for the MMBB. In one sense, it is a fulfillment of its original vision. Denominations have taken more specific institutional form since Morehouse called for support for retiring ministers. But Morehouse never clearly defined that the "old soldiers of the cross" should only be a particular denomination of Baptists. Rockefeller, too, had an expansive vision, one that might well have included a broader dimension of service. Over time, he developed an ecumenical view of religion as well as an expansive approach to other social concerns. His son John D. Rockefeller, Jr., clearly abandoned parochial approaches to social investment. It is, therefore, likely that the MMBB's most generous early donors would approve of its new direction of service beyond the American Baptist Churches/USA.

Therefore, at the end of its first one hundred years, the MMBB is in a period of "new creation." It seeks to remain faithful to its vision and charter of service to American Baptist ministers, while, at the same time, extending its service to other groups of ministers and those serving similar organizations with compatible purposes. It is a direction that seems consistent with its charter. It is also consistent with the prudent management and effective strategy that has always characterized the MMBB's actions.

In pursuing its second hundred years, the MMBB would seem to be approaching its future with the same qualities of good management, strong vision, prudent judgment, and effective strategy. To fully accomplish this, it may be important for the MMBB to remember another characteristic that enabled its success and that is hard to identify and even harder to quantify: a focus on personal connection with its membership while providing its service. Countless anecdotal and personal testimonies provide evidence that one of the Board's major benefits had nothing directly to do with money but instead with a demonstrated personal care and concern for its members. Therefore, a clear challenge is likely to be that of managing the balance between maintaining personal contact and providing efficient service. As the Board seeks to achieve its strategy of growth and enlargement, the personal connection that it has built will be harder to maintain but will be even more important to accomplish.

There are other challenges. Even as the MMBB celebrates its century of service, the American economic and social context in which it serves has deemphasized pensions and seeks, again, to make resources for retirement the responsibility of workers themselves. "Work until the grave" is once again becoming a potential reality and a common perspective in many professions and vocations. Already many churches or organizations are reluctant to provide the full coverage represented by the 16 percent of compensation retirement and disability program, or full coverage for health care. Reasons given are "we can't afford it" or "it is not normal." While the newly established strategy of growth for the MMBB offers much promise of growth in larger, critical mass, bigger resources and a broader base over which to diffuse expenses may be an increasing challenge.

Predictably, growth and expanded resources will also bring greater responsibility. More members and more funds will inevitably bring a need for an expanding staff and larger administrative expenses. Larger size and greater assets will, therefore, likely also magnify the effects of future crises and economic downturns. Therefore, not all numerical gains will serve to strengthen the organization. Except for those politically favored organizations able to expect "bailouts" in times of crisis, recent events have proved that "too big to fail" is a false premise.

Larger size and greater diversity of clientele will, in addition, bring another, very specific challenge for the MMBB's communication. In reviewing the publications the MMBB has sponsored over the decades, there is a noticeable trend, especially in the last twenty-five years, toward greater specific focus on financial education and awareness, and less focus on personal and professional concerns that once served to bond the MMBB with its members. Highly specific information regarding benefits and the provision of resources enabling members to be more effective managers of other assets, including their own personal resources, is valuable and consistent in advancing the MMBB's long-term commitment to a more educated membership. But the MMBB has succeeded, in part, because of the strong loyalty of its members who found benefit in its resources of education, inspiration, and encouragement that were broader and bigger than money.

Also, as MMBB communication has moved toward providing clear financial resource education and clarification of benefits, it has moved away from its prior tradition of concern for the total "maintenance of ministry." The loss of nonfinancial information is apparent: articles on what pastors might read, or how ministers' spouses handle the unique pressures of a partner's ministry, or features focusing on beloved ministers' activities in retirement, the personal qualities of new and retiring MMBB staff members, and especially, the inspirational articles that were often the most anticipated and most frequently read articles of previous publications. Morehouse's most often used language was rooted in the mission of the church served by its ministers and missionaries, and the needs of its most venerable servants, The "old soldiers of the cross." That is to say, the MMBB began as an organization imbued with the philosophy and values of what we now, more passively and impersonally, describe as a "faith-based organization." If an organization may be said to have a soul, the soul of the MMBB has been dedicated to the service of the ministry and has been, therefore, itself an agent of ministry. That has been, in part, a result of its effective, broad, and at times, spiritual communication.

The MMBB's recent pursuit of autonomy and broader service seems right and proper to enable its fulfillment of the purpose for which it was created. Its recent strategy of development is brilliant and likely effective to secure its own long-term viability and its ability to fulfill its charter. Indeed, if the MMBB follows its century-old pattern of excellence, that strategy will lead it to become bigger, better, and more highly successful in providing the financial resources that provide a safety net for its younger members and a comfortable landing for its senior ones.

But even if the MMBB were to become legendary as a highly regarded and successful financial service organization, but lost its vision of—and its connection to—serving those who serve the gospel in some way, it would lose much of what has made it unique. Rather, in a hundred years, an observer might hope that the MMBB will be found with vastly larger resources and a much-expanded impact in the care of those whom it serves. But we might also hope that Morehouse's favored phrase, "old soldiers of the cross," even if it sounds more quaint and charming to future ears than to our own, will still connect with those who know precisely what it means because it will still be the model on which the MMBB's purpose is delivered on personal terms.

Now that pensions are endangered in the present American social and economic climate, it may well be that at the end of the next century of MMBB service, the Board will stand alone, or if not alone, as a rare example of the very concept they pioneered. That is beyond our horizon of sight, of course, but the "old soldiers of the cross" of the future are just now being born. Some will face financial adversity, and all will grow older. If the MMBB follows the course of its first one hundred years, it will continue to be there as a steward to provide assistance for these "soldiers" as they face life's unpredictable disasters and a well-earned income when they retire.

NOTES

[1] MMBB was incorporated in New York state on March 24, 1913. Section 2 of the Act of Incorporation states, "The objects of the corporation shall be to administer its funds for the benefit of worthy Baptist ministers and Baptist missionaries, their wives and widows, and their dependent children, either directly or through the medium of related organizations; to cooperate with such organizations in securing, so far as practicable, uniformity in the methods for the extension of such aid; *to promote interest in the better maintenance of The Ministry*; and to adopt such measures to these ends as may be recommended by the Northern Baptist Convention" [*Annual Report* (1913)].

[2] MMBB was founded under the auspices of the then Northern Baptist Convention. At mid-century, that organization changed its name to the American Baptist Convention, and still later to the American Baptist Churches in the USA. As a general practice we shall use the name current at the time of events described. Generally, however, the denominational name is interchangeable.

[3] For Mather, benevolence was not solely defined by helping the poor. By Mather's time, financial charity had become commonplace. He believed that those in need might more urgently need spiritual correction and "admonitions of piety" than handouts. Thus, he could query, "Cannot you contrive to mingle a spiritual charity with your temporal bounty?" Cotton Mather, *Bonifacius*, or *Essays to Do Good* (1710):169.

[4] William Penn, 1682, "The Cross of Christ." For additional sources of Penn's humanitarianism see Frederick B. Tolles and E. Gordon Aldefer, eds.,*The Witness of William Penn* (1957)

[5] The contemporary challenge of Bill Gates and Warren Buffet to their wealthy colleagues to distribute their wealth for the good of the world continued in that same spirit.

[6] Robert H. Bremner, *American Philanthropy*, 2nd ed. (Chicago: University of Chicago Press, 1988):42.

[7] There was a certain logic to this development: by discouraging individual charity specifically to the individual poor, it did not directly reward sloth or indolence. Schools, for example, were perceived to establish worthy ideals and habits and thus avoid individual poverty.

[8] David Charles Laubach, *To Think That It Happened On Mulberry Street*, (Valley Forge, PA: Board of National Ministries, American Baptist Churches USA, 2007):4.

[9] For a more complete description of the establishment of the American Baptist Home Mission Society see David Charles Laubach, *American Baptist Home Mission Roots: 1824-2010* (Valley Forge, PA: American Baptist Home Mission Societies, 2010):4–12.

[10] In the South, institutions established for freed black slaves included Wayland Seminary (Washington, DC):which later became part of Virginia Union University, Shaw University, Morehouse College, Benedict College, Florida Memorial University, and others. In the North, the ABHMS was instrumental in founding a number of colleges and universities, including New York University (originally focused on immigrant education):Vassar College, Denison University, Kalamazoo College, Franklin College, and Bacone College in Oklahoma, created especially to provide educational opportunities for Native Americans. In the developing American West, Redlands University in California and Linfield College in Oregon were both established under Northern Baptist and ABHMS auspices and supported by benevolent gifts through their connections.

[11] Henry L. Morehouse, then with the American Baptist Home Mission Society, had earlier advised Rockefeller on revising the curriculum for Spelman Seminary (later Spelman College). He led in the creation of the American Baptist Education Society in 1888 and chose Frederick T. Gates as its first Corresponding Secretary. Morehouse's early biographer, Lathan A. Crandall, includes material to indicate that Morehouse was pivotal in persuading a vacillating William Rainey Harper to accept the Presidency of the new university. And according to Ron Chernow, it was Gates, along with William Rainey Harper, who vigorously championed the idea of a Baptist university in Chicago, urged Rockefeller to back the project and encouraged his continued support. Rockefeller particularly admired Gates' exhaustive research and thorough presentation and ultimately engaged him as his assistant. Morehouse's cordial connections with Rockefeller and Gates would later serve MMBB well. See Ron Chernow, *Titan: The Life of John D. Rockefeller, Senior* (New York, 1998):309, and Lathan A. Crandall, *Henry Lyman Morehouse: A Biography* (Philadelphia: American Baptist Publication Society, 1919):133–34.

[12] Robert H. Bremner, *The Public Good: Philanthropy and Welfare in the Civil War Era* (New York: Alfred Knopf, 1980):125.

[13] Robert H. Bremner, *American Philanthropy*, (University of Chicago Press, 1988):p 101-102. Bremner cites one English critic who proposed that Carnegie's perspective was strictly based on a "gospel of wealth," rather than the gospel of Christianity. Carnegie accepted the phrase and extended it, saying that little could be accomplished by imitating Christ in the modern world. Instead, he argued, left free, the able and energetic wealthy should dispose of their surplus. He believed that such distribution was but one step in the longer process of social evolution.

[14] Rockefeller and Carnegie differed in motives. Carnegie advanced the precepts of social Darwinism as a rationale for philanthropy while Rockefeller was a life-long Baptist and exhibited a traditional concept of Judeo-Christian charity. He believed that "the Good Lord gave me the money," that he had been given his wealth for a purpose and that he was expected to handle it with care. Rockefeller tried to be faithful to that trust, and felt obligated to personally investigate the worthiness of every organization to which he gave. Ultimately, this practice took too much time, and he engaged the young former Baptist minister, Frederick T. Gates, to assist him and ultimately to lead in the process of giving away his resources where they would do the most good. Later, Rockefeller determined to lay aside what he called "retail giving" and to move instead into what he designated as "wholesale philanthropy" by which he meant an intentional, organized approach to addressing social problems on a large scale. See Bremner, *American Philanthropy*, 105–107, and Chernow, *Titan*, 361ff.

[15] Both Carnegie and Rockefeller were social architects at heart. One result of the generosity of both of these iconic titans was to establish philanthropy on a grand and noble scale in public perception. Still another, though, was to recognize and establish a pattern of ongoing philanthropy by using approaches that would enable "gifts to keep on giving" well beyond the lifetime of the donor, thus assuring support for worthy work. This intent was actualized through "foundations." Ironically, a primary inspiration for this concept was not the later usefulness of foundations to avoid tax on income or wealth. Instead, it was the dawning recognition of the need to create a business model of support that went beyond annual appeals and random personal donations. One inspiration for this understanding was a woman who was not herself wealthy at all: Jane Addams. Addams was the founder and sustainer of Hull House in Chicago, and in every practical respect, founder of the "settlement house" movement. As one scholar phrased it, "while Carnegie proposed building ladders on which the ambitious poor could rise, Miss Addams and other settlement house leaders went to live with the poor." Addams created a prototype of the modern foundation to support Hull House. See Bremner, *American Philanthropy*, 108.

[16] Examples include: The Rockefeller Institute for Medical Research, General Education Board, and Carnegie Foundation for the Advancement of Teaching, the Milbank Memorial Fund, the Russell Sage Foundation, The Carnegie Corporation of New York, and the Rockefeller Foundation.

[17] Henry Allen, "What it Felt Like": "Living in the American Century, 1900-1910, Starting from Zero," *Washington Post*, September 20, 1999, p. C 1, C 8.

[18] Isaac Watts, "Am I a Soldier of the Cross?" appended to Watts, Isaac, *Sermons*, (c. 1721-1724):

[19] Consistent with the style of the time, Milo C. Treat was most frequently identified as "M.C. Treat." Treat was originally insistent upon anonymity and

was, therefore, also referred to by Henry Morehouse and other contemporary MMBB leaders as "A Man from Pennsylvania."

[20] Henry Lyman Morehouse was born on a farm near Bangall, in Dutchess County, New York, in 1834 and later moved with his family to East Avon, New York, in the Genesee Valley. His family heritage included both farmers and ministers. He was not attracted to farming, and instead followed an educational path. He graduated from the University of Rochester in its earliest days and later the Rochester Theological Seminary. He recounted a time of spiritual awakening while he was in college and during a period when Charles Grandison Finney was preaching in the area. After his graduation from theological school in 1864, Morehouse entered the service of the Christian Commission for about six weeks, working in Front Royal, Cold Harbor, Belle Plain, and Petersburg, Virginia. Having promised to investigate a pastoral opportunity in East Saginaw, Michigan, he accepted a call and began work there. During that pastorate he built up the church and helped them build a new building. In 1872 he became pastor of the East Avenue Baptist Church in Rochester where he remained for over six years before becoming Corresponding Secretary of the ABHMS in 1879.

[21] The emerging railroad industry soon developed as the most hierarchical and stratified of American businesses, encompassing a labor force of imported immigrants barely distinguishable from slavery at the lowest end, a great variety of skilled and semiskilled workers in the middle ranks, and highly skilled and well-compensated professionals of many types in the highest levels of management. The development of railroads and their organizations exerted a strong influence on both the American economy and its emerging corporate structures.

[22] By 1920 it is estimated that approximately 15 percent of the US labor force had some kind of pension program.

[23] The B&O plan was a well-developed example of what later became known as a defined benefit plan. It allowed workers who had worked for the railroad for at least ten years to retire at age 65 with benefits ranging from 20 to 35 percent of wages. Elizabeth Fee, Linda Shopes, and Linda Zeidman, *The Baltimore Book: New Views of Local History* (Philadelphia: Temple University Press, 1991):11–14.

[24] Eugene V. Debs was instrumental in founding or advocating on behalf of several railroad unions, most notably the Brotherhood of Locomotive Firemen and the American Railway Union. He was one of the founding members of the International Labor Union and the Industrial Workers of the World, often demonized in the press as the "Wobblies," and cast in unpatriotic and insurrectionist light. During the ARU's strike against the Pullman Palace Car Company in 1894, and after its spread to other states and regions, President Grover Cleveland used the US Army to break the strike, and Debs was later arrested and sentenced for failing to observe an injunction against the strike. In

jail, Debs became convinced that socialism offered the best alternative for workers' needs and later ran in several presidential elections on the ballot of the Social Democratic Party, a socialist ticket.

[25] The College Retirement Equities Fund (CREF) was established and added much later in 1952. It was a "variable annuity" addition to the mostly fixed-income investments that TIAA had originally developed. CREF was largely invested in common stocks and, therefore, offered balance to the theoretical protection from the inflationary trends that were evident after World War II. It later influenced a similar approach by MMBB.

[26] Everett T. Tomlinson, *The First Twenty Years: The Ministers and Missionaries Benefit Board of the Northern Baptist Convention* (MMBB, c. 1931):6.

[27] Ibid., 13.

[28] Ibid.

[29] Many early pension programs, however, were predicated on insufficient financial planning or actuarial information, or both. Most of the railroad pensions, for example, were inadequately funded and, by the Depression, created a national crisis requiring federal resolution.

[30] Physicians and other medical workers advanced economically with the development of prepaid medical certificates and insurance. Blue Cross/Blue Shield emerged as the dominant form of coverage for both hospital and physician services and benefited both practitioners and consumers. The prototype for prepaid hospital protection, upon which Blue Cross was later based, was created by Justin Ford Kimball in 1929 at Baylor University, a Southern Baptist institution. It progressed from only 1,300 subscribers to three million in ten years.

[31] Tomlinson, 11.

[32] There is a story, possibly apocryphal, that about this time emissaries representing the building of New York's Red Brick (Presbyterian) Church visited Carnegie seeking support for their new church building. Carnegie was unenthusiastic about the project, so he sought to discourage them by saying that he would give $1 million for the project if they could find a single donor who would match it. It seemed an impossible task. However, the committee experienced good fortune and found such a donor. They returned to Carnegie to announce their success. The chagrined Carnegie sat down to write a check and then paused to ask, "May I ask who is the matching donor?" The committee chair smiled and said, "Of course! It is Mrs. Carnegie." It was a rare time when the shrewd industrial giant was out-maneuvered in negotiations.

[33] Tomlinson, 11.

[34] Tomlinson, 15.

[35] Henry Allen, "What it Felt Like: Living in the American Century, 1910-1920, The View From Over There," *Washington Post*, September 21, 1999, C 1, C 8.

[36] Henry Allen, From A Series *What it Felt Like: Living in the American Century*, 1910–1920, The View from Over There," *The Washington Post*, 21 September 1999, C-1, C-8. Much of this section is quoted, re-phrased or adapted from Allen's article. Words or phrases in quotations are direct quotes from it.

[37] Ibid, C-8.

[38] Although Conwell was a conservative evangelical preacher, his achievements as pastor position him as a key figure in the development of the "institutional church" movement.

[39] Conwell was born in Massachusetts and attended Yale University and Albany Law School. After several years as a lawyer, lecturer, and writer, he was called, in 1882, to the pastorate of Grace Baptist Church of Philadelphia, and by 1889 the congregation had grown so large that a new building was constructed. The new building was frequently referred to as Grace Temple or Temple Baptist Church. Conwell achieved national fame, largely as an inspirational and motivational speaker. A frequent centerpiece of his talks focused on a little girl who had been excluded from his church's Sunday school because of shortage of space, and then saved up 57 cents, which she contributed to the church to build a new Sunday school building. She died shortly thereafter. Its touching quality had great effect in fund-raising. Conwell's most popular lecture was based on a sermon, "Acres of Diamonds," whose central theme was that opportunities to get rich were all around and had only to be claimed. In his book A *People's History of the United States,* Howard Zinn quotes a portion of the speech that underlined the moral superiority of the wealthy and, in contrast, the likelihood of God's punishment of those who were poor: "I say that you ought to get rich, and it is your duty to get rich.... The men who get rich may be the most honest men you find in the community. Let me say here clearly ... ninety-eight out of one hundred of the rich men of America are honest. That is why they are rich. That is why they are trusted with money. That is why they carry on great enterprises and find plenty of people to work with them. It is because they are honest men.... I sympathize with the poor, but the number of poor who are to be sympathised with is very small. To sympathize with a man whom God has punished for his sins ... is to do wrong.... let us remember there is not a poor person in the United States who was not made poor by his own shortcomings...." A *People's History of the United States: 1492 to the Present,* (Harper Collins, New York, 2010):262.

[40] Everett T. Tomlinson, *The First Twenty Years: The Ministers and Missionaries Benefit Board of the Northern Baptist Convention* (MMBB, c. 1931):16-17.

[41] Tomlinson, 16–17. A similar message written in pencil on tablet paper signed "A Man from Pennsylvania" is contained in MMBB Correspondence Files.

[42] The donor, M.C. Treat, desired anonymity out of a genuine spirit of humility. He was also a very private person and desired neither the publicity nor the inconvenience that public recognition of his generosity would bring. His

preference for anonymity continued through his continuing support of MMBB, Northern Baptist and several other institutions.

[43] Tomlinson, 17.

[44] So strong was Tomlinson's reputation as an educational administrator that William Rainey Harper, president of the fledgling University of Chicago—at its inception a Baptist-related institution—had sought to persuade him to head the preparatory school associated with the university (later called "The Laboratory School"). Tomlinson did not accept the invitation. During Tomlinson's career, he published more than one hundred books, mostly containing stories from the heroes of American history, which were of interest to young boys.

[45] Tomlinson, 23.

[46] Tomlinson, 24.

[47] Arthur M. Harris was the nephew of the firm's founder, Norman Wait Harris of Chicago. Harris, Forbes & Company specialized in marketing municipal bonds and had achieved notoriety by pioneering a door-to-door approach in selling them. Norman Harris' strategy was to make investment in municipal bonds possible for people of modest means, a market segment not served by the established investment firms. Harris, Forbes & Co. merged with Chase Bank in 1930. In 1913 Arthur Harris became MMBB Treasurer, and between 1921 and 1933 he was Chair of the Finance Committee. His leadership and financial acuity were critical, both to the Board's early development and to MMBB's long-term financial success. He also served a term as President of the Northern Baptist Convention beginning in 1928.

[48] *MMBB Board Minutes,* vol. 1, 19. The Act of Incorporation of the Ministers and Missionaries Benefit Board under Chapter 107 of the Laws of New York is also reprinted in detail in Tomlinson, 43–44. The incorporation further defined the relationship to the Northern Baptist Convention as one in which the Convention's confirmation was required for approval of bylaws and general policies, and the Board was required to make an annual report to the Convention. By the time of incorporation, the MMBB Board had expanded to twenty-one persons serving three-year terms (although at the time of incorporation three-year, two-year and one-year terms were designated to balance the process); the Convention retained the power to appoint seven of the members as their terms expired and also to appoint members to fulfill the terms of those who departed by "death, resignation or otherwise." The Board itself also had the power to fill such vacancies. All appointments required the official nomination of the Convention Executive Committee. The Board retained the power to buy, sell, and hold a variety of financial instruments, including real estate, and to conduct and manage its affairs as it deemed proper, subject to the laws of the United States.

[49] *Board Minutes,* vol. 1, 69.

[50] Tomlinson, 51–52. The Pittsburgh funds were known as the Jane Nichols Ministerial Relief Fund. Other funds voluntarily merged with those of the Board included the Baptist Ministers Relief Association of West Virginia; funds for relief of the Central Baptist Association of New Jersey; the Hudson River Central Baptist Association; the Iowa Baptist State Convention; the Lincoln Benevolent Society of Maine; the Long Island Baptist Association, the Pittsburgh Baptist Association, the Warren, Providence, Narragansett and Roger Williams Association of Rhode Island; the Swedish Baptist Ministers Pension and Aid Association, and the United Baptist Convention of Maine, Free Baptists. Later, the funds of the Norwegian and Danish Baptists were also transferred to MMBB. In Massachusetts, it was agreed that two funds given for ministerial aid remained to be administered by their boards, but it was agreed that the boards would no longer appeal to churches for funds. Instead, the MMBB would appeal for church support, and that henceforth funds raised from Massachusetts churches would be allocated on a percentage basis within the state.

[51] Swasey later increased the fund to $300,000.

[52] Tomlinson, 57.

[53] Tomlinson, 59.

[54] Ibid., 60.

[55] *Board Minutes*, vol. 1, 186–87.

[56] Tomlinson, 61. Tomlinson's figures included "profit from the money." Other figures suggest that the total grants were slightly less than $7 million. In any case, support from the Rockefeller family and foundations in fact ultimately was greater, especially including the family's role in acquiring the Interchurch Center property of which MMBB became a partner in developing.

[57] *Board Minutes,* vol. 1, 235.

[58] *Annual Report* (1920).

[59] Henry Allen, "What it Felt Like: Living in the American Century: 1920-1930, The Gin Before the Storm", *Washington Post*, September 22, 1999, p. C-1, C 10. This section, "A Sense of the Times," is significantly quoted, paraphrased or adapted from the Allen article, published at the turn of the millennium in 1999.

[60] M. Forest Ashbrook reported that in 1922 MMBB received $457,400 from churches and individuals, and in 1931 only received $309,583 from the same sources, a decrease of $147,818.

[61] *Board Minutes*, vol. 1, 342.

[62] In 1936 the subsidy was reduced to 58.5 percent and discontinued in 1945.

[63] One or more state pension funds for teachers had recently proved bankrupt. Tomlinson reports that this example caused the Board to be especially careful in devising the MMBB Retiring Fund and strengthened their resolve to base their plan on conservative financial assumptions. Tomlinson, 64.

[64] Ibid., 65-66.

[65] *Board Minutes*, vol. 1, 201ff.

[66] Even after adoption, there was significant confusion about the Plan's provisions. Tomlinson reports that one minister wrote to say he had heard of Mr. Rockefeller's large gift to Baptist ministers. He confessed that he was tired of preaching and would be glad to retire. He proposed to buy a farm and requested that a check be sent to him representing his share of Rockefeller's gift so that he could do so.

[67] *The Ministry*, May 1938.

[68] In the early years of the Retiring Pension Fund, "dues" and "premiums" were used interchangeably by many. Those who paid into the Fund most frequently used the word dues, possibly because of the influence of unions whose members paid dues, and because in order to participate in the pension program, one had to be an MMBB member. Membership implied dues. Later, especially after the introduction of the variable annuity style of fund, the word premium dominant.

[69] Specifically, beginning 1 January 1924, ministers for whom dues had been paid to age 65, and who at the age of 65 had served either for a minimum of thirty-five years in denominational churches, or if less than thirty-five years, had served their entire career in the denomination, and had retired without salary, parsonage or any other financial support, would have their pensions increase to no less than $500, except that in no case could it exceed the average annual salary the minister had received during his active ministry.

[70] *Annual Report* (1924).

[71] MMBB continued to keep a Registry of Ministers until about 1960. An extensive collection of registry materials, as well as later biographical materials about many American Baptist ministers and missionaries is available at the American Baptist Historical Society in Atlanta, Georgia.

[72] MMBB's role in placement was largely accidental and developed out of the practical reality that it possessed the only comprehensive list of all ABC ministers. By the mid-twentieth century, MMBB was serving as a kind of clearinghouse and matchmaker for ministers seeking positions, and for churches seeking ministers. This function was accomplished by keeping a basic profile of individual ministers, which included education, experience, and recommendations. A similar role was performed by many American Baptist-related seminaries for their graduates.

[73] *Board Minutes*, vol. 1, 275.

[74] Tomlinson, 77. Wright had served as Recording Secretary of the Board. Following his appointment as Associate Secretary of MMBB, the Rev. Clarence Gallup was elected as his successor. Gallup continued to serve on the Board until 1936.

[75] The Publication Society remained in Philadelphia, its long established location.

[76] It appears that the financial stresses on ministers created by the Depression helped motivate participation in this registry by ministers. During that period, MMBB was more frequently perceived as a "refuge" than a threat.

[77] The economic and social development of the far west was only accomplished after about 1850. Baptists had been generally successful in establishing churches in the western regions, but the affiliations and identities of those churches were not well defined. The American Baptist Publication Society and the American Baptist Home Mission Boards, for example, had collaborated in the use of railroad cars to help establish new churches near, or intersecting with, rail lines as the railroads were rapidly build in that period. Of the hundreds of churches and Sunday Schools initiated or encouraged by their efforts, relatively few were clearly affiliated with a particular Baptist body, and those who were, often followed the lead of the pastors who served them. A great many became independent or affiliated with the Southern Baptist Convention before the Northern Baptist Convention established a more clear presence in the area. See Wilma Rugh Taylor and Norman Thomas Taylor, *This Train is Bound for Glory: The Story of American Chapel Cars*, (Valley Forge, PA: Judson Press, 1999).

[78] Tomlinson, 92; *Annual Report* (1931).

[79] From 1927 to 1931, Tomlinson regularly went to the MMBB offices and offered his service, support, and counsel to both the Board and to P.C. Wright, his successor. During that time, he also compiled the first history of the MMBB, *The First Twenty Years*, published by MMBB in 1931. Tomlinson died on 30 October 1931. According to P.C. Wright, Tomlinson had finished the work on the history only a week before his death. In his tribute to Tomlinson, P.C. Wright said of him that "he gloried in the valor and victories of the old soldiers of the Cross ... for during recent years he himself cheerfully and bravely fought a good fight against the foes that came ... he went down with colors flying."

[80] Cress was reared in cattle country near Abilene, Kansas. He was ordained in 1898, prior to receiving his theological education, and embarked as a missionary to Rhodesia (now Zimbabwe). Ill health forced his return from South Africa. Following his return, Cress graduated from the Divinity School of the University of Chicago. He began his work with MMBB on 1 May 1930, at a salary of $4,500. *Annual Report* (1930): 5; *Board Minutes* (February 1951):85; *Tomorrow Magazine*, Spring, Second Quarter, (1945): 6.

[81] *Annual Report* (1935): 8.

[82] *The Ministry* began publication with an October 1922 issue and continued until 1941 when it was transformed into *Tomorrow Magazine*. See also Tomlinson, 75.

[83] The October 1925 issue of *The Ministry* carried a piece titled "A Warning from Business," which described the failure of a recent employee lawsuit against the Armour & Company, which had taken over Morris & Company. The suit sought to compel Armour to fulfill Morris employee pension expectations in a

non-contributory pension fund. It also noted that "even the great Carnegie Foundation which instituted free pensions for teachers, found its accrued liabilities so great that it was obliged to discontinue the system" and to replace it with a contributory plan. *The Ministry* 4, no. 1 (October 1925): 3.

[84] *The Ministry* 1, no. 4 (June 1923): 3.

[85] Ibid.

[86] In 1930 the Executive Committee of the Northern Baptist Convention asked MMBB to create and maintain a registry of the ministers and missionaries in the convention, which inevitably focused even greater attention on standards for accreditation and qualification for ministers. MMBB voted to establish a Bureau of Ministerial Records and established a Committee on *The Ministry* to over see this responsibility. *Board Committee Minutes*, vol. A 1930, 216 and *Annual Report* (1930).

[87] *The Ministry*, Vol. II, No. 2, January (1924): 1-2.

[88] *The Ministry*, Vol. IV, No. 3, April (1926): 4.

[89] In a later issue, it was reported that this same minister, then over ninety, was in such dire straights that he had requested additional emergency assistance from his denominational pension board.

[90] *The Ministry*, Vol. III, No. 3, April (1925): 4.

[91] See, for example, "Are Ministers Old at Fifty?" in *The Ministry* 8, no. 2 (January 1930): 2.

[92] *The Ministry* 4, no. 4 (June 1926): 2.

[93] *The Ministry* 7, no. 1 (October 1928): 2.

[94] *The Ministry*, Vol. VII, No. 1, October, 1928: 3.

[95] Ibid.

[96] Henry Allen, From a Series, *What it Felt Like Living in the American Century*, 1930–1940: A Crashing Silence Settles In," *The Washington Post*, 23 September 1999, C-1, C-8.

[97] Henry Allen, "What it Felt Like: Living in the American Century," 1940-1950, Exploding into a Brave New World" The Washington Post, September 24, 1999, p. C 1, C 8.

[98] Henry Allen, "What It Felt Like: Living in the American Century," 1940-1950: Exploding Into a Brave New World," *The Washington Post*, 24 September 1999, C-1.

[99] *The Ministry* 9, no. 4 (June 1931): 3.

[100] *The Ministry* 9, no. 3 (April 1931): 2.

[101] M. Forest Ashbrook, "Fifty Years of Service, Part II: The Story of the Next 30 years," (unpublished manuscript, MMBB Archives): 4. Ashbrook was Assistant to the Executive Secretary from 1935 to 1940, and following Peter C. Wright's retirement in 1940, was Executive Director from 1940 to 1961.

[102] Ashbrook, "Fifty Years," 6.

[103] *The Ministry* 9, no. 1 (October 1932): 3.

[104] Letter from Arthur M. Harris, MMBB Treasurer to W.A. Staub, Chairman, Finance Committee of the Northern Baptist Convention, 11 November 1931, quoted in Ashbrook, "Fifty Years," 6–7.

[105] *Board Minutes*, vol. B (1931): 40.

[106] *The Ministry* 10, no. 1 (October 1931): 2.

[107] Ashbrook, "Fifty Years," 12.

[108] The changes instituted for the new Retiring Pension Plan were described in *The Ministry* 14, no. 3 (May 1936): 2, and in *Annual Report* (1935).

[109] At the same time, those on the waiting list were given the opportunity to join the program at the older 6 percent level, and about three-fourths of the list did so. The cost of those who did was covered by a transfer from the Permanent Fund to the Retiring Pension Fund.

[110] The transfer of larger financial responsibilities for the pension payments to the churches did stimulate some objections and concerns. It was rumored in some areas that the reason for the increase was that MMBB had lost significant funds during the Depression, for example. And, in general, there was fear that churches could not bear the increased contribution required. In fact, MMBB assets had survived intact, and the churches responded amazingly well in accepting a greater percentage share of pension plan payments. See Ashbrook, "Fifty Years," 18.

[111] *Annual Report* (1935). In 1936 the Communion Fellowship Offering took in more than $15,000 and progressed in 1943 to $41,000; in 1953 to $87,000; and 1960 to $110,000.

[112] Ashbrook, "Fifty Years," 19. The stress of responding to emergency grants was considerable because funds for that purpose were limited.

[113] Letter from John D. Rockefeller to MMBB in Historical Correspondence Files. While this announcement was certainly unhappy news in light of the generosity Rockefeller had exhibited to the MMBB in the past, it was not without foundation. Rockefeller's philanthropic philosophy had evolved considerably. His early demonstrated commitment to tithing his income, first to his own church, and then to other Baptist causes and institutions, had greatly benefited Baptists, but Rockefeller had developed an increasingly global view of philanthropy, as well as an acute awareness of the unique role his wealth required of him. With regard to religious institutions in particular, his vision for the future was that churches ought not to compete, but to cooperate. It followed that support for particular denominational goals tended to enhance competition, not cooperation. His decision was, therefore, consistent with his business views and, in all likelihood, his understanding of the complexity of social needs.

[114] *Board Minutes*, vol. B (1934):138.

[115] Fulton began her work with MMBB in 1935, and formally retired in September 1953. However, following her retirement, she continued to provide services to the Board particularly writing a column "Women's Concerns" in

Tomorrow Magazine and speaking and writing in a variety of contexts for both MMBB and the denomination, especially to women's groups.

[116] *Annual Report* (1938) and *The Ministry* XVI, no. 3 (May 1938).

[117] *The Ministry* IX, no. 3 (June 1933): 4.

[118] *Annual Report* (1938).

[119] *Board Minutes*, vol. B, (1936):148.

[120] *The Ministry*, Vol IX, No. 2, January, 1931, p. 2. This article reported that in Missouri, 900 out of a total of 1600 Baptist ministers were out of work

[121] *The Ministry*, Vol XI, No. 2, January, 1933, 3

[122] Ministry, Vol. IX, No. 3, April 1931: 2.

[123] *The Ministry*, XI, No. 2, January, 1933: 4.

[124] *The Ministry*, Vol. XI, No. 3 (June, 1933): 5.

[125] *The Ministry* 12, no. 3 (May 1934): 3. In that example, MMBB responded with an emergency grant and an ongoing regular grant to provide for medical care and sufficient food.

[126] *Annual Report* (1932): 5.

[127] *The Ministry*, Vol. XI, No. 3 (June, 1933): 4.

[128] The 86-year -old considering retirement confessed that, "in 57 years of strict economy I had saved $1600 but lost it all a year ago. I have taken but fourteen vacations of two weeks each in 57 years." *The Ministry* 12, No. 3 (May, 1934): 3.

[129] "Whisky Sets an Example for the Christian Church," *The Ministry* XVII, no. 3 (May 1939): 4.

[130] *The Ministry* XII, no. 1 (October 1933): 4. The Convention address was presented by the Rev. James D. Morrison of Providence, Rhode Island, and the full address was included in *The Baptist World*, (1 June 1933). Morrison was a member of the MMBB Board at the time of his address.

[131] The title of Executive Secretary was changed to Executive Director when M. Forest Ashbrook assumed the responsibilities of the office. *Board Minutes*, vol. C (1940):116.

[132] *The Ministry* XIX, no. 1 (October 1940): 2. The same edition announced the election of Charles E. Wilson, President and Director of General Electric, as a member of the Board.

[133] The election of J. Herbert Case to these offices is further evidence of effective succession planning on the Board. Case was elected to the MMBB Board in 1922, and in all likelihood he had been identified for that role by Arthur M. Harris. Like Harris, Case was a long-standing member of the First-Park Baptist Church of Plainfield, New Jersey. Also like Harris, he had a distinguished career in financial management in several banking and investment firms. He served successively as Deputy Governor (1917–1930) and then Governor (1930–36):of the Federal Reserve Bank of New York. In 1942 he was elected as Vice President of the MMBB while also serving as Treasurer. He resigned from the Board in 1947,

but continued as an honorary member until his death in 1972. *Annual Reports* (1940):7; *Annual Reports* (1947):9; *Annual Reports* (1972):9. *Tomorrow*, Fourth Quarter (1944): 3.

[134] Ashbrook reported that only eight had been received in 1936 and 44 in 1937. Ashbrook, "Fifty Years," 32.

[135] *Annual Report* (1943):6; *Annual Report* (1944):8. *Minutes, Executive Committee Meeting*, item C918 (17 March 1942).

[136] Ashbrook, "Fifty Years," 43. As a related issue, Ashbrook recalls that there was a desire for the MMBB to merge the Communion Fellowship Offering with offerings received for the World Emergency Fund. Ashbrook recalled that he firmly resisted that proposal because he feared it would ultimately result in the long-term loss of the Communion Offering for the Board's work.

[137] The 20 percent reduction in dues was limited to compensation up to $5,000, or a maximum reduction of dues in dollar amount of $100. MMBB, therefore, provided 2 percent of the 10 percent total dues required. *Annual Report* (1942).

[138] *Tomorrow: The M & M Quarterly* (Winter 1944): 2.

[139] *Annual Report* (1945); Ashbrook, "Fifty Years," 50. The states with the highest percentages of participation were California, Utah, Montana, New Hampshire, North and South Dakota, Washington, and Wyoming.

[140] *Annual Report* (1946).

[141] *Board Minutes*, vols. C and D (1943): 275–76.

[142] *Tomorrow* (Winter 1944): 13. Part of the rapid rise in food costs was attributable to wartime scarcity, restrictions, and rationing.

[143] The World Mission Crusade was a denomination-wide fund-raising program to secure and advance a wide variety of Northern Baptist Convention (later American Baptist Convention) programs and goals, and with a financial goal of $14,000,000 to be raised in the years 1945–46 and 1946–47. It was part of an overall financial development program of the Northern Baptist Convention called The Crusade for Christ. *Yearbook of the Northern Baptist Convention* (1945):115.

[144] MMBB *Annual Reports* show receipts from the World Mission Crusade of $354,719.62 for 1946, $873,215.15 for 1947, $459,218.03 for 1948, and $82,841.81 for 1949. The greatest portion of WMC-derived funds was applied to increase the reserves of the Retiring Pension Fund. John Bone reported that through 1948 the amount added to those reserves from the WMC was $1,421,568.56. See John S. Bone, *The Better Maintenance of* The Ministry—*The First Seventy Five Years of the Ministers and Missionaries Benefit Board* (The Ministers and Missionaries Benefit Board, New York, 1987.):109.

[145] In 1915 the Baptist Ministers' Home Society had turned over significant assets to MMBB and agreed to eventual corporate mergers. By 1942 it was agreed that the Society could be disbanded, and MMBB received about $129,000 in

remaining funds. Likewise, The Baptist Ministers' Aid Society had agreed to merge with MMBB, but continuing obligations required its existence for many years. In 1938 the remaining residents of the Fenton Home in Michigan were transferred to the Baptist Old People's Home in Maywood, Illinois, with an agreement that MMBB would continue certain provisions for their support and care, as well as to continue several annuities contracted by that Society. Their remaining assets of $140,010 were transferred to MMBB. Ashbrook, "Fifty Years," 67.

[146] Provision for emergency grants in addition to grants to elderly ministers who had not been part of the Participating Retirement Fund continued to loom as a major challenge. *Annual Report* (1947).

[147] *Tomorrow* (Winter 1944): 11.

[148] *Board Minutes*, Vol. D (1947):163. This action was in part a result of a study 374 questionnaires sent to those receiving pensions of less than $500 joint, $300 single or $200 as a widow, in light of economic circumstances and inflationary experience.

[149] *Tomorrow,* Fourth Quarter (1945): 6.

[150] George W. Bovenizer, like Harris and Case before him, had a distinguished career in finance, was a partner in the firm of Kuhn, Loeb & Company, and was a Director of several corporations. *Annual Report* (1947): 9–10; *Tomorrow*, Third Quarter (1947): 5. Bovenizer served until 1961.

[151] In 1949, Dr. Avery Shaw also died. Shaw had served the Board for 29 years, 18 of which were as President.

[152] *Tomorrow,* Fourth Quarter (1948): 3.

[153] Henry Allen, (From a Series, "What It Felt Like") "Living in the American Century, 1950-1960, "The Split Level Years," The Washington Post, September 27, 1999, C 1, C 8.

[154] *Board Minutes*, vol. E (1951): 75–78. Huggins and Company was a Philadelphia-based consulting company founded by George A. Huggins, who was a distinguished actuary and one of the first specialists in clergy pensions. In 1951 Huggins and Company served at least twenty denominations' pension funds, as well as a large number of municipal and state employee pensions and many commercial and corporate pensions.

[155] It was Jenkins who encouraged Ashbrook to investigate a variable annuity style of pension investment structure that TIAA was considering at that time.

[156] *Board Minutes*, vol. F (1934): 65.

[157] *Tomorrow* (September 1955): 9.

[158] *Tomorrow* (May 1951): 12–13.

[159] MMBB's focus on financial practicalities generally kept it free of theological debate. Still, from the beginning, contentious opinions were expressed in or to the Board. For example, Milo C. Treat wrote to Everett

Tomlinson in 1918, "I wonder if your Board is clean and free from the German made Philosophy. Have you any who call themselves Liberals on the Board? If so people will not want such to handle money for Christ's work and his people. You see what it has done for some of our colleges." Correspondence, Treat to Tomlinson, 3 October 1918.

[160] *Board Minutes*, Vol. D (1945):37; John S. Bone, *The Better Maintenanc of The Ministry: The First Seventy-five Years,* (The Ministers and Missionaries Benefit Board, 1987), 104.

[161] *Board Minutes,* vol. D (1949): 261.

[162] Ibid, 269

[163] *Annual Report* (1950); *Tomorrow* (Winter 1950): 3.

[164] These achievements are discussed in greater detail below.

[165] *Annual Report* (1951).

[166] *Annual Report* (1951): 8–9.

[167] *Board Minutes,* Vol. F (1954): 45–46

[168] The new 11 percent plan became the standard plan for all new participants as of 1 July 1954. At that time, only 4 percent of the members of the previous plans had not converted to the new 11 percent plan. They were given until 31 December 1954, to convert, with only a $20 transfer payment that was applied to the upcoming dues.

[169] *Annual Report* (1954). Approximately nine hundred members received such supplements.

[170] Ashbrook, p. 111.

[171] *Board Minutes,* vol. G (1956): 25–26. Retired ministers and widows were not initially included. All retired foreign missionaries received the Senior Health Plan without cost as a result of a legacy provided by Marguerite T. Doane.

[172] M. Forest Ashbrook, "Fifty Years of Service, Part II: The Story of the Next 30 years," (unpublished manuscript, MMBB Archives):113.

[173] *Tomorrow* (September 1956): 16–17.

[174] By November 1957, the first year of operation, $487,324 was paid out in benefits for the Family and Senior plans.

[175] *Board Minutes,* Vol. G (1957): 128–130. The amounts provided to administer the Pension Plan and to build reserves were $10,000 for 1957 and $15,000 for 1958.

[176] *Annual Report* (1956): 14.

[177] The programs ultimately were popularly known as "Social Security" but were originally created as the Federal Old-Age, Survivors, and Disability Insurance system.

[178] *Annual Report* (1952).

[179] *Board Minutes,* vol. F (1953): 15.

[180] On several occasions the deadline for enrollment was extended or windows of opportunity were created for enrollment of ministers who had

originally not been covered, whether by neglect or, in many cases, reasons of conscience based on a misunderstanding of the voluntary, self-employment provisions of the amended law.

[181] *Board Minutes* (1954): 65.

[182] *Tomorrow* (September 1955): 5. This article noted that the self-employment tax for ministers in Social Security was 3 percent.

[183] *Tomorrow* (January 1958): 8–11.

[184] *Annual Report* (1955).

[185] Some churches reduced salary amounts by all, or a portion, of the amount required to cover the dues. Over time, however, churches or sponsoring agencies nearly universally assumed the burden of the Retiring Pension Fund dues.

[186] Non-contractual services at MMBB were generally perceived to be activities and programs such as emergency assistance, supplemental grants, educational grants, medical assistance, support for ministers' career development, programs to support or raise salaries, financial and retirement planning, annual "Thank You Offering" gift checks, and, from time-to-time, special programs to heighten awareness of emerging social or ministry challenges. Outlays for such non-contractual services for ministers and missionaries from 1912–2008 totaled nearly $210 million. Non-contractual programs for lay-employees from 1970–2008 totaled $15 million.

[187] In 1954 the MMBB Annual Report began reporting Convention and Offering receipts and their use.

[188] *Annual Report* (1956, 1957).

[189] *Annual Report* (1957): 6.

[190] Sturges was then pastor of the Central Baptist Church in Providence, Rhode Island, and was a member of the MMBB Board of Managers. His address was entitled "Fortieth Anniversary Advances." At the same dinner, Associate Director John L. Thomas led a panel discussion on the subject "Should Ministers Be Eligible for Social Security?" *Tomorrow* (May 1952): 9.

[191] In 1952, and in some subsequent years, funding was provided by a layman, who wished to offer his support in this way.

[192] *Annual Report* (1953).

[193] *Board Minutes*, Vol. G (1956): 13. In 1956–57 the salary for special promotional workers was $15,000 for salary and $7,500 for travel expenses.

[194] Other resources included limited service by the theological schools and seminaries, which kept files on graduates and sought to recommend their own graduates for placement opportunities.

[195] *Board Minutes*, Vol. G (1957): 125–128.

[196] The Boston office was later re-located to Valley Forge, Pennsylvania, following the opening of the new American Baptist headquarters building there.

[197] *Board Minutes*, Vol. H (1958): 103–04.

[198] *Tomorrow* (September 1959): 17–24. Examples of its contributions include conferences for ministers, regional and state presentations on subjects of ministry concern, conferences on *The Ministry*, strategies for recruitment of ministerial candidates, support of ministerial education, systems to improve placement of ministers, salary studies, training programs, and studies on standards for ordination and ministerial ethics

[199] Lynn Leavenworth, "Too Old at 55?" in *Tomorrow* (May, 1953): 18-21.

[200] *Tomorrow* (September 1958): 4-8.

[201] The Gift was continued and increased on several occasions using a formula that took into account years of service and the amount of the annuity. Following the introduction of the ABC Retirement Plan in 1964, the need for the Gift program declined. In 1974 the Board voted that any newly eligible annuitant born in or after 1910 would not receive a Gift, and the Gift for all annuitants was reduced by 10 percent.

[202] Ashbrook, "Fifty Years," 126.

[203] *Board Minutes*, Vol. H (1958): 68–69.

[204] Harold Stassen was a former Minnesota Governor and US presidential candidate, as well as President of the American Baptist Convention. He had been appointed by Eisenhower to the committee that framed the charter of the United Nations. Consequently, the vision for international and inter-denominational cooperation was highly visible and focused for many American Baptists.

[205] John D. Rockefeller, Jr., to William R. Conklin, 21 November 1945 in Correspondence Files.

[206] Ashbrook, "Fifty Years," 130.

[207] MMBB operated a branch office at the Valley Forge headquarters building for many years, primarily to serve the needs of the building's employees, but also to maintain a "presence" with the other agencies.

[208] Ashbrook, "Fifty Years," 135. Despite the occasional vicissitudes of the New York real estate market, MMBB's original investment in monetary terms has multiplied since the building's construction.

[209] Bartlett, "The Gospel Confronts the Contemporary, " (MMBB, 1958):in MMBB Archives.

[210] Henry Allen, (Form a series, *What It Felt Like*) "Living in the American Century, 1960–1970" In Sad Pursuit of Happiness," *The Washington Post*, 28 September 1999, C-1, C8. Much of the material in this section is an adaptation from Allen's piece and is a mixture of fact and fiction, image and reality.

[211] Ibid, C-2.

[212] *Board Minutes*, Vol. I (1960): 25. As amended, the revised bylaw specified that "not less than 50% of the book value of the assets" shall be invested in fixed-income securities. Since book value is frequently less than appreciated value, this change created wide latitude for future investment policy.

[213] *Board Minutes*, Vol. K (1965): 239–242.

[214] Ibid, 28–32.

[215] *Board Minutes*, Vol. K (1964): 109–113.

[216] *Board Minutes*, Vol. M (1968): 21–25, 50–53; *Supplemental Minutes*, item 549.

[217] Additional aspects of these proceedings will be referenced in the section on civil rights below.

[218] *Board Minutes*, Vol. I (1961): 140–41; *Tomorrow* (September 1961): 20.

[219] *Tomorrow* (September 1961): 16, 22. See this source, especially 4–5, 8–18, and 22–23, for additional biographical and testimonial information regarding Ashbrook's leadership.

[220] *Tomorrow* (September 1961): 7. Wright had previously graduated from Linfield College (McMinnville, Oregon) and Yale University Divinity School and had done graduate work at Columbia University.

[221] *Tomorrow* (January 1962): 9. After Tillinghast's death in 1998, Brown University honored him by creating the Tillinghast Chair of International Studies. An interesting piece of American corporate history and American language usage resulted from Tillinghast's appointment as CEO of TWA. At that time, a group of creditors were seeking to oust famous aviator, Howard Hughes, from control of the TWA Board and were involved in litigation with TWA. In order to gain Tillinghast's services TWA devised a contract containing clauses protecting Tillinghast financially in the event the creditors were successful in deposing Hughes and Tillinghast were to be removed as CEO. In describing that contract, *TIME* magazine, soon frequently to be copied, used the phrase "Golden Parachute" to describe the contract's protections for the first recorded time. The creditors failed, and Tillinghast went on to preside over the "golden era" of TWA.

[222] *Tomorrow* (September 1963): 25, 26, 28.

[223] *Tomorrow* (January 1966): 24; (October 1968): 19; and (October 1970): 22.

[224] *Board Minutes*, Vol. I (1961): 142–43. An additional provision of the changes allowed that changes to MMBB bylaws could be initiated by delegates of the annual meeting of the American Baptist Convention. That provision did not immediately affect Board operations or autonomy. A decade later, however, its implications were expanded.

[225] *Board Minutes*, Vol. J (1962): 19–21. The formula for "The Gift" was becoming complicated because of inflationary trends and the low pensions received by the earliest participants. For example, those receiving pensions who were born prior to 1886 and met the basic requirements received from The Gift a total annual amount of 50 percent of their pension in June, and an additional 25 percent in December. Rather than reflecting unusual generosity, this amount reflected the struggle to keep pace with rising costs in an equitable manner in light of length of service and longevity.

[226] *Board Minutes*, Vol. J (1962): 19–21.

[227] Ibid, 90–91.

[228] *Board Minutes*, Vol. J (1963):135–36; *Tomorrow* (May 1963): 4–11. In 1965 the name was changed from "Variable Annuity Supplement" (VAS):to "The Annuity Supplement" (TAS). *Board Minutes*, vol. K (1965): 243.

[229] *Annual Report* (1963):7.

[230] Ibid, 118–19, 217.

[231] Chaplains serving were required to be endorsed by the Committee on Chaplains of the American Baptist Convention. *Board Minutes*, vol. K (1965):169–70.

[232] *Board Minutes*, Vol. M (1969): 97.

[233] Ibid., 62–63.

[234] *Tomorrow* (May 1961): 5–19.

[235] As examples, see the articles, "About Minimum Salary Plans," by Charles N. Forsberg in *Tomorrow* (September 1961): [24-25 and "Adequate Compensation for the Pastoral Ministry," by Russell S. Orr, also in *Tomorrow* (September 1962): [4-9]. Similar articles appeared almost yearly.

[236] *Annual Report* (1968); *Board Minutes*, Vol. L (1967):160; *Supplemental Minutes*, item 537.

[237] *Board Minutes*, Vol. M (1969):121.

[238] *Tomorrow* (September 1965): 1–21. This issue was dedicated to ministerial compensation and thus demonstrates MMBB's approach to a number of expense categories, including housing.

[239] *Board Minutes*, Vol. J (1962):103; *Tomorrow* (September 1960): 3-8 ; *Tomorrow* (January 1961): 18-22 .

[240] Some churches opted to sell their parsonages and invest the funds to provide income to support housing allowances. Others retained the homes for rental or for use by other staff members. Ministerial home ownership remained a problem for both ministers and churches, however. In come communities, housing costs escalated so rapidly that ministers were unable to purchase homes. In such communities, it often proved difficult for churches to re-enter the housing market for subsequent pastors who preferred church-provided housing.

[241] *Tomorrow*, (May, 1962): 3-6.

[242] *Tomorrow*, (January, 1963): 4-10

[243] *Board Minutes*, Vol. K (1964): 24.

[244] *Board Minutes*, Vol. I (1960): 46, 120, 147.

[245] *Board Minutes*, Vol. J (1963): 203. The opening of this office was largely in response to growing tensions in Southern churches resulting from civil rights confrontations. In many material respects, it was a critical part of the establishment of the American Baptist presence in the South and, ultimately, the development of an ABC/USA administrative region.

[246] *Board Minutes*, Vol. J (1962): 87–88 and *Supplemental Minutes*, item 521.

[247] *Board Minutes*, Vol. I (1961): 121–23.

[248] Oren H. Baker, "Profile of the American Baptist Pastor: Summary of a Study (The Ministers and Missionaries Benefit Board, 1962," from the Foreword of the "Profile." ; "The Baker Study is Presented to the Board of Managers," *Tomorrow* (January 1963): 21.

[249] *Board Minutes*, Vol. L (1967): 165–166.

[250] *Board Minutes*, Vol. J (1963): 203; *Annual Report* (1992):13.

[251] *Board Minutes*, Vol. L (1967): 168.

[252] *Tomorrow* (January 1965): 27; *Board Minutes*, Vol. M (1968): 40; *Supplemental Minutes*, item 552.

[253] With a few exceptions, printed versions of the MMBB Luncheon addresses are available in the MMBB Archives and at the American Baptist Historical Society.

[254] William H. Brackney, "Baptists and Transformation: American Baptist Contributions," *American Baptist Quarterly* 28, no. 2 (Summer 2009): 153.

[255] *Board Minutes*, Vol. L (June 1963): 165.

[256] Ibid, 166.

[257] *Board Minutes* (September 1963): 167.

[258] England also maintained contact, and on occasion worked with, J. C. Herrin, who during that time was funded by the American Baptist Home Mission Society to work among churches in the South. Like England, Herrin was a native of the South who had become an American Baptist following his dismissal as Southern Baptist Chaplain at the University of North Carolina for advocating racial equality in his work with student groups. Following his dismissal, and prior to his association with the Home Mission Society, Herrin served briefly as an Associate Minister at the Scarsdale Community Baptist Church. Forest Ashbrook, former MMBB Executive Director, was a member, of that congregation, along with Forrest Smith, long-time Treasurer of the Home Mission Society, and several other denominational leaders.

[259] *Board Minutes*, Vol. K (1968): 24. England's work was ecumenical. His connections extended to black and white Baptist, Methodist, Presbyterian, Southern Baptists, and to non-religious groups such as SNIC, COFO, CORE, FDP, SCLC, SRC, and governmental offices such as OEO and VISTA. One grateful admirer said, "He knows more Catholic contacts than any Protestant I know."

[260] *Oral Memoirs of Jasper Martin England and Mabel Orr England*, interviewed by David Stricklin, Baylor University Institute for Oral History (1996):55. *Letter from a Birmingham Jail* was a galvanizing document in developing support for the civil rights effort, especially among religious leaders, and later became a classic of the rhetoric of the period. It is frequently included as a masterpiece in collections of American literature.

[261] *Board Minutes*, Vol. K (1965): 160–67, 250–51.

[262] Ibid, 76.

[263] Board Minutes, (1968): 21-25, 50-53.

[264] There was also a conflict of purpose contained in the dilemma. The MMBB, as chartered for a specific purpose, had legal requirements that were more limiting than other charitable society boards might have. And, were they to begin investing funds for the purpose of achieving social goals rather than its chartered purpose, they might not be "properly carrying out their duties and fiduciaries." See *Supplemental Minutes*, item 549, 6. David Rockefeller was born in 1915 and was the youngest son of John D. Rockefeller, Jr. Although never active in Baptist affairs or the MMBB, he provided the Board with information and advice on several occasions. David Rockefeller assumed the role of Chief Executive Officer and Chairman of the Board of Chase Manhattan Bank in 1969. The bank later became JPMorgan Chase.

[265] The banks ultimately chosen for investments, mostly in the form of savings accounts of Certificates of Deposit, held as few as $829,013 in assets (Connecticut Savings & Loan Association in Hartford):to as much as $27,210,281 (the Freedom National Bank in New York City). In addition, other banks were located in the poorer sections of Richmond, Los Angeles, Nashville, Denver, Seattle, Philadelphia, Cleveland, Chicago, Detroit, Atlanta, Milwaukee, Baltimore, Washington, DC, Greensboro, North Carolina, and Roxbury, Massachusetts (near Boston). Amounts deposited were $15,000 in each bank, except for three banks with deposits of $10,000. In each case, an African-American pastor or leader was the contact person/consultant. Prominent examples in that group included David T. Shannon, Floyd Massey, Jr., Samuel B. McKinney, Martin Luther King, Sr., Harold A. Carter, and Samuel D. Proctor.

[266] *Tomorrow* (January 1969):23.

[267] *Board Minutes*, Vol. K (1964):49.

[268] Ibid, 98–99.

[269] *Annual Report* (1964):5. One percent of members' salary contribution was supplemented by Endowment Funds to enable lower-paid ministers to have the health benefit and pension programs.

[270] Among those who reported lower-than-actual salaries for this purpose were some of the ABC national boards and agencies, for whom the increased costs would create a budget crisis. As another tactic, the Board had approved in 1965 the Ministerial Support Program (Shared Protection):being offered by the Executive Director to those boards and agencies based on need. See *Board Minutes*, Vol. K (1965):124–25.

[271] *Board Minutes*, Vol. K (1965):152.

[272] In 1967 the Board voted that administrative expenses of the M & M Medical Plan would be paid by the MMBB. *Board Minutes*, Vol. L (1967):130–31.

[273] *Supplemental Minutes*, Vol. 15, item 577.

[274] In 1966 the Board discontinued the Annuitant Medical Plan following the introduction of Medicare and, instead, paid for the medical portion of Medicare

at $3 per month. Later in the same year they introduced the M & M Medicare Supplement, which was offered without charge. See *Board Minutes*, Vol. L (1966):23–24, 50–52.

[275] *Board Minutes*, Vol. M (1968):54–55.

[276] *Board Minutes*, Vol. L (1966):9.

[277] *Annual Report* (1966).

[278] *Board Minutes*, Vol. L (1966): 71, 90-93.

[279] *Annual Report* (1969): 7.

[280] Henry Allen, (From a Series, *What it Felt Like):"*Living in the American Century, 1970–1980: The Decade That Taste Forgot," *The Washington Post*, 29 September 1999, C-1, C10. Some portions of this section are adapted from Allen's article.

[281] Martin Marty, "Dangerous Future or Quiet Turning: The Shape of Religion in the Eighties," an address delivered at the biennial luncheon of the Ministers and Missionaries Benefit Board, at Carbondale, Illinois, 6 June 1979.

[282] *Board Minutes*, Vol. P-Q (1974):26.

[283] *Annual Report* (1970): 7; *Board Minutes*, Vol. N (1971):117–18. As of 1970, the Board had also decided to report the market value of funds held, rather than the book value.

[284] *Board Minutes*, Vol. P-Q (1974):14, See also "Chronology of a Benefactor," *Supplemental Minutes*, item 617.

[285] *Board Minutes*, Vol. O (1972):8, 19, and *Supplemental Minutes*, item 600.

[286] See "John W. Reed, President" in *Tomorrow* (September 1971): 3–9.

[287] *Board Minutes*, Vol. S (1976): 44–45. Oliver J. Troster was a partner in Troster, Singer & Co., one of the nation's largest investment securities firms. Troster represented the continuing tradition of including on the Board highly competent leaders in the financial and investment community. In addition, he had been a strong supporter of Baptist concerns: Trotter had served as President of the New York City Societies, was a member of the Executive Council of the American Baptist Men, had been President of the American Baptist Assembly at Green Lake, and had generously supported several its development projects.

[288] Soto-Fontanez had also served as the first Director of Spanish Speaking Work in New York City for the ABC.

[289] *Tomorrow* (October 1970): 22.

[290] Ibid., 22. Eads had been Director of the Department of Church and Ministry at Colgate Rochester Divinity School and had been the Pastor of the University Baptist Church at State College, Pennsylvania. Sillen was a Trustee of Andover Newton Theological School and had served several churches in Massachusetts and Ohio, and was the first Director of the Baptist Graduate House at the University of Chicago.

[291] Jones had served on the staffs of the Los Angeles City Mission Society and the St. John Mission Baptist Church of Long Beach, California.

[292] *Board Minutes*, Vol. O (1972):32. Ballesteros had served on special assignment to assist pastors in Baja California, had been pastor in the North Baptist Church of Jersey City, where a large number of Spanish speaking persons resided, and had later become, at the request of the New Jersey Executive Minister Joe Heartberg, the Coordinator of Anglo and Hispanic Ministries in Camden and Jersey City, New Jersey. Ballesteros was the second staff Hispanic member on the MMBB staff, having been preceded by the Rev. Adam Morales. Ballesteros served the MMBB for more than twenty years and retired in 1995.

[293] Adams had a long career as a pastor and denominational executive and served for a time as the Chairman of the Board of Trustees of the Berkeley Baptist Divinity School. *Tomorrow* (May 1970): 16.

[294] *Board Minutes*, Vol. S (1976):6–12; *Yesterday, Today, Tomorrow* (1977): 15. *Tomorrow* had ceased regular publication with the May 1972, issue. A similar magazine was re-established and published beginning in 1977 under the title of *Yesterday, Today and Tomorrow*.

[295] Ibid. Freiert was among the few women ordained by American Baptists in the mid-twentieth century. She had previously served as Assistant to the Executive Secretary of the American Baptist Churches of New York.

[296] Ibid.

[297] *Board Minutes*, Vol. M (1970):8–17.

[298] Examples include such determinations as, if the member is survived by a spouse who is living on the first month following the member's death, the spouse would receive a single-life annuity with 120 payments certain. Also provided the clarification of qualifying beneficiaries, proof required for payments of death benefits, and other definitions. See *Board Minutes*, Vol. N (1971): 77–80.

[299] *Board Minutes*, Vol. N (1970):47–49, 101–103; also *Board Minutes*, Vol. T (1977):28, and *Board Minutes*, Vol. U (1978):15–16.

[300] *Board Minutes*, Vol. R (1975):13–28.

[301] *Annual Report* (1978). From 1971–78 the Board's supplementation of annuities totaled $1,601,619.

[302] *Board Minutes*, Vol. R (1975): 51–52.

[303] *Board Minutes*, Vol. U (1979): 39ff.

[304] *Board Minutes*, Vol. W (1980): 16–18.

[305] *Board Minutes*, Vol. V (1979): 42–46.

[306] *Board Minutes*, Vol. W (1979): 21-22; *Supplemental Minutes*, item 704.

[307] *Board Minutes*, Vol. S (1976): 50–55; *Annual Report* (1977, 1978).

[308] *Board Minutes*, Vol. V (1979): 16.

[309] *Board Minutes*, Vol. Y (1982): 36–37.

[310] *Board Minutes*, Vol. P-Q (1974): 40.

[311] *Annual Report* (1992).

[312] *Board Minutes*, (1971): 111.

[313] *Board Minutes*, Vol. N (1972): 46–47.

[314] *Tomorrow* (May 1971): 9–12.

[315] *Board Minutes*, Vol. S (1976): 26–28.

[316] *Board Minutes*, Vol. W (1980): 2.

[317] The MMBB was specifically assigned this administrative responsibility by the General Council of the ABC in 1970. *Board Minutes*, Vol. N (1970):20–21 and *Annual Report* (1970): 7.

[318] *Tomorrow* (May 1971): 3–8.

[319] *Board Minutes*, Vol. T (1977): 34–36; *Tomorrow* (Summer-Fall 1980): 13.

[320] *Supplemental Minutes*, item 811. The Church Alliance served a critical function again in 1986 during a period of Congressional tax reform that threatened pension board procedures and ministerial tax considerations.

[321] *Annual Report of the Executive Director* (1972):6; *Board Minutes*, Vol. N (1971):111.

[322] *Report of the StudyCommission on Denominational Structure*, in Board Minutes (1972, Vol. O): 28-30.

[323] *Report of the Study Commission on Denominational Structure* ([1972 2. This document, along with other minutes and records of the American Baptist Convention and the American Baptist Churches, USA, can be found at the American Baptist Historical Society.

[324] *Report of the Study Commission on Denominational Structure* (1972. Board Minutes, 1972 (Vol O): 28-30.

[325] Ibid., 43–44.

[326] It remains unclear what unofficial conversations led to MMBB acquiescence to this proposal.

[327] MMBB Annual Reports and Board Minutes do not reflect the degree of debate that likely occurred regarding SCODS, but it must have been considerable. The MMBB had always perceived itself as part of the "American Baptist family," and, therefore, desired to be a cooperative participant in change. However, the reduction of the MMBB's governing board size, and, the reduction of its authority to select and continue board members was a departure from its first fifty years of successful operation and was likely to have been the cause of grave concern "off the record."

[328] *Board Minutes*, Vol. T (1977): 10.

[329] *Board Minutes*, Vol. U (1978): 19.

[330] Board Minutes, Vol. U (1978): 33.

[331] *Board Minutes*, Vol. U (1978): 19–20.

[332] It is not clear whether the recommendations of the Task Force were persuasive. However, recommendations regarding account owner's choices in investment types, the amount of the death benefit, the development of regional Pre-Retirement Seminars, and several others were reflected in later programs and services of the MMBB. See *Supplemental Minutes*, Vol. 21, item 713.

[333] *Annual Report* (1978).

[334] Senator Sam Nunn, Personal Comments, Washington DC "Blitz Build," Habitat for Humanity, May, 1991.

[335] Henry Allen, (From a series *What It Felt Like, Living in the American Century, 1980-1990*: "Song in the Key of Me," *The Washington Post*, 30 September 1999, C1-C6. Portions of this section are quoted or adapted from this material.

[336] Martin E. Marty, "Dangerous Future or Quiet Turning: The Shape of Religion in the Eighties," MMBB Biennial Luncheon Address, June 1979. (Published in pamphlet format by MMBB). This address, and other MMBB luncheon addresses is available in the MMBB Archives, or at the American Baptist Historical Society, Atlanta, GA._. Martin E. Marty was, at that time, the Fairfax M. Cone Distinguished Service Professor of Modern Christian History at the Divinity School of the University of Chicago, and also an Associate Professor in the Department of History. Through a variety of scholarly publications, newsletters, columns, and modes of expression, Marty became a popular and pervasive observer and commentator of religious trends in the United States.

[337] O'Driscoll was, at that time, the Dean and Rector of Christ Church Cathedral in Vancouver, British Columbia. A native of Cork, Ireland, O'Driscoll combined a winsome Irish narrative style in both speaking and writing and possessed the ability to bring biblical texts to life in contemporary contexts. He was a popular preacher and lecturer in North America, and had published a number of books and articles.

[338] T. Herbert O'Driscoll, "People of the Apocalypse – Children of the Covenant," Biennial Luncheon Address, 1981. Published in Pamphlet Form by MMBB and available in MMBB Archives and at ABHS, Atlanta, GA.

[339] *Board Minutes*, Vol. Y (1982): 10–14. Prior to the implementation of the SCODS and later SCORE reforms, ministers were much more likely to serve in positions of leadership on national and local denominational and agency boards. While the reforms accomplished a broad inclusion of lay persons and minority groups in leadership roles, it diminished the number of ordained ministers and the frequency of their service.

[340] Morikawa was a Japanese American who, because of his racial-ethnic identity, had been detained during World War II by the federal government.

[341] *Board Minutes*, Vol. Y (1981): 7–8.

[342] *Board Minutes*, Vol. Y (1982): 18.

[343] *Board Minutes*, Vol. BB (1985): 25. The minutes of the May 1985, MMBB meeting provide a comprehensive insight into the process of discussion and considerations regarding the use of investments as a tool to express displeasure with South African's apartheid policies. The Board considered the potential effectiveness of divesting its portfolio of corporations not willing to sign and operate according to the "Sullivan Principles." The four Sullivan principles dealt with the rights of black businesses to locate in the South African's urban areas,

the importance of influencing other companies to follow equal rights standards and principles, to support the freedom of mobility of black workers in seeking employment, to provide for adequate housing for families of employees within proximity of workers' employment, and to support the ending of all apartheid laws. A full summary review of the discussion and considerations is found in the *Board Minutes*, Vol. BB (1985):3–15.

[344] Ibid., 25.

[345] *Board Minutes*, Vol. BB (1985):31–32. J. Andy Smith was the then Director of Social and Ethical Responsibility in Investments of the Board of National Ministries, ABC/USA.

[346] *Annual Report* (1986).

[347] *Board Minutes*, Vol. X (1981):16–17, 30–32.

[348] *Board Minutes*, Vol. Z (1983):22–23.

[349] Board Minutes, Vol. BB (1985):16–18. The previous short-term benefit of $250 was replaced. Instead, after three months, disability income payments would equal 2/3 of compensation; after nine months, MMBB payments were to be coordinated with Social Security long-term and/or other government disability to equal 2/3 of compensation combined, and would increase 5 percent annually

[350] *Board Minutes*, Vol. EE (1988):6.

[351] *Board Minutes*, Vol. CC (1986):12-14.

[352] *Board Minutes*, Vol. CC (1986):14-15.

[353] *Tomorrow* (Winter-Spring 1984): 4–5.

[354] Hella Mears Hugh, a member of the Board, made the gift and thus stimulated Board commitment to the project through 1983. *Board Minutes*, Vol. Z (1983):36. See also *Tomorrow* (Winter-Spring 1984): 8–9.

[355] *Tomorrow* (Winter-Spring 1984): 2–3.

[356] *Board Minutes*, Vol. EE (1988): 27–28.

[357] *Board Minutes*, Vol. X (1983): 27–28.

[358] The minister was the present author, Everett C. Goodwin, then serving as Senior Minister of the First Baptist Church of the City of Washington, DC.

[359] Rodney M. Romney, speaking at an MMBB HIV/AIDS Workshop at The First Baptist Church of the City of Washington, DC. Romney was then the Senior Minister of the First Baptist Church of Seattle, Washington.

[360] *Board Minutes*, Vol. EE (1989): 26–27. Craig Darling had founded the AIDS Pastoral Care Network in Chicago, and later offered similar leadership in Seattle.

[361] Gardner C. Taylor, "Civil Rights Events of the 60s: A Retrospective and Forward Look," MMBB Biennial Luncheon Address, 1985, published by MMBB in pamphlet form. This and other MMBB Luncheon addresses are available in the MMBB Archives and at the ABHS in Atlanta, GA.

[362] Gardner C. Taylor, "Civil Rights Events of the 1960's: A Retrospective and Forward Look," MMBB Luncheon Address,, 1985, published in pamphlet form and available at MMBB Archives or at the ABHS at Atlanta, GA., (1985):5.

[363] John H. Buchanan, Jr., "Baptist Heritage: Champions of Religious Liberty," MMBB Biennial Luncheon Address,1987, published in pamphlet form and available at the MMBB Archives or at the ABHS, Atlanta, GA. p. 5]

[364] John H. Buchanan, Jr., "Baptist Heritage: Champions of Religious Liberty," MMBB Biennial Luncheon Address, 1987. Published in Pamphlet form by MMBB. Southern Baptists were among the most notable in their swing toward the most extreme positions of right-wing politics, as well as literalistic biblical interpretation. In their political shift, many Southern Baptist leaders had indicated a willingness to compromise the Baptist principal of separation of church and state in order to guarantee some programs and to conserve preferred values. Buchanan had risen above the identities and limits of both impulses. In response, he suggested that separation of church and state was what made the state great and true religion possible.

[365] Howard R. Moody, "Unfinished Reformations: Looking Back to see the Future," MMBB Biennial Luncheon Address, (1991): 4. This and other MMBB Biennial Luncheon addresses may be found in the MMBB Archives or at the American Baptist Historical Society in Atlanta, GA.

[366] John S. Bone, *The Better Maintenance of* The Ministry: *The First Seventy-five Years of the Ministers and Missionaries Benefit Board*, (MMBB, 1987).

[367] *Board Minutes*, Vol. G (1990):19-b.

[368] *Tomorrow* (Summer 1990): 1.

[369] Ibid., 4–8. See also *Supplemental Minutes*, item 839.

[370] Henry Allen, From a series "What It Felt Like Living in the American Century: 1990-2000: Decade of Indifference. Whatever," *The Washington Post*, 1 October 1999, C-1. Portions of this section are quoted or adapted from this piece.

[371] Ibid., C8.

[372] See Memo to Dr. George Tooze and Dr. Sumner Grant, Ministers and Missionaries Benefit Board of American Baptists Churches from Bernard F. O'Hare and Jessica S. Carter, of Patterson, Belknap, Webb and Tyler, 4 February 2004, in MMBB correspondence files.

[373] Margaret Cowden recalled that toward the end of the search process members of the search committee spoke with her and assured her that she was thought highly qualified, but young and perhaps not yet experienced enough. Therefore, the Board was considering Gordon Smith to be a "transitional executive" who would serve a few years, thus allowing Cowden to gain more experience, after which time she would likely be elected. At that time, she was 39, the same age that Dean Wright had been at his selection as Executive Director. Conversation with Margaret Cowden, 8 November 2011.

[374] Conversation with Richard Huber, 9 March 2011.

[375] It is not clear whether the Board chose not to pursue Wright's preference, or whether Wright changed his mind regarding a successor. There was some indication that Wright thought that Smith supported Cowden's candidacy, and that Wright was caught by surprise when Smith, instead, declared his own interest in the position.

[376] Margaret Cowden continued to serve the MMBB for four years and left in 1994 to take a sabbatical. She later became the President (Chief Executive Officer) of the American Baptist Extension Corporation, a denominational lending organization for development of church and other program facilities. Another female candidate considered a contender for leadership, Cheryl Wade, had served as Assistant Treasurer and was made MMBB Treasurer after Gordon Smith's selection as Executive Director. Wade resigned as MMBB Treasurer on 31 December 1992 and subsequently became Treasurer of the ABC/USA. See *Tomorrow* (Spring 1993): 22 and *Tomorrow* (Summer 1994): 26.

[377] Conversation with MMBB Board Chair, George Tooze, 28 October 2011.

[378] *Board Minutes*, Vol. JJ (October 1993): 19.

[379] *Board Minutes*, Vol. JJ (May 1993): 6–7; See *Board Minutes*, Vol. II (October 1992):23–26 for the report of the recommendation from the National Commission on *The Ministry*.

[380] "Executive Director's Report to the Board of Managers," *Board Minutes*, Vol. KK, Appendix B (17 May 1994): 2–3.

[381] *Board Minutes*, Vol. JJ (May 1993):19 and *Tomorrow* (Summer 1993): 26–27.

[382] *Tomorrow* (Summer 1992): 1–3. Fisher was, by that time, a highly visible and well-regarded member of the New York financial community, having become Chairman of the Board of the Morgan Stanley Group. Later Fisher presided over Morgan Stanley's acquisition of several other financial organizations and emerged as one of the leading investment and banking institutions in the country.

[383] Ibid., 4–6. Morong, the son of a Baptist minister and educator, and long-time active member of Baptist churches, was the Senior Vice President and Investment Manager in charge of domestic active investments for TIAA-CREF Investment Management, Inc. He began his service to the Board in 1980 and served primarily on the Finance Committee.

[384] *Tomorrow* (Winter 1995): 2–8. In addition to Reed's credentials and accomplishments as a lawyer, honored professor of law, and his leadership gifts in several contexts, he was also a long-term member of the First Baptist Church of Ann Arbor, Michigan, where he served as Moderator and on several boards and committees, in addition to being the Director of the church's choir, which was described as "one of the finest choirs in the state of Michigan."

[385] Purcell had been elected to the MMBB in 1985 and had served as Vice President in 1993. She had been president of both the American Association and

the International Federation of University Women and had been a member of several other national organizations. *Tomorrow* (Summer 1995): 2–3.

[385] *Board Minutes*, Vol. HH (October 1991):9–10.

[386] *Tomorrow* (Winter 1998–99): 18–19. Accumulation units, which represent net asset value, are translated into annuity units at retirement, which are the basis for annual and monthly annuity payments.

[387] *Board Minutes*, Vol. HH (October 1991): 9–10.

[388] *Annual Report* (1995).

[389] *Board Minutes*, Vol. LL (May 1995):10–11. This was an administrative action, not a plan provision.

[390] Examples of "non-steeple" clients could include schools, colleges, retirement homes, hospitals, and other such organizations that had been founded by church or church-related organizations for benevolent purposes.

[391] *Board Minutes*, Vol. NN (May 1997):5–8.

[392] *Board Minutes*, Vol. CC (1986):28. See also *Supplemental Minutes*, item 791.

[393] *Board Minutes*, Vol. GG (November 1990):2. See also *Supplemental Minutes*, item No. 850.

[394] *Board Minutes*, Vol. GG (November 1990):12–13; *Board Minutes*, Vol. JJ (1993):18–19.

[395] *Budget Letter*, 30 June 1997; "Contractual Plans/ABC Medical Dental Plan" in *Supplemental Minutes*, Vol. 31 Item # 435.

[396] *Board Minutes*, Vol. MM (May 1996): 2–3.

[397] *Board Minutes*, Vol. MM (November 1996): 10–12.

[398] *Board Minutes*, Vol. MM (November 1996): 6–8.

[399] *Board Minutes*, Vol. PP (May 1999): 11.

[400] *Board Minutes*, Vol. SS (May 2002). Attachment A.

[401] Nola M. Falcone had, at that time, been the long-time President of the Evergreen Mutual Funds, a highly rated family of mutual funds, where her success as a value-oriented fund manager was nationally notable. Falcone was a member of the Scarsdale Community Baptist Church in Scarsdale, New York, and had previously been a member of the First Baptist Church of White Plains, New York.

[402] *Supplemental Minutes*, Vol. 27, item 866, 44.

[403] *Board Minutes*, Vol. GG (May 1990): 8. The Baptist Joint Committee, an educational and advocacy organization supported by a number of Baptist denominations and bodies, had lost significant funding support from the Southern Baptist Convention following that denomination's decision to pursue a separate path as a result of theological and political disagreement.

[404] *Board Minutes*, Vol. RR (2001):7–8; *Board Minutes*, Vol. SS (2002): 4.

[405] Conversation with Sumner Grant, July 11, 2011.

[406] *Board Minutes*, Vol. LL (May 1995): 17–18.

[407] Howard Moody, "Reflections on 26 Years of M&M Service," Exhibit I, in *Board Minutes*, Vol. MM (November 1996): 4.

[408] *Tomorrow* (Winter 1998–99): 3.

[409] *Board Minutes*, Vol. OO–PP (May 1998): 1–4.

[410] Private interviews with Board members.

[411] Interviews with Sumner Grant.

[412] The Board of Educational Ministries had, by this time, been dissolved and its functions absorbed by the other boards and agencies.

[413] *Board Minutes*, Vol. TT (May 2005): 14.

[414] *Board Minutes*, Vol. RR (November 2001): 8–11.

[415] Dreyfus Retirement Services provided the record keeping for the PIC program and a number of administrative functions, such as loan administration, partial and minimum distributions, rollovers, and a variety of tax record and other record-keeping functions were also turned over to Dreyfus Services for administration.

[416] *Report of the Executive Director* (19 May 1999).

[417] *Report of the Executive Director* (10 November 1999): 3.

[418] Both the Alliance of Baptists and the Cooperative Baptist Fellowship were comprised of former Southern Baptist Churches that had opted to leave the SBC, or, in the case of the Cooperative Baptist Fellowship, to additionally affiliate with a new or more moderate fellowships.

[419] *Report of the Executive Director* (8 November 2000): 1–2.

[420] Ibid., 3–4.

[421] *Report of the Executive Director* (8 November 2001): 1.

[422] *Business Week*, 6 May 2002.

[423] *Report of the Executive Director* (8 November 2001): 1.

[424] *Report of the Executive Director* (22 May 2002): 1.

[425] *Report of the Executive Director* (7 November 2002): 3–4.

[426] *Report of the Executive Director* (6 November 2003): 1–3.

[427] *Report of the Executive Director* (11 May 2005): 1.

[428] *Report of the Executive Director* (8 November 2006): 2.

[429] "Benefits for Life" included The Pension Plan, the Death Benefit Plan, disability insurance, and a variety of other services and benefit guarantees available to qualifying ABC/USA members.

[430] *Report of the Executive Director* (11 May 2005): 2.

[431] Ronald Heifetz, Alexander Grashow, and Marty Linsky, "Leadership in a Permanent Crisis," *Harvard Business Review* (July-August 2009): 62-69.

[432] *Report of the Executive Director* (3 November 2009): 1.

[433] *Board Minutes*, (May 2010):4.

[434] Ibid., 6–7.

[435] *Report of the Executive Director* (5 May 2010): 1.

[436] *Board Minutes* (2–3 November 2010):6–10. The plan modifications also addressed a number of non-crisis related clarifications and changes regarding the various plans that had developed over time.

[437] *Report of the Executive Director* (2 November 2010): 1.

[438] Private message to the author, 29 October 2011.

[439] The ABC/USA bylaw revisions reflected more independent roles also for the Board of International Ministry, and for the Board of National Ministries, which had recently taken back its historic name: The American Baptist Home Mission Societies. In some respects, it appeared that they had been inspired by— and had learned from—MMBB's efforts to retain autonomy while fulfilling their purpose.

[440] H. Pierson Hammond quoted in *Board Minutes*, Vol. N (1971): 123–24, in a summary and review of sixty years of Board history.

[441] Howard, Moody, reflections on his retirement from the MMBB Board, 12 November 1996, MMBB Archives.

[442] "The Image," Miriam Corbett, Special Representative at a Staff Conference, September 1968; *Supplemental Minutes*, item 552, 3.

INDEX

ABC People, 174, 187, 197, 238

ABC/USA. *See* American Baptist Churches in the USA

Abernathy, Ralph, 156

ABHMS. *See* American Baptist Home Mission Society

accountable plans for qualified expenses, 238

accumulation plan, 159

accumulation units, 174, 230, 231, 310n386

accumulation unit values, 230

"Acres of Diamonds" (Conwell), 42

actuarial soundness, 64, 74, 88, 90, 110

Adams, Elmer C., 170

Addams, Jane, 283n15

Adopt a Beneficiary, 93–94

Affiliated Retirement Programs, 252

African-American churches, 141, 150, 152, 156, 170, 176, 255, 261

age discrimination against ministers, 27, 31, 37, 78, 96–98, 125–26

Allen, Henry, xviii

Alliance of Baptists, 255, 311n418

almsgiving, 5, 15, 16

American Baptist Churches of Michigan, 183

American Baptist Churches of the Pacific Southwest, 177

American Baptist Churches in the USA, 183; Board of Educational Ministries, programs transferred to, 226; Board of International Ministry, 312n439; Board of National Ministries, 312n439; criticisms of, used to rally personal support, 185; increasingly going to MMBB for financial assistance, 240; Inter-Board Task Force on AIDS, 210; intrusion of, into MMBB, 240–42, 248–50; Pastoral Relations Committee, 204;

reorganization of, 221; theological division in, 262–63

American Baptist Committee on Chaplains, 143

American Baptist Convention; attempting to retain control of MMBB, 141–42; black churchmen seeking reparations from, 157; centralization of, attempted, 182–83; concept behind, 181; considering reorganization, 163; developing a Lay Workers Pension Plan, 117; Division of World Mission Support, 162; growing diversity of, 169; increased membership in the South, 156; investment policies of, 137–38; name change to, 113; renamed American Baptist Churches in the USA, 183; reorganization of, affecting MMBB, 168; Study Commission on Denominational Structure (SCODS), 167, 168; trying to unite operations in one location, 129; Valley Forge headquarters, 129–30, 136–37, 147, 163, 226–27, 240–42, 59

American Baptist Education Society, 282n11

American Baptist Foreign Mission Society, 8, 36, 94, 129–30, 181

American Baptist Historical Society (ABHS), 240

American Baptist Home and Foreign Missions, 34

American Baptist Home Mission Board, 290n77

American Baptist Home Mission Society (ABHMS), 8, 9, 36, 44–45, 129, 152, 181, 301n258, 312n439; approving enrollment of missionaries in the Retiring Pension Fund, 94; Morehouse's role with, 10, 25;

extended to, 118–20. *See also* Social
Security; supporting, challenges of,
76–77; taxation of, 204–5;
unemployment among, 95–96
Ministers Aid Society, 52
Ministers Council, 122, 124–25, 177, 130–
31, 147, 163, 183, 226, 227
Ministers Life and Casualty Union of
Minneapolis, 116, 161
Ministers' Luncheons, 131. *See also*
MMBB Luncheons
Ministers and Missionaries Benefit
Board. *See* MMBB
ministers' wives, 31, 91, 149
ministry. *See also* ministers;
development of, as a profession,
147; rising dropout rate in, 147;
women in, 178–79. *See also* women
in ministry; Women in Ministry
Ministry, The, 72–75, 195–96, 197;
celebrating MMBB's 15th
anniversary, 79; continuing series on
ordained men no longer in ministry,
76; educating laity and clergy about
nonfinancial problems within
ministry, 78; educating readers
about a variety of giving methods,
94–95; emphasizing wills and
bequests, 89; encouraging higher
salaries for ministers, 122–23;
explaining the MMBB's programs,
78–79; on perceiving ministry as a
career, 77–78; presenting counsel
and advice to ministers, 120–21;
printing excerpts from grateful
beneficiaries, 93; reporting on
unemployed ministers, 95–96;
urging communication with the
MMBB if a member couldn't pay
dues, 95; using humor to make its
point, 76–77
missionaries; applying for membership
in the Retiring Pension Fund, 65;
dues of, paid for by sponsoring
boards, 94; economic insecurity of,
29
mission movement, 8

Mission Partners, 240
mission societies, influence of, 10
M&M Annuitant Medical Plan, 161–62
MMBB; ABC move to Valley Forge,
involvement in, 137; ABC/USA
going to, for financial assistance,
240; ABC/USA involvement in
leadership selection, 248–50;
adequacy of reserves, 103; adjusting
for pension erosion, 127, 158–59;
administrative development of, 68–
71; advocacy role of, 73; advocating
for better financial support for
ministers, 126, 144–45, 176;
advocating for competence and
professional quality for the ministry,
76; advocating for women in
ministry, 179; African-American
membership in, 150, 156; as
anomaly in the American Baptist
structure, 137; asset retention,
problem of, 261–62; assets of, 70–71,
79, 87, 111, 139, 167–68, 188–89, 199,
214–15, 230, 242, 243, 244, 253, 259–
62, 270, 267; basing aid on services
rendered, not on ordination status,
54; beneficiaries of, 1; benefits and
services of, 87, 88, 111, 114–15, 142–
44, 170–75, 201–3, 215, 230–37, 251,
254, 257, 266, 269, 307n349; birth of,
in spirit, 43; Board appointed
largely by denominational control,
249–50; Board members, numbers
of, 183, 250–51, 287n48; building
relationships with churches and
pastors, 93–95; challenges facing, in
its next one hundred years, 278–80;
changed relationship with the
Convention, 182–83 ; chartering of,
1; civil rights involvement of, 134,
167. *See also* socially responsible
investing; Committee on
Applications, 53; concerned with
ministers' low salaries, 92, 115, 115,
122–23, 126, 144–45, 176; concerned
about its public perception, 196–97;
contributing to building the